Better Homes and Gardens®

BIGGEST BOOK OF
SLOW
COOKER
RECIPES

Houghton Mifflin Harcourt

Boston New York

Copyright © 2002 by Meredith Corporation, Des Moines, Iowa. First Edition.
All rights reserved.

Published by Houghton Mifflin Harcourt Publishing Company

Published simultaneously in Canada

For information about permission to reproduce selections from this book,
please write Permissions, Houghton Mifflin Harcourt Publishing Company,
215 Park Avenue South NY NY 10003.

www.hmhco.com

Library of Congress Control Number: 2002102028
ISBN-13: 978-0-696-21546-9 (tradepaper)
ISBN-13: 978-0-696-21835-4 (comb bound)

Printed in China

OGP 10 9
4500518402

Publisher: Natalie Chapman
Associate Publisher: Jessica Goodman
Executive Editor: Anne Ficklen

Biggest Book of Slow Cooker Recipes
Editors: Chuck Smothermon, Carrie Holcomb Mills
Senior Associate Design Director: John Eric Seid
Copy Chief: Terri Fredrickson
Copy and Production Editor: Victoria Forlini
Editorial Operations Manager: Karen Schirm
Managers, Book Production: Pam Kvitne, Marjorie J. Schenkelberg
Contributing Copy Editor: Shelly Moses
Contributing Proofreaders: Gretchen Kauffman, Elise Marton, Donna Segal
Illustrator: Jim Swanson
Indexer: Elizabeth Parson
Electronic Production Coordinator: Paula Forest
Editorial and Design Assistants: Karen McFadden, Mary Lee Gavin
Test Kitchen Director: Lynn Blanchard
Test Kitchen Product Supervisor: Marilyn Cornelius

Our Better Homes and Gardens® Test Kitchen seal on the back cover of this book assures you that every recipe in the *Biggest Book of Slow Cooker Recipes* has been tested in the Better Homes and Gardens® Test Kitchen. This means that each recipe is practical and reliable, and meets our high standards of taste appeal. We guarantee your satisfaction with this book for as long as you own it..

TABLE OF CONTENTS

BONUS CHAPTERS

INTRODUCTION

Slow cookers are hot. They always have been, of course, technically speaking. While there's a greater selection of colors, sizes, and shapes than ever before, the basic mission of the slow cooker has not changed: *to make your life easier and your meals tastier.*

In addition to incredible convenience, a slow cooker offers other benefits. A slow cooker can turn an inexpensive, less-than-tender cut of meat into prime eating. Foods come out moist, flavorful, and falling-off-the-bone tender.

Slow cookers may be associated with the one-pot meal — and there's no shortage of delicious one-dish dinners in this book that feature beef, pork, lamb, and poultry — and there's also a great selection of recipes for Appetizers & Beverages, Desserts, Meatless Main Dishes, Side Dishes, and Soups & Stews.

So come home to savor a great meal — and the extra time you have because you didn't have to watch the pot.

APPETIZERS & BEVERAGES

Keep this party-perfect dip warm in a slow cooker for up to two hours after cooking. Stir just before serving.

ASIAGO CHEESE DIP

PREP:

15 minutes

COOK:

Low 3 hours, High 1¹/₂ hours

MAKES:

28 (¹/₄ cup) servings

SLOW COOKER:

3¹/₂- to 4-quart

1	cup chicken broth or water
4	ounces dried tomatoes (not oil-packed)
4	8-ounce cartons dairy sour cream
1¹/₄	cups mayonnaise
¹/₂	of an 8-ounce package cream cheese, cut up
1	cup sliced fresh mushrooms
1	cup thinly sliced green onions
6	ounces shredded Asiago cheese (1¹/₂ cups)
	Thinly sliced green onions
	Toasted baguette slices

1 In a medium saucepan bring the chicken broth or water to boiling. Remove from heat and add the dried tomatoes. Cover and let stand for 5 minutes. Drain, discard the liquid, and chop the tomatoes (about 1¹/₄ cups).

2 Meanwhile, in a 3¹/₂- to 4-quart slow cooker combine the sour cream, mayonnaise, cream cheese, mushrooms, 1 cup green onions, and Asiago cheese. Stir in the chopped tomatoes. Cover and cook on low-heat setting for 3 to 4 hours or on high-heat setting for 1¹/₂ to 2 hours. Stir before serving and sprinkle with additional green onions. Keep warm on low-heat setting for 1 to 2 hours. Serve warm with toasted baguette slices.

Nutrition Facts per serving: 195 cal., 19 g total fat (8 g sat. fat), 31 mg chol., 242 mg sodium, 5 g carbo., 1 g fiber, 4 g pro. **Daily Values:** 8% vit. A, 4% vit. C, 10% calcium, 3% iron

Serve crispy scoopers such as corn chips or toasted baguette slices with this sharply flavored dip.

BACON-HORSERADISH DIP

3 8-ounce packages cream cheese, softened and cut up
3 cups shredded cheddar cheese (12 ounces)
1 cup half-and-half or light cream
⅓ cup chopped green onions
3 tablespoons prepared horseradish
1 tablespoon Worcestershire sauce
3 cloves garlic, minced
½ teaspoon coarse-ground pepper
12 slices bacon, crisp-cooked, cooled, and finely crumbled (1 cup)
Corn chips, toasted baguette slices, toasted pita wedges, or assorted crackers

1 In a 3½- to 4-quart slow cooker combine cream cheese, cheddar cheese, half-and-half, green onions, horseradish, Worcestershire sauce, garlic, and pepper. Cover and cook on low-heat setting for 4 to 5 hours or on high-heat setting for 2 to 2½ hours, stirring once halfway through cooking. Stir in the bacon. Serve with corn chips, baguette slices, pita wedges, or assorted crackers.

Nutrition Facts per serving: 227 cal., 21 g total fat (13 g sat. fat), 63 mg chol., 282 mg sodium, 2 g carbo., 0 g fiber, 8 g pro. **Daily Values:** 15% vit. A, 1% vit. C, 17% calcium, 4% iron

PREP:
25 minutes
COOK:
Low 4 hours, High 2 hours
MAKES:
20 (¼ cup) servings
SLOW COOKER:
3½- to 4-quart

Tote this zesty appetizer to a tailgate party or serve it while watching a game on TV.
Be sure to whisk it before serving to smooth out the dip and distribute the flavors.

CHIPOTLE CON QUESO DIP

PREP:

10 minutes

COOK:

Low 3 hours, High 1½ hours

MAKES:

16 (4½ tablespoons) servings

SLOW COOKER:

3½- to 4-quart

2 pounds packaged process cheese spread, cubed

1 10-ounce can chopped tomatoes and green chile peppers

1 to 3 chipotle peppers in adobo sauce, chopped

1 tablespoon Worcestershire sauce

Tortilla chips

1 In a 3½- to 4-quart slow cooker combine the cheese spread, undrained tomatoes, chipotle peppers in adobo sauce, and Worcestershire sauce. Cover and cook on low-heat setting for 3 to 3½ hours or on high-heat setting for 1½ to 1¾ hours. Whisk before serving. Serve warm with tortilla chips. Keep warm on low-heat setting.

Nutrition Facts per serving: 352 cal., 22 g total fat (11 g sat. fat), 47 mg chol., 1,030 mg sodium, 24 g carbo., 2 g fiber, 15 g pro. **Daily Values:** 27% vit. A, 4% vit. C, 36% calcium, 3% iron

Take this classic to a party and you'll be a hit — it's a tried-and-true favorite.
Chopped red sweet pepper gives this version a festive confetti look and a sweet crunch too.

HOT ARTICHOKE DIP

2   medium leeks, thinly sliced (²/₃ cup)

1   tablespoon olive oil

2   14-ounce cans artichoke hearts, drained and coarsely chopped

2   cups light mayonnaise dressing (do not use regular mayonnaise)

1   cup chopped red sweet pepper

1   cup finely shredded Parmesan cheese

1   teaspoon Mediterranean seasoning or lemon-pepper seasoning
     Finely shredded Parmesan cheese
     Toasted pita wedges

In a large skillet cook leeks in hot olive oil over medium heat until tender. Place in a 3¹/₂- to 4-quart slow cooker. Stir in the artichoke hearts, light mayonnaise, sweet pepper, 1 cup Parmesan cheese, and seasoning. Cover and cook on low-heat setting for 3 to 4 hours until cheese is melted and mixture is heated through.

To serve, stir mixture, sprinkle with additional Parmesan cheese, and keep warm on low-heat setting for up to 1 hour. Serve on toasted pita wedges.

Nutrition Facts per serving: 129 cal., 10 g total fat (3 g sat. fat), 14 mg chol., 361 mg sodium, 6 g carbo., 1 g fiber, 3 g pro. **Daily Values:** 11% vit. A, 22% vit. C, 8% calcium, 5% iron

PREP:
20 minutes
COOK:
Low 3 hours
MAKES:
about 20 (¹/₄ cup) servings
SLOW COOKER:
3¹/₂- to 4-quart

Surprise guests with their favorite pizza flavors served in a spicy dip. If there are any leftovers, they can be frozen and served later.

SPICY SAUSAGE PIZZA DIP

PREP:

20 minutes

COOK:

Low 5 hours, High 2 1/2 hours

MAKES:

28 (1/4 cup) servings

SLOW COOKER:

3 1/2- to 4-quart

LEFTOVERS
After cooling, transfer any leftovers to freezer containers and freeze for up to 3 months. Thaw and reheat in a saucepan.

1	pound bulk Italian sausage
2/3	cup chopped onion
4	cloves garlic, minced
2	15-ounce cans tomato sauce
1	14 1/2-ounce can tomatoes, cut up
1	6-ounce can tomato paste
4	teaspoons dried oregano, crushed
1	tablespoon dried basil, crushed
2	teaspoons sugar
1/4	teaspoon ground red pepper
1/2	cup chopped, pitted ripe olives

Dippers—breadsticks, breaded mozzarella cheese sticks, and green sweet pepper strips

1 In a large skillet cook sausage, onion, and garlic until meat is brown and onion is tender; drain well.

2 In a 3 1/2- to 4-quart slow cooker combine sausage mixture, tomato sauce, undrained tomatoes, tomato paste, oregano, basil, sugar, and red pepper. Stir ingredients, cover, and cook on low-heat setting for 5 to 6 hours or on high-heat setting for 2 1/2 to 3 hours.

3 Stir in olives. Serve with dippers.

Nutrition Facts per serving: 70 cal., 4 g total fat (2 g sat. fat), 11 mg chol., 275 mg sodium, 4 g carbo., 1 g fiber, 3 g pro. **Daily Values:** 3% vit. A, 6% vit. C, 2% calcium, 4% iron

If you have finicky eaters in your family, they'll love this spin on one of their favorite foods. Serve this pizza-flavored fondue for a graduation party or birthday party.

SUPREME PIZZA FONDUE

4	ounces Italian sausage
1	small onion, finely chopped
1	clove garlic, minced
1	28-ounce jar meatless spaghetti sauce
1	cup sliced fresh mushrooms
⅔	cup chopped pepperoni or Canadian-style bacon
1	teaspoon dried basil or oregano, crushed
½	cup sliced, pitted ripe olives (optional)
¼	cup chopped green sweet pepper (optional)
	Dippers: focaccia or Italian bread cubes, mozzarella or provolone cheese cubes, or cooked tortellini or ravioli

1 Remove casings from sausage, if present. In a large skillet cook the sausage, onion, and garlic until meat is brown. Drain off fat.

2 In a 3½- to 4-quart slow cooker combine spaghetti sauce, mushrooms, pepperoni or Canadian-style bacon, and basil or oregano. Stir in the sausage mixture.

3 Cover and cook on low-heat setting for 3 hours. If desired, stir in ripe olives and sweet pepper. Cover and cook on low-heat setting for 15 minutes more. To serve, spear the dippers with fondue forks and dip them into the fondue.

Nutrition Facts per serving: 254 cal., 12 g total fat (4 g sat. fat), 39 mg chol., 738 mg sodium, 24 g carbo., 0 g fiber, 13 g pro. **Daily Values:** 31% vit. C, 15% calcium, 11% iron

PREP:
20 minutes

COOK:
Low 3¼ hours

MAKES:
10 servings (about 5½ cups)

SLOW COOKER:
3½- to 4-quart

PUT COOKING ON HOLD
Have there been times when you were concerned about not returning home until well after the slow cooker dinner was finished? Here's a remedy: Use an automatic timer to start the cooker. When using a timer, be sure all ingredients are well chilled when you place them in the cooker. Never use this method with frozen fish or poultry. The food should not stand for longer than 2 hours before cooking begins.

And you thought these wonders could be enjoyed only in restaurants. Slow cooking makes this hot, hearty hors d'oeuvre a snap to make at home.

THAI CHICKEN WINGS WITH PEANUT SAUCE

PREP:

25 minutes

COOK:

Low 5 hours, High 2¹/₂ hours

MAKES:

12 servings

SLOW COOKER:

3¹/₂- to 4-quart

24	chicken wing drummettes (about 2¹/₄ pounds)
¹/₂	cup bottled salsa
2	tablespoons creamy peanut butter
1	tablespoon lime juice
2	teaspoons soy sauce
2	teaspoons grated fresh ginger
¹/₄	cup sugar
¹/₄	cup creamy peanut butter
3	tablespoons soy sauce
3	tablespoons water
2	cloves garlic, minced

1 Place chicken in a 3¹/₂- to 4-quart slow cooker. Combine salsa, 2 tablespoons peanut butter, lime juice, 2 teaspoons soy sauce, and ginger. Pour over chicken wings. Toss to coat.

2 Cover and cook on low-heat setting for 5 to 6 hours or on high-heat setting for 2¹/₂ to 3 hours.

3 Meanwhile, for the peanut sauce, in a small saucepan use a whisk to combine sugar, ¹/₄ cup creamy peanut butter, 3 tablespoons soy sauce, water, and garlic. Heat over medium-low heat until sugar is dissolved and mixture is smooth; set aside (mixture will thicken as it cools).

4 Drain chicken, discarding cooking liquid. Return chicken to slow cooker. Gently stir in peanut sauce. Keep chicken warm in a covered cooker on low-heat setting for up to 2 hours.

Nutrition Facts per serving: 189 cal., 13 g total fat (3 g sat. fat), 58 mg chol., 392 mg sodium, 6 g carbo., 1 g fiber, 12 g pro. **Daily Values:** 1% vit. A, 2% vit. C, 1% calcium, 1% iron

Vegetables, spices, and sweet mango contribute big taste to these beefy appetizer-size tacos.

ZESTY BEEF-FILLED TACOS

1	medium onion, cut into wedges
1	medium carrot, quartered
12	ounces beef flank steak
1/4	cup snipped fresh cilantro
1/2	to 1 teaspoon crushed red pepper
1/2	teaspoon salt
1	14 1/2-ounce can diced tomatoes with roasted garlic
1/2	cup water
24	miniature taco shells
	Finely chopped mango (about 1 cup)
	Toppings—snipped cilantro, sliced green onion, chopped tomato, and/or finely shredded lettuce

PREP:
25 minutes

COOK:
Low 7 hours, High 4 hours; plus 15 minutes on High

MAKES:
24 servings

SLOW COOKER:
3 1/2- to 4-quart

1 Place onion and carrot in a 3 1/2- to 4-quart slow cooker. Place beef over vegetables. Sprinkle with 1/4 cup cilantro, crushed red pepper, and salt; add the undrained tomatoes and water. Cover and cook on low-heat setting for 7 to 9 hours or on high-heat setting for 4 to 5 hours.

2 Remove meat from cooker. Shred meat with a fork, cutting into shorter shreds, if desired. Drain vegetable mixture well; discard liquid. Transfer vegetable mixture to a food processor bowl or blender container. Process with several on/off turns until chopped. Return meat and chopped vegetable mixture to slow cooker; cook, covered, on high for 15 to 30 minutes or until heated through. Spoon mixture into miniature taco shells. Top with mango and desired toppings.

Nutrition Facts per serving: 53 cal., 2 g total fat (1 g sat. fat), 6 mg chol., 145 mg sodium, 5 g carbo., 1 g fiber, 4 g pro. **Daily Values:** 14% vit. A, 5% vit. C, 1% calcium, 2% iron

Garlic, onion, tomatoes, and meat are the basic picadillo quartet; this sassy pita dip takes on Mediterranean flair by mingling with olives, almonds, and raisins.

PICADILLO PITA WEDGES

PREP:

20 minutes

COOK:

Low 6 hours, High 3 hours

MAKES:

16 (1/4 cup) servings

SLOW COOKER:

3 1/2- to 4-quart

1	pound ground beef, cooked and drained
1	medium onion chopped
3	cloves garlic, minced
1	16-ounce jar salsa
1/2	cup raisins
1/4	cup chopped pimiento-stuffed olives
2	tablespoons red wine vinegar
1/2	teaspoon ground cinnamon
1/2	teaspoon ground cumin
1/4	cup slivered almonds, toasted
	Slivered almonds, toasted
	Toasted pita wedges or bagel chips

1 In a 3 1/2- to 4-quart slow cooker stir together the beef, onion, garlic, salsa, raisins, olives, vinegar, cinnamon, and cumin. Cover and cook on low-heat setting for 6 to 8 hours or on high-heat setting for 3 to 4 hours. Stir in 1/4 cup almonds. Sprinkle with additional almonds and serve as a dip with toasted pita wedges.

Nutrition Facts per serving: 94 cal., 5 g total fat (2 g sat. fat), 18 mg chol., 190 mg sodium, 6 g carbo., 1 g fiber, 6 g pro. **Daily Values:** 4% vit. A, 8% vit. C, 2% calcium, 6% iron

This perfect party appetizer can be held in the slow cooker for up to 2 hours.
For a variation, substitute cocktail wieners or Polish sausage pieces.

SWEET 'N' SOUR HAM BALLS

2	eggs, lightly beaten
1	cup graham cracker crumbs
¼	cup milk
1	pound ground cooked ham
1	pound uncooked ground pork
	Nonstick cooking spray
2	9- or 10-ounce bottles sweet and sour sauce (1½ cups)
⅔	cup unsweetened pineapple juice
⅔	cup packed brown sugar
½	teaspoon ground ginger

1 For meatballs, in a large bowl combine eggs, graham cracker crumbs, and milk. Add ground ham and pork; mix well. Shape into sixty 1-inch meatballs. Lightly coat a 15×10×1-inch baking pan with cooking spray. Arrange meatballs in a single layer in pan. Bake in 375° oven for 18 to 20 minutes or until an instant-read thermometer registers 160° when inserted in the center of a meatball.

2 Meanwhile, in a 3½- to 4-quart slow cooker stir together sweet and sour sauce, pineapple juice, brown sugar, and ground ginger.

3 Add cooked meatballs to cooker; stir to coat with sauce. Cover; cook on low-heat setting for 3 to 4 hours or on high-heat setting for 1½ to 2 hours. Serve immediately or keep warm on low-heat setting for up to 2 hours.

Nutrition Facts per serving: 128 cal., 5 g total fat (2 g sat. fat), 45 mg chol., 468 mg sodium, 18 g carbo., 0 g fiber, 9 g pro. **Daily Values:** 1% vit. A, 2% vit. C, 2% calcium, 5% iron

PREP:
35 minutes

BAKE:
18 minutes

COOK:
Low 3 hours, High 1½ hours

OVEN:
375°

MAKES:
20 servings

SLOW COOKER:
3½- to 4-quart

Make the meatballs ahead of time and store them in the freezer. On party day it will take only minutes to combine the fixings in a slow cooker.

PINEAPPLE MEATBALLS & SAUSAGES

PREP:

35 minutes

BAKE:

15 minutes

COOK:

High 2 hours

OVEN:

350°

MAKES:

30 appetizer servings

SLOW COOKER:

3¹/₂- to 5-quart

MAKE-AHEAD TIP

Bake meatballs as directed. Place on a tray; cover and freeze for 30 minutes. Transfer meatballs to a freezer bag or wrap in foil. Seal, label, and freeze for up to 3 months. To use, transfer frozen meatballs to slow cooker and continue as directed above, except cook 3 hours on high-heat setting.

1   beaten egg

1   medium onion, finely chopped

¹/₃   cup finely chopped green sweet pepper

¹/₄   cup fine dry bread crumbs

3   tablespoons soy sauce

1   pound ground beef

1   16-ounce package small cooked smoked sausage links

1   cup chopped green sweet pepper

1   12-ounce jar pineapple ice cream topping or pineapple or apricot preserves

1   cup hot-style or regular vegetable juice

1   tablespoon quick-cooking tapioca

¹/₂   to 1 teaspoon crushed red pepper

1 In a large bowl combine egg, onion, ¹/₃ cup sweet pepper, the bread crumbs, and 1 tablespoon of the soy sauce. Add ground beef; mix well. Shape into 1-inch meatballs. Place meatballs in a 15×10×1-inch baking pan. Bake for 15 to 18 minutes or until an instant-read thermometer registers 160° when inserted in the center of a meatball.

2 Transfer meatballs to a 3¹/₂- to 5-quart slow cooker. Add sausage links and 1 cup sweet pepper. In a bowl combine ice cream topping or preserves, vegetable juice, remaining 2 tablespoons soy sauce, the tapioca, and crushed red pepper. Pour over meatballs and sausages; stir gently to coat.

3 Cover and cook on high-heat setting for 2 to 3 hours. Serve immediately or keep warm on low-heat setting for up to 2 hours longer. Use toothpicks to serve.

Nutrition Facts per serving: 124 cal., 7 g total fat (3 g sat. fat), 27 mg chol., 274 mg sodium, 10 g carbo., 0 g fiber, 5 g pro. **Daily Values:** 2% vit. A, 11% vit. C, 1% calcium, 3% iron

When stuffing mix is unavailable, use croutons and lightly crush them with a rolling pin. To make the recipe even quicker, substitute 2 pounds frozen cooked appetizer-size meatballs, thawed, for homemade.

ZESTY COCKTAIL MEATBALLS

1	beaten egg
1	10½-ounce can condensed French onion soup
2	cups herb-seasoned stuffing mix
2	pounds ground beef
1	15-ounce can tomato sauce
⅓	cup packed brown sugar
2	tablespoons Worcestershire sauce
2	tablespoons vinegar

1 In a large bowl combine egg, soup, and stuffing mix. Add ground beef; mix well. Shape into fifty 1-inch meatballs. Place meatballs in a 15×10×1-inch baking pan. Bake in a 350° oven for 15 to 18 minutes or until no longer pink (meat thermometer registers 160°). Drain fat off meatballs and transfer to a 3½- to 5-quart slow cooker.

2 In a bowl combine the remaining ingredients. Pour over meatballs; stir gently to coat.

3 Cover; cook on high-heat setting for 2 hours. Serve immediately or keep warm on low-heat setting for up to 2 hours. Use toothpicks to serve.

Nutrition Facts per serving: 178 cal., 8 g total fat (3 g sat. fat), 49 mg chol., 430 mg sodium, 13 g carbo., 1 g fiber, 13 g pro. **Daily Values:** 1% vit. C, 2% calcium, 10% iron

PREP:
30 minutes

BAKE:
15 minutes

COOK:
High 2 hours

OVEN:
350°

MAKES:
About 50 meatballs (16 servings)

SLOW COOKER:
3½- to 5-quart

Conversation will cease and guests will swoon when this arrives at the table. Dipping fruit, berries, cake, or brownies in this rum-laced confection is a completely luscious pleasure.

BUTTERSCOTCH FONDUE

PREP:

10 minutes

COOK:

Low 3 hours

MAKES:

about 21 (¼ cup) servings

SLOW COOKER:

3½- to 4-quart

2 14-ounce cans sweetened condensed milk

2 cups packed brown sugar

1 cup butter, melted

⅔ cup light corn syrup

1 teaspoon vanilla

¼ cup rum or milk

   Apple slices, fresh whole strawberries, cubed sponge cake, and/or cubed brownies

1 In a 3½- to 4-quart slow cooker stir together the sweetened condensed milk, brown sugar, butter, corn syrup, and vanilla. Cover and cook on low-heat setting for 3 hours (do not cook on high-heat setting). Whisk in rum or milk until smooth. Keep warm on low-heat setting for up to 2 hours, stirring occasionally.

2 Serve with apple slices, strawberries, sponge cake, and/or brownies.

Nutrition Facts per serving: 317 cal., 13 g total fat (8 g sat. fat), 38 mg chol., 163 mg sodium, 49 g carbo., 0 g fiber, 3 g pro. **Daily Values:** 9% vit. A, 2% vit. C, 13% calcium, 3% iron

Set bowls of these spirited nuts on a party buffet, sprinkle them on a salad, or serve them on small plates with crunchy pear slices for a light, healthful dessert.

FIVE-SPICE PECANS

1	pound pecan halves, toasted* (4 cups)
1/4	cup butter or margarine, melted
2	tablespoons soy sauce
1	teaspoon five-spice powder
1/2	teaspoon garlic powder
1/2	teaspoon ground ginger
1/4	teaspoon ground red pepper

1 Place toasted pecans in a 3¹/₂- to 4-quart slow cooker. In a small bowl combine the remaining ingredients. Pour over nuts and stir to coat.

2 Cover; cook on low-heat setting for 2 hours. Stir nuts. Spread in a single layer on waxed paper to cool. (Nuts appear soft after cooking, but will crisp upon cooling.) Store in a tightly covered container.

Nutrition Facts per serving: 225 cal., 23 g total fat (4 g sat. fat), 8 mg chol., 146 mg sodium, 4 g carbo., 3 g fiber, 3 g pro. **Daily Values:** 3% vit. A, 1% vit. C, 2% calcium, 4% iron

PREP:

10 minutes

COOK:

Low 2 hours

COOL:

1 hour

MAKES:

16 (¹/₄-cup) servings

SLOW COOKER:

3¹/₂- to 4-quart

*NOTE
To toast pecans, place in a single layer in a shallow baking pan. Bake in a 350° oven for 5 to 10 minutes, stirring once so nuts don't burn.

Make this snack to have on hand when you crave something crunchy. Store the roasted nuts in the refrigerator for up to one week.

SUGAR-ROASTED ALMONDS

PREP:

20 minutes

COOK:

Low 4 hours

MAKES:

22 (^{1}/$_4$ cup) servings

SLOW COOKER:

3^1/$_2$- to 4-quart

*NOTE
To toast nuts, place in a single layer in a shallow baking pan. Bake in a 350° oven for 5 to 10 minutes, stirring once so nuts don't burn.

4   cups whole, unblanched almonds or mixed nuts, toasted*

1   egg white

1   teaspoon water

^{1}/$_3$ cup granulated sugar

^{1}/$_3$ cup packed brown sugar

2   teaspoons ground cinnamon

^{1}/$_2$ teaspoon salt

1 Place the nuts in a 3^1/$_2$- to 4-quart slow cooker. In a medium mixing bowl beat the egg white and water with a wire whisk or rotary beater until frothy. Stir in remaining ingredients. Pour over nuts and stir gently to coat.

2 Cover and cook on low-heat setting for 4 to 4^1/$_2$ hours, stirring once halfway through cooking. Spread on waxed paper, separating into small clusters to cool. Store in a tightly covered container in the refrigerator for up to 1 week.

Nutrition Facts per serving: 182 cal., 13 g total fat (1 g sat. fat), 0 mg chol., 57 mg sodium, 12 g carbo., 3 g fiber, 6 g pro. **Daily Values:** 8% calcium, 7% iron

Vary this rich and delicious drink with flavored creamers and liqueurs. For a party, hold it for up to one hour in the cooker.

CHOCOLATE CREAM COCOA

1	9.6-ounce package nonfat dry milk powder (about 3½ cups)
1	cup powdered sugar
1	cup plain powdered nondairy creamer
¾	cup unsweetened cocoa powder
8	cups water
½	cup crème de cacao (optional)
	Sweetened whipped cream

1 In a 3½- to 5-quart slow cooker combine dry milk powder, powdered sugar, nondairy creamer, and cocoa powder. Gradually add water; stir well to dissolve.

2 Cover; cook on low-heat setting for 3 to 4 hours or on high-heat setting for 1½ to 2 hours. Hold on low for up to 1 hour, if desired.

3 If desired, stir in the crème de cacao. Stir mixture before serving. Ladle into mugs; top with whipped cream.

Nutrition Facts per serving: 210 cal., 6 g total fat (4 g sat. fat), 14 mg chol., 132 mg sodium, 29 g carbo., 0 g fiber, 9 g pro. **Daily Values:** 13% vit. A, 2% vit. C, 35% calcium, 4% iron

PREP:

10 minutes

COOK:

Low 3 hours, High 1½ hours

MAKES:

about 12 (6-ounce) servings

SLOW COOKER:

3½- to 5-quart

This wassail, which is Norse for "be in good health," is bound to become a holiday favorite. Garnish each serving with a slice of fresh orange.

HOLIDAY WASSAIL

PREP:

10 minutes

COOK:

Low 4 hours, High 2 hours

MAKES:

16 (6-ounce) servings

SLOW COOKER:

4- to 6-quart

MAKING A SPICE BAG
Removing whole spices and fruit peel from a mixture is quick when they are bundled together. Cut a 6- or 8-inch square from a double thickness of 100-percent-cotton cheesecloth and place the whole spices and peels in the center. Bring up the corners of the cheesecloth and tie it closed with clean kitchen string.

6 inches stick cinnamon, broken
12 whole cloves
6 cups water
1 12-ounce can frozen cranberry juice cocktail concentrate
1 12-ounce can frozen raspberry juice blend concentrate
1 12-ounce can frozen apple juice concentrate
1 cup brandy or rum
$\frac{1}{3}$ cup lemon juice
$\frac{1}{4}$ cup sugar
Orange slices (optional)

1 For spice bag, cut a 6-inch square from a double thickness of 100-percent-cotton cheesecloth. Place cinnamon and cloves in center of square, bring up corners, and tie closed with a clean kitchen string.

2 In a 4- to 6-quart slow cooker combine water, juice concentrates, brandy, lemon juice, and sugar. Add the spice bag to juice mixture.

3 Cover; cook on low-heat setting for 4 to 6 hours or on high-heat setting for 2 to 3 hours. Remove the spice bag and discard. To serve, ladle beverage into cups. If desired, float an orange slice on each serving.

Nutrition Facts per serving: 178 cal., 0 g total fat (0 g sat. fat), 0 mg chol., 12 mg sodium, 37 g carbo., 0 g fiber, 0 g pro. **Daily Values:** 85% vit. C, 1% calcium, 2% iron

Fire up this toasty drink—it's a wonderful treat at a bonfire buffet, winter open house, or Sunday afternoon game party.

HOT BUTTERED APPLE RUM

4	inches stick cinnamon, broken*
1	teaspoon whole allspice
1	teaspoon whole cloves
7	cups apple juice
1½	to 2 cups rum
⅓	to ½ cup packed brown sugar
	Butter

1 To make a spice bag, cut a 6-inch square from a double thickness of 100-percent-cotton cheesecloth. Place cinnamon, allspice, and cloves in center of square. Bring up corners of the cheesecloth and tie closed with clean kitchen string.

2 In a 3½- to 6-quart slow cooker, combine spice bag, apple juice, rum, and brown sugar. Cover; cook on low-heat setting for 7 to 8 hours or on high-heat setting for 3 to 4 hours.

3 Remove and discard spice bag. Ladle hot punch into cups; float about ½ teaspoon butter on each serving.

Nutrition Facts per serving: 214 cal., 2 g total fat (1 g sat. fat), 5 mg chol., 29 mg sodium, 27 g carbo., 0 g fiber, 0 g pro. **Daily Values:** 2% vit. A, 3% vit. C, 2% calcium, 4% iron

PREP:
10 minutes

COOK:
Low 7 hours, High 3 hours

MAKES:
10 (6-ounce) servings

SLOW COOKER:
3½- to 6-quart

*NOTE
To break cinnamon sticks, place in a heavy plastic bag and pound sticks with a meat mallet.

Put your hands around a hot drink, pass one to a friend — there's nothing better to ward off a cold-weather chill. Wine, fruit, and spices combine in this easy punch.

HOT AND SPICY CRANBERRY PUNCH

PREP:

10 minutes

COOK:

Low 4 hours, High 2 hours

MAKES:

18 ($\frac{1}{2}$ cup) servings

SLOW COOKER:

3$\frac{1}{2}$- to 6-quart

8　whole cardamom pods

16　inches stick cinnamon, broken

12　whole cloves

4　cups dry red wine

3　cups water

1　11$\frac{1}{2}$- or 12-ounce can frozen cranberry juice concentrate

$\frac{1}{3}$　cup honey

　Orange slices, halved (optional)

　Whole cloves (optional)

1 Cut a 6-inch square from a double thickness of 100-percent-cotton cheesecloth for a spice bag. Pinch cardamom pods to break. Center the cardamom, cinnamon, and 12 whole cloves on the cheesecloth square, bring up corners, and tie closed with clean kitchen string.

2 In a 3$\frac{1}{2}$- to 6-quart slow cooker combine spice bag, wine, water, frozen juice concentrate, and honey. Cover and cook on low-heat setting for 4 to 6 hours or on high-heat setting for 2 to 2$\frac{1}{2}$ hours.

3 Remove and discard spice bag. If desired, stud orange slices with additional whole cloves. Ladle punch into cups and float an orange slice on each serving.

Nutrition Facts per serving: 91 cal., 0 g total fat (0 g sat. fat), 0 mg chol., 5 mg sodium, 15 g carbo., 0 g fiber, 0 g pro. **Daily Values:** 24% vit. C, 1% calcium, 2% iron

Use processed cider from the grocery shelf; unprocessed cider from the refrigerated section will separate and appear curdled when heated.

MULLED CIDER

Peel from ½ orange, cut into pieces

6 inches stick cinnamon, broken*

1 1-inch piece fresh ginger, peeled and thinly sliced

1 teaspoon whole allspice

8 cups apple cider or apple juice

1 cup apple brandy (optional)

¼ cup honey or packed brown sugar

1 For spice bag, cut a 6- or 8-inch square from a double thickness of 100-percent-cotton cheesecloth. Place orange peel, cinnamon, ginger, and allspice in center of cheesecloth square, bring up the corners, and tie it closed with clean kitchen string.

2 In a 3½- to 5-quart slow cooker combine apple cider or apple juice, apple brandy (if desired), and honey or brown sugar. Add spice bag to cider mixture.

3 Cover; cook on low-heat setting for 4 to 6 hours or on high-heat setting for 2 to 3 hours. Remove and discard spice bag. Ladle cider into cups.

Nutrition Facts per serving: 148 cal., 0 g total fat (0 g sat. fat), 0 mg chol., 8 mg sodium, 38 g carbo., 0 g fiber, 0 g pro. **Daily Values:** 4% vit. C, 2% calcium, 5% iron

PREP:

10 minutes

COOK:

Low 4 hours, High 2 hours

MAKES:

8 or 9 (1 cup) servings

SLOW COOKER:

3½- to 5-quart

*NOTE
To break cinnamon sticks, place in a heavy plastic bag and pound sticks with a meat mallet.

With a libation like this, your guests will linger at the party. It's a great starter for dinner, brunch, or an evening of appetizers and good cheer.

MULLED CRANBERRY CIDER

PREP:

15 minutes

COOK:

Low 5 hours, High 2^1/$_2$ hours

MAKES:

10 (6-ounce) servings

SLOW COOKER:

3^1/$_2$- to 5-quart

1	small orange
8	cups cranberry-raspberry drink
^{1}/$_4$	cup packed brown sugar
6	inches stick cinnamon, broken
3	star anise
1	teaspoon whole cloves
	Orange peel strips (optional)

1 Remove the orange portion of the orange peel using a vegetable peeler. Cut peel into strips. Squeeze juice from orange; discard seeds and pulp. In a 3^1/$_2$- to 5-quart slow cooker combine orange juice, cranberry-raspberry drink, and brown sugar.

2 For spice bag, place the orange peel, cinnamon, star anise, and whole cloves on a double-thick, 8-inch square of 100-percent-cotton cheesecloth. Bring corners of cheesecloth together and tie with clean kitchen string. Add to slow cooker.

3 Cover; cook on low-heat setting for 5 to 6 hours or on high-heat setting for 2^1/$_2$ to 3 hours. To serve, remove spice bag and discard. Ladle cider into cups. If desired, garnish with additional orange peel.

Nutrition Facts per serving: 152 cal., 0 g total fat (0 g sat. fat), 0 mg chol., 30 mg sodium, 37 g carbo., 0 g fiber, 0 g pro. **Daily Values:** 85% vit. C, 3% iron

The unusual combination of fruit juices and wine will be a delicious hit at your next gathering.

SPICY SURPRISE SIPPER

Peel of 1 lemon, cut into strips

5 inches stick cinnamon, broken

1 teaspoon whole allspice

1 teaspoon whole cloves

4 cups water

1 12-ounce can frozen pineapple-orange juice concentrate

¼ cup honey

1 750-milliliter bottle dry white wine (3¼ cups)

1 Place lemon peel, cinnamon, allspice, and cloves on a 6-inch square of 100-percent-cotton cheesecloth. Bring corners of cheesecloth together and tie with clean kitchen string. In a 3½- to 6-quart slow cooker combine spice bag, water, juice concentrate, and honey. Stir in wine.

2 Cover and cook on low-heat setting for 5 to 7 hours or on high-heat setting for 2½ to 3 hours. Remove and discard spice bag.

Nutrition Facts per serving: 121 cal., 0 g total fat (0 g sat. fat), 0 mg chol., 15 mg sodium, 20 g carbo., 0 g fiber, 1 g pro. **Daily Values:** 95% vit. C, 2% calcium, 1% iron

PREP:
10 minutes

COOK:
Low 5 hours, High 2½ hours

MAKES:
12 (6-ounce) servings

SLOW COOKER:
3½- to 6-quart

A perfect starter for the next brunch or tailgate party, this sipper has just the right amount of spice. Garnish with celery sticks or a dill pickle spear.

SPICY TOMATO SIPPER

PREP:

10 minutes

COOK:

Low 4 hours, High 2 hours

MAKES:

8 (6-ounce) servings

SLOW COOKER:

3¹/₂- to 4-quart

1	46-ounce can vegetable juice
1	stalk celery, halved crosswise
2	tablespoons brown sugar
2	tablespoons lemon juice
1¹/₂	teaspoons prepared horseradish
1	teaspoon Worcestershire sauce
¹/₂	teaspoon bottled hot pepper sauce
	Celery sticks (optional)

1 In a 3¹/₂- to 4-quart slow cooker combine vegetable juice, halved celery stalk, brown sugar, lemon juice, horseradish, Worcestershire sauce, and hot pepper sauce.

2 Cover; cook on low-heat setting for 4 to 5 hours or on high-heat setting for 2 to 2¹/₂ hours. Discard celery. Ladle beverage into cups. If desired, garnish each serving with a celery stick.

Nutrition Facts per serving: 46 cal., 0 g total fat (0 g sat. fat), 0 mg chol., 456 mg sodium, 10 g carbo., 1 g fiber, 1 g pro. **Daily Values:** 29% vit. A, 75% vit. C, 3% calcium, 5% iron

PARTY TIME
When it's cold and damp outside, greet guests with the enticing aroma of a simmering spiced cocktail. Keep the beverage on low-heat setting and encourage guests to help themselves to sipping-temperature refills.

Fix this mellow drink to savor on fall and winter afternoons while cheering your favorite football team on to victory.

SPICED WINE TODDY

16	whole cloves
8	inches stick cinnamon, broken
6	cups apple juice
2	cups water
1½	cups Burgundy
⅔	cup instant lemon-flavored tea powder
2	tablespoons brown sugar

1 Tie cloves and cinnamon in a 6-inch square of 100-percent-cotton cheesecloth. Gather the corners of the cloth and tie it closed with clean kitchen string. In a 3½- to 6-quart slow cooker combine all ingredients. Cover; cook on low-heat setting for 4 to 6 hours or on high-heat setting for 2 to 3 hours. Remove and discard spice bag.

Nutrition Facts per serving: 90 cal., 0 g total fat (0 g sat. fat), 0 mg chol., 9 mg sodium, 18 g carbo., 0 g fiber, 0 g pro. **Daily Values:** 2% vit. C, 1% calcium, 4% iron

PREP:
10 minutes

COOK:
Low 4 hours, High 2 hours

MAKES:
12 (6-ounce) servings

SLOW COOKER:
3½- to 6-quart

The cinnamon scent and flavor of this alternative to dark or milk chocolate are as enticing as its creamy texture.

WHITE HOT CHOCOLATE

PREP:

10 minutes

COOK:

Low 4 hours, High 2 hours

MAKES:

8 servings

SLOW COOKER:

3¹/₂- to 4-quart

6 inches stick cinnamon, broken

8 cardamom pods

1 vanilla bean, split, or 2 teaspoons vanilla

3 cups half-and-half or light cream

3 cups milk

1¹/₂ cups white baking pieces

❶ Place the cinnamon, cardamom, and vanilla bean, if using, on a square of 100-percent-cotton cheesecloth. Bring up corners of cheesecloth and tie with clean kitchen string.

❷ In a 3¹/₂- to 4-quart slow cooker stir together the cream, milk, and baking pieces. Add spice bag. Cover and cook on low-heat setting for 4 to 5 hours or on high-heat setting for 2 to 2¹/₂ hours, stirring halfway through cooking time. Remove and discard spice bag. Stir in vanilla, if using.

Nutrition Facts per serving: 403 cal., 24 g total fat (18 g sat. fat), 40 mg chol., 142 mg sodium, 35 g carbo., 0 g fiber, 6 g pro. **Daily Values:** 12% vit. A, 3% vit. C, 21% calcium, 1% iron

SOUPS & STEWS

This full-flavored soup calls for surprisingly few ingredients. If desired, substitute ground turkey for the ground beef and chicken broth for the beef broth.

EASY VEGETABLE-BEEF SOUP

PREP:

20 minutes

COOK:

Low 7 hours, High 3$\frac{1}{2}$ hours

MAKES:

4 to 6 servings

SLOW COOKER:

3$\frac{1}{2}$- to 4-quart

1	pound ground beef
1	14-ounce can beef broth (1$\frac{2}{3}$ cups)
1$\frac{1}{4}$	cups water
1	10-ounce package frozen mixed vegetables
1	14$\frac{1}{2}$-ounce can tomatoes, cut up
1	10$\frac{3}{4}$-ounce can condensed tomato soup
1	tablespoon dried minced onion
1	teaspoon dried Italian seasoning, crushed
$\frac{1}{4}$	teaspoon garlic powder

1 In a large skillet cook beef until brown. Drain off fat.

2 Transfer meat to a 3$\frac{1}{2}$- to 4-quart slow cooker. Add the remaining ingredients to the cooker.

3 Cover; cook on low-heat setting for 7 to 8 hours or on high-heat setting for 3$\frac{1}{2}$ to 4 hours.

Nutrition Facts per serving: 314 cal., 12 g total fat (4 g sat. fat), 71 mg chol., 1,011 mg sodium, 26 g carbo., 5 g fiber, 27 g pro. **Daily Values:** 81% vit. A, 33% vit. C, 8% calcium, 26% iron

Turn this into a lamb soup by substituting lamb stew meat for the beef and replacing the thyme and basil with ¾ teaspoon dried rosemary and ¾ teaspoon dried mint.

BEEF & RICE SOUP

1½	pounds lean beef stew meat
1	tablespoon cooking oil
2	medium yellow summer squash, halved lengthwise and cut into ½-inch slices (2½ cups)
2	medium carrots, cut into ½-inch slices (1 cup)
1	cup chopped onions
1	clove garlic, minced
¾	teaspoon dried thyme, crushed
¾	teaspoon dried basil, crushed
6	cups beef broth
¼	cup dry red or white wine (optional)
2	cups chopped fresh spinach
½	cup quick-cooking rice

1 Cut any large pieces of stew meat. In a large skillet brown meat, half at a time, in hot oil. Drain off the fat.

2 In a 4- to 6-quart slow cooker place squash, carrots, onions, garlic, thyme, and basil. Place meat on vegetables. Pour broth and, if desired, wine over all.

3 Cover; cook on low-heat setting for 8 to 10 hours or on high-heat setting for 4 to 5 hours.

4 Stir in spinach and rice. Cover and cook 5 to 10 minutes more or until rice is tender.

Nutrition Facts per serving: 278 cal., 9 g total fat (2 g sat. fat), 54 mg chol., 748 mg sodium, 15 g carbo., 3 g fiber, 33 g pro. **Daily Values:** 116% vit. A, 21% vit. C, 5% calcium, 24% iron

PREP:

20 minutes

COOK:

Low 8 hours, High 4 hours; plus 5 minutes

MAKES:

6 servings

SLOW COOKER:

4- to 6-quart

This rich and satisfying chili-flavored soup has chunks of beef and a basketful of vegetables. Stewing the bones adds beefy flavor and body to the broth. Accompany it with slices of crusty bread.

BEEF & GARDEN VEGETABLE SOUP

PREP:

30 minutes

COOK:

Low 8 hours, High 4 hours

MAKES:

6 to 8 servings

SLOW COOKER:

3¹/₂- to 6-quart

2	to 2¹/₂ pounds meaty beef shank crosscuts
2	medium carrots, bias-sliced
2	medium stalks celery, sliced
1	large potato, peeled and cubed
1	cup coarsely chopped cabbage
1	small onion, coarsely chopped
3	cups water
2	cups tomato juice
2	tablespoons instant beef bouillon granules
1	tablespoon Worcestershire sauce
1	teaspoon chili powder
2	bay leaves

1 Cut meat into 1-inch cubes, reserving bones and trimming off fat.

2 In a 3¹/₂- to 6-quart slow cooker place the carrots, celery, potato, cabbage, onion, beef, and beef bones. Add the remaining ingredients. Cover; cook on low-heat setting for 8 to 10 hours or on high-heat setting for 4 to 5 hours.

3 Remove and discard bones and bay leaves. Skim off fat.

Nutrition Facts per serving: 305 cal., 13 g total fat (4 g sat. fat), 64 mg chol., 1,463 mg sodium, 14 g carbo., 2 g fiber, 33 g pro. **Daily Values:** 115% vit. A, 42% vit. C, 6% calcium, 25% iron

*Soup lovers can't resist this combination of spicy tomato base, beef, and vegetables.
Complete the meal with cheesy corn bread.*

ZESTY BEEF & SLAW SOUP

1	pound ground beef
½	cup chopped onion
2	cloves garlic, minced
2	cups pre-shredded coleslaw mix
1	10-ounce package frozen whole kernel corn
1	9-ounce package frozen cut green beans
4	cups hot-style vegetable juice
1	14½-ounce can Italian-style stewed tomatoes
1	tablespoon Worcestershire sauce
1	teaspoon dried basil, crushed
¼	teaspoon pepper

1 In a large skillet cook ground beef, onion, and garlic until meat is brown and onion is tender. Drain off fat.

2 In a 3½- to 5-quart slow cooker combine meat mixture and the remaining ingredients.

3 Cover; cook on low-heat setting for 8 to 10 hours or on high-heat setting for 4 to 5 hours.

Nutrition Facts per serving: 324 cal., 16 g total fat (6 g sat. fat), 56 mg chol., 750 mg sodium, 28 g carbo., 4 g fiber, 18 g pro. **Daily Values:** 33% vit. A, 75% vit. C, 8% calcium, 16% iron

PREP:

15 minutes

COOK:

Low 8 hours, High 4 hours

MAKES:

6 servings

SLOW COOKER:

3½- to 5-quart

Pumpkin, plus a dash of nutmeg, lends a fall harvest flair to this pasta-filled soup. If fresh pumpkin is unavailable, use butternut squash.

BEEFY PUMPKIN & PASTA SOUP

PREP:

20 minutes

COOK:

Low 10 hours, High 5 hours

MAKES:

6 servings

SLOW COOKER:

3½- to 5-quart

1½	pounds beef stew meat, cut into 1-inch cubes
1	10-ounce package frozen whole kernel corn
1½	cups peeled, seeded, and cubed pumpkin or butternut squash
1½	cups water
1	8-ounce can tomato sauce
¾	cup chopped onion
½	cup chopped green sweet pepper
1	clove garlic, minced
½	teaspoon salt
¼	teaspoon black pepper
⅛	teaspoon ground nutmeg
2	ounces dried medium shell macaroni or cavatelli
¼	cup snipped fresh parsley

1 In a 3½- to 5-quart slow cooker combine meat, corn, pumpkin or squash, water, tomato sauce, onion, sweet pepper, garlic, salt, black pepper, and nutmeg.

2 Cover; cook on low-heat setting for 10 to 12 hours or on high-heat setting for 5 to 6 hours.

3 Cook pasta according to package directions; drain. Stir pasta into the soup. Ladle soup into bowls; sprinkle with parsley.

Nutrition Facts per serving: 301 cal., 9 g total fat (3 g sat. fat), 82 mg chol., 467 mg sodium, 26 g carbo., 2 g fiber, 31 g pro. **Daily Values:** 32% vit. C, 3% calcium, 29% iron

Beer is a prominent ingredient in this hearty soup. For a light beer flavor, use a pale beer. Use a darker variety for pronounced beer taste.

BEEF & BEER VEGETABLE SOUP

3	medium onions, sliced
1	pound carrots, cut into ½-inch slices
4	parsnips, cut into ½-inch slices
4	cloves garlic, minced
2	bay leaves
1	tablespoon snipped fresh thyme or 1 teaspoon dried thyme, crushed
¾	teaspoon salt
½	teaspoon pepper
2	tablespoons quick-cooking tapioca
1½	pounds beef stew meat, cut into 1-inch cubes
1	14-ounce can beef broth
1	12-ounce can beer

1 In a 5- to 6-quart slow cooker place onions, carrots, parsnips, garlic, bay leaves, dried thyme (if using), salt, and pepper. Sprinkle with tapioca. Place meat on vegetables. Add beef broth and beer.

2 Cover; cook on low-heat setting for 10 to 12 hours or on high-heat setting for 5 to 6 hours. To serve, remove bay leaves; stir in fresh thyme, if using.

Nutrition Facts per serving: 344 cal., 7 g total fat (2 g sat. fat), 54 mg chol., 637 mg sodium, 38 g carbo., 7 g fiber, 29 g pro. **Daily Values:** 341% vit. A, 37% vit. C, 8% calcium, 20% iron

PREP:
25 minutes
COOK:
Low 10 hours, High 5 hours
MAKES:
6 servings
SLOW COOKER:
5- to 6-quart

COOKING UNDER COVER
Because slow cookers cook food at such low temperatures, removing the lid can dramatically reduce the temperature inside the cooker. When you lift the cover to stir or to add ingredients, replace the lid as quickly as possible, especially when cooking on low-heat setting. An uncovered cooker can lose up to 200° of cooking heat in as little as 2 minutes. A quick peek, however, lowers the temperature only 1 or 2 degrees. If you have no reason to peek—don't!

Purchased spaghetti sauce rounds out the flavor and provides robust color to this hearty soup.

RICH BEEF & BARLEY SOUP

PREP:

30 minutes

COOK:

Low 9 hours, High 4^1/$_2$ hours

MAKES:

6 to 8 servings

SLOW COOKER:

3^1/$_2$- to 6-quart

1^1/$_2$	pounds beef stew meat
1	tablespoon cooking oil
1	cup thinly sliced carrots
1	cup sliced celery
1	medium onion, thinly sliced
^{1}/$_2$	cup coarsely chopped green sweet pepper
4	cups beef broth
1	14^1/$_2$-ounce can tomatoes, cut up
1	cup spaghetti sauce
^{2}/$_3$	cup pearl barley
1^1/$_2$	teaspoons dried basil, crushed
^{1}/$_2$	teaspoon salt
^{1}/$_4$	teaspoon black pepper
^{1}/$_4$	cup snipped fresh parsley

1 Cut meat into 1-inch cubes. In a large skillet brown meat, half at a time, in hot oil. Drain well.

2 Meanwhile, in a 3^1/$_2$- to 6-quart slow cooker combine carrots, celery, onion, and sweet pepper. Add broth, undrained tomatoes, spaghetti sauce, barley, basil, salt, and black pepper. Stir in browned meat.

3 Cover; cook on low-heat setting for 9 to 10 hours or on high-heat setting for 4^1/$_2$ to 5 hours. Skim off fat. Stir in parsley.

Nutrition Facts per serving: 408 cal., 19 g total fat (7 g sat. fat), 72 mg chol., 998 mg sodium, 30 g carbo., 6 g fiber, 29 g pro. **Daily Values:** 116% vit. A, 45% vit. C, 8% calcium, 25% iron

When you're hungry for the beefy taste of steak without the heavy meal that goes with it, this soup is the perfect dinner solution.

STEAK & VEGETABLE SOUP

2	tablespoons all-purpose flour
1	teaspoon ground chipotle peppers or chili powder
1	pound beef stew meat, cut into ½-inch cubes
2	tablespoons cooking oil
1	cup sliced fresh mushrooms
½	cup chopped carrot
½	cup chopped onion
1	cup frozen succotash
1	teaspoon dried oregano, crushed
2	14-ounce cans beef broth

PREP:
25 minutes

COOK:
Low 10 hours, High 5 hours

MAKES:
4 servings

SLOW COOKER:
3½- to 4-quart

1 Place flour and chipotle peppers or chili powder in a plastic bag. Add meat cubes and shake until meat is coated with flour mixture. In a large skillet brown meat, half at a time, in hot oil.

2 In a 3½- to 4-quart slow cooker layer mushrooms, carrot, onion, and succotash. Add meat and oregano. Pour beef broth over all.

3 Cover and cook on low-heat setting for 10 to 12 hours or on high-heat setting for 5 to 6 hours. Ladle into bowls to serve.

Nutrition Facts per serving: 318 cal., 15 g total fat (4 g sat. fat), 54 mg chol., 817 mg sodium, 16 g carbo., 3 g fiber, 30 g pro. **Daily Values:** 84% vit. A, 9% vit. C, 4% calcium, 21% iron

Combine pork, hominy, and chili powder to make a flavorful rendition of pozole. Hominy, dried corn that has had the hulls removed, is in the canned vegetable sections of supermarkets.

PORK & HOMINY SOUP

PREP:

30 minutes

COOK:

Low 8 hours, High 4 hours

MAKES:

6 servings

SLOW COOKER:

3¹/₂- to 4-quart

1	pound boneless pork shoulder
1	tablespoon cooking oil
1	medium red or green sweet pepper, cut into ¹/₂-inch pieces
1	medium tomato, chopped
¹/₂	cup chopped onion
4	cloves garlic, minced
2	14¹/₂-ounce cans golden hominy, drained
1	4-ounce can diced green chile peppers
1	tablespoon chili powder
¹/₂	teaspoon dried oregano, crushed
2	14-ounce cans chicken broth
	Tortilla chips (optional)
	Sour cream (optional)

1 Trim fat from meat; cut pork into 1-inch cubes. In a large skillet brown pork, half at a time, in hot oil. Drain off fat.

2 Transfer pork to a 3¹/₂- to 4-quart slow cooker. Add sweet pepper, tomato, onion, garlic, hominy, chile peppers, chili powder, and oregano. Pour broth over all.

3 Cover; cook on low-heat setting for 8 to 10 hours or on high-heat setting for 4 to 5 hours. If desired, serve with tortilla chips and sour cream.

Nutrition Facts per serving: 277 cal., 11 g total fat (3 g sat. fat), 51 mg chol., 1,015 mg sodium, 26 g carbo., 5 g fiber, 19 g pro. **Daily Values:** 32% vit. A, 71% vit. C, 5% calcium, 14% iron

Enjoy this easy-to-make version of a Mexican classic anytime by stocking the ingredients in your pantry or freezer.

SAUSAGE & BLACK BEAN SOUP

12	ounces bulk pork sausage
2	14-ounce cans reduced-sodium chicken broth
1	15-ounce can black beans, rinsed and drained
1	14½-ounce can golden hominy, rinsed and drained
1	14½-ounce can Mexican-style stewed tomatoes, cut up
1	cup frozen loose-pack diced hash brown potatoes
1	small green sweet pepper, chopped (½ cup)
1	small onion, chopped (⅓ cup)
1	clove garlic, minced
1	teaspoon dried oregano, crushed
½	teaspoon chili powder

1 In a large saucepan brown the sausage, breaking sausage into small pieces; drain off fat. Place in a 3½- to 6-quart slow cooker.

2 Stir in the chicken broth, black beans, hominy, undrained tomatoes, hash brown potatoes, sweet pepper, onion, garlic, oregano, and chili powder. Cover; cook on low-heat setting for 4 to 5 hours or on high-heat setting for 2 to 2½ hours.

Nutrition Facts per serving: 356 cal., 17 g total fat (7 g sat. fat), 32 mg chol., 1,085 mg sodium, 33 g carbo., 7 g fiber, 15 g pro. **Daily Values:** 9% vit. A, 25% vit. C, 7% calcium, 13% iron

PREP:
15 minutes

COOK:
Low 4 hours, High 2 hours

MAKES:
6 servings

SLOW COOKER:
3½- to 6-quart

Substitute a pound of purchased bean mix or a pound of any of the beans for this soup. For thicker soup, mash part of the beans before serving.

HAM & MIXED BEAN SOUP

PREP:
25 minutes

COOK:
Low 8 hours, High 4 hours

MAKES:
8 servings

SLOW COOKER:
4- to 6-quart

½ cup dry navy or Great Northern beans

½ cup dry black beans or kidney beans

½ cup dry lima beans

½ cup dry garbanzo beans

6 cups water

2 cups cooked ham cut into ½-inch pieces (about 10 ounces)

1 cup chopped onions (2 medium)

1 cup chopped carrots (2 medium)

½ cup dry split peas

1 teaspoon dried basil, crushed

1 teaspoon dried oregano, crushed

¾ teaspoon salt

¼ teaspoon pepper

2 bay leaves

6 cups water

Salt

Pepper

1 Rinse beans; drain. In a Dutch oven combine the beans and 6 cups water. Bring to boiling; reduce heat. Simmer, uncovered, for 10 minutes. Cover and let stand for 1 hour. Drain and rinse beans.

2 Meanwhile, in a 4- to 6-quart slow cooker combine ham, onions, carrots, peas, basil, oregano, ¾ teaspoon salt, ¼ teaspoon pepper, and bay leaves. Stir in drained beans and the remaining 6 cups fresh water.

3 Cover; cook on low-heat setting for 8 to 10 hours or on high-heat setting for 4 to 5 hours. Discard the bay leaves. If desired, mash beans slightly. Season to taste with additional salt and pepper.

Nutrition Facts per serving: 289 cal., 5 g total fat (1 g sat. fat), 21 mg chol., 786 mg sodium, 41 g carbo., 13 g fiber, 22 g pro. **Daily Values:** 78% vit. A, 5% vit. C, 8% calcium, 21% iron

Substitute curly endive or another mildly bitter green for the escarole, if you like. Endive has a stronger flavor than escarole.

SPICY SAUSAGE & ESCAROLE SOUP

1	beaten egg
2	tablespoons milk
¾	cup soft bread crumbs (1 slice)
1	pound bulk Italian sausage
	Nonstick cooking spray
2	15-ounce cans Great Northern beans, rinsed and drained
2	medium carrots, cut into ½-inch pieces
2	medium tomatoes, chopped
½	cup chopped onion (1 medium)
2	cloves garlic, minced
1	teaspoon dried Italian seasoning, crushed
½	teaspoon crushed red pepper
5	cups chicken broth
4	cups chopped escarole
	Grated Parmesan cheese (optional)

PREP:
1 hour

COOK:
Low 10 hours, High 5 hours

MAKES:
8 servings

SLOW COOKER:
4- to 6-quart

1 For meatballs, in a large bowl combine egg, milk, and bread crumbs. Add sausage and mix well. Shape into 1-inch meatballs. Lightly coat a 12-inch skillet with cooking spray. Add meatballs and brown on all sides over medium heat. Drain meatballs.

2 In a 4- to 6-quart slow cooker place beans, carrots, tomatoes, onion, garlic, Italian seasoning, and red pepper. Add meatballs to cooker. Pour broth over all.

3 Cover; cook on low-heat setting for 10 to 11 hours or on high-heat setting for 5 to 5½ hours. Stir in escarole. Ladle soup into bowls and, if desired, sprinkle with grated Parmesan cheese.

Nutrition Facts per serving: 356 cal., 15 g total fat (6 g sat. fat), 65 mg chol., 848 mg sodium, 31 g carbo., 7 g fiber, 21 g pro. **Daily Values:** 110% vit. A, 19% vit. C, 11% calcium, 18% iron

Smoked turkey sausage can be used in place of the ham. Rice is the surprising addition to this old-fashioned soup.

SPLIT PEA & RICE SOUP WITH HAM

PREP:

25 minutes

COOK:

Low 8 hours, High 4 hours

STAND:

5 minutes

MAKES:

6 servings

SLOW COOKER:

3^1/$_2$- to 5-quart

2	cups cubed cooked ham
1	cup dry split peas
1	cup chopped onions (2 medium)
1	cup chopped celery with leaves
1	cup shredded carrots (2 medium)
2	tablespoons snipped fresh parsley
^{1}/$_2$	teaspoon dried thyme, crushed
^{1}/$_4$	teaspoon pepper
4	cups chicken broth
2	cups water
1	cup quick-cooking rice

1 In a 3^1/$_2$- to 5-quart slow cooker combine ham, peas, onions, celery, carrots, parsley, thyme, and pepper. Pour broth and water over all.

2 Cover; cook on low-heat setting for 8 to 10 hours or on high-heat setting for 4 to 5 hours. Stir in rice. Cover; let stand 5 minutes or until rice is tender.

Nutrition Facts per serving: 293 cal., 7 g total fat (2 g sat. fat), 26 mg chol., 1,292 mg sodium, 39 g carbo., 10 g fiber, 19 g pro. **Daily Values:** 96% vit. A, 10% vit. C, 4% calcium, 15% iron

If you use the wine option in this classic bean and sausage soup, buy a good-quality red wine that you also can serve with dinner.

SAUSAGE, VEGETABLE, & BEAN SOUP

1¼	cups dry Great Northern beans
1	14½-ounce can whole Italian-style tomatoes or low-sodium tomatoes, cut up
1	14-ounce can beef broth
¾	pound fresh Italian sausage links, cut into ½-inch slices
1	medium onion, chopped
⅓	cup dry red wine or water
1	clove garlic, minced
½	teaspoon dried Italian seasoning, crushed
½	of a 10-ounce package frozen chopped spinach, thawed
1	large yellow summer squash or zucchini, sliced
	Grated Parmesan cheese (optional)

1 Rinse beans; place in a large saucepan. Add enough water to cover beans by 2 inches. Bring to boiling; reduce heat. Simmer, uncovered, for 10 minutes. Remove from heat. Cover and let stand for 1 hour. (Or place beans and water in a large saucepan. Cover and let soak in a cool place overnight.) Drain and rinse beans.

2 In a 3½- to 4-quart slow cooker combine beans, undrained tomatoes, beef broth, Italian sausage, onion, wine or water, garlic, and Italian seasoning.

3 Cover; cook on low-heat setting for 11 to 12 hours or on high-heat setting for 6 to 8 hours. Squeeze excess liquid from spinach. Stir spinach and squash or zucchini into soup. Cover and let stand for 10 minutes. To serve, ladle soup into bowls. If desired, sprinkle with Parmesan cheese.

Nutrition Facts per serving: 460 cal., 17 g total fat (6 g sat. fat), 49 mg chol., 1,118 mg sodium, 47 g carbo., 7 g fiber, 28 g pro. **Daily Values:** 42% vit. C, 17% calcium, 38% iron

PREP:
25 minutes

COOK:
Low 11 hours, High 6 hours

STAND:
10 minutes

MAKES:
4 to 5 servings

SLOW COOKER:
3½- to 4-quart

Boost the flavor of split pea soup with curry and rich cream. For optimum curry flavor, use fresh curry powder; the fragrance will determine whether it's fresh.

SPLIT PEA CURRY SOUP

PREP:

20 minutes

COOK:

Low 10 hours, High 4 hours

MAKES:

5 servings

SLOW COOKER:

3¹/₂- to 5-quart

1¹/₄	cups dry green split peas
1	small meaty ham bone or 2 smoked pork hocks
1	cup coarsely chopped onions (2 medium)
1	cup coarsely chopped celery
1	cup coarsely chopped carrots (2 medium)
1	tablespoon curry powder
1	tablespoon snipped fresh marjoram or thyme or 1 teaspoon dried marjoram or thyme, crushed
1	bay leaf
5	cups chicken broth
1	cup half-and-half or light cream
	Salt and pepper

1 Rinse split peas; drain. Place drained peas in a 3¹/₂- to 5-quart slow cooker. Add the ham bone or pork hocks, onions, celery, carrots, curry powder, dried marjoram or thyme (if using), and bay leaf. Pour chicken broth over all.

2 Cover; cook on low-heat setting for 10 to 12 hours or on high-heat setting for 4 to 5 hours. Remove ham bone or pork hocks. When cool enough to handle, cut meat off bones; finely chop meat. Discard the bones and bay leaf.

3 Return meat to cooker. Stir in half-and-half or light cream and, if using, the fresh marjoram or thyme. Season to taste with salt and pepper.

Nutrition Facts per serving: 369 cal., 10 g total fat (5 g sat. fat), 38 mg chol., 1,381 mg sodium, 43 g carbo., 5 g fiber, 29 g pro. **Daily Values:** 11% vit. C, 11% calcium, 26% iron

Any variety of winter squash—acorn, butternut, hubbard, or turban—will furnish this classic Italian vegetable soup with bright color and gentle sweetness.

ITALIAN SQUASH & VEGETABLE SOUP

1	pound uncooked Italian or pork sausage links, cut into ¾-inch slices
2½	cups peeled winter squash, such as butternut squash, cut into 1-inch cubes
1½	cups cubed potatoes
2	medium fennel bulbs, trimmed and cut into 1-inch pieces
1	large onion, chopped
2	cloves garlic, minced
1	15-ounce can red kidney beans, rinsed and drained
½	teaspoon dried sage, crushed
4	cups chicken broth or vegetable broth
1	cup dry white wine
4	cups chopped kale or fresh spinach

1 In a large skillet cook the sausage until brown; drain well.

2 In a 5- to 6-quart slow cooker place squash, potatoes, fennel, onion, garlic, beans, and sage. Top with sausage. Pour broth and wine over all.

3 Cover and cook on low-heat setting for 8 to 10 hours or on high-heat setting for 4 to 5 hours. Stir in kale or spinach. Cover and cook for 5 minutes more.

Nutrition Facts per serving: 315 cal., 14 g total fat (5 g sat. fat), 38 mg chol., 933 mg sodium, 27 g carbo., 14 g fiber, 16 g pro. **Daily Values:** 69% vit. C, 11% calcium, 13% iron

PREP:
40 minutes

COOK:
Low 8 hours, High 4 hours; plus 5 minutes

MAKES:
8 servings

SLOW COOKER:
5- to 6-quart

Plan this soup for days that start hectic and stay that way. It takes only minutes to assemble in the morning and will be ready to serve at the end of the day.

POLISH SAUSAGE & CABBAGE SOUP

PREP:

15 minutes

COOK:

Low 10 hours, High 5 hours

MAKES:

6 servings

SLOW COOKER:

3¹/₂- to 6-quart

2   cups cubed peeled potatoes

4   cups packaged shredded cabbage with carrot (coleslaw mix)

1   large onion, chopped

2   teaspoons caraway seeds, crushed

1   pound cooked Polish sausage, halved lengthwise and cut into ¹/₂-inch slices

4   cups reduced-sodium chicken broth

❶ In a 3¹/₂- to 6-quart slow cooker place potatoes, coleslaw mix, onion, caraway seeds, and sausage. Pour broth over all.

❷ Cover and cook on low-heat setting for 10 to 12 hours or on high-heat setting for 5 to 6 hours. Ladle into bowls.

Nutrition Facts per serving: 322 cal., 22 g total fat (8 g sat. fat), 53 mg chol., 1,087 mg sodium, 16 g carbo., 3 g fiber, 15 g pro. **Daily Values:** 42% vit. C, 5% calcium, 11% iron

BROTH OPTIONS

Canned broths and bouillon granules and cubes are handy alternatives to homemade chicken, beef, or vegetable broth. Canned chicken, beef, and vegetable broth are ready to use. Instant bouillon granules and cubes can be purchased in beef, chicken, vegetable, and onion flavors. Mixing one cube or 1 teaspoon of granules with 1 cup of boiling water is an easy way to make broth. If you're watching sodium intake, use a lower-sodium broth and adjust the seasoning in the recipe to taste.

Lentils, Canadian bacon, and cheese-filled tortellini make this soup a hearty meal. Round it out with a small salad or breadsticks.

SPINACH & LENTIL TORTELLINI SOUP

½ cup dry lentils

2 cups coarsely shredded carrots

1 large onion, finely chopped

4 ounces chopped cooked ham or Canadian-style bacon

2 cloves garlic, minced

2 tablespoons snipped fresh basil or 2 teaspoons dried basil, crushed

1½ tablespoons snipped fresh thyme or 1½ teaspoons dried thyme, crushed

¼ teaspoon pepper

5 cups reduced-sodium chicken broth

1 cup water

1 9-ounce package refrigerated cheese-filled tortellini

4 cups torn fresh spinach

PREP:

20 minutes

COOK:

Low 6½ hours, High 3¼ hours; plus 30 minutes on High

MAKES:

6 servings

SLOW COOKER:

3½- to 5-quart

1 Rinse lentils; drain. Place lentils in a 3½- to 5-quart slow cooker. Add the carrots, onion, ham or bacon, garlic, dried basil and thyme (if using), and pepper. Pour broth and water over all.

2 Cover; cook on low-heat setting for 6½ to 7 hours or on high-heat setting for 3¼ to 3½ hours. If using low-heat setting, turn to high-heat setting. Stir in tortellini. Cover and cook 30 minutes more. To serve, stir in spinach and, if using, the fresh basil and thyme.

Nutrition Facts per serving: 245 cal., 5 g total fat (1 g sat. fat), 30 mg chol., 1,023 mg sodium, 35 g carbo., 4 g fiber, 16 g pro. **Daily Values:** 25% vit. C, 12% calcium, 20% iron

Savor the flavors of sun-drenched Tuscany with this hearty vegetable soup. Serve focaccia wedges or thick slices of buttery garlic bread with the soup.

ITALIAN BEAN SOUP WITH SAUSAGE

PREP:

20 minutes

COOK:

Low 9 hours, High 5 hours; plus 10 minutes on High

STAND:

1 hour

MAKES:

6 servings

SLOW COOKER:

3^1/$_2$- to 5-quart

1^1/$_4$ cups dry Great Northern beans

4 cups cold water

8 ounces uncooked Italian sausage links, cut into ^{1}/$_2$- to ^{3}/$_4$-inch slices

2^1/$_4$ cups water

2 14-ounce cans beef broth

1 large onion, chopped

2 cloves garlic, minced

1 teaspoon dried Italian seasoning, crushed

1 medium yellow summer squash or zucchini, sliced (about 1^1/$_2$ cups)

^{1}/$_3$ cup dry red wine or water

^{1}/$_2$ of a 10-ounce package frozen chopped spinach, thawed and well drained

1 14^1/$_2$-ounce can low-sodium diced tomatoes

Grated Parmesan cheese (optional)

1 Rinse dry beans. In a Dutch oven combine beans and the 4 cups cold water. Bring to boiling; reduce heat. Simmer for 10 minutes. Remove from heat. Cover and let stand 1 hour. Drain and rinse beans.

2 Meanwhile, in a medium skillet cook Italian sausage until brown. Drain well on paper towels.

3 In a 3^1/$_2$- to 5-quart slow cooker combine the drained beans, drained sausage, the 2^1/$_4$ cups water, broth, onion, garlic, Italian seasoning, squash, and wine. Cover and cook on low-heat setting for 9 to 10 hours or on high-heat setting for 5 to 6 hours or until beans are tender.

4 If using low-heat setting, turn to high-heat setting. Stir spinach and undrained tomatoes into soup. Cover and cook 10 to 15 minutes more on high-heat setting or until heated through. If desired, sprinkle each serving with Parmesan cheese.

Nutrition Facts per serving: 329 cal., 14 g total fat (5 g sat. fat), 31 mg chol., 841 mg sodium, 33 g carbo., 10 g fiber, 17 g pro. **Daily Values:** 20% vit. C, 12% calcium, 16% iron

For a pretty and tasty garnish, sprinkle crumbled crisp-cooked bacon and a little chopped hard-cooked egg onto each bowl of soup.

CHICKEN-SAUSAGE-SAUERKRAUT SOUP

8   ounces skinless, boneless chicken breast halves, cut into 1-inch pieces

8   ounces smoked Polish sausage links, coarsely chopped

1   small potato, cut into ½-inch pieces (¾ cup)

1   medium carrot, cut into ½-inch pieces (½ cup)

½   cup chopped onion (1 medium)

½   cup sliced celery

1   10¾-ounce can condensed cream of mushroom soup

1   8-ounce can sauerkraut, rinsed and drained

1   4-ounce can sliced mushrooms, drained

1   tablespoon vinegar

½   teaspoon dried dillweed

¼   teaspoon pepper

1   14-ounce can reduced-sodium chicken broth

1¾   cups water

PREP:
20 minutes
COOK:
Low 10 hours, High 5 hours
MAKES:
4 servings
SLOW COOKER:
3½- to 5-quart

1 In a 3½- to 5-quart slow cooker combine chicken, Polish sausage, potato, carrot, onion, and celery. Add mushroom soup, sauerkraut, mushrooms, vinegar, dillweed, and pepper. Stir in chicken broth and water.

2 Cover; cook on low-heat setting for 10 to 11 hours or on high-heat setting for 5 to 5½ hours.

Nutrition Facts per serving: 389 cal., 23 g total fat (8 g sat. fat), 73 mg chol., 1,826 mg sodium, 19 g carbo., 4 g fiber, 26 g pro. **Daily Values:** 78% vit. A, 28% vit. C, 7% calcium, 18% iron

This sophisticated and tasty soup is packed full of winter vegetables. Adding fresh spinach before serving lends a touch of color and a boost of nutrition.

SPICY PORK & VEGETABLE SOUP

PREP:

30 minutes

COOK:

Low 10 hours, High 5 hours

MAKES:

6 servings

SLOW COOKER:

3$^1/_2$- to 4-quart

1	pound boneless pork or beef stew meat
1	tablespoon cooking oil
$^1/_2$	cup chopped onion
2	cloves garlic, minced
1	teaspoon paprika
3	cups water
2	medium parsnips or 3 medium carrots, cut into $^1/_4$-inch pieces (1$^1/_2$ cups)
$^1/_2$	pound winter squash, peeled and cut into $^1/_2$-inch pieces (1$^1/_2$ cups)
1	medium sweet potato, peeled and cut into $^1/_2$-inch pieces (1$^1/_3$ cups)
1	8$^3/_4$-ounce can whole kernel corn
4	teaspoons instant beef bouillon granules
$^1/_2$	teaspoon salt
$^1/_4$	teaspoon ground red pepper
2	cups torn fresh spinach

❶ Cut meat into $^1/_2$-inch cubes. In a large skillet brown half of the meat in hot oil. Remove meat; set aside. Brown remaining meat with onion, garlic, and paprika.

❷ Meanwhile, in a 3$^1/_2$- to 4-quart slow cooker place water, parsnips or carrots, squash, sweet potato, undrained corn, beef bouillon granules, salt, and red pepper. Stir in all of the meat and onion mixture. Cover; cook on low-heat setting for 10 to 11 hours or on high-heat setting for 5 to 5$^1/_2$ hours.

❸ Before serving, add torn spinach to soup and stir until slightly wilted.

Nutrition Facts per serving: 243 cal., 9 g total fat (2 g sat. fat), 51 mg chol., 907 mg sodium, 25 g carbo., 5 g fiber, 18 g pro. **Daily Values:** 146% vit. A, 32% vit. C, 7% calcium, 15% iron

Escaping south of the border is as cinchy as soup: Tap your pantry and freezer for the ingredients, toss them in the cooker, and you're there with each spoonful.

HAM & SALSA SOUP WITH LIME

2¼ cups dry black beans (about 1 pound)

2 cups chopped cooked smoked ham

1 cup chopped yellow and/or red sweet pepper

3½ cups water

1 16-ounce jar purchased lime-garlic salsa

Dairy sour cream (optional)

Lime wedges (optional)

1 Rinse beans; place in a large saucepan. Add enough water to cover beans by 2 inches. Bring to boiling; reduce heat. Simmer, uncovered, for 10 minutes. Remove from heat. Cover; let stand about 1 hour. Drain and rinse beans.

2 In a 3½- to 4-quart slow cooker combine the beans, ham, sweet pepper, and 3½ cups fresh water. Cover and cook on low-heat setting for 11 to 13 hours or on high-heat setting for 5½ to 6½ hours or until beans are tender. If desired, use a potato masher to mash beans slightly while in the cooker. Stir salsa into soup.

3 If desired, serve with sour cream and lime wedges.

Nutrition Facts per serving: 341 cal., 4 g total fat (1 g sat. fat), 28 mg chol., 1,176 mg sodium, 49 g carbo., 12 g fiber, 29 g pro. **Daily Values:** 6% vit. A, 93% vit. C, 12% calcium, 24% iron

PREP:

20 minutes

COOK:

Low 11 hours, High 5½ hours

STAND:

1 hour

MAKES:

6 servings

SLOW COOKER:

3½- to 4-quart

The lemon-pine flavor of rosemary permeates this wonderful winter-dinner dish.
Serve with crusty baguette slices.

FRENCH COUNTRY SOUP

PREP:

20 minutes

COOK:

Low 8 hours, High 4 hours

STAND:

1 hour

MAKES:

6 servings

SLOW COOKER:

3¹/₂- to 6-quart

¹/₂	pound dry navy, Great Northern, or cannellini beans
6	cups water
1	pound lamb or beef stew meat, cut into 1-inch cubes
2	medium carrots, peeled and cut into 1-inch pieces
2	stalks celery, cut into 1-inch pieces
1	large onion, cut into wedges
6	cloves garlic, minced
4	cups reduced-sodium chicken broth
1	cup dry white wine
3	bay leaves
1¹/₂	teaspoons dried rosemary, crushed
¹/₂	teaspoon salt
¹/₄	teaspoon pepper

1 Rinse and drain beans. In a 4-quart Dutch oven combine beans and water. Bring to boiling; reduce heat. Simmer 10 minutes. Remove from heat. Cover and let stand for 1 hour.

2 Drain soaked beans; rinse in colander. In a 3¹/₂- to 6-quart slow cooker combine the beans, stew meat, and remaining ingredients. Cover; cook on low-heat setting for 8 to 10 hours or on high-heat setting for 4 to 5 hours. Remove bay leaves before serving.

Nutrition Facts per serving: 389 cal., 17 g total fat (7 g sat. fat), 54 mg chol., 516 mg sodium, 30 g carbo., 11 g fiber, 24 g pro. **Daily Values:** 115% vit. A, 30% vit. C, 11% calcium, 25% iron

Look for lean lamb at the supermarket or buy extra (2¹/₂ pounds) and trim it yourself. Beef and pork substitute deliciously for the lamb as well.

LAMB & BARLEY VEGETABLE SOUP

1¹/₂	pounds lamb stew meat, cut into 1-inch cubes
2	cups sliced fresh mushrooms
¹/₂	cup pearl barley
1	cup chopped onion (1 medium)
1	medium carrot, cut into ¹/₂-inch pieces
1	large parsnip, peeled and cut into ¹/₂-inch pieces
1	14¹/₂-ounce can Italian-style stewed tomatoes
2	cloves garlic, minced
1	teaspoon dried marjoram, crushed
¹/₂	teaspoon salt
¹/₄	teaspoon pepper
1	bay leaf
4	cups beef broth

PREP:
25 minutes
COOK:
Low 6 hours, High 3 hours
MAKES:
8 servings
SLOW COOKER:
3¹/₂- to 6-quart

1 In a 3¹/₂- to 6-quart slow cooker place meat, mushrooms, barley, onion, carrot, parsnip, undrained tomatoes, garlic, marjoram, salt, pepper, and bay leaf. Pour beef broth over all.

2 Cover; cook on low-heat setting for 6 to 8 hours or on high-heat setting for 3 to 4 hours. Discard bay leaf.

Nutrition Facts per serving: 212 cal., 4 g total fat (1 g sat. fat), 53 mg chol., 643 mg sodium, 20 g carbo., 4 g fiber, 23 g pro. **Daily Values:** 39% vit. A, 8% vit. C, 4% calcium, 16% iron

For this recipe, substitute low-sodium soup and broth if desired. The Mexican flavors will still wake up your taste buds.

CREAMY CHICKEN CHOWDER

PREP:

20 minutes

COOK:

Low 4 hours, High 2 hours

STAND:

5 minutes

MAKES:

6 servings

SLOW COOKER:

3¹/₂- to 4-quart

1 pound skinless, boneless chicken breasts, cut into ¹/₂-inch pieces

1 11-ounce can whole kernel corn with sweet peppers, drained

1 10³/₄-ounce can condensed cream of potato soup

1 4-ounce can diced green chile peppers

2 tablespoons snipped fresh cilantro

1 1¹/₄-ounce envelope taco seasoning mix

3 cups chicken broth

1 8-ounce carton dairy sour cream

¹/₂ of an 8-ounce package cheese spread with jalapeño peppers, cubed

1 In a 3¹/₂- to 4-quart slow cooker combine chicken, corn, soup, undrained chile peppers, cilantro, and taco seasoning mix. Stir in chicken broth. Cover; cook on low-heat setting for 4 to 6 hours or on high-heat setting for 2 to 3 hours.

2 Stir about 1 cup of the hot soup into the sour cream. Stir sour cream mixture and cheese into the mixture in cooker; cover and let stand 5 minutes. Stir with a whisk until combined.

Nutrition Facts per serving: 327 cal., 15 g total fat (8 g sat. fat), 74 mg chol., 1,906 mg sodium, 23 g carbo., 2 g fiber, 25 g pro. **Daily Values:** 16% vit. A, 21% vit. C, 18% calcium, 8% iron

This recipe goes together easily for a soup that's deserving of guests. Serve it with submarine sandwiches.

TURKEY SAUSAGE & TORTELLINI SOUP

6   ounces cooked smoked turkey sausage, halved lengthwise
    and cut into $\frac{1}{2}$-inch slices

2   cups packaged shredded cabbage with carrot (coleslaw mix)

1   cup loose-pack frozen cut green beans or Italian-style
    green beans

2   14$\frac{1}{2}$-ounce cans Italian-style stewed tomatoes

1   10$\frac{1}{2}$-ounce can condensed French onion soup

3   cups water

1   9-ounce package refrigerated cheese-filled tortellini
    Grated Parmesan cheese

PREP:

10 minutes

COOK:

*Low 8 hours, High 4 hours;
plus 15 minutes on High*

MAKES:

6 servings

SLOW COOKER:

3$\frac{1}{2}$- to 5-quart

1 In a 3$\frac{1}{2}$- to 5-quart slow cooker place sausage, coleslaw mix, green beans, undrained tomatoes, soup, and water.

2 Cover; cook on low-heat setting for 8 to 10 hours or on high-heat setting for 4 to 5 hours.

3 If using low-heat setting, turn to high-heat setting. Stir in tortellini. Cover and cook for 15 minutes more. Ladle soup into bowls. Sprinkle with grated Parmesan cheese.

Nutrition Facts per serving: 257 cal., 7 g total fat (3 g sat. fat), 45 mg chol., 1,134 mg sodium, 36 g carbo., 4 g fiber, 13 g pro. **Daily Values:** 17% vit. A, 29% vit. C, 15% calcium, 11% iron

This streamlined soup version of the classic French specialty is delicious served with crusty bread.

EASY CASSOULET SOUP

PREP:

20 minutes

COOK:

Low 7 hours, High 3¹/₂ hours

MAKES:

6 to 8 servings

SLOW COOKER:

3¹/₂- to 5-quart

8   ounces skinless, boneless chicken thighs

2   medium carrots, cut into ¹/₂-inch pieces

1   medium red or green sweet pepper, cut into ¹/₂-inch pieces

1   cup chopped onion

3   cloves garlic, minced

2   15-ounce cans cannellini beans or Great Northern beans, rinsed and drained

1   14¹/₂-ounce can Italian-style stewed tomatoes

8   ounces cooked smoked turkey sausage, halved lengthwise and cut into ¹/₂-inch slices

1¹/₂ cups chicken broth

¹/₂ cup dry white wine or chicken broth

1   tablespoon snipped fresh parsley

1   teaspoon dried thyme, crushed

¹/₈ to ¹/₄ teaspoon ground red pepper

1   bay leaf

1 Cut chicken into 1-inch pieces.

2 In a 3¹/₂- to 5-quart slow cooker place carrots, sweet pepper, onion, garlic, beans, undrained tomatoes, chicken, and sausage.

3 Add chicken broth, wine, parsley, thyme, red pepper, and bay leaf.

4 Cover; cook on low-heat setting for 7 to 8 hours or on high-heat setting for 3¹/₂ to 4 hours. Discard bay leaf.

Nutrition Facts per serving: 248 cal., 6 g total fat (2 g sat. fat), 55 mg chol., 969 mg sodium, 31 g carbo., 9 g fiber, 23 g pro. **Daily Values:** 133% vit. A, 64% vit. C, 8% calcium, 17% iron

Pea pods, cabbage, and a well-beaten egg added toward the end of cooking transform this version of classic chicken soup into distinctively Asian cuisine.

ASIAN-STYLE CHICKEN SOUP

1	pound skinless, boneless chicken breast halves, cut into bite-size pieces
2	14-ounce cans chicken broth
1	cup water
1	tablespoon soy sauce
1	teaspoon grated fresh ginger
$1/8$	teaspoon crushed red pepper
1	medium red sweet pepper, cut into $3/4$-inch pieces
1	medium carrot, sliced
$1/3$	cup thinly sliced green onions
1	cup fresh pea pods, halved crosswise, or $1/2$ of a 6-ounce package frozen pea pods, thawed and halved crosswise
2	cups shredded napa cabbage
1	well-beaten egg

PREP:

25 minutes

COOK:

Low 5 hours, High $2^{1}/_{2}$ hours; plus 10 minutes on High

MAKES:

4 servings

SLOW COOKER:

$3^{1}/_{2}$- to 4-quart

1 Place the chicken in a $3^{1}/_{2}$- to 4-quart slow cooker. Stir in the chicken broth, water, soy sauce, ginger, crushed red pepper, sweet pepper, carrot, and green onions. Cover; cook on low-heat setting for 5 to 6 hours or on high-heat setting for $2^{1}/_{2}$ to 3 hours.

2 If using low-heat setting, increase to high-heat setting. Stir in pea pods and cabbage. Slowly pour in the well-beaten egg; stir gently. Cover and cook 10 minutes more.

Nutrition Facts per serving: 208 cal., 5 g total fat (1 g sat. fat), 119 mg chol., 1,195 mg sodium, 8 g carbo., 3 g fiber, 32 g pro. **Daily Values:** 122% vit. A, 102% vit. C, 7% calcium, 9% iron

For a weeknight supper or weekend get-together, this hearty dish is sure to get rave reviews. Saffron-flavored rice gives it beautiful color and terrific flavor.

CHICKEN & SAFFRON RICE SOUP

PREP:

15 minutes

COOK:

Low 4 hours, High 2 hours; plus 15 minutes on High

MAKES:

4 to 6 main-dish servings

SLOW COOKER:

3½- to 4-quart

1	pound skinless, boneless chicken breast halves, cut into 1-inch pieces
1	medium onion, chopped (½ cup)
1	clove garlic, minced
1	14½-ounce can diced tomatoes
1	14-ounce can reduced-sodium chicken broth
1	14-ounce can whole artichokes, drained and quartered
½	of a 7.25-ounce jar roasted red sweet peppers, drained and cut into strips (½ cup)
½	cup frozen peas
1	5-ounce package saffron-flavored yellow rice mix
2	tablespoons slivered almonds, toasted

1 Place chicken in a 3½- to 4-quart slow cooker. Stir in onion, garlic, tomatoes, broth, artichokes, and sweet peppers. Cover; cook on low-heat setting for 4 to 5 hours or on high-heat setting for 2 to 2½ hours. If using low-heat setting, turn to high-heat setting. Stir in frozen peas. Cook, covered, for 15 minutes more.

2 Meanwhile, prepare rice mix according to package directions.

3 To serve, divide soup among serving bowls. Mound the cooked rice in the center of each bowl. Sprinkle with almonds.

Nutrition Facts per serving: 415 cal., 10 g total fat (1 g sat. fat), 66 mg chol., 1,315 mg sodium, 44 g carbo., 9 g fiber, 35 g pro. **Daily Values:** 6% vit. A, 129% vit. C, 10% calcium, 32% iron

This delicious broth is lower in sodium than canned versions. Try it in any recipe that calls for chicken broth, especially chicken noodle soup.

SLOW-STEWED CHICKEN WITH BROTH

4	to 4½ pounds meaty chicken pieces (breasts, thighs, and/or drumsticks)
4	stalks celery with leaves, cut up
1	small onion, sliced
2	sprigs fresh parsley
1	bay leaf
¾	teaspoon salt
½	teaspoon dried thyme or marjoram, crushed
¼	teaspoon black pepper
4	cups cold water

1 In a 5- to 6-quart slow cooker combine all ingredients; pour water over all.

2 Cover; cook on low-heat setting for 7 to 10 hours or on high-heat setting for 3½ to 5 hours.

3 Remove chicken from cooker. Strain broth through a large sieve or colander lined with two layers of 100-percent-cotton cheesecloth. Discard cheesecloth and solids.

4 If using broth immediately, skim off fat. If storing broth for later use, chill broth in a bowl for 6 hours or overnight. Lift off fat. Pour broth into an airtight container; seal. Chill in the refrigerator for up to 3 days or freeze for up to 3 months.

5 When chicken is cool enough to handle, remove meat from bones. Discard skin and bones. Place meat in an airtight container; seal. Chill in the refrigerator for up to 3 days or freeze for up to 3 months.

Nutrition Facts per serving: 264 cal., 17 g total fat (5 g sat. fat), 70 mg chol., 296 mg sodium, 2 g carbo., 24 g pro.

PREP:
20 minutes

COOK:
Low 7 hours, High 3½ hours

MAKES:
5 to 6 cups broth and 4 to 5 cups cooked meat

SLOW COOKER:
5- to 6-quart

Lemongrass, a popular herb used in Thai cooking, resembles a very large green onion. Use only the fibrous white bulb, which contains lemon fragrance and flavor.

THAI-STYLE COCONUT-CHICKEN SOUP

PREP:

20 minutes

COOK:

Low 6 hours, High 3 hours

STAND:

5 minutes

MAKES:

6 servings

SLOW COOKER:

3¹/₂- to 5-quart

1 pound skinless, boneless chicken breasts or thighs, rinsed and cut into ³/₄-inch pieces

4 cups chicken broth

2 cups bias-sliced carrots

1 large onion, chopped

2 tablespoons grated fresh ginger

3 cloves garlic, minced

2 stalks lemongrass, cut into 1-inch pieces, or 1 teaspoon finely shredded lemon peel

¹/₂ teaspoon crushed red pepper

1 15-ounce can unsweetened coconut milk

1 medium red, yellow, and/or green sweet pepper, cut into ¹/₂-inch pieces

2 4-ounce cans straw or button mushrooms, drained

¹/₄ cup snipped fresh cilantro

¹/₃ cup chopped roasted peanuts

1 In a 3¹/₂- to 5-quart slow cooker combine the chicken, broth, carrots, onion, ginger, garlic, lemongrass or lemon peel, and crushed red pepper.

2 Cover; cook on low-heat setting for 6 to 7 hours or on high-heat setting for 3 to 3¹/₂ hours. If necessary, skim off fat. Stir coconut milk, sweet pepper, mushrooms, and cilantro into chicken mixture. Cover; let stand 5 to 10 minutes. Remove and discard lemongrass (if using). Ladle soup into bowls. Sprinkle peanuts over each serving.

Nutrition Facts per serving: 328 cal., 20 g total fat (13 g sat. fat), 40 mg chol., 764 mg sodium, 15 g carbo., 4 g fiber, 23 g pro. **Daily Values:** 39% vit. C, 3% calcium, 16% iron

Numerous varieties of cooked smoked turkey are available in supermarket delis. You may also want to check the selection of turkey sausage at the meat counter.

SAVORY SPLIT PEA & TURKEY SOUP

2	cups dry yellow split peas (1 pound)
2	cups chopped cooked smoked turkey or sliced cooked turkey sausage
1½	cups coarsely shredded carrots
½	cup chopped chives
1	clove garlic, minced
1	tablespoon snipped fresh basil or 1 teaspoon dried basil, crushed
1	tablespoon snipped fresh oregano or 1 teaspoon dried oregano, crushed
5	cups chicken broth
2	cups water
½	cup snipped dried tomatoes (not oil-packed)

1 Rinse split peas; drain.

2 In a 3½- to 4-quart slow cooker combine the split peas, turkey or turkey sausage, carrots, chives, garlic, dried basil, and oregano (if using). Pour chicken broth and water over all.

3 Cover; cook on low-heat setting for 6 to 8 hours or on high-heat setting for 3 to 4 hours. Stir in dried tomatoes; cover and let stand for 10 minutes. If using, stir in fresh basil and oregano.

Nutrition Facts per serving: 204 cal., 2 g total fat (1 g sat. fat), 22 mg chol., 1,313 mg sodium, 26 g carbo., 5 g fiber, 22 g pro. **Daily Values:** 13% vit. C, 4% calcium, 15% iron

PREP:
20 minutes

COOK:
Low 6 hours, High 3 hours

STAND:
10 minutes

MAKES:
6 to 8 servings

SLOW COOKER:
3½- to 4-quart

"Deviled" refers to food that is seasoned with such piquant ingredients as red pepper, hot pepper sauce—or as in this dish, mustard. Add more or less to your liking.

DEVILED CHICKEN & VEGETABLE SOUP

PREP:

20 minutes

COOK:

Low 8 hours, High 4 hours

MAKES:

6 servings

SLOW COOKER:

3¹/₂- to 4-quart

1	pound skinless, boneless chicken thighs
1	large red potato, chopped
¹/₂	of a 16-ounce package (1¹/₂ cups) frozen whole kernel corn
1	medium onion, chopped
¹/₂	cup chopped celery
3	tablespoons Dijon-style mustard
¹/₄	teaspoon pepper
¹/₈	teaspoon garlic powder
2¹/₂	cups vegetable juice
1	14-ounce can reduced-sodium chicken broth

1 Rinse chicken. Cut into bite-size pieces.

2 In a 3¹/₂- to 4-quart slow cooker combine the chicken, potato, corn, onion, celery, mustard, pepper, and garlic powder. Pour vegetable juice and chicken broth over all.

3 Cover; cook on low-heat setting for 8 to 10 hours or on high-heat setting for 4 to 5 hours.

Nutrition Facts per serving: 192 cal., 5 g total fat (1 g sat. fat), 36 mg chol., 800 mg sodium, 23 g carbo., 1 g fiber, 15 g pro. **Daily Values:** 59% vit. C, 2% calcium, 12% iron

FIX IT AND FREEZE AHEAD

With a large-capacity slow cooker, you can cook once and have enough leftovers for two or three more dinners. To freeze leftovers, cool the hot food by placing it in a bowl set over another bowl filled with ice water. Transfer the cooled food to freezer-safe containers. Label and freeze for up to six months. Do not use a slow cooker to reheat the frozen food. Place the frozen food in an appropriate-size saucepan; cook and stir over low heat until boiling. Or place food in an oven-safe casserole dish and bake in a 400° oven for 1 to 2 hours, stirring once during baking.

Fennel has a creamy-white bulblike base, pale green stalks, and feathery green leaves. It has a light licorice flavor and a texture that is similar to celery.

FENNEL-CHICKEN-GARBANZO SOUP

1	cup dry garbanzo beans
1	pound skinless, boneless chicken breasts or thighs
2½	cups sliced carrots
1	medium fennel bulb, trimmed and cut into ¼-inch slices, or 1½ cups sliced celery
1	large onion, chopped
1	tablespoon snipped fresh marjoram or 1 teaspoon dried marjoram, crushed
1	tablespoon snipped fresh thyme or 1 teaspoon dried thyme, crushed
1	tablespoon instant chicken bouillon granules
¼	teaspoon salt
¼	teaspoon pepper
4	cups water
1	cup shredded fresh spinach or escarole
	Fresh thyme (optional)

PREP:

20 minutes

COOK:

Low 8 hours, High 4 hours

STAND:

1 hour, 5 minutes

MAKES:

6 servings

SLOW COOKER:

3½- to 5-quart

1 Rinse the garbanzo beans; place in a large saucepan. Add enough water to cover the beans by 2 inches. Bring to boiling; reduce heat. Simmer, uncovered, for 10 minutes. Remove from heat. Cover and let stand for 1 hour. (Or place beans in water in a large saucepan. Cover and let soak in a cool place overnight.) Drain and rinse beans.

2 Place beans and chicken in a 3½- to 5-quart slow cooker. Add carrots, fennel or celery, onion, dried marjoram and thyme (if using), bouillon granules, salt, and pepper. Pour water over all.

3 Cover; cook on low-heat setting for 8 to 10 hours or on high-heat setting for 4 to 5 hours. Remove the chicken; cool slightly. Cut the meat into bite-size pieces. Return to cooker. Add the spinach or escarole and, if using, the fresh marjoram and thyme. Let stand 5 minutes before serving.

4 To serve, ladle soup into bowls. If desired, garnish with sprigs of fresh thyme.

Nutrition Facts per serving: 205 cal., 4 g total fat (1 g sat. fat), 40 mg chol., 625 mg sodium, 23 g carbo., 9 g fiber, 20 g pro. **Daily Values:** 149% vit. A, 12% vit. C, 6% calcium, 18% iron

Easily turn this hearty recipe into a tasty meatless version by omitting the chicken.

BEAN SOUP WITH CHICKEN & VEGGIES

PREP:

30 minutes

COOK:

Low 8 hours, High 4 hours; plus 30 minutes on High

STAND:

1 hour

MAKES:

6 servings

SLOW COOKER:

4- to 5-quart

1	cup dry Great Northern beans
6	cups water
1	cup chopped onion
1	medium fennel bulb, trimmed and cut into ½-inch pieces
2	medium carrots, chopped
2	cloves garlic, minced
1	teaspoon dried thyme, crushed
1	teaspoon dried marjoram, crushed
¼	teaspoon pepper
3	14-ounce cans chicken broth
2½	cups chopped cooked chicken
1	14½-ounce can diced tomatoes
2	tablespoons snipped fresh parsley

1 Rinse beans; drain. In a Dutch oven, combine beans and the 6 cups water. Bring to boiling; reduce heat. Simmer, uncovered, for 2 minutes. Remove from heat. Cover and let stand for 1 hour. (Or place beans and water in Dutch oven. Cover and let soak overnight in a cool place.) Drain and rinse beans.

2 Meanwhile, in a 4- to 5-quart slow cooker, combine onion, fennel, carrots, garlic, thyme, marjoram, and pepper. Place beans over vegetables. Pour chicken broth over all.

3 Cover; cook on low-heat setting for 8 to 10 hours or on high-heat setting for 4 to 5 hours.

4 If using low-heat setting, turn to high-heat setting. Stir in chicken and tomatoes. Cover and cook 30 minutes longer. Stir in parsley.

Nutrition Facts per serving: 299 cal., 6 g total fat (2 g sat. fat), 52 mg chol., 834 mg sodium, 31 g carbo., 9 g fiber, 29 g pro. **Daily Values:** 107% vit. A, 327% vit. C, 13% calcium, 20% iron

When you know the morning will be hectic, cut up the turkey and vegetables the night before and refrigerate them in separate plastic bags.

MUSHROOM, TURKEY, & RICE SOUP

2	cups sliced fresh mushrooms, such as shiitake or button
1½	cups sliced bok choy
1	medium onion, chopped
2	medium carrots, cut into bite-size strips (1 cup)
1	pound turkey breast tenderloins or skinless, boneless chicken breast halves, cut into 1-inch pieces
2	14½-ounce cans reduced-sodium chicken broth
2	tablespoons reduced-sodium soy sauce
1	tablespoon toasted sesame oil (optional)
4	cloves garlic, minced
2	teaspoons grated fresh ginger
1	cup instant rice

1 In a 3½- to 4-quart slow cooker place mushrooms, bok choy, onion, and carrots. Add turkey or chicken to cooker. Combine chicken broth, soy sauce, sesame oil (if desired), garlic, and ginger. Pour over vegetables and turkey.

2 Cover and cook on low-heat setting for 8 to 10 hours or on high-heat setting for 4 to 5 hours. Stir in rice. Cover and let stand for 5 to 10 minutes. Ladle into bowls.

Nutrition Facts per serving: 186 cal., 1 g total fat (0 g sat. fat), 47 mg chol., 584 mg sodium, 20 g carbo., 1 g fiber, 24 g pro. **Daily Values:** 19% vit. C, 4% calcium, 11% iron

PREP:
25 minutes

COOK:
Low 8 hours, High 4 hours

STAND:
5 minutes

MAKES:
6 servings

SLOW COOKER:
3½- to 4-quart

FOR A 5- TO 6-QUART COOKER
Recipe may be doubled.

All the world loves the comforting, restorative quality of chicken noodle soup. Why not expand your horizons and your health? Next time you need a lift, try the soup Eastern-style.

ASIAN CHICKEN SOUP WITH NOODLES

PREP:

20 minutes

COOK:

Low 8 hours, High 4 hours; plus 5 minutes

MAKES:

6 servings

SLOW COOKER:

3¹/₂- to 4-quart

2   cups sliced fresh mushrooms, such as shiitake or button

1   medium onion, cut into thin wedges (¹/₂ cup)

2   medium carrots, bias-sliced (1 cup)

1   pound skinless, boneless chicken breast halves, cut into 1-inch pieces

2   cloves garlic, minced

2   teaspoons grated fresh ginger

2   14-ounce cans reduced-sodium chicken broth

2   tablespoons soy sauce

3   cups shredded Swiss chard leaves or shredded fresh spinach

8   ounces Chinese egg noodles or rice sticks

    Cilantro leaves (optional)

    Chile oil (optional)

1 In a 3¹/₂- to 4-quart slow cooker place mushrooms, onion, and carrots. Add chicken to cooker. Combine garlic, ginger, chicken broth, and soy sauce. Pour over vegetables and chicken.

2 Cover and cook on low-heat setting for 8 to 10 hours or on high-heat setting for 4 to 5 hours. Stir in Swiss chard or spinach. Cover and cook 5 minutes more. Meanwhile, cook noodles or rice sticks according to package directions. Divide noodles among serving bowls. Ladle soup over noodles. If desired, top with cilantro leaves and chile oil.

Nutrition Facts per serving: 285 cal., 3 g total fat (1 g sat. fat), 80 mg chol., 758 mg sodium, 39 g carbo., 3 g fiber, 27 g pro. **Daily Values:** 114% vit. A, 11% vit. C, 4% calcium, 14% iron

To save time and retain nutrients, leave the peels on the potatoes. Simply scrub them and cut into cubes.

MANHATTAN-STYLE CLAM CHOWDER

2	6½-ounce cans minced clams or one 10-ounce can baby clams
2	medium potatoes, peeled and cut into ½-inch cubes
1	cup chopped onions (2 medium)
1	cup chopped celery with leaves
½	cup chopped green sweet pepper (1 small)
1	14½-ounce can Italian-style stewed tomatoes
1½	cups hot-style tomato juice or hot-style vegetable juice
½	teaspoon dried thyme, crushed
1	bay leaf
4	slices bacon, crisp-cooked, drained, and crumbled, or ¼ cup cooked bacon pieces

1 Drain clams, reserving liquid (about ⅔ cup liquid). Place clams in a small bowl; cover and chill.

2 In a 3½- to 4-quart slow cooker combine reserved clam liquid, potatoes, onions, celery, sweet pepper, undrained tomatoes, juice, thyme, and bay leaf. Cover; cook on low-heat setting for 8 to 10 hours or on high-heat setting for 4 to 5 hours.

3 If using low-heat setting, turn to high-heat setting. Stir in clams. Cover and cook 5 minutes more. Discard bay leaf. Ladle soup into bowls. Sprinkle each serving with crumbled bacon.

Nutrition Facts per serving: 238 cal., 5 g total fat (1 g sat. fat), 34 mg chol., 719 mg sodium, 30 g carbo., 4 g fiber, 17 g pro. **Daily Values:** 19% vit. A, 92% vit. C, 10% calcium, 78% iron

PREP:

20 minutes

COOK:

Low 8 hours, High 4 hours; plus 5 minutes on High

MAKES:

4 servings

SLOW COOKER:

3½- to 4-quart

Thick and chunky, this chowder measures up. Halibut and haddock are fine substitutes for the cod.

HEARTY FISH CHOWDER

PREP:

25 minutes

COOK:

*Low 6 hours, High 3 hours;
plus 1 hour on High*

MAKES:

6 servings

SLOW COOKER:

3¹/₂- to 4-quart

2 medium potatoes, finely chopped (2 cups)

1 cup chopped onions (2 medium)

2 cloves garlic, minced

1 10³/₄-ounce can condensed cream of celery soup

1 10-ounce package frozen whole kernel corn

1 10-ounce package frozen baby lima beans or 2 cups loose-pack frozen baby lima beans

1¹/₂ cups chicken broth

¹/₃ cup dry white wine or chicken broth

1 teaspoon lemon-pepper seasoning

1 pound cod or other whitefish fillets

1 14¹/₂-ounce can stewed tomatoes

¹/₃ cup nonfat dry milk powder

1 In a 3¹/₂- to 4-quart slow cooker combine potatoes, onion, garlic, condensed soup, corn, lima beans, broth, white wine, and lemon-pepper seasoning.

2 Cover; cook on low-heat setting for 6 to 7 hours or on high-heat setting for 3 to 3¹/₂ hours. Place fish on the mixture in the cooker. If using low-heat setting, turn to high-heat setting. Cover and cook for 1 hour more.

3 Add undrained tomatoes and dry milk powder to cooker, stirring gently to break up the fish.

Nutrition Facts per serving: 295 cal., 4 g total fat (1 g sat. fat), 39 mg chol., 955 mg sodium, 40 g carbo., 6 g fiber, 23 g pro. **Daily Values:** 8% vit. A, 25% vit. C, 12% calcium, 15% iron

This golden broth is the perfect base for many meatless soups and stews. To have it handy, freeze portions for up to three months.

VEGETABLE STOCK

2   tomatoes, chopped

2   medium onions, cut up

4   medium carrots, cut up

1   turnip or 2 parsnips, cut up

1   medium stalk celery with leaves, cut up

1   medium potato, halved lengthwise and cut into $^1/_2$-inch slices

6   unpeeled cloves garlic

6   sprigs parsley

1   teaspoon salt

$^1/_2$ teaspoon dried thyme, crushed

$^1/_4$ teaspoon whole black peppercorns

1   bay leaf

6   cups water

1 In a $3^1/_2$- to 5-quart slow cooker combine the tomatoes, onions, carrots, turnip or parsnips, celery, potato, garlic, parsley, salt, thyme, peppercorns, and bay leaf. Stir in the water.

2 Cover; cook on low-heat setting for 12 to 14 hours or on high-heat setting for 6 to 7 hours. Strain stock through a large sieve or colander lined with 2 layers of 100-percent-cotton cheesecloth. Discard the solids.

Nutrition Facts per serving: 44 cal., 0 g total fat (0 g sat. fat), 0 mg chol., 319 mg sodium, 10 g carbo., 1 g pro.

PREP:

30 minutes

COOK:

Low 12 hours, High 6 hours

MAKES:

about 6 cups stock

SLOW COOKER:

$3^1/_2$- to 5-quart

In a melody, Paul Simon and Art Garfunkel immortalized the seasonings of this lovely, chill-warming pantry soup. "Parsley, sage, rosemary, and thyme...."

WINTER VEGETABLE SOUP

PREP:

30 minutes

COOK:

Low 10 hours, High 4½ hours

MAKES:

6 servings

SLOW COOKER:

3½- to 4-quart

2	medium parsnips, peeled, halved lengthwise, and cut into 1-inch pieces
1	large onion, chopped
1	medium turnip, peeled and cut into ¾-inch pieces
1	medium potato, cut into ¾-inch pieces
2	cups water
1	14½-ounce can diced tomatoes
¼	cup dry red wine or water
1	teaspoon salt
½	teaspoon dried thyme, crushed
¼	teaspoon dried sage, crushed
¼	teaspoon dried rosemary, crushed
4	cloves garlic, minced
2	15-ounce cans Great Northern or navy beans, rinsed and drained
¼	cup snipped fresh parsley

1 In a 3½- to 4-quart slow cooker place the parsnips, onion, turnip, and potato. Stir in water, undrained tomatoes, wine, salt, thyme, sage, rosemary, and garlic. Stir in beans.

2 Cover; cook on low-heat setting for 10 to 11 hours or on high-heat setting for 4½ to 5 hours. Stir in parsley just before serving.

Nutrition Facts per serving: 211 cal., 1 g total fat (0 g sat. fat), 0 mg chol., 853 mg sodium, 41 g carbo., 11 g fiber, 9 g pro. **Daily Values:** 3% vit. A, 44% vit. C, 18% calcium, 18% iron

Italian-style tomato paste provides wonderful flavor to this meatless soup. Freeze leftover servings and reheat them for quick warm-ups.

ITALIAN HERBED VEGETABLE SOUP

1	10-ounce package frozen whole kernel corn (about 2 cups)
1	cup chopped onions (2 medium)
1	cup finely chopped carrots (2 medium)
1	cup coarsely chopped zucchini
2	cloves garlic, minced
6	cups vegetable broth or chicken broth
1	6-ounce can Italian-style tomato paste
1/2	teaspoon dried basil, crushed
1	9-ounce package frozen Italian-style green beans
1	cup tiny shell macaroni
2	tablespoons snipped fresh parsley

PREP:

20 minutes

COOK:

Low 7 hours, High 3 1/2 hours; plus 45 minutes on High

MAKES:

6 to 8 main-dish servings

SLOW COOKER:

3 1/2- to 5-quart

1 In a 3 1/2- to 5-quart slow cooker combine frozen corn, onions, carrots, zucchini, and garlic. Add broth, tomato paste, and basil. Stir to combine.

2 Cover; cook on low-heat setting for 7 to 8 hours or on high-heat setting for 3 1/2 to 4 hours. If using low-heat setting, turn to high-heat setting. Add green beans and pasta; cover and cook 45 minutes more. Stir in parsley before serving.

Nutrition Facts per serving: 198 cal., 2 g total fat (0 g sat. fat), 0 mg chol., 1,269 mg sodium, 41 g carbo., 5 g fiber, 8 g pro. **Daily Values:** 113% vit. A, 25% vit. C, 4% calcium, 11% iron

Combine lentils with vegetables to make a thick, satisfying soup—perfect for a cold-weather meal.

LENTIL-VEGGIE SOUP

PREP:

20 minutes

COOK:

Low 12 hours, High 5 hours

MAKES:

6 servings

SLOW COOKER:

3¹/₂- to 4-quart

1	cup dry lentils
1	cup chopped carrots (2 medium)
1	cup chopped celery (2 stalks)
1	cup chopped onions (2 medium)
2	cloves garlic, minced
¹/₂	teaspoon dried basil, crushed
¹/₂	teaspoon dried oregano, crushed
¹/₄	teaspoon dried thyme, crushed
1	bay leaf
2	14-ounce cans vegetable broth or chicken broth (3¹/₂ cups)
1¹/₂	cups water
1	14¹/₂-ounce can Italian-style stewed tomatoes
¹/₄	cup snipped fresh parsley

1 Rinse lentils. In a 3¹/₂- to 4-quart slow cooker place lentils, carrots, celery, onions, garlic, basil, oregano, thyme, and bay leaf. Stir in broth, water, and undrained tomatoes.

2 Cover; cook on low-heat setting for 12 hours or on high-heat setting for 5 to 6 hours. Discard bay leaf. Stir in parsley.

Nutrition Facts per serving: 165 cal., 1 g total fat (0 g sat. fat), 0 mg chol., 713 mg sodium, 30 g carbo., 12 g fiber, 11 g pro. **Daily Values:** 126% vit. A, 20% vit. C, 7% calcium, 20% iron

The hearty barley grain adds bulk and staying power to savory vegetable soup—you'll feel full and satisfied long after enjoying it.

BARLEY VEGETABLE SOUP

1   15-ounce can red beans, rinsed and drained

1   10-ounce package frozen whole kernel corn

½   cup medium pearl barley

1   14½-ounce can stewed tomatoes

2   cups sliced fresh mushrooms

1   cup chopped onions (2 medium)

1   medium carrot, coarsely chopped (½ cup)

1   stalk celery, coarsely chopped (½ cup)

3   cloves garlic, minced

2   teaspoons dried Italian seasoning, crushed

¼   teaspoon pepper

5   cups vegetable broth or chicken broth

1 In a 3½- to 5-quart slow cooker place beans, corn, barley, undrained tomatoes, mushrooms, onions, carrot, celery, garlic, Italian seasoning, and pepper. Pour broth over all.

2 Cover; cook on low-heat setting for 8 to 10 hours or on high-heat setting for 4 to 5 hours.

Nutrition Facts per serving: 220 cal., 2 g total fat (0 g sat. fat), 0 mg chol., 1,167 mg sodium, 47 g carbo., 9 g fiber, 12 g pro. **Daily Values:** 60% vit. A, 16% vit. C, 6% calcium, 11% iron

PREP:

25 minutes

COOK:

Low 8 hours, High 4 hours

MAKES:

6 servings

SLOW COOKER:

3½- to 5-quart

Look for basil-flavored pesto on the grocery shelf or in the refrigerator section next to fresh pasta.

PESTO, TOMATO, & RICE SOUP

PREP:

15 minutes

COOK:

Low 8 hours, High 4 hours

STAND:

7 minutes

MAKES:

6 to 8 servings

SLOW COOKER:

3¹/₂- to 4-quart

1	cup chopped onions (2 medium)
1	cup shredded carrots (2 medium)
3	stalks celery with leaves, chopped (1½ cups)
1	14½-ounce can Italian-style stewed tomatoes
1	6-ounce can Italian-style tomato paste
½	teaspoon dried oregano, crushed
¼	teaspoon dried thyme, crushed
¼	teaspoon pepper
3	cups water
1	14-ounce can chicken broth or vegetable broth
1	cup quick-cooking rice
¼	cup pesto
	Grated Parmesan cheese (optional)

1 In a 3¹/₂- to 4-quart slow cooker combine onions, carrots, celery, undrained tomatoes, tomato paste, oregano, thyme, and pepper. Stir in water and broth.

2 Cover; cook on low-heat setting for 8 to 10 hours or on high-heat setting for 4 to 5 hours.

3 Turn off cooker. Stir in rice and pesto. Cover; let stand 7 to 10 minutes or until rice is tender. Ladle soup into bowls. If desired, sprinkle with grated Parmesan cheese.

Nutrition Facts per serving: 206 cal., 7 g total fat (1 g sat. fat), 2 mg chol., 811 mg sodium, 30 g carbo., 3 g fiber, 5 g pro. **Daily Values:** 105% vit. A, 16% vit. C, 7% calcium, 10% iron

A saucy mix of garden vegetables and olives—ratatouille—makes this an extra-satisfying soup. Serve it with a green salad and buttered slices of crusty bread.

RATATOUILLE SOUP WITH BEANS

1   medium onion, coarsely chopped (1/2 cup)

2   cups peeled eggplant, cut into 3/4-inch cubes

2   medium zucchini, halved lengthwise and sliced 1/4 inch thick (2 1/2 cups)

1   medium red sweet pepper, coarsely chopped (3/4 cup)

1   medium green sweet pepper, coarsely chopped (3/4 cup)

1   15- to 19-ounce can cannellini or Great Northern beans, rinsed and drained

1   cup hot-style vegetable juice or vegetable juice

1   14 1/2-ounce can diced tomatoes with basil, oregano, and garlic

1   14-ounce can reduced-sodium chicken broth

1   2 1/4-ounce can sliced, pitted ripe olives, drained

6   tablespoons finely shredded Parmesan cheese

PREP:
20 minutes
COOK:
Low 8 hours, High 4 hours
MAKES:
6 servings
SLOW COOKER:
3 1/2- to 4-quart

1 In a 3 1/2- to 4-quart slow cooker place onion, eggplant, zucchini, sweet peppers, and beans. Pour vegetable juice, undrained tomatoes, and broth over vegetables and beans.

2 Cover and cook on low-heat setting for 8 to 10 hours or on high-heat setting for 4 to 5 hours. Stir in olives before serving. Ladle into bowls; top with Parmesan cheese.

Nutrition Facts per serving: 148 cal., 3 g total fat (1 g sat. fat), 6 mg chol., 945 mg sodium, 25 g carbo., 6 g fiber, 10 g pro. **Daily Values:** 43% vit. A, 101% vit C, 15% calcium, 15% iron

Chock-full of nutty-tasting garbanzo beans, red potatoes, and chunks of eggplant, this curried soup can be served as a meatless entrée or a substantial side dish.

INDIAN-STYLE CURRY SOUP

PREP:

30 minutes

COOK:

Low 8 hours, High 4 hours

MAKES:

6 to 8 servings

SLOW COOKER:

4- to 6-quart

1	medium eggplant, cut into ½-inch cubes (5 to 6 cups)
1	pound red potatoes, cut into 1-inch pieces (3 cups)
2	cups chopped tomatoes or one 14½-ounce can low-sodium tomatoes, cut up
1	15-ounce can garbanzo beans, rinsed and drained
1	tablespoon grated fresh ginger
1½	teaspoons mustard seeds
1½	teaspoons ground coriander
1	teaspoon curry powder
¼	teaspoon pepper
4	cups vegetable broth or chicken broth
2	tablespoons snipped fresh cilantro

1 In a 4- to 6-quart slow cooker combine eggplant, potatoes, undrained tomatoes, and garbanzo beans.

2 Sprinkle the ginger, mustard seeds, coriander, curry powder, and pepper over vegetables. Pour vegetable broth or chicken broth over all.

3 Cover and cook on low-heat setting 8 to 10 hours or on high-heat setting for 4 to 5 hours. Ladle into bowls and sprinkle with cilantro.

Nutrition Facts per serving: 162 cal., 2 g total fat (0 g sat. fat), 0 mg chol., 889 mg sodium, 30 g carbo., 7 g fiber, 8 g pro. **Daily Values:** 33% vit. C, 4% calcium, 10% iron

Float thick slices of buttered garlic toast on this hearty meat-free soup. Three kinds of beans—Great Northern, red beans, and Italian-style green beans—provide plenty of protein and vitamins.

MIXED-BEAN ITALIAN SOUP

1	cup dry Great Northern beans
1	cup dry red beans or pinto beans
4	cups water
1	medium onion, chopped
2	tablespoons instant beef bouillon granules
2	cloves garlic, minced
2	teaspoons dried Italian seasoning, crushed
1/4	teaspoon pepper
1	28-ounce can tomatoes, cut-up
1	9-ounce package frozen Italian green beans or cut green beans, thawed
2	tablespoons margarine or butter
1/4	teaspoon garlic powder
1/4	teaspoon dried Italian seasoning, crushed
12	1/2-inch-thick slices baguette-style French bread

PREP:

15 minutes

COOK:

Low 11 hours, High 5 1/2 hours; plus 30 minutes on High

STAND:

1 hour

MAKES:

6 servings

SLOW COOKER:

3 1/2- to 6-quart

1 Rinse dry beans. In a Dutch oven combine rinsed beans and 5 cups cold water. Bring to boiling; reduce heat. Simmer for 10 minutes. Remove from heat. Cover and let stand for 1 hour. Drain and rinse beans.

2 In a 3 1/2- to 6-quart slow cooker combine beans, 4 cups fresh water, onion, bouillon granules, garlic, the 2 teaspoons Italian seasoning, and the pepper.

3 Cover and cook on low-heat setting for 11 to 13 hours or on high-heat setting for 5 1/2 to 6 1/2 hours or until beans are almost tender. If using low-heat setting, turn to high-heat setting. Stir undrained tomatoes and thawed green beans into soup. Cover and cook about 30 minutes more or until beans are tender.

4 Meanwhile, stir together margarine, garlic powder, and the 1/4 teaspoon Italian seasoning. Spread on one side of each bread slice. Place bread, spread side up, on the unheated rack of a broiler pan. Broil 4 to 5 inches from the heat for 1 to 2 minutes or until crisp and light brown. To serve, ladle soup into bowls. Float 2 pieces of herb toast in each bowl of soup. Serve immediately.

MAKE-AHEAD TIP
Instead of simmering dry beans and soaking them for 1 hour, soak the beans for 12 hours in cold water in a covered Dutch oven. Drain and rinse the beans, then prepare the soup as directed.

Nutrition Facts per serving: 432 cal., 6 g total fat (1 g sat. fat), 0 mg chol., 1,619 mg sodium, 75 g carbo., 15 g fiber, 20 g pro. **Daily Values:** 29% vit. C, 15% calcium, 30% iron

Top bowls of hot soup with fluffy cornmeal dumplings. To ensure proper cooking, avoid lifting the cooker lid until it's time to test dumplings for doneness.

BEAN SOUP WITH DUMPLINGS

PREP:

25 minutes

COOK:

Low 10 hours, High 5 hours; plus 30 minutes on Low or 20 minutes on High

MAKES:

6 servings

SLOW COOKER:

3¹/₂- to 4-quart

3 cups water

1 15-ounce can red kidney beans, rinsed and drained

1 15-ounce can black beans, pinto beans, or Great Northern beans, rinsed and drained

1 14¹/₂-ounce can Mexican-style stewed tomatoes

1 10-ounce package frozen whole kernel corn

1 cup sliced carrots

1 large onion, chopped

1 4-ounce can diced green chile peppers

2 tablespoons instant beef or chicken bouillon granules

1 to 2 teaspoons chili powder

2 cloves garlic, minced

¹/₃ cup all-purpose flour

¹/₄ cup yellow cornmeal

1 teaspoon baking powder

Dash black pepper

1 beaten egg white

2 tablespoons milk

1 tablespoon cooking oil

1 In a 3¹/₂- to 4-quart slow cooker combine water, beans, undrained tomatoes, corn, carrots, onion, undrained chile peppers, bouillon granules, chili powder, and garlic. Cover and cook on low-heat setting for 10 to 12 hours or on high-heat setting for 5 to 6 hours.

2 For dumplings, in a medium mixing bowl stir together flour, cornmeal, baking powder, and black pepper. In a small mixing bowl combine egg white, milk, and oil. Add to flour mixture; stir with a fork just until combined.

3 Drop dumpling mixture in 6 mounds onto the bubbling soup. Cover and cook on low-heat setting for 30 minutes more or on high-heat setting for 20 minutes more or until a wooden toothpick inserted in center comes out clean. (Do not lift lid while dumplings are cooking.) Ladle soup into bowls and top with a dumpling.

Nutrition Facts per serving: 263 cal., 4 g total fat (1 g sat. fat), 1 mg chol., 1,434 mg sodium, 51 g carbo., 11 g fiber, 15 g pro. **Daily Values:** 17% vit. C, 15% calcium, 15% iron

A small amount of sour cream heightens the flavor of this main-dish soup. Spoon it on each bowl just before serving.

CREAMY-STYLE LENTIL SOUP

$3/4$ cup dry lentils, rinsed and drained

2 medium carrots, sliced (1 cup)

2 stalks celery, sliced (1 cup)

1 medium onion, chopped ($1/2$ cup)

3 cups water

1 $10^{3}/4$-ounce can condensed cream of mushroom soup

2 teaspoons instant beef bouillon granules

$1/4$ cup snipped fresh parsley

Dairy sour cream

1 In a $3^{1}/2$- to 4-quart slow cooker combine lentils, carrots, celery, and onion. Stir in water, mushroom soup, and bouillon granules.

2 Cover; cook on low-heat setting for 6 to 8 hours or on high-heat setting for $3^{1}/2$ to $4^{1}/2$ hours. Stir in parsley. Top each serving with sour cream.

Nutrition Facts per serving: 228 cal., 6 g total fat (2 g sat. fat), 1 mg chol., 999 mg sodium, 32 g carbo., 13 g fiber, 12 g pro. **Daily Values:** 158% vit. A, 19% vit. C, 7% calcium, 20% iron

PREP:

15 minutes

COOK:

Low 6 hours, High $3^{1}/2$ hours

MAKES:

4 main-dish servings

SLOW COOKER:

$3^{1}/2$- to 4-quart

FOR 5- TO 6-QUART SLOW COOKER
Recipe may be doubled.

To reduce the amount of heat in this south-of-the-border soup, use Monterey Jack cheese without the jalapeño peppers.

SPICY BEAN SOUP

PREP:

15 minutes

COOK:

Low 8 hours, High 4 hours

MAKES:

8 servings

SLOW COOKER:

$3^1/_2$- to 6-quart

1	15-ounce can red kidney beans, rinsed and drained
1	15-ounce can garbanzo beans, rinsed and drained
1	15-ounce can navy beans, rinsed and drained
1	10-ounce package frozen lima beans
1	9-ounce package frozen cut green beans
1	cup chopped onions (2 medium)
4	teaspoons chili powder
$1^1/_2$	teaspoons dried basil, crushed
$^1/_2$	teaspoon dried oregano, crushed
2	14-ounce cans beef broth
$^3/_4$	cup water
4	ounces Monterey Jack cheese with jalapeño peppers, shredded (1 cup)

1 In a $3^1/_2$- to 6-quart slow cooker combine canned and frozen beans, onions, chili powder, basil, and oregano. Stir in beef broth and water.

2 Cover; cook on low-heat setting for 8 to 9 hours or on high-heat setting for 4 to $4^1/_2$ hours. Stir in shredded cheese until melted. Ladle into soup bowls.

Nutrition Facts per serving: 284 cal., 6 g total fat (3 g sat. fat), 12 mg chol., 861 mg sodium, 42 g carbo., 12 g fiber, 20 g pro. **Daily Values:** 16% vit. A, 13% vit. C, 20% calcium, 20% iron

Two classic soup favorites—cheese and vegetables—get mixed up for a winning Mexican-style variation. Serve it hot with Mexican beer and lime wedges.

CHEESY MEXICAN-STYLE SOUP

2 cups chopped zucchini

¾ cup chopped red or green sweet pepper (1 medium)

½ cup chopped onion (1 medium)

1 15-ounce can black beans, rinsed and drained

1 10-ounce package frozen whole kernel corn, thawed

1 14½-ounce can diced tomatoes with green chiles

1 16-ounce jar cheddar cheese pasta sauce

1 cup reduced-sodium chicken broth or vegetable broth

Coarsely crushed tortilla chips (optional)

1 In a 3½- to 4-quart slow cooker place zucchini, sweet pepper, onion, beans, and corn. Pour undrained tomatoes over vegetables and beans. Combine cheese sauce and broth; pour over all.

2 Cover and cook on low-heat setting for 6 to 8 hours or on high-heat setting for 3 to 4 hours. Ladle into bowls and, if desired, sprinkle with crushed tortilla chips.

Nutrition Facts per serving: 287 cal., 14 g total fat (5 g sat. fat), 35 mg chol., 1,391 mg sodium, 36 g carbo., 7 g fiber, 12 g pro. **Daily Values:** 43% vit. A, 90% vit. C, 17% calcium, 11% iron

PREP:

15 minutes

COOK:

Low 6 hours, High 3 hours

MAKES:

5 to 6 servings

SLOW COOKER:

3½- to 4-quart

Indian cuisine has a lovely way with vegetables: slightly hot, slightly sweet, saucy, and fresh. The flavor is sublime in this soup. Stretch leftover soup by serving it with hot rice.

CREAMY CURRIED VEGETABLE SOUP

PREP:

25 minutes

COOK:

Low 8 hours, High 4 hours

MAKES:

6 to 8 servings

SLOW COOKER:

3½- to 6-quart

1	pound potatoes, peeled and cut into 1-inch pieces (3 cups)
3	cups cauliflower florets
1½	cups sliced carrots (3 medium)
¾	cup coarsely chopped red sweet pepper (1 medium)
½	cup chopped onion (1 medium)
1	15-ounce can garbanzo beans, rinsed and drained
2	to 3 teaspoons curry powder
2	teaspoons grated fresh ginger
½	teaspoon salt
⅛	teaspoon crushed red pepper
2	14-ounce cans chicken broth or vegetable broth (3½ cups total)
1	14-ounce can unsweetened coconut milk
2	tablespoons snipped fresh cilantro

1 In a 3½- to 6-quart slow cooker combine potatoes, cauliflower, carrots, sweet pepper, onion, and beans. Sprinkle curry powder, ginger, salt, and red pepper over vegetables and beans. Pour broth over all.

2 Cover and cook on low-heat setting for 8 to 10 hours or on high-heat setting for 4 to 5 hours. Stir in coconut milk. Ladle into bowls and sprinkle with cilantro.

Nutrition Facts per serving: 293 cal., 16 g total fat (13 g sat. fat), 0 mg chol., 1,030 mg sodium, 31 g carbo., 7 g fiber, 9 g pro. **Daily Values:** 176% vit. A, 103% vit. C, 7% calcium, 22% iron

If you love the warm, piquant tang of German-style potato salad, you'll be glad to find the taste in a soup bowl. Thick slices of hearty rye bread are a nice accompaniment.

GERMAN-STYLE POTATO SOUP

4   medium potatoes, peeled and chopped

2   stalks celery, sliced

1   medium onion, chopped

8   ounces cooked smoked sausage, sliced

4   cups beef broth

2   tablespoons vinegar

1   tablespoon sugar

¼   teaspoon celery seed

½   teaspoon dry mustard

¼   teaspoon pepper

2   cups packaged shredded cabbage with carrot (coleslaw mix)
     Snipped fresh parsley

PREP:

20 minutes

COOK:

Low 8 hours, High 4 hours; plus 15 minutes

MAKES:

4 main-dish servings

SLOW COOKER:

3½- to 4-quart

1 In a 3½- to 4-quart slow cooker combine potatoes, celery, onion, and sausage.

2 In a bowl combine broth, vinegar, sugar, celery seed, dry mustard, and pepper. Pour over potato mixture.

3 Cover and cook on low-heat setting for 8 to 9½ hours or on high-heat setting for 4 to 4½ hours. Stir in cabbage mixture. Cover and cook 15 to 30 minutes more. Top each serving with parsley.

Nutrition Facts per serving: 404 cal., 18 g total fat (6 g sat. fat), 39 mg chol., 1,542 mg sodium, 38 g carbo., 4 g fiber, 22 g pro. **Daily Values:** 2% vit. A, 64% vit. C, 7% calcium, 16% iron

A medley of mushrooms makes this sherry-flavored soup extra special. If using shiitake mushrooms, remove and discard the tough stems before slicing the caps.

SHERRIED BEEF & MUSHROOM STEW

PREP:

20 minutes

COOK:

Low 8 hours, High 4 hours

MAKES:

6 servings

SLOW COOKER:

4- to 6-quart

4   cups sliced assorted fresh mushrooms, such as button, crimini, and shiitake

3   medium carrots, cut into ½-inch slices (1½ cups)

1   cup sliced celery

1   6-ounce package long grain and wild rice mix with seasoning packet

1   pound beef stew meat, cut into 1-inch cubes

6   cups beef broth

½   cup dry sherry

1 In a 4- to 6-quart slow cooker place mushrooms, carrots, celery, and rice mix with seasoning packet. Place meat on top of vegetables. Pour broth and sherry over all.

2 Cover and cook on low-heat setting for 8 to 10 hours or on high-heat setting for 4 to 5 hours.

Nutrition Facts per serving: 279 cal., 5 g total fat (2 g sat. fat), 43 mg chol., 1,394 mg sodium, 30 g carbo., 2 g fiber, 24 g pro. **Daily Values:** 8% vit. C, 2% calcium, 20% iron

MARVELOUS MUSHROOMS

Varieties have mushroomed in recent years—you'll find several types in supermarket produce aisles. White or brown mushrooms, often called button mushrooms, are readily available and very mild in flavor. Morels, shiitakes, and portobellos have a rich, earthy flavor.

The best way to clean all types of mushrooms is to brush them with a clean, soft vegetable brush and wipe them with a clean, damp cloth. Do not soak fresh mushrooms or run them under water because they absorb liquid like sponges, ruining their texture.

Cook this classic French stew for a delicious weeknight meal. Accompany it with a loaf of rustic bread and a crisp mixed green salad tossed with vinaigrette.

BEEF BOURGUIGNON

1	pound boneless beef chuck roast, cut into ¾-inch cubes
2	tablespoons cooking oil
1	large onion, chopped
1	clove garlic, minced
3	cups whole fresh mushrooms
4	medium carrots, cut into ¾-inch pieces
8	ounces pearl onions or 2 cups frozen small, whole onions
3	tablespoons quick-cooking tapioca
1	teaspoon dried thyme, crushed
¾	teaspoon dried marjoram, crushed
½	teaspoon salt
¼	teaspoon pepper
2	bay leaves
1¼	cups Burgundy
½	cup beef broth
2	slices bacon, crisp-cooked, drained, and crumbled
3	cups hot cooked noodles

PREP:
40 minutes
COOK:
Low 10 hours, High 5 hours
MAKES:
6 servings
SLOW COOKER:
3½- to 4-quart

1 In a large saucepan brown half of the meat in 1 tablespoon of the hot oil; remove meat from pan. Add remaining oil, remaining meat, chopped onion, and garlic. Cook until meat is brown and onion is tender. Drain off fat.

2 In a 3½- to 4-quart slow cooker layer mushrooms, carrots, and pearl onions. Sprinkle with tapioca. Place meat mixture over vegetables. Add thyme, marjoram, salt, pepper, and bay leaves. Pour Burgundy and beef broth over meat and vegetables.

3 Cover and cook on low-heat setting for 10 to 12 hours or on high-heat setting for 5 to 6 hours or until tender. Discard bay leaves. To serve, stir in bacon. Serve with noodles.

Nutrition Facts per serving: 446 cal., 19 g total fat (7 g sat. fat), 80 mg chol., 367 mg sodium, 39 g carbo., 4 g fiber, 22 g pro. **Daily Values:** 12% vit. C, 6% calcium, 24% iron

If jalapeño pinto beans are unavailable, add one finely chopped jalapeño pepper—seeded if you want less heat.

BEEF STEW WITH A KICK

PREP:

20 minutes

COOK:

Low 10 hours, High 5 hours; plus 30 minutes on High

MAKES:

6 servings

SLOW COOKER:

4- to 6-quart

1	pound beef chuck pot roast
2	14$\frac{1}{2}$-ounce cans Mexican-style stewed tomatoes
3$\frac{1}{2}$	cups beef broth
1	6-ounce can tomato paste
4	teaspoons chili powder
1	tablespoon dried Italian seasoning, crushed
$\frac{1}{4}$	teaspoon crushed red pepper
$\frac{1}{8}$	teaspoon ground cloves
$\frac{1}{8}$	teaspoon ground allspice
$\frac{1}{8}$	teaspoon ground cinnamon
1$\frac{1}{2}$	cups coarsely chopped onions
1	15-ounce can pinto beans or jalapeño pinto beans, rinsed and drained
1	medium zucchini, halved lengthwise and cut into $\frac{1}{2}$-inch pieces
1	medium yellow or green sweet pepper, cut into 1-inch pieces

1 Trim fat from meat. Cut meat into 1-inch cubes.

2 In a 4- to 6-quart slow cooker combine undrained tomatoes, beef broth, tomato paste, chili powder, Italian seasoning, crushed red pepper, cloves, allspice, and cinnamon. Add meat, onions, and beans. Cover; cook on low-heat setting for 10 to 12 hours or on high-heat setting for 5 to 6 hours.

3 If using low-heat setting, turn to high-heat setting. Add zucchini and sweet peppers. Cover and cook 30 minutes more.

Nutrition Facts per serving: 272 cal., 5 g total fat (2 g sat. fat), 48 mg chol., 1,201 mg sodium, 34 g carbo., 8 g fiber, 25 g pro. **Daily Values:** 42% vit. A, 116% vit. C, 10% calcium, 26% iron

Mexican-style stewed tomatoes, salsa, and tortillas lend a south-of-the-border accent to this beef stew. Complete the meal with a colorful salad of romaine, orange sections, and avocado slices.

GREEN SALSA BEEF & POTATO STEW

1½	pounds boneless beef chuck pot roast
1	tablespoon cooking oil
4	medium unpeeled potatoes, cut into 1-inch pieces
1	large onion, coarsely chopped
1	green sweet pepper, cut into ½-inch pieces
1	14½-ounce can Mexican-style stewed tomatoes
1	15- or 16-ounce can pinto beans, rinsed and drained
1	cup bottled mild or medium green salsa
2	cloves garlic, minced
1	teaspoon ground cumin
6	flour tortillas

1 Trim fat from meat. Cut beef into 1-inch pieces. In a large skillet brown half of the beef at a time in hot oil over medium-high heat. Drain off fat.

2 In a 3½- to 5-quart slow cooker combine beef, potatoes, onion, sweet pepper, undrained tomatoes, beans, salsa, garlic, and cumin. Cover and cook on low-heat setting for 8 to 9 hours or on high-heat setting for 5 to 6 hours. Serve with warmed tortillas.

Nutrition Facts per serving: 465 cal., 12 g total fat (3 g sat. fat), 72 mg chol., 709 mg sodium, 56 g carbo., 8 g fiber, 33 g pro. **Daily Values:** 51% vit. C, 11% calcium, 31% iron

PREP:
30 minutes

COOK:
Low 8 hours, High 5 hours

MAKES:
6 servings

SLOW COOKER:
3½- to 5-quart

When peeling fresh beets, wear latex gloves to prevent staining your hands. Remember to serve the stew with sour cream, the customary garnish for this traditional Russian dish.

BEEF & BORSCHT STEW

PREP:

40 minutes

COOK:

Low 8 hours, High 4 hours; plus 30 minutes on High

MAKES:

6 to 8 servings

SLOW COOKER:

4- to 5-quart

1	pound cubed beef stew meat
1	tablespoon cooking oil
4	medium beets, peeled and cut into ½-inch pieces, or one 16-ounce can diced beets, drained
2	medium tomatoes, coarsely chopped
2	medium potatoes, peeled and cut into ½-inch pieces
2	medium carrots, shredded
1	medium onion, chopped
3	cloves garlic, minced
4	cups beef broth
1	6-ounce can tomato paste
2	tablespoons red wine vinegar
1	tablespoon brown sugar
1	teaspoon salt
½	teaspoon dried dillweed
¼	teaspoon pepper
1	bay leaf
3	cups shredded cabbage
	Dairy sour cream or plain yogurt

1 Cut up any large pieces of stew meat. In a large skillet brown beef, half at a time, in hot oil. Drain off fat.

2 Meanwhile, in a 4- to 5-quart slow cooker combine beets, tomatoes, potatoes, carrots, onion, and garlic. Add meat.

3 In a large bowl combine beef broth, tomato paste, vinegar, brown sugar, salt, dillweed, pepper, and bay leaf. Add to cooker. Cover; cook on low-heat setting for 8 to 10 hours or on high-heat setting for 4 to 4½ hours.

4 If using low-heat setting, turn to high-heat setting. Stir in cabbage. Cover and cook 30 minutes more. Discard bay leaf. Ladle into bowls. Garnish each serving with sour cream or yogurt.

Nutrition Facts per serving: 277 cal., 9 g total fat (3 g sat. fat), 40 mg chol., 954 mg sodium, 24 g carbo., 5 g fiber, 25 g pro. **Daily Values:** 111% vit. A, 53% vit. C, 7% calcium, 20% iron

Combine a trio of vegetables with top round steak in this hearty Belgian-inspired stew. Either dark or light beer, depending on personal preference, works well in this recipe.

CARBONNADE-STYLE BEEF

2	pounds boneless beef top round steak, cut into 1-inch cubes
2	12-ounce cans beer
1/4	cup red wine vinegar
3	tablespoons brown sugar
2	tablespoons instant beef bouillon granules
4	cloves garlic, minced
2	bay leaves
2	teaspoons dried thyme, crushed
2	teaspoons Worcestershire sauce
1/2	teaspoon pepper
3	large leeks or medium onions, sliced (1 1/2 cups)
4	medium carrots, peeled and cut diagonally into 1/2-inch slices
2	parsnips, peeled and cut diagonally into 1/2-inch slices
1/4	cup cornstarch
	Hot mashed potatoes

PREP:

30 minutes

COOK:

Low 8 hours, High 4 hours; plus 30 minutes on High

MAKES:

8 servings

SLOW COOKER:

3 1/2- to 4-quart

1 In a 3 1/2- to 4-quart slow cooker place the beef cubes. Reserve 1/4 cup beer in refrigerator. Add the remaining beer, vinegar, brown sugar, bouillon granules, garlic, bay leaves, thyme, Worcestershire sauce, and pepper to slow cooker. Stir in the leeks, carrots, and parsnips. Cover; cook on low-heat setting for 8 to 10 hours or on high-heat setting for 4 to 5 hours. Remove bay leaves.

2 If cooking on low-heat setting, turn cooker to high-heat setting. Combine cornstarch and reserved beer; stir into cooker. Cover and cook 30 minutes more or until thickened and bubbly.

3 Serve over mashed potatoes.

Nutrition Facts per serving: 353 cal., 7 g total fat (4 g sat. fat), 57 mg chol., 1,160 mg sodium, 39 g carbo., 5 g fiber, 27 g pro. **Daily Values:** 160% vit. A, 24% vit. C, 8% calcium, 19% iron

Look for Jerusalem artichokes, also called sunchokes, from fall through winter in the produce department of the grocery store.

SPICED BEEF & SUNCHOKE STEW

PREP:

30 minutes

COOK:

Low 9 hours, High 4 hours

MAKES:

5 servings

SLOW COOKER:

3 1/2- to 4-quart

1 1/4	pounds boneless beef chuck steak, cut into 3/4-inch cubes
1	tablespoon olive oil or cooking oil
8	whole allspice
1/2	teaspoon dillseed
1	bay leaf
1	14 1/2-ounce can tomatoes, cut up
1	8-ounce can tomato sauce
2	tablespoons cider vinegar
2	cloves garlic, minced
1/4	teaspoon celery salt
1/4	teaspoon pepper
1	pound Jerusalem artichokes, red potatoes, or new potatoes, cut into 1/4-inch-thick slices
2	cups frozen pearl onions or 1 medium onion, cut into thin wedges
8	ounces fresh mushrooms, halved

1 In a large skillet brown meat, half at a time, in hot oil. Drain off fat.

2 For spice bag, place allspice, dillseed, and bay leaf in the center of a square of 100-percent-cotton cheesecloth. Bring up the corners and tie them with clean kitchen string. Set aside.

3 In a bowl stir together undrained tomatoes, tomato sauce, vinegar, garlic, celery salt, and pepper.

4 In a 3 1/2- to 4-quart slow cooker place Jerusalem artichokes, onions, and mushrooms. Add meat and spice bag. Pour tomato mixture over all.

5 Cover; cook on low-heat setting for 9 to 10 hours or on high-heat setting for 4 to 5 hours. Remove and discard spice bag before serving.

Nutrition Facts per serving: 296 cal., 12 g total fat (3 g sat. fat), 60 mg chol., 574 mg sodium, 23 g carbo., 3 g fiber, 26 g pro. **Daily Values:** 9% vit. A, 33% vit. C, 8% calcium, 32% iron

Purchase chunks of stew meat from the butcher or select a beef chuck or shoulder roast and cut it into 1- to 1½-inch pieces.

SUPER-SIMPLE BEEF STEW

12	ounces small red potatoes, quartered (about 2 cups)
4	medium carrots, cut into ½-inch pieces (2 cups)
1	small red onion, cut into wedges (⅓ cup)
1	pound beef stew meat
1	10¾-ounce can condensed cream of mushroom or cream of celery soup
1	cup beef broth
½	teaspoon dried marjoram or thyme, crushed
1	9-ounce package frozen cut green beans, thawed

1 In a 3½- to 4-quart slow cooker place potatoes, carrots, onion, meat, condensed soup, broth, and marjoram or thyme. Stir to combine.

2 Cover; cook on low-heat setting for 8 to 9 hours or on high-heat setting for 4 to 4½ hours. If using low-heat setting, turn to high-heat setting. Stir in thawed green beans. Cover and cook for 10 to 15 minutes more.

Nutrition Facts per serving: 316 cal., 11 g total fat (3 g sat. fat), 38 mg chol., 766 mg sodium, 31 g carbo., 6 g fiber, 24 g pro. **Daily Values:** 313% vit. A, 40% vit. C, 8% calcium, 20% iron

PREP:
15 minutes

COOK:
Low 8 hours, High 4 hours; plus 10 minutes on High

MAKES:
4 servings

SLOW COOKER:
3½- to 4-quart

This inviting stew comes from a region of Switzerland near the border of Italy. Swiss cooking is among the heartiest in Europe—and the use of polenta is traditional.

BEEF STEW WITH POLENTA

PREP:

40 minutes

COOK:

Low 8 hours, High 4 hours

MAKES:

8 servings

SLOW COOKER:

3¹/₂- to 4-quart

¹/₄	cup all-purpose flour
1	teaspoon dried thyme, crushed
1	teaspoon dried basil, crushed
¹/₂	teaspoon salt
¹/₂	teaspoon pepper
2¹/₂	pounds boneless beef chuck steak, cut into 1-inch pieces
2	tablespoons olive oil
8	ounces boiling onions, peeled
4	medium carrots, cut into ¹/₂-inch chunks
6	cloves garlic, minced
1	teaspoon snipped fresh rosemary or ¹/₄ teaspoon dried rosemary, crushed
1	14-ounce can beef broth
1¹/₂	cups dry red wine
1	recipe Polenta
¹/₂	cup snipped fresh flat-leaf parsley
¹/₄	cup tomato paste
	Flat-leaf parsley (optional)

1 In a medium bowl stir together flour, thyme, basil, salt, and pepper. Coat meat with flour mixture. In a 4-quart Dutch oven brown half the meat in hot oil over medium-high heat. Remove meat from Dutch oven and place in a 3¹/₂- to 4-quart slow cooker. Repeat with remaining meat; add more oil if necessary. Add onions, carrots, garlic, and dried rosemary, if using, to cooker. Add broth and wine to cooker; stir to combine.

2 Cover; cook on low-heat setting for 8 to 10 hours or on high-heat setting for 4 to 5 hours. Meanwhile, prepare Polenta. Just before serving, stir the parsley, fresh rosemary (if using), and tomato paste into beef mixture in cooker. Serve in bowls with Polenta. If desired, garnish with flat-leaf parsley.

POLENTA: In a large saucepan bring 2³/₄ cups water to boiling. Meanwhile, in a bowl combine 1 cup cornmeal, 1 cup cold water, and ¹/₂ teaspoon salt. Slowly add cornmeal mixture to boiling water, stirring constantly. Cook and stir until mixture returns to boiling. Reduce heat to low. Cook for 10 to 15 minutes or until mixture is very thick, stirring occasionally. Makes 3¹/₂ cups.

Nutrition Facts per serving: 365 cal., 10 g total fat (3 g sat. fat), 86 mg chol., 506 mg sodium, 26 g carbo., 4 g fiber, 33 g pro. **Daily Values:** 199% vit. A, 19% vit. C, 5% calcium, 29% iron

This rich broth is well worth the effort it requires. Use the cooked meat for barbecue sandwiches or add it to soups, stews, or casseroles that call for cooked beef.

FORK-TENDER BEEF WITH BROTH

2	large onions, sliced (2 cups)
4	cloves garlic, halved
8	sprigs fresh parsley
4	large bay leaves
8	whole black peppercorns
1½	teaspoons salt
3	pounds meaty beef soup bones (beef shank crosscuts or short ribs)
5	cups water
1	egg white (optional)
1	eggshell, crushed (optional)
¼	cup water (optional)

1 In a 4- to 6-quart slow cooker combine onions, garlic, parsley, bay leaves, peppercorns, and salt. Add soup bones and the 5 cups water.

2 Cover; cook on low-heat setting for 10 to 12 hours or on high-heat setting for 5 to 6 hours.

3 Remove bones from cooker. Strain broth through a large sieve or colander lined with two layers of 100-percent-cotton cheesecloth. Discard solids in cheesecloth. If desired, clarify broth by combining egg white, eggshell, and ¼ cup water in a large saucepan. Add hot broth. Bring to boiling; let stand 5 minutes. Strain broth through two layers of 100-percent-cotton cheesecloth.

4 If using broth right away, skim off fat. If storing broth for later use, chill broth in a bowl for 6 hours. Lift off fat. Pour broth into an airtight container; discard residue in the bottom of the bowl; seal. Chill in the refrigerator for up to 3 days or freeze for up to 3 months.

5 When bones are cool enough to handle, remove meat from bones. Discard bones. Place the meat in an airtight container; seal. Chill in the refrigerator for up to 3 days or freeze for up to 3 months.

Nutrition Facts per 1-cup serving of broth: 0 cal., 0 g total fat (0 g sat. fat), 0 mg chol., 705 mg sodium, 0 g carbo., 0 g fiber, 0 g pro. **Daily Values:** 1% calcium

PREP:
20 minutes

COOK:
Low 10 hours, High 5 hours

STAND:
5 minutes

MAKES:
5 to 5½ cups broth and 2½ to 3½ cups cooked meat

SLOW COOKER:
4- to 6-quart

Hungarian paprika is lighter in color and more pungent in flavor than other paprikas. The Hungarian type may be labeled as sweet (mild) or hot. Look for it in specialty markets.

HUNGARIAN-STYLE GOULASH

PREP:

15 minutes

COOK:

Low 10 hours, High 5 hours

STAND:

10 minutes

MAKES:

6 servings

SLOW COOKER:

3^1/$_2$- to 5-quart

3	medium potatoes, cut into 1-inch cubes
2	medium onions, chopped
2	cloves garlic, minced
1^1/$_2$	pounds beef stew meat, cut into 1-inch cubes
1	14^1/$_2$-ounce can beef broth
1	14-ounce can chunky tomatoes with garlic and spices
1	6-ounce can tomato paste
2	tablespoons hot-style Hungarian paprika or paprika
1	teaspoon caraway seeds or fennel seeds
^{1}/$_2$	teaspoon salt
1	9-ounce package frozen artichoke hearts, thawed
3	cups hot cooked noodles
^{1}/$_3$	cup dairy sour cream

1 In a 3^1/$_2$- to 5-quart slow cooker place potatoes, onions, and garlic. Add beef. In a bowl combine broth, undrained tomatoes, tomato paste, paprika, caraway or fennel seeds, and salt. Pour over all.

2 Cover; cook on low-heat setting for 10 to 12 hours or on high-heat setting for 5 to 6 hours.

3 Stir thawed artichoke hearts into cooker. Cover and let stand for 10 minutes. Serve over hot cooked noodles. Top each serving with a spoonful of sour cream.

Nutrition Facts per serving: 501 cal., 13 g total fat (5 g sat. fat), 121 mg chol., 820 mg sodium, 58 g carbo., 5 g fiber, 38 g pro. **Daily Values:** 64% vit. C, 9% calcium, 53% iron

To include beef as part of a low-fat diet, choose lean meat that is trimmed of excess fat, or trim the meat yourself.

BEEF RAGOUT WITH GREMOLATA

1½ pounds beef stew meat, cut into 1-inch cubes

1 tablespoon olive oil

2 medium onions, cut into wedges

3 medium carrots, cut into ½-inch slices

1 14½-ounce can diced tomatoes

½ cup beef broth

2 cloves garlic, minced

1½ teaspoons dried thyme, crushed

¼ teaspoon salt

¼ teaspoon pepper

1 medium zucchini, halved lengthwise and cut into ¼-inch slices

6 ounces fresh green beans, cut into 2-inch pieces (1¾ cups)

4½ cups hot cooked couscous

1 recipe Gremolata

PREP:
25 minutes

COOK:
Low 7 hours, High 3½ hours; plus 30 minutes on High

MAKES:
6 servings

SLOW COOKER:
3½- to 4-quart

1 In a large skillet brown meat, half at a time, in hot oil. Drain off fat. Transfer meat to a 3½- to 4-quart slow cooker. Add onions and carrots. In a bowl stir together the undrained tomatoes, broth, garlic, thyme, salt, and pepper. Pour over all.

2 Cover; cook on low-heat setting for 7 to 9 hours or on high-heat setting for 3½ to 4½ hours. If using low-heat setting, turn to high-heat setting. Stir in zucchini and green beans. Cover; cook for 30 minutes more. Serve over hot couscous. Top each serving with Gremolata.

GREMOLATA: Stir together ¼ cup snipped parsley, 1 tablespoon finely shredded lemon peel, and 2 cloves garlic, minced.

Nutrition Facts per serving: 413 cal., 11 g total fat (4 g sat. fat), 82 mg chol., 404 mg sodium, 43 g carbo., 9 g fiber, 34 g pro. **Daily Values:** 34% vit. C, 6% calcium, 33% iron

In the depths of winter when temperatures plunge and darkness comes early, welcome the family home with bowls of this all-time favorite.

TRADITIONAL BEEF STEW

PREP:

25 minutes

COOK:

Low 10 hours, High 5 hours

MAKES:

4 to 6 servings

SLOW COOKER:

3 1/2- to 4-quart

*NOTE

Substitute 2 cups of frozen mixed vegetables for the beans and the corn.

FOR A 6-QUART COOKER

Recipe may be doubled.

2	tablespoons all-purpose flour
1	pound beef or pork stew meat, cut into 3/4-inch cubes
2	tablespoons cooking oil
2 1/2	cups cubed potatoes
1	cup frozen cut green beans*
1	cup frozen whole kernel corn*
1	cup sliced carrot
1	medium onion, cut into thin wedges
2	teaspoons instant beef bouillon granules
2	teaspoons Worcestershire sauce
1	teaspoon dried oregano, crushed
1/2	teaspoon dried marjoram or basil, crushed
1/4	teaspoon pepper
1	bay leaf
2 1/2	cups vegetable juice or hot-style vegetable juice

1 Place flour in a plastic bag. Add meat cubes and shake until meat is coated with flour. In a Dutch oven brown half of the meat in 1 tablespoon of hot oil, turning to brown evenly. Brown remaining meat in remaining oil. Drain off fat.

2 In a 3 1/2- to 4-quart slow cooker layer potatoes, green beans, corn, carrot, and onion. Add meat. Add bouillon granules, Worcestershire sauce, oregano, marjoram, pepper, and bay leaf. Pour vegetable juice over all.

3 Cover and cook on low-heat setting for 10 to 12 hours or on high-heat setting for 5 to 6 hours or until meat and vegetables are tender. Discard bay leaf. Ladle into bowls.

Nutrition Facts per serving: 525 cal., 28 g total fat (10 g sat. fat), 77 mg chol., 953 mg sodium, 42 g carbo., 6 g fiber, 27 g pro. **Daily Values:** 119% vit. C, 7% calcium, 29% iron

Argentina is known for its excellent beef. This vegetable-filled beef stew is a favorite of this South American country.

ARGENTINA-STYLE STEW

4 slices bacon

1½ pounds beef stew meat, cut into 1-inch cubes

3 medium carrots, cut into 1-inch pieces

3 medium onions, coarsely chopped

3 medium tomatoes, peeled and cut into wedges

2 medium potatoes, peeled and cut into eighths

8 ounces winter squash or pumpkin, peeled and cut into 1½-inch cubes (1½ cups)

1 medium green sweet pepper, chopped

1 tablespoon snipped fresh thyme or 1 teaspoon dried thyme, crushed

1 clove garlic, minced

1 14-ounce can beef broth

½ small head of cabbage, coarsely chopped (3 cups)

PREP:

35 minutes

COOK:

Low 8 hours, High 4 hours; plus 15 minutes on High

MAKES:

6 servings

SLOW COOKER:

5- to 6-quart

1 In a large skillet cook bacon until crisp. Remove bacon, reserving drippings. Drain bacon on paper towels. Crumble bacon; chill until serving time. Brown beef, half at a time, in hot drippings. Drain off fat.

2 In a 5- to 6-quart slow cooker place carrots, onions, tomatoes, potatoes, squash or pumpkin, sweet pepper, dried thyme (if using), and garlic. Add meat. Pour broth over all.

3 Cover; cook on low-heat setting for 8 to 10 hours or on high-heat setting for 4 to 5 hours.

4 If using low-heat setting, turn to high-heat setting. Stir in the cabbage and, if using, the fresh thyme. Cover and cook for 15 to 20 minutes more or until cabbage is just tender. To serve, sprinkle each serving with crumbled bacon.

Nutrition Facts per serving: 341 cal., 11 g total fat (4 g sat. fat), 86 mg chol., 386 mg sodium, 29 g carbo., 5 g fiber, 33 g pro. **Daily Values:** 91% vit. C, 6% calcium, 35% iron

Ginger, molasses, and raisins provide pleasant sweetness to this savory stew. Serve the stew with a salad of mixed greens, grapes, and toasted walnuts.

SWEET 'N' SNAPPY BEEF STEW

PREP:

35 minutes

COOK:

Low 8 hours, High 4 hours; plus 30 minutes

MAKES:

8 servings

SLOW COOKER:

3¹/₂- to 6-quart

2	pounds lean beef stew meat, cut into 1-inch cubes
4	carrots, sliced
2	medium parsnips, sliced
1	medium onion, sliced
1	stalk celery, sliced
¹/₄	cup quick-cooking tapioca
1	tablespoon grated fresh ginger or ¹/₂ teaspoon ground ginger
1	teaspoon salt
¹/₂	teaspoon pepper
1	14¹/₂-ounce can diced tomatoes
¹/₄	cup cider vinegar
¹/₄	cup molasses
¹/₂	cup raisins

1 In a 3¹/₂- to 6-quart slow cooker place meat, carrots, parsnips, onion, and celery. Sprinkle tapioca, ginger, salt, and pepper over mixture. Add undrained tomatoes, vinegar, and molasses.

2 Cover; cook on low-heat setting for 8 to 9 hours or on high-heat setting for 4 to 4¹/₂ hours. Stir in raisins; cover and continue cooking for 30 minutes more.

Nutrition Facts per serving: 302 cal., 7 g total fat (2 g sat. fat), 54 mg chol., 486 mg sodium, 34 g carbo., 4 g fiber, 27 g pro. **Daily Values:** 155% vit. A, 20% vit. C, 7% calcium, 20% iron

For a change from Mom's old-fashioned beef stew, try this delicious variation. The green olives and raisins make it unusually attractive and tasty.

SAUCY BEEF WITH A TWIST

2	tablespoons all-purpose flour
1	pound beef stew meat, cut into 1-inch cubes
2	tablespoons cooking oil
5	medium carrots, sliced into ½-inch pieces
2	medium parsnips, sliced into ½-inch pieces
12	ounces boiling onions, peeled and halved
1	14½-ounce can diced tomatoes
1	14-ounce can beef broth
2	cloves garlic, minced
1	bay leaf
1	tablespoon snipped fresh thyme or 1 teaspoon dried thyme, crushed
¼	teaspoon pepper
½	cup almond- or pimiento-stuffed green olives
⅓	cup golden raisins

PREP:

35 minutes

COOK:

Low 8 hours, High 4 hours

MAKES:

4 servings

SLOW COOKER:

3½- to 4-quart

1 Place flour in a plastic bag. Add meat cubes, a few at a time, shaking to coat meat. In a large skillet brown meat, half at a time, in hot oil. Drain off fat.

2 In a 3½- to 4-quart slow cooker place carrots, parsnips, and onions. Add meat, undrained tomatoes, broth, garlic, bay leaf, dried thyme (if using), and pepper.

3 Cover; cook on low-heat setting for 8 to 10 hours or on high-heat setting for 4 to 5 hours. Remove and discard bay leaf. To serve, stir in olives, raisins, and, if using, fresh thyme.

Nutrition Facts per serving: 394 cal., 11 g total fat (3 g sat. fat), 69 mg chol., 899 mg sodium, 45 g carbo., 8 g fiber, 29 g pro. **Daily Values:** 480% vit. A, 56% vit. C, 13% calcium, 29% iron

Simple ingredients add up to a wonderful wintertime stew. Apples and apple cider lend subtly sweet flavor while thyme offers a minty-lemon complement.

GOLDEN BEEF & APPLE CIDER STEW

PREP:

35 minutes

COOK:

Low 8 hours, High 4 hours

MAKES:

5 servings

SLOW COOKER:

3^1/2- to 5-quart

TYPES OF SLOW COOKING APPLIANCES

Continuous slow cooker/crockery cooker: This type of electric cooker cooks foods at a very low wattage. The heating coils or elements wrap around the sides of the cooker and remain on continuously. This type of appliance has two fixed settings—low (about 200°F) and high (about 300°F), and in some models, automatic (cooker shifts from high to low automatically). The ceramic liner may or may not be removable. All crockery recipes in this book were tested in this type of appliance. **Intermittent slow cooker:** This type of cooker has the heating element or coil located below the food container. It cycles on and off during operation and has a dial indicating temperatures in degrees. Because the recipes in this book need continuous slow cooking, they will not cook properly in this type of appliance.

1	pound beef or lamb stew meat, cut into 1-inch cubes
1	tablespoon cooking oil
4	carrots or parsnips, chopped
2	medium red potatoes, chopped
2	onions, halved and sliced
2	small apples, cored and cut into ^{1}/2-inch pieces
1	stalk celery, chopped
2	tablespoons quick-cooking tapioca
1	cup apple cider or apple juice
1	cup water
2	teaspoons instant beef bouillon granules
1	teaspoon snipped fresh thyme or ^{1}/4 teaspoon dried thyme, crushed
^{1}/4	teaspoon pepper

1 In a large skillet brown meat, half at a time, in hot oil. Drain off fat.

2 In a 3^1/2- to 5-quart slow cooker place carrots or parsnips, potatoes, onions, apples, and celery. Sprinkle tapioca over vegetables. Add meat. In a bowl combine the cider, water, bouillon granules, dried thyme (if using), and pepper; pour over meat.

3 Cover; cook on low-heat setting for 8 to 10 hours or on high-heat setting for 4 to 5 hours. To serve, stir in fresh thyme, if using.

Nutrition Facts per serving: 366 cal., 16 g total fat (5 g sat. fat), 58 mg chol., 432 mg sodium, 36 g carbo., 5 g fiber, 20 g pro. **Daily Values:** 247% vit. A, 29% vit. C, 5% calcium, 19% iron

Impress guests with this elegant entrée accompanied by chilled asparagus spears drizzled with raspberry vinaigrette.

STEWED VEAL IN PASTRY

1½	pounds veal or pork stew meat, cut into 1-inch cubes
2	tablespoons cooking oil
4	medium parsnips and/or large carrots, bias-sliced into ½-inch pieces
1	medium red onion, chopped
2	cloves garlic, minced
3	tablespoons snipped fresh basil or 1 teaspoon dried basil, crushed
¼	teaspoon pepper
1	cup beef broth
⅓	cup dry white wine or beef broth
2	tablespoons cornstarch
1½	cups quartered fresh mushrooms
1½	cups halved seedless red grapes
6	baked individual pastry shells

1 In a large skillet brown meat, half at a time, in hot oil. Drain off fat.

2 In a 3½- to 5-quart slow cooker place parsnips or carrots, onion, and garlic. Add meat. Sprinkle with dried basil (if using) and pepper. Pour the 1 cup broth over all. Cover; cook on low-heat setting for 6 to 8 hours or on high-heat setting for 3 to 4 hours.

3 If using low-heat setting, turn to high-heat setting. Stir together wine and cornstarch; stir into stew. Cover; cook 30 minutes more or until thickened. Stir in mushrooms. Cover; cook for 10 minutes more. Stir grapes and, if using, fresh basil into stew.

4 To serve, place pastry shells on serving plates. Spoon stew into and around the pastry shells.

Nutrition Facts per serving: 498 cal., 22 g total fat (2 g sat. fat), 92 mg chol., 382 mg sodium, 44 g carbo., 5 g fiber, 29 g pro. **Daily Values:** 26% vit. C, 4% calcium, 12% iron

PREP:

25 minutes

COOK:

Low 6 hours, High 3 hours; plus 40 minutes on High

MAKES:

6 servings

SLOW COOKER:

3½- to 5-quart

This hearty stew of Panamanian origin is mildly spiced with chili powder and chile peppers. The yams or sweet potatoes sweetly complement the flavors.

PANAMA PORK STEW

PREP:

20 minutes

COOK:

Low 7 hours, High 3¹/₂ hours

MAKES:

6 to 8 servings

SLOW COOKER:

3¹/₂- to 5-quart

3	medium yams or sweet potatoes, peeled and cut into 2-inch pieces
1	large green sweet pepper, cut into strips
1	cup frozen whole kernel corn
1	medium onion, sliced and separated into rings
3	cloves garlic, minced
1¹/₂	pounds boneless pork shoulder, cut into ³/₄-inch cubes
1	teaspoon chili powder
³/₄	teaspoon ground coriander
¹/₂	teaspoon salt
2	cups water
1	10-ounce can chopped tomatoes with green chile peppers
1	9-ounce package frozen cut green beans

1 In a 3¹/₂- to 5-quart slow cooker place yams or sweet potatoes, sweet pepper, corn, onion, and garlic. Add pork, chili powder, coriander, and salt. Pour the water and the undrained tomatoes over all.

2 Cover; cook on low-heat setting for 7 to 8 hours or on high-heat setting for 3¹/₂ to 4 hours, adding the frozen green beans during the last 15 minutes of cooking time.

Nutrition Facts per serving: 299 cal., 12 g total fat (4 g sat. fat), 74 mg chol., 446 mg sodium, 26 g carbo., 3 g fiber, 23 g pro. **Daily Values:** 54% vit. C, 5% calcium, 14% iron

Dish up down-home cooking. Try this hearty stew that features familiar Southern standbys—collard greens, black-eyed peas, okra, and hominy.

DIXIE HAM STEW

1½ cups dry black-eyed peas (about 9½ ounces)
4   cups water
2   cups cubed cooked ham
1   15-ounce can white hominy, rinsed and drained
1   10-ounce package frozen cut okra
1   large onion, chopped
4   cloves garlic, minced
1   to 2 teaspoons Cajun or Creole seasoning
¼   teaspoon pepper
4½ cups water
4   cups chopped collard greens or fresh spinach
1   14½-ounce can stewed tomatoes

1 Rinse peas; drain. In a large saucepan combine peas and the 4 cups water. Bring to boiling; reduce heat. Simmer, uncovered, for 10 minutes. Drain and rinse peas.

2 In a 3½- to 6-quart slow cooker combine peas, ham, hominy, frozen okra, onion, garlic, Cajun seasoning, and pepper. Stir in 4½ cups fresh water. Cover and cook on low-heat setting for 8 to 10 hours or on high-heat setting for 4 to 5 hours.

3 If using low-heat setting, turn to high-heat setting. Stir in collard greens and undrained tomatoes. Cover and cook about 10 minutes more. Ladle into bowls.

Nutrition Facts per serving: 245 cal., 5 g total fat (1 g sat. fat), 20 mg chol., 673 mg sodium, 35 g carbo., 7 g fiber, 16 g pro. **Daily Values:** 21% vit. C, 11% calcium, 21% iron

PREP:
20 minutes

COOK:
Low 8 hours, High 4 hours; plus 10 minutes on High

MAKES:
8 servings

SLOW COOKER:
3½- to 6-quart

Poblano peppers are mild to medium-hot. They're long, deep green, and have an irregular bell-pepper shape. Remove the membranes and seeds for the mildest flavor.

POBLANO PORK STEW

PREP:

30 minutes

COOK:

Low 8 hours, High 4 hours

MAKES:

6 servings

SLOW COOKER:

3 1/2- to 4-quart

*NOTE

Because fresh chile peppers contain pungent oils (the membranes and the seeds carry the heat), protect your hands when handling them. Wear plastic gloves or put sandwich bags over your hands. Wash your hands and nails thoroughly in hot, soapy water after handling chile peppers.

1	pound boneless pork shoulder roast, cut into 1-inch cubes
1	tablespoon cooking oil
1	pound whole, tiny new potatoes, quartered
2	medium onions, chopped
2	fresh poblano peppers, seeded and cut into 1-inch pieces*
1	fresh jalapeño pepper, seeded and chopped*
4	cloves garlic, minced
2	inches stick cinnamon
3	cups chicken broth
1	14 1/2-ounce can diced tomatoes
1	tablespoon chili powder
1	teaspoon dried oregano, crushed
1/4	teaspoon black pepper
1/4	cup snipped fresh cilantro or parsley
	Hot cooked basmati or long grain rice (optional)

1 In a large skillet brown meat, half at a time, in hot oil. Drain off fat.

2 In a 3 1/2- to 4-quart slow cooker place potatoes, onions, poblano peppers, jalapeño pepper, garlic, and stick cinnamon. Add meat. In a bowl combine chicken broth, undrained tomatoes, chili powder, oregano, and black pepper; pour over all.

3 Cover; cook on low-heat setting for 8 to 10 hours or on high-heat setting for 4 to 5 hours. Discard stick cinnamon. Stir in cilantro or parsley. If desired, serve stew over hot cooked rice.

Nutrition Facts per serving: 285 cal., 11 g total fat (3 g sat. fat), 50 mg chol., 753 mg sodium, 28 g carbo., 3 g fiber, 19 g pro. **Daily Values:** 202% vit. C, 5% calcium, 21% iron

Unlike dry beans, lentils simmer to perfection in the slow cooker without precooking. In this soup, lemon peel and spinach enhance the mild, nutty flavor of the lentils.

HAM & LENTIL SOUP

1	cup dry lentils
4	cups water
1	medium onion, chopped
1	cup chopped celery
1	cup sliced carrot
2	teaspoons instant chicken bouillon granules
1	teaspoon bottled minced garlic or 2 cloves garlic, minced
$\frac{1}{2}$	teaspoon finely shredded lemon peel
$\frac{1}{8}$	to $\frac{1}{4}$ teaspoon ground red pepper
1	cup cubed cooked ham
2	cups chopped fresh spinach

1 Rinse and drain lentils. In a $3\frac{1}{2}$- to 4-quart slow cooker combine lentils, water, onion, celery, carrot, bouillon granules, garlic, lemon peel, and red pepper.

2 Cover and cook on low-heat setting for 7 to 8 hours or on high-heat setting for $3\frac{1}{2}$ to 4 hours. If using low-heat setting, turn to high-heat setting. Add ham. Cover and cook for 10 minutes more. Stir in spinach. Ladle into bowls and serve immediately.

Nutrition Facts per serving: 235 cal., 4 g total fat (1 g sat. fat), 21 mg chol., 815 mg sodium, 33 g carbo., 6 g fiber, 18 g pro. **Daily Values:** 20% vit. C, 9% calcium, 27% iron

PREP:

15 minutes

COOK:

Low 7 hours, High $3\frac{1}{2}$ hours; plus 10 minutes on High

MAKES:

4 to 6 servings

SLOW COOKER:

$3\frac{1}{2}$- to 4-quart

A FULL POT
Unlike cooking in a saucepan, the heat in a slow cooker comes from coils that wrap around the sides of the pot. Therefore, a cooker that is at least half full will cook more efficiently. When you remove the meat from the cooker, the juices likely will fill the cooker less than halfway. To thicken juices, transfer them to a saucepan rather than leaving them in the cooker.

If you haven't thought about parsnips since you last read about Peter Rabbit, it's time to give this nutty-tasting root a try. Look for small to medium parsnips that are firm with fairly smooth skin and few rootlets.

HARVEST PORK & PARSNIP STEW

PREP:

25 minutes

COOK:

Low 7 hours, High 3¹/₂ hours

MAKES:

4 servings

SLOW COOKER:

3¹/₂- to 4-quart

1	pound boneless pork shoulder
2	cups cubed, peeled sweet potatoes
2	medium parsnips, peeled and cut into ¹/₂-inch pieces (1³/₄ cups)
2	small cooking apples, cored and cut into ¹/₄-inch slices (1³/₄ cups)
1	medium onion, chopped
³/₄	teaspoon dried thyme, crushed
¹/₂	teaspoon dried rosemary, crushed
¹/₂	teaspoon salt
¹/₄	teaspoon pepper
2	cups apple cider or apple juice

1 Trim fat from meat. Cut pork into 1-inch cubes.

2 In a 3¹/₂- to 4-quart slow cooker layer potatoes, parsnips, apples, and onion. Sprinkle with thyme, rosemary, salt, and pepper. Add meat to cooker. Pour apple cider or juice over all.

3 Cover and cook on low-heat setting for 7 to 8 hours or on high-heat setting for 3¹/₂ to 4 hours or until meat and vegetables are tender. Ladle into bowls.

Nutrition Facts per serving: 365 cal., 8 g total fat (3 g sat. fat), 76 mg chol., 392 mg sodium, 37 g carbo., 7 g fiber, 24 g pro. **Daily Values:** 242% vit. A, 40% vit. C, 7% calcium, 16% iron

Early Virginia settlers made this hearty stew with squirrel meat. This updated version features chicken and ham that simmer all day in a slow cooker.

BRUNSWICK-STYLE STEW

3	medium onions, cut into thin wedges
2	pounds meaty chicken pieces, skinned
1½	cups diced cooked ham (8 ounces)
1	teaspoon dry mustard
1	teaspoon dried thyme, crushed
¼	teaspoon black pepper
1	14½-ounce can diced tomatoes
1	14-ounce can chicken broth
4	cloves garlic, minced
1	tablespoon Worcestershire sauce
¼	teaspoon bottled hot pepper sauce
1	10-ounce package frozen sliced okra (2 cups)
1	cup frozen baby lima beans
1	cup frozen whole kernel corn

PREP:

20 minutes

COOK:

Low 8 hours, High 4 hours; plus 45 minutes on High

MAKES:

6 servings

SLOW COOKER:

3½- to 5-quart

1 In a 3½- to 5-quart slow cooker place onions. Top with chicken and ham. Sprinkle with mustard, thyme, and black pepper. Add undrained tomatoes, broth, garlic, Worcestershire sauce, and hot pepper sauce.

2 Cover and cook on low-heat setting for 8 to 10 hours or on high-heat setting for 4 to 5 hours.

3 If desired, remove chicken; cool slightly. (Replace lid on cooker.) Remove meat from chicken bones and cut meat into bite-size pieces. Discard bones; return chicken to cooker.

4 Add okra, lima beans, and corn to cooker. If using low-heat setting, turn to high-heat setting. Cover and cook 45 minutes more or until vegetables are tender.

Nutrition Facts per serving: 310 cal., 10 g total fat (3 g sat. fat), 81 mg chol., 960 mg sodium, 23 g carbo., 5 g fiber, 31 g pro. **Daily Values:** 2% vit. A, 24% vit. C, 11% calcium, 16% iron

When there's no time to make the dumplings, serve corn muffins or slices of corn bread with the stew—eliminating the extra 50 minutes of cooking time called for in the recipe.

BEER-STEWED PORK & DUMPLINGS

PREP:

30 minutes

COOK:

Low 9 hours, High 4 hours; plus 50 minutes on High

MAKES:

4 servings

SLOW COOKER:

3¹/₂- to 4-quart

FOR 5- TO 6-QUART SLOW COOKER
Use 1¹/₂ pounds boneless pork shoulder roast, 5 medium carrots, and 3 medium potatoes. Leave remaining ingredient amounts the same. Prepare as directed, except drop cornmeal mixture to make 12 dumplings. Makes 6 servings.

1 pound boneless pork shoulder
1 clove garlic, minced
1 tablespoon cooking oil
4 medium carrots, cut into ¹/₂-inch pieces (2 cups)
2 medium potatoes, peeled and cubed (2 cups)
1 cup beer
¹/₄ cup quick-cooking tapioca
1 tablespoon sugar
1 tablespoon Worcestershire sauce
2 bay leaves
1 teaspoon dried thyme, crushed
¹/₂ teaspoon salt
¹/₄ teaspoon ground nutmeg
¹/₄ teaspoon pepper
1 28-ounce can tomatoes, cut up
1 recipe Cornmeal Dumplings

1 Trim fat from meat. Cut pork into 1-inch cubes. In a large skillet brown half of the pork and the garlic in hot oil, turning to brown evenly. Remove from skillet. Brown remaining pork, adding more oil if necessary. Drain off fat.

2 In a 3¹/₂- to 4-quart slow cooker combine carrots, potatoes, beer, tapioca, sugar, Worcestershire sauce, bay leaves, thyme, salt, nutmeg, and pepper. Stir in browned meat and undrained tomatoes. Cover; cook on low-heat setting for 9 to 11 hours or on high-heat setting for 4 to 5 hours.

3 If using low-heat setting, turn cooker to high-heat setting. Prepare Cornmeal Dumplings. Remove bay leaves from stew. Stir stew; drop dumplings by tablespoons onto stew to make 8 dumplings. Cover; cook for 50 minutes more (do not lift cover).

CORNMEAL DUMPLINGS: In a medium bowl stir together ¹/₂ cup all-purpose flour, ¹/₂ cup shredded cheddar cheese, ¹/₃ cup yellow cornmeal, 1 teaspoon baking powder, ¹/₄ teaspoon salt, and a dash of pepper. Combine 1 beaten egg, 2 tablespoons milk, and 2 tablespoons cooking oil. Add to flour mixture; stir with a fork just until combined.

Nutrition Facts per serving: 625 cal., 24 g total fat (7 g sat. fat), 142 mg chol., 1,102 mg sodium, 64 g carbo., 7 g fiber, 35 g pro. **Daily Values:** 339% vit. A, 73% vit. C, 29% calcium, 32% iron

Pork and apples are perfect complements in this hearty dish that you'll enjoy time and again. The deep, nutty kick comes from a sprinkling of caraway seeds.

PORK CIDER STEW

2	pounds pork shoulder roast
3	medium potatoes, cubed (2½ cups)
3	medium carrots, cut into ½-inch pieces (1½ cups)
2	medium onions, sliced
1	medium apple, cored and coarsely chopped (1 cup)
½	cup coarsely chopped celery
3	tablespoons quick-cooking tapioca
2	cups apple cider or apple juice
1	teaspoon salt
1	teaspoon caraway seeds
¼	teaspoon pepper

1 Cut meat into 1-inch cubes. In a 3½- to 6-quart slow cooker combine meat, potatoes, carrots, onions, apple, celery, and tapioca. Stir in apple cider or juice, salt, caraway seeds, and pepper.

2 Cover; cook on low-heat setting for 10 to 12 hours or high-heat setting for 5 to 6 hours.

Nutrition Facts per serving: 273 cal., 8 g total fat (3 g sat. fat), 76 mg chol., 395 mg sodium, 26 g carbo., 3 g fiber, 24 g pro. **Daily Values:** 116% vit. A, 22% vit. C, 4% calcium, 14% iron

PREP:
20 minutes
COOK:
Low 10 hours, High 5 hours
MAKES:
8 servings
SLOW COOKER:
3½- to 6-quart

The sweet-tart taste of chopped apple and the licorice-like flavor of fennel seeds make this stew complex and lively. Serve it with wedges of hearty bread or drop in slices of yesterday's crusty sourdough.

SMOKED SAUSAGE & CABBAGE STEW

PREP:

20 minutes

COOK:

Low 7 hours, High 3 1/2 hours

MAKES:

4 servings

SLOW COOKER:

3 1/2- to 4-quart

4	cups packaged shredded cabbage with carrot (coleslaw mix) or coarsely chopped cabbage
1 1/2	cups peeled, cubed potatoes
1	cup sliced carrots
1	cup cored and coarsely chopped red apple
12	ounces cooked cheese smoked sausage, sliced
3/4	teaspoon fennel seeds, crushed
2 1/4	cups reduced-sodium chicken broth
1/3	cup apple juice

1 In a 3 1/2- to 4-quart slow cooker place coleslaw mix, potatoes, carrots, and apple. Place sausage on top of vegetables. Sprinkle with fennel seeds. Pour broth and apple juice over all.

2 Cover and cook on low-heat setting for 7 to 8 hours or on high-heat setting for 3 1/2 to 4 hours. Spoon into bowls.

Nutrition Facts per serving: 413 cal., 26 g total fat (13 g sat. fat), 56 mg chol., 1,395 mg sodium, 31 g carbo., 5 g fiber, 16 g pro. **Daily Values:** 96% vit. C, 13% calcium, 9% iron

Scotch broth is one of the more familiar uses of barley in America. This stew, traditionally made with lamb, is equally good with beef stew meat.

SCOTCH BROTH TAKEN SLOW

12	ounces lamb or beef stew meat, cut into 1-inch cubes
1	large leek, halved lengthwise and sliced (about ½ cup)
1	large turnip, peeled and cut into ½-inch pieces (1 cup)
2	medium carrots, sliced ½ inch thick (about 1 cup)
3	14-ounce cans beef broth
1	12-ounce bottle dark beer
⅔	cup pearl barley
½	teaspoon freshly ground pepper
2	tablespoons snipped fresh parsley

1 In a 3½- to 4-quart slow cooker place the stew meat, leek, turnip, and carrots. Stir in the broth, beer, barley, and pepper. Cover; cook on low-heat setting for 8 to 10 hours or on high-heat setting for 4 to 5 hours.

2 Stir in parsley before serving.

Nutrition Facts per serving: 441 cal., 19 g total fat (8 g sat. fat), 60 mg chol., 1,107 mg sodium, 39 g carbo., 7 g fiber, 22 g pro. **Daily Values:** 173% vit. A, 24% vit. C, 6% calcium, 20% iron

PREP:
25 minutes

COOK:
Low 8 hours, High 4 hours

MAKES:
4 to 5 main-dish servings

SLOW COOKER:
3½- to 4-quart

Yellow split peas are a classic ingredient in Persian stew. During cooking, the peas soften and fall apart, thickening the stew.

PERSIAN-STYLE LAMB & SPLIT PEA STEW

PREP:

25 minutes

COOK:

Low 8 hours, High 4 hours; plus 10 minutes on High

MAKES:

6 to 8 servings

SLOW COOKER:

3¹/₂- to 5-quart

1½	to **2** pounds lamb or beef stew meat, cut into 1-inch cubes
1	tablespoon cooking oil
3	leeks, cut into 1-inch pieces
1	large onion, chopped
½	cup dry yellow split peas
4	cloves garlic, sliced
2	bay leaves
1	tablespoon snipped fresh oregano or 1 teaspoon dried oregano, crushed
1½	teaspoons ground cumin
¼	teaspoon pepper
3	cups chicken broth
⅓	cup raisins
2	tablespoons lemon juice
3	cups hot cooked bulgur or rice

1 In a large skillet brown meat, half at a time, in hot oil. Drain off fat. Transfer meat to a 3½- to 5-quart slow cooker. Stir in leeks, onion, split peas, garlic, bay leaves, dried oregano (if using), cumin, and pepper. Pour chicken broth over all.

2 Cover; cook on low-heat setting for 8 to 10 hours or on high-heat setting for 4 to 5 hours. If using low-heat setting, turn to high-heat setting. Stir raisins into stew. Cover; cook for 10 minutes more. Remove bay leaves. Stir in lemon juice and, if using, the fresh oregano. Serve with hot bulgur or rice.

Nutrition Facts per serving: 357 cal., 9 g total fat (2 g sat. fat), 58 mg chol., 449 mg sodium, 42 g carbo., 7 g fiber, 29 g pro. **Daily Values:** 12% vit. C, 6% calcium, 33% iron

Ragout (rah-goo) is a French term for a rich stew that contains meat, vegetables, and wine. With lamb, artichoke hearts, and zucchini, this stew is fit for all your royal guests.

FRENCH-STYLE LAMB RAGOUT

1½ to 2 pounds lamb stew meat, cut into 1-inch cubes

1 tablespoon cooking oil

2 cups coarsely chopped onions

2 medium tomatoes, chopped

2 medium carrots, cut into ½-inch slices

3 cloves garlic, minced

2 tablespoons quick-cooking tapioca

1 cup beef broth

¼ cup dry red wine or water

1 teaspoon dried Italian seasoning or oregano, crushed

½ teaspoon salt

¼ teaspoon pepper

2 small zucchini, halved lengthwise and cut into ¼-inch slices

1 9-ounce package frozen artichoke hearts, thawed and quartered

3 cups hot cooked couscous or rice

PREP:
30 minutes

COOK:
Low 8 hours, High 4 hours; plus 30 minutes on High

MAKES:
6 servings

SLOW COOKER:
3½- to 5-quart

1 In a large skillet brown meat, half at a time, in hot oil. Drain off fat. Transfer meat to a 3½- to 5-quart slow cooker. Add the onions, tomatoes, carrots, and garlic. Sprinkle with tapioca. Combine beef broth, wine or water, Italian seasoning or oregano, salt, and pepper. Pour over all. Stir to combine.

2 Cover; cook on low-heat setting for 8 to 10 hours or on high-heat setting for 4 to 5 hours.

3 If using low-heat setting, turn to high-heat setting. Stir in the zucchini and thawed artichoke hearts. Cover; cook for 30 minutes more. Serve over couscous or rice.

Nutrition Facts per serving: 373 cal., 8 g total fat (3 g sat. fat), 61 mg chol., 456 mg sodium, 47 g carbo., 6 g fiber, 28 g pro. **Daily Values:** 37% vit. C, 6% calcium, 23% iron

Pearl barley adds a slightly chewy texture to this stew. "Pearl" refers to the process of polishing the hulled grain. It is sold in regular and quick-cooking forms.

TENDER LAMB STEW WITH BARLEY

PREP:

20 minutes

COOK:

Low 8 hours, High 4 hours

MAKES:

6 servings

SLOW COOKER:

3¹/₂- to 5-quart

1¹/₂	pounds lamb stew meat, cut into 1-inch cubes
2	tablespoons cooking oil
1	medium onion, chopped
4	cloves garlic, minced
2¹/₂	cups chicken broth
1	14¹/₂-ounce can diced tomatoes
¹/₂	cup pearl barley (regular)
¹/₄	cup dry white wine (optional)
2	tablespoons snipped fresh dill or 1¹/₂ teaspoons dried dillweed
¹/₂	teaspoon salt
¹/₄	teaspoon ground black pepper
1¹/₂	7-ounce jars roasted red sweet peppers, drained and thinly sliced (about 1¹/₂ cups)
¹/₄	cup snipped fresh mint

1 In a large skillet brown half of the meat in hot oil; remove meat from skillet. Add remaining meat, onion, and garlic. Cook until meat is brown and onion is tender. Drain off fat.

2 In a 3¹/₂- to 5-quart slow cooker combine the broth, undrained tomatoes, barley, wine (if desired), dried dillweed (if using), salt, and black pepper. Stir in the meat mixture.

3 Cover; cook on low-heat setting for 8 to 10 hours or on high-heat setting for 4 to 5 hours. To serve, stir in the roasted peppers and fresh mint. If using, stir in the fresh dill.

Nutrition Facts per serving: 266 cal., 11 g total fat (3 g sat. fat), 58 mg chol., 709 mg sodium, 19 g carbo., 4 g fiber, 23 g pro. **Daily Values:** 193% vit. C, 3% calcium, 24% iron

Prepare this recipe during chilly fall and winter months when you crave hearty meals and long for sweet summer fruits.

STEWED LEG OF LAMB WITH FRUIT

1	to 2 teaspoons crushed red pepper
³⁄₄	teaspoon ground turmeric
³⁄₄	teaspoon ground ginger
³⁄₄	teaspoon ground cinnamon
¹⁄₂	teaspoon salt
2	pounds boneless leg of lamb or beef bottom round roast, well trimmed and cut into 1- to 1¹⁄₂-inch pieces
2	tablespoons olive oil or cooking oil
2	large onions, chopped
3	cloves garlic, minced
1	14-ounce can beef broth
1	tablespoon cornstarch
2	tablespoons cold water
1	cup pitted dates
1	cup dried apricots
	Hot cooked couscous or rice
¹⁄₄	cup slivered almonds, toasted

1 In a shallow bowl combine crushed red pepper, turmeric, ginger, cinnamon, and salt. Coat meat with seasoning mixture. In a large skillet heat oil over medium-high heat. Brown meat, a third at a time, in the hot oil. Drain off fat. Transfer meat to a 3¹⁄₂- to 4-quart slow cooker. Add onions and garlic; stir to combine. Pour beef broth over all.

2 Cover and cook on low-heat setting for 7 to 9 hours or on high-heat setting for 3¹⁄₂ to 4¹⁄₂ hours or until meat is tender.

3 Skim fat from the surface of the juices in the cooker. Stir cornstarch into water; stir into cooker. Add dates and apricots; stir to combine. If using low-heat setting, turn to high-heat setting. Cover and cook 30 minutes more or until mixture is slightly thickened and bubbly.

4 To serve, spoon stew over hot couscous or rice. Sprinkle stew with slivered almonds.

Nutrition Facts per serving: 550 cal., 14 g total fat (3 g sat. fat), 76 mg chol., 475 mg sodium, 75 g carbo., 12 g fiber, 34 g pro. **Daily Values:** 7% vit. C, 6% calcium, 29% iron

PREP:

30 minutes

COOK:

Low 7 hours, High 3¹⁄₂ hours; plus 30 minutes on High

MAKES:

6 to 8 servings

SLOW COOKER:

3¹⁄₂- to 4-quart

If sodium is a concern in your diet, use low-sodium soy sauce. For a fun Asian-style dinner, start the meal with egg rolls or pot stickers.

SOY-GINGER SOUP WITH CHICKEN

PREP:

20 minutes

COOK:

High 2 hours, 8 minutes

MAKES:

6 servings

SLOW COOKER:

3 1/2- to 5-quart

1   pound skinless, boneless chicken thighs, cut into 1-inch pieces

1   cup coarsely shredded carrots (2 medium)

2   tablespoons dry sherry (optional)

1   tablespoon soy sauce

1   tablespoon rice vinegar

1   teaspoon grated fresh ginger or 1/2 teaspoon ground ginger

1/4   teaspoon pepper

3   14-ounce cans chicken broth

1   cup water

2   ounces dried medium noodles

1   6-ounce package frozen snow pea pods, thawed and halved diagonally

1 In a 3 1/2- to 5-quart slow cooker combine chicken, carrots, sherry (if desired), 1 tablespoon soy sauce, vinegar, ginger, and pepper. Stir in chicken broth and water. Cover; cook on high-heat setting for 2 to 3 hours.

2 Stir in noodles and pea pods. Cover and cook for 8 minutes more. Serve with additional soy sauce.

Nutrition Facts per serving: 175 cal., 5 g total fat (1 g sat. fat), 72 mg chol., 1,246 mg sodium, 12 g carbo., 2 g fiber, 19 g pro. **Daily Values:** 95% vit. A, 29% vit. C, 3% calcium, 8% iron

Smoked turkey sausage has all the flavor of traditional pork sausage with fewer calories. Team this stew with a green salad to present a healthful weeknight meal.

TURKEY SAUSAGE & SWEET POTATO STEW

1	pound cooked smoked turkey sausage
2	small sweet potatoes, peeled and cut into $1/2$-inch pieces (about 1 pound; $2^1/2$ cups)
1	medium green sweet pepper, cut into 1-inch pieces ($3/4$ cup)
1	large stalk celery, cut into $1/2$-inch pieces ($3/4$ cup)
$1/2$	cup chopped onion
2	tablespoons quick-cooking tapioca
1	$14^1/2$-ounce can diced tomatoes with roasted garlic
1	15-ounce can garbanzo beans, rinsed and drained
1	cup beef broth

PREP:

15 minutes

COOK:

Low 8 hours, High 4 hours

MAKES:

4 servings

SLOW COOKER:

$3^1/2$- to 6-quart

1 Cut sausage in half lengthwise; cut into 1-inch slices. In a $3^1/2$- to 6-quart slow cooker combine sausage pieces, sweet potatoes, sweet pepper, celery, onion, and tapioca. Add undrained tomatoes, garbanzo beans, and beef broth.

2 Cover and cook on low-heat setting for 8 to 10 hours or on high-heat setting for 4 to 5 hours.

Nutrition Facts per serving: 499 cal., 11 g total fat (3 g sat. fat), 76 mg chol., 1,915 mg sodium, 72 g carbo., 10 g fiber, 28 g pro. **Daily Values:** 414% vit. A, 97% vit. C, 12% calcium, 24% iron

Mushrooms, wild and brown rice, leeks, and rosemary give a fragrant, earthy quality to this classic, hearty fare.

CHICKEN & RICE STEW GONE WILD

PREP:

20 minutes

COOK:

Low 7 hours, High 3¹/₂ hours

MAKES:

6 servings

SLOW COOKER:

3¹/₂- to 6-quart

3	cups quartered button mushrooms (8 ounces)
2	medium carrots, sliced (1 cup)
2	medium leeks, sliced (²/₃ cup)
¹/₂	cup uncooked brown rice
¹/₂	cup uncooked wild rice, rinsed and drained
12	ounces skinless, boneless chicken breasts, cut into ³/₄-inch pieces
1	teaspoon dried thyme, crushed
¹/₂	teaspoon dried rosemary, crushed
¹/₄	teaspoon coarse ground pepper
3	14-ounce cans reduced-sodium chicken broth (5¹/₄ cups)
1	10³/₄-ounce can condensed cream of mushroom soup

1 In a 3¹/₂- to 6-quart slow cooker place mushrooms, carrots, leeks, and rices. Place chicken on vegetables and rices. Top with thyme, rosemary, and pepper. Pour broth over all.

2 Cover and cook on low-heat setting for 7 to 8 hours or on high-heat setting for 3¹/₂ to 4 hours. Stir in cream of mushroom soup at end of cooking.

Nutrition Facts per serving: 264 cal., 6 g total fat (2 g sat. fat), 33 mg chol., 908 mg sodium, 32 g carbo., 3 g fiber, 22 g pro. **Daily Values:** 104% vit. A, 6% vit. C, 4% calcium, 10% iron

This warming chili really is full of beans—refried and chili beans! Top it with a spoonful of sour cream and serve corn bread on the side.

REFRIED BEAN CHILI

2	pounds ground beef
1	cup chopped onion
2	15¾-ounce cans chili beans with chili gravy
1	16-ounce jar thick and chunky salsa
1	16-ounce can refried beans
1	12-ounce can beer or 14-ounce can beef broth
2	tablespoons chili powder
1	tablespoon ground cumin
2	tablespoons lime juice
	Dairy sour cream (optional)

1 In a large skillet cook beef and onion until meat is brown and onion is tender, stirring occasionally, and leaving some of the beef in larger pieces. Drain off fat.

2 In a 5- to 6-quart slow cooker place the beef mixture, chili beans with gravy, salsa, refried beans, beer, chili powder, and cumin. Cover; cook on low-heat setting for 6 to 8 hours or on high-heat setting for 3 to 4 hours. Stir in lime juice at the end of cooking.

3 To serve, ladle chili into bowls. If desired, garnish with a spoonful of sour cream.

Nutrition Facts per serving: 482 cal., 22 g total fat (8 g sat. fat), 86 mg chol., 960 mg sodium, 36 g carbo., 10 g fiber, 30 g pro. **Daily Values:** 21% vit. A, 25% vit. C, 8% calcium, 26% iron

PREP:
20 minutes

COOK:
Low 6 hours, High 3 hours

MAKES:
8 to 10 main-dish servings

SLOW COOKER:
5- to 6-quart

With a slow cooker, traditional-style chili made with chunks of beef stew meat is as easy to prepare as the ground-beef version.

BEEF CHILI STEW

PREP:

20 minutes

COOK:

Low 8 hours, High 4 hours; plus 15 minutes on High

MAKES:

10 servings

SLOW COOKER:

6-quart

MAKE-AHEAD TIP

Cut or chop the vegetables and meat up to 24 hours ahead. Place vegetables and meat in separate containers; cover and refrigerate. The next day, place ingredients in the cooker in the order specified in the recipe. Cover and cook as directed.

1	28-ounce can tomatoes, cut up
1	10-ounce can chopped tomatoes and green chile peppers
2	cups vegetable juice or tomato juice
1	to 2 tablespoons chili powder
1	teaspoon ground cumin
1	teaspoon dried oregano, crushed
3	cloves garlic, minced
1½	pounds beef or pork stew meat, cut into 1-inch cubes
2	cups chopped onions
1½	cups chopped celery
1	cup chopped green sweet pepper
2	15-ounce cans black, kidney, and/or garbanzo beans, rinsed and drained

Toppers: shredded Mexican cheese or cheddar cheese, dairy sour cream, thinly sliced green onions, snipped fresh cilantro, thinly sliced jalapeño peppers, and/or sliced, pitted ripe olives (optional)

1 In a 6-quart slow cooker combine both cans of undrained tomatoes, vegetable or tomato juice, chili powder, cumin, oregano, and garlic. Stir in the meat, onions, celery, and sweet pepper.

2 Cover and cook on low-heat setting for 8 to 10 hours or on high-heat setting for 4 to 5 hours.

3 If using low-heat setting, turn to high-heat setting. Stir in the beans. Cover and cook 15 minutes more. Spoon into bowls. If desired, serve with toppers.

Nutrition Facts per serving: 224 cal., 6 g total fat (2 g sat. fat), 49 mg chol., 807 mg sodium, 24 g carbo., 6 g fiber, 24 g pro. **Daily Values:** 66% vit. C, 7% calcium, 28% iron

A double-bean salad makes this chili stand out from the rest. Dressed in lime and garlic, the salad is a refreshing complement to the spiciness of the chili.

CHILI WITH TWO-BEAN SALAD

1	pound boneless beef top round steak
1	tablespoon cooking oil
2	14$\frac{1}{2}$-ounce cans diced tomatoes
1	14-ounce can beef broth
1	large onion, chopped
1	or 2 fresh jalapeño or serrano peppers, finely chopped
2	cloves garlic, minced
2	tablespoons cornmeal
4	teaspoons chili powder
1	tablespoon brown sugar
1$\frac{1}{2}$	teaspoons dried oregano, crushed
$\frac{1}{2}$	teaspoon ground cumin
$\frac{1}{4}$	teaspoon black pepper
1	recipe Two-Bean Salad
	Dairy sour cream (optional)

PREP:
25 minutes

COOK:
Low 10 hours, High 5 hours

MAKES:
6 servings

SLOW COOKER:
3$\frac{1}{2}$- to 4-quart

1 Trim fat from meat. Thinly slice meat across the grain into bite-size pieces. In a large skillet brown meat, half at a time, in hot oil. Drain off fat.

2 In a 3$\frac{1}{2}$- to 4-quart slow cooker combine undrained tomatoes, beef broth, onion, jalapeño or serrano peppers, garlic, cornmeal, chili powder, brown sugar, oregano, cumin, and black pepper. Stir in meat.

3 Cover; cook on low-heat setting for 10 to 12 hours or on high-heat setting for 5 to 6 hours. Serve chili in bowls with Two-Bean Salad on the side. If desired, top chili with sour cream.

TWO-BEAN SALAD: In a bowl combine one 15-ounce can pinto beans and one 15-ounce can black beans, rinsed and drained. Add $\frac{1}{2}$ teaspoon finely shredded lime peel, 1 tablespoon lime juice, 1 tablespoon salad oil, and 1 clove garlic, minced. Toss to mix.

Nutrition Facts per serving: 315 cal., 9 g total fat (2 g sat. fat), 48 mg chol., 1,049 mg sodium, 33 g carbo., 8 g fiber, 28 g pro. **Daily Values:** 47% vit. C, 9% calcium, 33% iron

Fresh jalapeño peppers ignite the fire in this meaty chili. Douse the flames with glasses of cold beer. For a milder chili, substitute a can of diced mild chile peppers.

FIRECRACKER CHILI

PREP:

20 minutes

COOK:

Low 8 hours, High 4 hours

MAKES:

4 to 6 servings

SLOW COOKER:

3¹/₂- to 5-quart

1	pound bulk pork sausage or ground beef
1	15-ounce can red kidney beans, drained
1	cup chopped celery
1	large onion, chopped
¹/₂	cup chopped green sweet pepper
1	to 2 fresh jalapeño peppers, seeded and chopped
1	14¹/₂-ounce can tomatoes, cut up
1	10-ounce can chopped tomatoes and green chile peppers
1	cup hot-style vegetable juice or vegetable juice
1	6-ounce can low-sodium tomato paste
2	cloves garlic, minced
3	to 4 teaspoons chili powder
¹/₂	teaspoon ground cumin
¹/₂	cup shredded cheddar cheese (2 ounces)
¹/₄	to ¹/₃ cup dairy sour cream

1 In a large skillet cook the sausage or beef until brown. Drain off fat.

2 In a 3¹/₂- to 5-quart slow cooker combine cooked meat, beans, celery, onion, sweet pepper, and jalapeño peppers. Add undrained tomatoes, vegetable juice, tomato paste, garlic, chili powder, and cumin.

3 Cover and cook on low-heat setting for 8 to 10 hours or on high-heat setting for 4 to 5 hours. Ladle into bowls. Pass cheese and sour cream with chili.

Nutrition Facts per serving: 665 cal., 41 g total fat (18 g sat. fat), 85 mg chol., 1,432 mg sodium, 44 g carbo., 12 g fiber, 30 g pro. **Daily Values:** 115% vit. C, 27% calcium, 25% iron

When winter winds chill your spirit, it's time for a bowl of this hearty southwestern-style chili.

SOUTHWESTERN WHITE CHILI

1	cup chopped onion
4	cloves garlic, minced
2	teaspoons ground cumin
1	teaspoon dried oregano, crushed
1/4	teaspoon ground red pepper
3	15 1/2-ounce cans Great Northern beans, drained and rinsed
2	4-ounce cans diced green chile peppers
4	cups chicken broth or reduced-sodium chicken broth
3	cups chopped cooked chicken
2	cups shredded Monterey Jack cheese (8 ounces)
	Dairy sour cream (optional)
	Canned diced green chile peppers (optional)

PREP:
20 minutes
COOK:
Low 7 hours, High 3 1/2 hours
MAKES:
8 servings
SLOW COOKER:
3 1/2- to 6-quart

1 In a 3 1/2- to 6-quart slow cooker place the onion, garlic, cumin, oregano, red pepper, beans, 2 cans chile peppers, broth, and cooked chicken. Stir to combine.

2 Cover and cook on low heat setting for 7 to 8 hours or on high-heat setting for 3 1/2 to 4 hours. Stir in the cheese until melted.

3 Ladle the chili into 8 bowls. If desired, top with sour cream and sprinkle with additional chile peppers.

Nutrition Facts per serving: 431 cal., 14 g total fat (7 g sat. fat), 72 mg chol., 671 mg sodium, 39 g carbo., 9 g fiber, 38 g pro. **Daily Values:** 7% vit. A, 21% vit. C, 36% calcium, 22% iron

Control the level of heat in this chunky chili by choosing mild or spicy salsa. Serve it with warm cornmeal biscuits.

VEGETARIAN CHILI

PREP:

25 minutes

COOK:

Low 8 hours, High 4 hours

MAKES:

6 servings

SLOW COOKER:

3¹/₂- to 5-quart

1 medium zucchini, halved lengthwise and cut into ¹/₂-inch slices (1¹/₂ cups)

1 medium green sweet pepper, coarsely chopped (³/₄ cup)

¹/₂ cup chopped onion (1 medium)

¹/₂ cup thinly sliced celery

2 to 3 teaspoons chili powder

1 teaspoon dried oregano, crushed

¹/₂ teaspoon ground cumin

2 14¹/₂-ounce cans diced tomatoes

1 10-ounce package frozen whole kernel corn

1 15-ounce can black beans, rinsed and drained

1 cup bottled salsa

³/₄ cup shredded cheddar cheese (3 ounces)

Dairy sour cream

1 In a 3¹/₂- to 5-quart slow cooker combine zucchini, green sweet pepper, onion, celery, chili powder, oregano, and cumin. Stir in undrained tomatoes, corn, drained beans, and salsa.

2 Cover; cook on low-heat setting for 8 to 10 hours or on high-heat setting for 4 to 5 hours. To serve, ladle the chili into bowls and top with cheese and sour cream.

Nutrition Facts per serving: 203 cal., 6 g total fat (3 g sat. fat), 15 mg chol., 598 mg sodium, 32 g carbo., 7 g fiber, 11 g pro. **Daily Values:** 67% vit. C, 21% calcium, 14% iron

SIDE DISHES

Use any combination of beans for sweet and tangy results. A variety of beans makes an attractive dish.

MOLASSES BAKED BEANS

PREP:

15 minutes

COOK:

Low 5 hours, High 2 1/2 hours

MAKES:

10 servings

SLOW COOKER:

3 1/2- to 4-quart

4	15-ounce cans Great Northern beans, red or white kidney beans, black beans, and/or butter beans, rinsed and drained
1	8-ounce can tomato sauce
3/4	cup diced cooked ham or Canadian-style bacon (3 1/2 ounces)
1/4	cup molasses
2	tablespoons vinegar
2	teaspoons dry mustard
1/4	teaspoon ground ginger
1/4	teaspoon pepper

1 In a 3 1/2- to 4-quart slow cooker combine all ingredients.

2 Cover; cook on low-heat setting for 5 to 6 hours or on high-heat setting for 2 1/2 to 3 hours.

Nutrition Facts per serving: 185 cal., 2 g total fat (0 g sat. fat), 6 mg chol., 668 mg sodium, 32 g carbo., 9 g fiber, 10 g pro. **Daily Values:** 4% vit. A, 5% vit. C, 16% calcium, 18% iron

Keep the kitchen cool by baking beans in a slow cooker. This saucy bean dish makes an ideal potluck accompaniment.

SAUCY BAKED BEANS

1	pound dry navy beans or dry Great Northern beans (2⅓ cups)
8	cups cold water
1	cup chopped onion
¼	pound salt pork, chopped, or 6 slices bacon, cooked, drained, and crumbled
1¼	cups water
¼	cup packed brown sugar
¼	cup molasses or dark corn syrup
¼	cup Worcestershire sauce
1	teaspoon dry mustard
¼	teaspoon pepper

PREP:
10 minutes

COOK:
1 hour on cooktop; plus Low 8 hours, High 4 hours

STAND:
1 hour

MAKES:
12 servings

SLOW COOKER:
3½- to 4-quart

1 Rinse beans; drain. In a Dutch oven combine beans and the 8 cups water. Bring to boiling; reduce heat. Simmer for 2 minutes. Remove from heat. Cover and let stand for 1 hour. (Or omit simmering; soak beans in cold water overnight in a covered Dutch oven.) Drain and rinse. In the same Dutch oven combine beans and 8 cups fresh water. Bring to boiling; reduce heat. Simmer, covered, for 1 hour or until beans are tender, stirring occasionally.

2 Drain beans. In a 3½ to 4-quart slow cooker combine drained beans, onion, and salt pork or bacon. Add the remaining ingredients. Stir to combine.

3 Cover; cook on low-heat setting for 8 to 10 hours or on high-heat setting for 4 to 5 hours. Stir before serving.

Nutrition Facts per serving: 242 cal., 8 g total fat (3 g sat. fat), 8 mg chol., 200 mg sodium, 34 g carbo., 9 g fiber, 9 g pro. **Daily Values:** 4% vit. C, 8% calcium, 15% iron

Serve this squash dish, rich in flavor and color, with autumnal entrées such as roasted pork tenderloin or pork chops.

ACORN SQUASH & CRANBERRY-ORANGE SAUCE

PREP:

15 minutes

COOK:

Low 6 hours, High 3 hours

MAKES:

4 to 6 servings

SLOW COOKER:

3¹/₂- to 4-quart

2   medium acorn squash (about 2 pounds)

1   16-ounce can jellied cranberry sauce

¹/₄   cup orange marmalade

¹/₄   cup raisins

¹/₄   teaspoon ground cinnamon

    Salt and pepper

1 Cut each squash in half lengthwise; remove and discard seeds. Cut squash into 1-inch-thick wedges. Arrange squash in a 3¹/₂- to 4-quart slow cooker.

2 In a small saucepan heat and stir cranberry sauce, marmalade, raisins, and cinnamon until smooth. Pour over squash pieces.

3 Cover; cook on low-heat setting for 6 to 7 hours or on high-heat setting for 3 to 3¹/₂ hours. Season to taste with salt and pepper.

Nutrition Facts per serving: 328 cal., 0 g total fat (0 g sat. fat), 0 mg chol., 220 mg sodium, 83 g carbo., 5 g fiber, 2 g pro. **Daily Values:** 12% vit. A, 30% vit. C, 7% calcium, 9% iron

Deep-orange mashed sweet potatoes are beautiful on the table and plate; the addition of a few parsnips makes the taste sophisticated.

MASHED SWEET POTATOES & PARSNIPS

Nonstick cooking spray

1½ pounds sweet potatoes, peeled and cubed (about 4 cups)

3 medium parsnips, peeled and cubed (about 2½ cups)

½ cup chicken broth

2 tablespoons butter or margarine, melted

½ teaspoon ground sage

½ teaspoon onion salt

1 Lightly coat the inside of a 3½- to 4-quart slow cooker with nonstick cooking spray. Add sweet potatoes, parsnips, broth, melted butter, sage, and onion salt.

2 Cover and cook on low-heat setting for 7 to 8 hours or on high-heat setting for 3½ to 4 hours or until very tender. Mash with potato masher.

Nutrition Facts per serving: 166 cal., 5 g total fat (3 g sat. fat), 11 mg chol., 273 mg sodium, 30 g carbo., 5 g fiber, 2 g pro. **Daily Values:** 298% vit. A, 35% vit. C, 4% calcium, 4% iron

PREP:

20 minutes

COOK:

Low 7 hours, High 3½ hours

MAKES:

6 to 8 servings

SLOW COOKER:

3½- to 4-quart

When you need more servings for a holiday meal, double the ingredients and cook them in a 5- to 6-quart slow cooker.

COCONUT SWEET POTATOES WITH PECANS

PREP:

20 minutes

COOK:

Low 3 hours, High 1 1/2 hours

MAKES:

6 to 8 servings

SLOW COOKER:

3 1/2- to 4-quart

2 pounds sweet potatoes, peeled and shredded (8 cups)

2 tablespoons brown sugar

2 tablespoons butter or margarine, melted

2 tablespoons water

1/4 cup flaked coconut

1/4 teaspoon ground cinnamon

1/4 cup broken pecans, toasted

Toasted coconut (optional)

1 In a 3 1/2- to 4-quart slow cooker combine sweet potatoes, brown sugar, melted butter, water, coconut, and cinnamon.

2 Cover; cook on low-heat setting for 3 to 4 hours or on high-heat setting for 1 1/2 to 2 hours. Stir in pecans. Sprinkle with toasted coconut, if desired.

Nutrition Facts per serving: 216 cal., 9 g total fat (5 g sat. fat), 11 mg chol., 71 mg sodium, 32 g carbo., 4 g fiber, 3 g pro. **Daily Values:** 396% vit. A, 29% vit. C, 3% calcium, 5% iron

Serve this salad as an accompaniment to pork or take it along to a potluck. Stirring in the bacon at the last minute keeps it crisp.

HOT GERMAN-STYLE POTATO SALAD

6	cups peeled potatoes, cut into ¾-inch cubes
1	cup chopped onion
1	cup water
⅔	cup cider vinegar
¼	cup sugar
2	tablespoons quick-cooking tapioca
1	teaspoon salt
¼	teaspoon celery seed
¼	teaspoon pepper
6	slices bacon, crisp-cooked, drained, and crumbled

1 In a 3½- to 4-quart slow cooker combine potatoes and onion. In a bowl combine water, vinegar, sugar, tapioca, salt, celery seed, and pepper; pour over potatoes.

2 Cover; cook on low-heat setting for 8 to 9 hours or on high-heat setting for 4 to 4½ hours. Stir in bacon.

Nutrition Facts per serving: 160 cal., 2 g total fat (1 g sat. fat), 4 mg chol., 374 mg sodium, 32 g carbo., 2 g fiber, 4 g pro. **Daily Values:** 28% vit. C, 2% calcium, 6% iron

PREP:
25 minutes
COOK:
Low 8 hours, High 4 hours
MAKES:
8 servings
SLOW COOKER:
3½- to 4-quart

Ample time and low heat transform sliced onions into golden, sweet, edible delights. Combining them with creamy potatoes is an ideal match for full-flavored entrées such as beef tenderloin and salmon.

CARAMELIZED ONIONS & POTATOES

PREP:

15 minutes

COOK:

Low 6 hours, High 3 hours

MAKES:

6 servings

SLOW COOKER:

3¹/₂- to 4-quart

2	large sweet onions (Vidalia), thinly sliced (2 cups)
1¹/₂	pounds tiny new potatoes, halved
¹/₄	cup butter, melted
¹/₂	cup beef or chicken broth
3	tablespoons brown sugar
¹/₂	teaspoon salt
¹/₄	teaspoon freshly ground pepper

1 In a 3¹/₂- to 4-quart slow cooker place onions and potatoes.

2 In a small bowl combine melted butter, broth, brown sugar, salt, and pepper. Pour mixture over onions and potatoes in cooker.

3 Cover and cook on low-heat setting for 6 to 7 hours or on high-heat setting for 3 to 3¹/₂ hours. Stir gently before serving. Serve with a slotted spoon.

Nutrition Facts per serving: 194 cal., 8 g total fat (5 g sat. fat), 22 mg chol., 356 mg sodium, 28 g carbo., 3 g fiber, 3 g pro. **Daily Values:** 6% vit. A, 29% vit. C, 3% calcium, 10% iron

Everyone who loves potatoes will love them even more with the increased flavor from chopped prosciutto, leeks, smoked Gouda, and provolone.

EASY CHEESY POTATOES

1	28-ounce package frozen loose-pack diced hash brown potatoes with onion and peppers, thawed
1	10¾-ounce can condensed cream of chicken with herbs soup
1	cup finely shredded smoked Gouda cheese (4 ounces)
1	cup finely shredded provolone cheese (4 ounces)
1	8-ounce package cream cheese, cut into cubes
¾	cup milk
¼	cup finely chopped leek or thinly sliced green onions
¼	cup chopped prosciutto or 4 slices bacon, crisp-cooked and crumbled
½	teaspoon black pepper
2	tablespoons snipped fresh chives

1 In a 3½- to 4-quart slow cooker combine thawed potatoes, soup, cheeses, milk, leek or green onions, prosciutto (if using), and pepper.

2 Cover and cook on low-heat setting for 5 to 6 hours. Gently stir in chives and bacon, if using, before serving.

Nutrition Facts per serving: 216 cal., 14 g total fat (8 g sat. fat), 39 mg chol., 534 mg sodium, 16 g carbo., 2 g fiber, 8 g pro. **Daily Values:** 12% vit. A, 14% vit. C, 18% calcium, 6% iron

PREP:

20 minutes

COOK:

Low 5 hours

MAKES:

12 servings

SLOW COOKER:

3½- to 4-quart

Bits of dried apricot are sun-flavored jewels in this pretty, earthy side dish. Pair it with roast chicken or broiled salmon and steamed broccoli for an easy and colorful meal.

CREAMY WILD RICE PILAF

PREP:

20 minutes

COOK:

Low 7 hours, High 3 1/2 hours

MAKES:

12 servings

SLOW COOKER:

3 1/2 - to 4-quart

1	cup wild rice, rinsed and drained
1	cup regular brown rice
1	cup shredded carrots (2 medium)
1	cup sliced fresh mushrooms
1/2	cup thinly sliced celery (1 stalk)
1/3	cup chopped onion (1 small)
1/4	cup snipped dried apricots
1	10 3/4-ounce can condensed cream of mushroom with roasted garlic or condensed golden mushroom soup
1	teaspoon dried thyme, crushed
1	teaspoon poultry seasoning
3/4	teaspoon salt
1/2	teaspoon pepper
5 1/2	cups water
1/2	cup dairy sour cream

1 In a 3 1/2- to 4-quart slow cooker combine uncooked wild rice, uncooked brown rice, carrots, mushrooms, celery, onion, dried apricots, soup, thyme, poultry seasoning, salt, and pepper. Stir in water.

2 Cover; cook on low-heat setting for 7 to 8 hours or on high-heat setting for 3 1/2 to 4 hours. Stir in sour cream.

Nutrition Facts per serving: 165 cal., 4 g total fat (2 g sat. fat), 4 mg chol., 339 mg sodium, 28 g carbo., 2 g fiber, 4 g pro. **Daily Values:** 52% vit. A, 3% vit. C, 4% calcium, 6% iron

Brilliantly colored beets sparkle in this tart-tangy side dish, which is packed with nutritive value. Some call it beauty food.

CRANBERRY-ORANGE SAUCED BEETS

2	pounds medium beets, peeled and quartered
1/2	teaspoon ground nutmeg
1	cup cranberry juice
1	teaspoon finely shredded orange peel
2	tablespoons butter
2	tablespoons sugar
4	teaspoons cornstarch

1 Peel and quarter beets. Place in a 3½- to 4-quart slow cooker. Sprinkle nutmeg on beets. Add cranberry juice and orange peel; dot with butter.

2 Cover and cook on low-heat setting for 6 to 7 hours or on high-heat setting for 3 to 3½ hours or until beets are tender. If using low-heat setting, turn to high-heat setting.

3 In a small bowl combine sugar and cornstarch. Remove ½ cup of the cooking liquid from the cooker and stir into the cornstarch mixture; stir mixture into cooker. Cover and cook 15 to 30 minutes more or until sauce is thickened.

Nutrition Facts per serving: 127 cal., 4 g total fat (3 g sat. fat), 11 mg chol., 117 mg sodium, 22 g carbo., 2 g fiber, 2 g pro. **Daily Values:** 4% vit. A, 31% vit. C, 2% calcium, 5% iron

PREP:
25 minutes

COOK:
Low 6 hours, High 3 hours; plus 15 minutes on High

MAKES:
6 servings

SLOW COOKER:
3½- to 4-quart

Make this next time your oven is filled with ham for Sunday's dinner. If you like your food spicy, use Monterey Jack cheese with jalapeño peppers.

SPICY CREAMED CORN

PREP:

15 minutes

COOK:

Low 5 hours, High 2½ hours

STAND:

10 minutes

MAKES:

12 servings

SLOW COOKER:

3½- to 4-quart

2	16-ounce packages frozen white whole kernel corn (shoepeg), thawed
1	14¾-ounce can cream-style corn
2	cups shredded Monterey Jack cheese (8 ounces)
1	cup chopped tomato (1 large)
⅓	cup chopped onion
1	4½-ounce can diced green chile peppers
1½	teaspoons chili powder
½	teaspoon salt
1	16-ounce container dairy sour cream
2	tablespoons snipped fresh cilantro

1 In a 3½- to 4-quart slow cooker combine thawed whole kernel corn, cream-style corn, shredded cheese, tomato, onion, undrained chile peppers, chili powder, and salt.

2 Cover; cook on low-heat setting for 5 to 6 hours or on high-heat setting for 2½ to 3 hours. Gently stir in sour cream and snipped fresh cilantro. Let stand 10 minutes before serving.

Nutrition Facts per serving: 250 cal., 15 g total fat (9 g sat. fat), 33 mg chol., 350 mg sodium, 25 g carbo., 2 g fiber, 9 g pro. **Daily Values:** 15% vit. A, 21% vit. C, 20% calcium, 4% iron

Diced ham cooks with the vegetables in this slow cooker side dish, giving it a wonderfully rich flavor.

SIMPLE SUCCOTASH WITH HAM

1	16-ounce package frozen baby lima beans, thawed
1	16-ounce package frozen whole kernel corn, thawed
2	cups diced cooked ham (about 12 ounces)
1	cup coarsely chopped red or green sweet pepper
½	cup chopped onion
½	cup chopped celery
2	cloves garlic, minced
¼	teaspoon black pepper
1	14-ounce can chicken broth

PREP:
20 minutes
COOK:
Low 7 hours, High 3½ hours
MAKES:
8 to 10 servings
SLOW COOKER:
3½- to 4-quart

1 In a 3½- to 4-quart slow cooker combine lima beans, corn, ham, sweet pepper, onion, celery, garlic, and black pepper. Pour broth over all.

2 Cover; cook on low-heat setting for 7 to 9 hours or on high-heat setting for 3½ to 4½ hours. Serve with a slotted spoon.

Nutrition Facts per serving: 191 cal., 4 g total fat (1 g sat. fat), 21 mg chol., 719 mg sodium, 26 g carbo., 5 g fiber, 15 g pro. **Daily Values:** 24% vit. A, 69% vit. C, 3% calcium, 9% iron

For convenience, combine the ingredients in a large bowl before placing them in the cooker. Serve this saucy side dish in small bowls.

CREAMY CORN & BROCCOLI

PREP:

10 minutes

COOK:

Low 5 hours, High 2$\frac{1}{2}$ hours

MAKES:

8 to 10 servings

SLOW COOKER:

4- to 5-quart

Nonstick cooking spray

1   16-ounce bag frozen cut broccoli

1   16-ounce bag frozen corn

1   10$\frac{3}{4}$-ounce can cream of chicken soup

1   cup shredded American cheese

$\frac{1}{2}$ cup shredded cheddar cheese

$\frac{1}{4}$ cup milk

1 Lightly coat the inside of a 4- to 5-quart slow cooker with cooking spray. In a very large mixing bowl combine all ingredients. Place in slow cooker.

2 Cover and cook on low-heat setting for 5 to 6 hours or on high-heat setting for 2$\frac{1}{2}$ to 3 hours.

Nutrition Facts per serving: 191 cal., 10 g total fat (5 g sat. fat), 25 mg chol., 548 mg sodium, 19 g carbo., 3 g fiber, 9 g pro. **Daily Values:** 51% vit. C, 19% calcium, 5% iron

This side dish, made super easy by using a jar of cheese pasta sauce, is perfect for your next potluck.

CHEESY CAULIFLOWER FOR A CROWD

8	cups cauliflower florets
1	large onion, thinly sliced
1/2	teaspoon fennel seeds, crushed
1	14- to 16-ounce jar cheddar cheese pasta sauce
	Cracked black pepper

1 In a 3½- to 4-quart slow cooker place cauliflower, onion, and fennel seeds. Pour pasta sauce over all.

2 Cover and cook on low-heat setting for 6 to 7 hours or on high-heat setting for 3 to 3½ hours. Stir gently. Sprinkle with cracked black pepper before serving.

Nutrition Facts per serving: 59 cal., 6 g total fat (2 g sat. fat), 16 mg chol., 329 mg sodium, 8 g carbo., 2 g fiber, 3 g pro. **Daily Values:** 3% vit. A, 54% vit. C, 7% calcium, 3% iron

PREP:
15 minutes
COOK:
Low 6 hours, High 3 hours
MAKES:
10 to 12 servings
SLOW COOKER:
3½- to 4-quart

This warming soup suits a chilly autumn day. Look for pumpkin seeds (pepitas) in large supermarkets or health food stores.

HOT 'N' SPICY PUMPKIN SOUP

PREP:

20 minutes

COOK:

Low 6 hours, High 3 hours

MAKES:

6 to 8 servings

SLOW COOKER:

3¹/₂- to 4-quart

1	15-ounce can pumpkin
1	cup chopped celery (2 stalks)
¹/₂	cup chopped carrot (1 medium)
¹/₂	cup chopped onion (1 medium)
¹/₄	teaspoon salt
¹/₂	teaspoon dried oregano, crushed
¹/₂	teaspoon dried rosemary, crushed
¹/₄	teaspoon ground red pepper
¹/₄	teaspoon ground ginger
2	14-ounce cans vegetable broth or chicken broth
2	medium tomatoes, chopped (1¹/₂ cups)
¹/₄	cup whipping cream
	Toasted shelled pumpkin seeds or dry-roasted, shelled sunflower seeds (optional)

1 In a 3¹/₂- to 4-quart slow cooker place pumpkin, celery, carrot, onion, salt, oregano, rosemary, ground red pepper, and ginger. Stir in broth. Cover; cook on low-heat setting for 6 to 8 hours or on high-heat setting for 3 to 4 hours.

2 Stir in chopped tomatoes and cream. Ladle into bowls. Sprinkle with seeds, if desired.

Nutrition Facts per serving: 94 cal., 5 g total fat (2 g sat. fat), 14 mg chol., 713 mg sodium, 13 g carbo., 4 g fiber, 3 g pro. **Daily Values:** 376% vit. A, 24% vit. C, 4% calcium, 8% iron

Fit this classic French dish into your schedule by cooking it as little as 2½ hours or as long as 10 hours.

FRENCH ONION SOUP

4	to 6 onions, thinly sliced (4 to 6 cups)
1	clove garlic, minced
3	tablespoons butter or margarine
4½	cups beef broth
1½	teaspoons Worcestershire sauce
⅛	teaspoon pepper
6	to 8 one-inch slices French bread
6	to 8¾-ounce slices Swiss or Gruyère cheese

1 In a large skillet cook onions and garlic in hot butter or margarine, covered, over medium-low heat about 20 minutes or until tender, stirring occasionally.

2 Transfer onion mixture to a 3½- to 4-quart slow cooker. Add beef broth, Worcestershire sauce, and pepper. Cover; cook on low-heat setting for 5 to 10 hours or on high-heat setting for 2½ to 3 hours.

3 Before serving soup, toast bread slices. Arrange toast slices on a baking sheet and top each with a slice of cheese; broil 3 to 4 inches from the heat for 2 to 3 minutes or until cheese is light brown and bubbly. Ladle soup into bowls; top with toast.

Nutrition Facts per serving: 246 cal., 13 g total fat (8 g sat. fat), 36 mg chol., 777 mg sodium, 20 g carbo., 2 g fiber, 13 g pro. **Daily Values:** 8% vit. A, 7% vit. C, 24% calcium, 7% iron

PREP:

30 minutes

COOK:

Low 5 hours, High 2½ hours

MAKES:

6 to 8 servings

SLOW COOKER:

3½- to 4-quart

FOR 5- TO 6-QUART SLOW COOKER
Use 6 to 8 thinly sliced onions (6 to 8 cups), 1 clove minced garlic, ¼ cup butter or margarine, 6 cups beef broth, 2 teaspoons Worcestershire sauce, ⅛ teaspoon pepper, 10 to 12 slices French bread, and 10 to 12 slices Swiss or Gruyère cheese. Prepare as directed, except use a very large skillet to cook onions and garlic. Makes 10 to 12 servings.

This soup is an ideal accompaniment to lunchtime sandwiches. If you don't have shell macaroni, substitute any other small pasta.

SLOW COOKER MINESTRONE

PREP:

15 minutes

COOK:

Low 8 hours, High 4 hours; plus 30 minutes on High

MAKES:

8 servings

SLOW COOKER:

3^1/$_2$- to 6-quart

1	15-ounce can navy beans, rinsed and drained
1	cup shredded cabbage
½	cup sliced carrot
½	cup sliced celery
½	cup chopped onion
1	14½-ounce can diced tomatoes with basil, oregano, and garlic
1	14-ounce can beef broth
3	cups water
¼	teaspoon salt
¼	teaspoon black pepper
8	ounces fresh green beans, cut into 2-inch pieces
½	cup tiny shell macaroni
2	tablespoons snipped fresh parsley
½	cup finely shredded Parmesan cheese

1 In a 3½- to 6-quart slow cooker place navy beans, cabbage, carrot, celery, and onion. Stir in undrained tomatoes, beef broth, water, salt, and pepper. Cover; cook on low-heat setting for 8 to 10 hours or on high-heat setting for 4 to 5 hours.

2 If using low-heat setting, turn to high-heat setting. Stir green beans and macaroni into soup mixture. Cover; cook for 30 minutes more. Stir in parsley. Ladle into soup bowls. Sprinkle each serving with Parmesan cheese.

Nutrition Facts per serving: 157 cal., 2 g total fat (1 g sat. fat), 6 mg chol., 847 mg sodium, 25 g carbo., 5 g fiber, 9 g pro. **Daily Values:** 51% vit. A, 21% vit. C, 15% calcium, 14% iron

There's nothing fancy or surprising about this simple soup—it's tried and true. Kids of all ages call it a favorite.

CHEESY POTATO SOUP

6	medium potatoes, peeled and chopped (6 cups)
2½	cups water
½	cup chopped onion
2	teaspoons instant chicken bouillon granules
¼	teaspoon pepper
1½	cups shredded American cheese (6 ounces)
1	12-ounce can evaporated milk (1½ cups)

1 In a 3½- to 4-quart slow cooker combine potatoes, water, onion, bouillon granules, and pepper. Cover; cook on low-heat setting for 8 to 9 hours or on high-heat setting for 4 to 4½ hours.

2 Stir cheese and milk into mixture in cooker. Cover; cook on low-heat setting for 1 hour more or on high-heat setting for 30 minutes more. Mash potatoes slightly, if desired.

Nutrition Facts per serving: 308 cal., 13 g total fat (8 g sat. fat), 43 mg chol., 765 mg sodium, 35 g carbo., 3 g fiber, 14 g pro. **Daily Values:** 10% vit. A, 38% vit. C, 34% calcium, 8% iron

PREP:

20 minutes

COOK:

Low 8 hours, High 4 hours; plus 1 hour on Low or 30 minutes on High

MAKES:

6 servings

SLOW COOKER:

3½- to 4-quart

FOR 5- TO 6-QUART SLOW COOKER
Use 8 medium potatoes, peeled and chopped; 4 cups water; ¾ cup chopped onion; 1 tablespoon instant chicken bouillon granules; ¼ teaspoon pepper; 2 cups shredded American cheese (8 ounces); and one 12-ounce can evaporated milk plus one 5-ounce can evaporated milk. Prepare as directed. Makes 10 to 12 side-dish servings.

A package of frozen hash brown potatoes frees the time it takes to peel and chop potatoes. Slice a loaf of pumpernickel bread and serve it with this extra-easy, extra-creamy soup.

CREAMY POTATO-LEEK SOUP

PREP:

15 minutes

COOK:

Low 7 hours, High 3½ hours; plus 10 minutes on High

MAKES:

10 to 12 servings

SLOW COOKER:

3½- to 4-quart

ADVICE FOR NIGHT OWLS

If you're not a morning person, get a head start on slow cooker meals the night before. For recipes that call for cooked meat or poultry, cook it the night before, or brown ground beef, ground poultry, or ground sausage. Wait to brown meat cubes, poultry pieces, and roasts, however, until right before placing them in the cooker. Ground meats are completely cooked when browned and are then safe to refrigerate overnight; larger cuts of meat are not cooked through after browning. Clean and chop vegetables.
Store the prepared ingredients in separate containers in the refrigerator overnight. In the morning, assemble the recipe, turn on the cooker, and be on your way.

3   cups water

1   1.8-ounce envelope white sauce mix

1   28-ounce package frozen loose-pack diced hash brown potatoes with onion and peppers

3   medium leeks, sliced (about 1 cup)

1   cup diced Canadian-style bacon or cooked ham

1   12-ounce can evaporated milk

½   teaspoon dried dillweed

1   8-ounce carton dairy sour cream

    Snipped fresh parsley or sliced leek (optional)

1 In a 3½- to 4-quart slow cooker gradually stir water into white sauce mix until mixture is smooth. Stir in frozen potatoes, leeks, Canadian-style bacon or ham, evaporated milk, and dillweed.

2 Cover and cook on low-heat setting for 7 to 9 hours or on high-heat setting for 3½ to 4½ hours.

3 If using low-heat setting, turn to high-heat setting. In a medium bowl stir about 2 cups of the hot potato mixture into the sour cream. Return sour cream mixture to cooker. Cover and cook about 10 minutes more on high-heat setting or until heated through. Ladle into bowls. If desired, sprinkle with parsley or additional sliced leek.

Nutrition Facts per serving: 212 cal., 10 g total fat (5 g sat. fat), 28 mg chol., 476 mg sodium, 23 g carbo., 1 g fiber, 8 g pro. **Daily Values:** 14% vit. C, 13% calcium, 7% iron

Looking for a soup and sandwich supper? Pair this full-flavored soup with your family's favorite sandwiches, such as grilled cheese, tuna salad, or submarines.

FENNEL & ZUCCHINI SOUP WITH BARLEY

2	medium fennel bulbs, trimmed and chopped (2 cups)
2	medium zucchini, chopped (2½ cups)
1	large onion, chopped
½	cup regular barley
2	cloves garlic, minced
1	tablespoon snipped leafy tops of fennel
¼	teaspoon pepper
4	cups reduced-sodium vegetable juice or hot-style vegetable juice
2	cups water
1	14-ounce can vegetable broth or chicken broth

PREP:
25 minutes

COOK:
Low 8 hours, High 4 hours

MAKES:
8 servings

SLOW COOKER:
3½- to 4-quart

1 In a 3½- to 4-quart slow cooker combine fennel, zucchini, onion, barley, garlic, fennel tops, and pepper. Stir in vegetable juice, water, and broth.

2 Cover and cook on low-heat setting for 8 to 10 hours or on high-heat setting for 4 to 5 hours.

Nutrition Facts per serving: 95 cal., 1 g total fat (0 g sat. fat), 0 mg chol., 296 mg sodium, 21 g carbo., 9 g fiber, 3 g pro. **Daily Values:** 62% vit. C, 5% calcium, 7% iron

Show off this pretty dish by ladling it into small glass bowls. Gently spiced, it's also versatile and makes a nice match spooned over pork, pancakes or waffles, or ice cream.

SCANDINAVIAN FRUIT SOUP

PREP:

15 minutes

COOK:

Low 6 hours, High 3 hours

MAKES:

10 to 12 servings

SLOW COOKER:

3¹/₂- to 4-quart

2	7-ounce packages mixed dried fruit bits (about 3 cups)
¹/₂	cup snipped pitted dates or snipped dried figs
¹/₂	cup dried cranberries or dried cherries
¹/₄	cup granulated sugar
¹/₄	cup packed brown sugar
2	tablespoons quick-cooking tapioca
1	medium orange, sliced
2	3-inch pieces stick cinnamon
1¹/₂	teaspoons finely chopped crystallized ginger
	Dash ground cloves
	Dash ground nutmeg
6	cups water

1 In a 3¹/₂- to 4-quart slow cooker combine mixed dried fruit bits, dates or figs, dried cranberries or cherries, granulated sugar, brown sugar, tapioca, orange slices, stick cinnamon, crystallized ginger, cloves, and nutmeg. Pour water over all; stir to mix.

2 Cover; cook on low-heat setting for 6 to 7 hours or on high-heat setting for 3 to 4 hours. Remove orange slices and stick cinnamon before serving.

Nutrition Facts per serving: 203 cal., 0 g total fat (0 g sat. fat), 0 mg chol., 36 mg sodium, 53 g carbo., 1 g fiber, 2 g pro. **Daily Values:** 1% vit. C, 2% calcium, 4% iron

Cooking stuffing in a slow cooker allows space in the oven for other dishes—a lifesaver during holidays that involve lots of cooking.

SAVORY STUFFING WITH FRUIT & PECANS

$1/2$	cup apple juice
1	6-ounce package mixed dried fruit bits ($1^{1}/2$ cups)
1	cup finely chopped celery
$1/2$	cup sliced green onions
$1/2$	cup butter or margarine
2	tablespoons snipped fresh parsley
1	teaspoon dried sage, crushed
$1/2$	teaspoon dried thyme, crushed
$1/2$	teaspoon dried marjoram, crushed
$1/2$	teaspoon salt
$1/4$	teaspoon pepper
10	cups dry bread cubes*
$1/2$	cup broken pecans, toasted
1	to $1^{1}/2$ cups chicken broth

PREP:

25 minutes

COOK:

Low $4^{1}/2$ hours, High $2^{1}/4$ hours

MAKES:

10 to 12 servings

SLOW COOKER:

$3^{1}/2$- to 4-quart

1 In a small saucepan heat apple juice until boiling. Stir in dried fruit. Remove from heat; cover and let stand until needed.

2 Meanwhile, in a medium saucepan cook celery and onions in butter over medium heat until tender but not brown; remove from heat. Stir in parsley, sage, thyme, marjoram, salt, and pepper.

3 Place dry bread cubes in a large bowl. Add undrained fruit, vegetable mixture, and pecans. Drizzle with enough of the broth to moisten, tossing lightly. Transfer stuffing mixture to a $3^{1}/2$- to 4-quart slow cooker.

4 Cover; cook on low-heat setting for $4^{1}/2$ to 5 hours or on high-heat setting for $2^{1}/4$ to $2^{1}/2$ hours.

Nutrition Facts per serving: 279 cal., 15 g total fat (7 g sat. fat), 27 mg chol., 528 mg sodium, 33 g carbo., 2 g fiber, 4 g pro. **Daily Values:** 9% vit. A, 5% vit. C, 6% calcium, 10% iron

*NOTE
To prepare the 10 cups dry bread cubes, cut 14 to 16 slices of bread into $1/2$-inch cubes and spread in a large roasting pan. Bake in a 300° oven for 10 to 15 minutes or until dry, stirring twice.

If the oven is full when you prepare a holiday dinner, and you don't want to stuff the turkey, fix this slow-cooker version of dressing.

SLOW COOKER DRESSING

PREP:

20 minutes

COOK:

Low 4¹/₂ hours, High 2¹/₄ hours

MAKES:

8 to 10 servings

SLOW COOKER:

4- to 5-quart

12	to 16 slices white sandwich bread
¹/₂	cup butter
2	cups sliced celery
¹/₂	cup finely chopped onion
¹/₄	cup snipped fresh parsley
1¹/₂	teaspoons dried sage, crushed
¹/₂	teaspoon dried marjoram, crushed
¹/₄	teaspoon pepper
1¹/₂	cups chicken broth

1 Cut bread in ¹/₂-inch cubes to get 12 cups of bread cubes. Toast in a 350° oven for 10 to 13 minutes or until lightly browned.

2 In a large skillet melt butter over medium heat; add celery and onion and cook until tender; remove from heat. Stir in parsley, sage, marjoram, and pepper.

3 Place dry bread cubes in a very large bowl. Add vegetable mixture. Drizzle with broth to moisten, tossing lightly. Transfer dressing mixture to a 4- to 5-quart slow cooker.

4 Cover; cook on low-heat setting for 4¹/₂ to 5 hours or on high-heat setting for 2¹/₄ to 2¹/₂ hours.

Nutrition Facts per serving: 224 cal., 14 g total fat (8 g sat. fat), 33 mg chol., 541 mg sodium, 21 g carbo., 2 g fiber, 4 g pro. **Daily Values:** 12% vit. A, 8% vit. C, 6% calcium, 9% iron

This bread tastes great slathered with butter and served with a baked-bean casserole or a main-dish salad.

"SLOW-BAKED" BOSTON BROWN BREAD

½ cup whole wheat flour

⅓ cup all-purpose flour

¼ cup cornmeal

½ teaspoon baking powder

¼ teaspoon baking soda

⅛ teaspoon salt

1 beaten egg

¾ cup buttermilk or sour milk

¼ cup molasses

2 tablespoons brown sugar

1 tablespoon butter, melted

2 tablespoons raisins, finely chopped

½ cup warm water

PREP:
20 minutes

COOK:
High 2 hours

COOL:
10 minutes

MAKES:
2 loaves (6 servings per loaf)

SLOW COOKER:
4- to 6-quart

1 In a bowl stir together flours, cornmeal, baking powder, baking soda, and salt.

2 In a small bowl combine egg, buttermilk or sour milk, molasses, brown sugar, and melted butter. Add egg mixture to flour mixture, stirring just until combined. Stir in raisins.

3 Pour mixture into 2 well-greased, 1-pint, straight-sided, wide-mouth canning jars; cover the jars tightly with foil.* Immediately set jars in a 4- to 6-quart slow cooker. Pour the warm water into the cooker around the jars.

4 Cover; cook on high-heat setting about 2 hours or until a wooden toothpick inserted near the center comes out clean. Remove jars from cooker; cool 10 minutes. Carefully remove bread from jars. Cool on wire rack. Serve warm or at room temperature.

*SEE TIP, PAGE 388.

Nutrition Facts per serving: 89 cal., 2 g total fat (1 g sat. fat), 21 mg chol., 102 mg sodium, 17 g carbo., 1 g fiber, 2 g pro. **Daily Values:** 2% vit. A, 5% calcium, 5% iron

Bread in the slow cooker? You bet. Serve the round slices of this sweet bread with soft-style cream cheese.

APPLE BREAD

PREP:

20 minutes

COOK:

High 1³/₄ hours

COOL:

10 minutes

MAKES:

2 loaves (6 servings per loaf)

SLOW COOKER:

4- to 6-quart

1	cup all-purpose flour
1¹/₂	teaspoons baking powder
1	teaspoon apple pie spice
¹/₄	teaspoon salt
¹/₂	cup packed brown sugar
2	tablespoons cooking oil or melted butter
2	eggs, slightly beaten
¹/₂	cup applesauce
¹/₂	cup chopped walnuts, toasted

1 Grease well two 1-pint straight-sided, wide-mouth canning jars; flour the greased jars. Set aside.

2 In a medium bowl combine flour, baking powder, apple pie spice, and salt. Make a well in the center of the flour mixture; set aside.

3 In a small bowl combine brown sugar, oil, eggs, and applesauce; mix well. Add applesauce mixture all at once to the flour mixture. Stir just until moistened. Stir in walnuts.

4 Divide mixture between the prepared canning jars. Cover the jars tightly with greased foil, greased side in. Place the jars in a 4- to 6-quart slow cooker. Pour ¹/₂ cup warm water into the cooker around the jars.

5 Cover; cook on high-heat setting about 1³/₄ to 2 hours or until a long wooden skewer inserted near the center comes out clean. Remove jars from cooker; cool 10 minutes. Carefully remove bread from jars. Serve warm.

Nutrition Facts per serving: 146 cal., 7 g total fat (1 g sat. fat), 35 mg chol., 113 mg sodium, 20 g carbo., 1 g fiber, 3 g pro. **Daily Values:** 1% vit. A, 1% vit. C, 5% calcium, 6% iron

BEEF, PORK, & LAMB

Flavorful gravy is the finishing touch to this slow-cooked tender meat. If you have leftovers, shred the meat for sandwiches the following day.

BRISKET IN ALE

PREP:

25 minutes

COOK:

Low 10 hours, High 5 hours

MAKES:

10 servings

SLOW COOKER:

3¹/₂- to 6-quart

1	3- to 4-pound fresh beef brisket
2	medium onions, thinly sliced and separated into rings
1	bay leaf
1	12-ounce can beer
¼	cup chili sauce
2	tablespoons brown sugar
½	teaspoon dried thyme, crushed
¼	teaspoon salt
¼	teaspoon pepper
1	clove garlic, minced
2	tablespoons cornstarch
2	tablespoons cold water

1 Trim fat from brisket. If necessary, cut brisket to fit into cooker. In a 3¹/₂- to 6-quart slow cooker place onions, bay leaf, and brisket. In a medium bowl combine beer, chili sauce, sugar, thyme, salt, pepper, and garlic; pour over brisket. Cover; cook on low-heat setting for 10 to 12 hours or on high-heat setting for 5 to 6 hours.

2 Transfer brisket and onions to a platter using a slotted spoon; keep warm. Discard bay leaf. For gravy, skim fat from cooking liquid. Measure 2¹/₂ cups liquid; discard remaining liquid. In a medium saucepan stir together the cornstarch and water; stir in the cooking liquid. Cook and stir until thickened and bubbly; cook and stir 2 minutes more. Pass gravy with meat.

Nutrition Facts per serving: 227 cal., 7 g total fat (2 g sat. fat), 78 mg chol., 242 mg sodium, 8 g carbo., 1 g fiber, 30 g pro. **Daily Values:** 1% vit. A, 3% vit. C, 2% calcium, 16% iron

Serve this smoke-flavored beef on buns or rolls. Complete the hearty meal with baked beans, coleslaw, and dessert.

SMOKY BARBECUED BEEF BRISKET

1	2- to 3-pound fresh beef brisket
1	teaspoon chili powder
½	teaspoon garlic powder
¼	teaspoon celery seed
⅛	teaspoon pepper
½	cup catsup
½	cup chili sauce
¼	cup packed brown sugar
2	tablespoons vinegar
2	tablespoons Worcestershire sauce
1½	teaspoons liquid smoke
½	teaspoon dry mustard
⅓	cup water
3	tablespoons all-purpose flour

PREP:
15 minutes

COOK:
Low 10 hours, High 5 hours

MAKES:
6 to 8 servings

SLOW COOKER:
3½- to 4-quart

1 Trim fat from brisket. Cut brisket to fit into slow cooker. Combine chili powder, garlic powder, celery seed, and pepper. Rub the mixture evenly over meat. Place meat in a 3½- to 4-quart slow cooker.

2 For sauce, combine catsup, chili sauce, brown sugar, vinegar, Worcestershire sauce, liquid smoke, and dry mustard. Pour over brisket. Cover; cook on low-heat setting for 10 to 11 hours or on high-heat setting for 5 to 5½ hours.

3 Remove meat from cooker. Skim and discard fat from juices in cooker; measure 2½ cups juices. In a medium saucepan stir water into flour; add cooking juices. Cook and stir until thickened and bubbly; cook and stir for 1 minute more. Cutting across the grain, cut the brisket into thin slices. Serve sauce with meat.

Nutrition Facts per serving: 305 cal., 8 g total fat (2 g sat. fat), 87 mg chol., 681 mg sodium, 24 g carbo., 2 g fiber, 34 g pro. **Daily Values:** 10% vit. A, 12% vit. C, 3% calcium, 22% iron

For a time-saver, freeze half of this plentiful main course. It will be ready in minutes for dinner on a busy day.

SPICED BEEF BRISKET

PREP:

15 minutes

COOK:

Low 10 hours, High 5 hours

MAKES:

10 to 12 servings

SLOW COOKER:

3$1/2$- to 4-quart

SERVING SUGGESTION
Serve with tiny new potatoes.

1	3$1/2$- to 4-pound fresh beef brisket
2	cups water
$1/4$	cup catsup
1	envelope ($1/2$ of a **2.2**-ounce package) onion soup mix
2	tablespoons Worcestershire sauce
$1/2$	teaspoon ground cinnamon
$1/2$	teaspoon bottled minced garlic
$1/4$	teaspoon pepper
$1/4$	cup cold water
3	tablespoons all-purpose flour

1 Place beef brisket in a 3$1/2$- to 4-quart slow cooker, cutting to fit if necessary.

2 In a bowl combine the 2 cups water, catsup, soup mix, Worcestershire sauce, cinnamon, garlic, and pepper. Pour over brisket. Cover; cook on low-heat setting for 10 to 11 hours or on high-heat setting for 5 to 5$1/2$ hours.

3 Remove beef; keep warm. Pour juices into a glass measuring cup. Skim fat. Measure 1$1/2$ cups cooking liquid; discard remaining liquid. For gravy, in a small saucepan stir the $1/4$ cup cold water into the flour. Stir in the 1$1/2$ cups cooking liquid. Cook and stir until thickened and bubbly. Cook and stir 1 minute more.

4 Slice beef thinly across the grain. Serve with the hot gravy.

Nutrition Facts per serving: 247 cal., 9 g total fat (3 g sat. fat), 76 mg chol., 338 mg sodium, 5 g carbo., 0 g fiber, 33 g pro. **Daily Values:** 1% vit. A, 2% vit. C, 2% calcium, 19% iron

Leave the peels on the potatoes. You'll save time as well as valuable nutrients and fiber provided by the skins.

BEEF TIP ROAST & VEGETABLES

1	2- to 2½-pound beef round tip roast
1½	pounds small potatoes (about 10), halved, or medium potatoes (about 4), quartered
2	medium carrots, cut into 1-inch pieces (1 cup)
1	large onion, sliced
1	bay leaf
¼	teaspoon pepper
1	10-ounce can condensed beef broth
3	tablespoons all-purpose flour
3	tablespoons butter, melted
1	10-ounce package frozen cut green beans

1 Trim fat from roast. If necessary, cut roast to fit into slow cooker. In a 5- to 6-quart slow cooker place potatoes, carrots, and onion. Add bay leaf and pepper. Place roast over vegetables.

2 Pour broth over roast. Cover; cook on low-heat setting for 12 to 14 hours or on high-heat setting for 6 to 7 hours. In a small bowl combine flour and butter. Remove roast from cooker and set aside. Stir flour mixture and green beans into cooker. Return roast to cooker; cover, and cook 1 hour more.

3 To serve, discard bay leaf. Arrange roast and vegetables on a warm serving platter. Skim fat from gravy. Spoon some of the gravy over roast; pass remaining gravy with roast and vegetables.

Nutrition Facts per serving: 447 cal., 21 g total fat (9 g sat. fat), 112 mg chol., 521 mg sodium, 28 g carbo., 4 g fiber, 35 g pro. **Daily Values:** 123% vit. A, 33% vit. C, 4% calcium, 26% iron

PREP:

20 minutes

COOK:

Low 12 hours, High 6 hours; plus 1 hour

MAKES:

6 servings

SLOW COOKER:

5- to 6-quart

The old-fashioned goodness of this recipe will have your family asking for seconds. Mashed potatoes are a good alternative to noodles.

SAUCY POT ROAST WITH NOODLES

PREP:

25 minutes

COOK:

Low 10 hours, High 4 hours

MAKES:

6 to 8 servings

SLOW COOKER:

$3^{1}/_{2}$- to 4-quart

1	2- to $2^{1}/_{2}$-pound beef chuck roast
1	tablespoon cooking oil
2	medium carrots, coarsely chopped (1 cup)
2	stalks celery, sliced (1 cup)
1	medium onion, sliced
2	cloves garlic, minced
1	tablespoon quick-cooking tapioca
1	$14^{1}/_{2}$-ounce can Italian-style stewed tomatoes
1	6-ounce can Italian-style tomato paste
1	tablespoon brown sugar
$^{1}/_{2}$	teaspoon salt
$^{1}/_{4}$	teaspoon pepper
1	bay leaf
$4^{1}/_{2}$	to 6 cups cooked noodles ($^{3}/_{4}$ cup per serving)

1 Trim fat from pot roast. If necessary, cut roast to fit into slow cooker. In a large skillet brown roast on all sides in hot oil.

2 In a $3^{1}/_{2}$- to 4-quart slow cooker place carrots, celery, onion, and garlic. Sprinkle tapioca over vegetables. Place meat to cover vegetables.

3 In a bowl combine undrained tomatoes, tomato paste, brown sugar, salt, pepper, and bay leaf; pour over the meat.

4 Cover; cook on low-heat setting for 10 to 12 hours or on high-heat setting for 4 to 5 hours. Discard bay leaf. Skim off fat. Serve with hot cooked noodles.

Nutrition Facts per serving: 569 cal., 27 g total fat (10 g sat. fat), 127 mg chol., 693 mg sodium, 48 g carbo., 4 g fiber, 32 g pro. **Daily Values:** 103% vit. A, 15% vit. C, 6% calcium, 32% iron

This seasoned gravy is tasty over mashed potatoes too. Begin the meal with a leaf lettuce salad topped with your favorite vinaigrette.

HERBED PORT POT ROAST

1   2½- to 3-pound beef chuck pot roast
½   cup chopped onion
½   cup port wine or apple juice
1   8-ounce can tomato sauce
3   tablespoons quick-cooking tapioca
1   tablespoon Worcestershire sauce
1   teaspoon dried thyme, crushed
1   teaspoon dried oregano, crushed
2   cloves garlic, minced
4   cups hot cooked noodles

1 Trim fat from pot roast. If necessary, cut roast to fit into a 3½- to 4-quart slow cooker. Place meat in cooker.

2 In a small bowl combine onion, port or apple juice, tomato sauce, tapioca, Worcestershire, thyme, oregano, and garlic. Pour over pot roast.

3 Cover; cook on low-heat setting for 8 to 10 hours or on high-heat setting for 4 to 5 hours. Transfer roast to a serving platter. Skim fat from gravy. Pass gravy with meat. Serve with hot cooked noodles.

Nutrition Facts per serving: 426 cal., 20 g total fat (7 g sat. fat), 104 mg chol., 229 mg sodium, 29 g carbo., 1 g fiber, 27 g pro. **Daily Values:** 1% vit. A, 2% vit. C, 3% calcium, 25% iron

PREP:
15 minutes
COOK:
Low 8 hours, High 4 hours
MAKES:
8 to 10 servings
SLOW COOKER:
3½- to 4-quart

Nothing is more comforting on a chilly day than a hearty, melt-in-your-mouth pot roast. Mashed potatoes and fresh basil are special touches.

POT ROAST WITH WINTER VEGETABLES

PREP:

25 minutes

COOK:

Low 8 hours, High 4 hours

STAND:

10 minutes

MAKES:

6 servings

SLOW COOKER:

3$\frac{1}{2}$- to 4-quart

2	carrots, cut into $\frac{1}{2}$-inch pieces
1	medium turnip, peeled and cubed (1 cup)
1	small onion, chopped
$\frac{1}{2}$	cup snipped dried tomatoes (not oil-packed)
1	clove garlic, minced
1	teaspoon instant beef bouillon granules
$\frac{1}{2}$	teaspoon dried basil, crushed
$\frac{1}{2}$	teaspoon dried oregano, crushed
$\frac{1}{8}$	teaspoon pepper
1	1$\frac{1}{2}$- to 2-pound boneless beef chuck pot roast
1	cup water
1	10-ounce package frozen lima beans or whole kernel corn
1	cup frozen peas
1	20-ounce package refrigerated mashed potatoes
1	tablespoon finely snipped fresh basil

1 In a 3$\frac{1}{2}$- to 4-quart slow cooker combine the carrots, turnip, onion, dried tomatoes, garlic, bouillon granules, dried basil, dried oregano, and pepper. Trim fat from meat. If necessary, cut roast to fit into cooker. Place meat on top of vegetables. Pour water over all.

2 Cover; cook on low-heat setting for 8 to 10 hours or on high-heat setting for 4 to 5 hours. Stir in lima beans or corn and peas. Let stand, covered, for 10 minutes.

3 Meanwhile, prepare mashed potatoes according to package directions, except stir the 1 tablespoon fresh basil into potatoes just before serving. Remove meat and vegetables from cooker with a slotted spoon. If desired, reserve cooking juices. Serve meat and vegetables over hot mashed potatoes. If desired, serve cooking juices over meat.

Nutrition Facts per serving: 436 cal., 12 g total fat (5 g sat. fat), 87 mg chol., 497 mg sodium, 46 g carbo., 8 g fiber, 35 g pro. **Daily Values:** 12% vit. C, 4% calcium, 34% iron

A combination of ginger, curry, and turmeric takes this roast beyond the ordinary. Serve it with gravy made from the cooking juices.

CURRIED POT ROAST

1	2½-pound boneless beef chuck pot roast
1	teaspoon ground ginger
1	teaspoon curry powder
1	teaspoon ground turmeric
½	teaspoon salt
¼	teaspoon pepper
2	cups chopped onions
6	medium carrots, cut into 1-inch pieces
2	cloves garlic, minced
½	teaspoon dried thyme, crushed
1	14½-ounce can diced tomatoes
½	cup beef broth
1	bay leaf
¼	cup all-purpose flour
½	cup cold water

PREP:
35 minutes
COOK:
Low 8 hours, High 4 hours
MAKES:
6 servings
SLOW COOKER:
3½- to 4-quart

1 Trim fat from meat. In a small bowl stir together the ginger, curry powder, turmeric, salt, and pepper. Rub over surface of meat. In a 3½- to 4-quart slow cooker place the onions, carrots, and garlic. Place the meat on the vegetables. Sprinkle with thyme; add undrained tomatoes, beef broth, and bay leaf.

2 Cover; cook on low-heat setting for 8 to 10 hours or on high-heat setting for 4 to 5 hours. Remove bay leaf. Transfer meat and vegetables to a platter, reserving juices. Keep meat and vegetables warm.

3 For gravy, measure juices; skim fat. If necessary, add enough water to equal 1½ cups. Add juices to a small saucepan. Combine flour and cold water. Stir into juices. Cook and stir until thickened and bubbly. Cook and stir for 1 minute more. Serve gravy with meat and vegetables.

Nutrition Facts per serving: 348 cal., 10 g total fat (4 g sat. fat), 120 mg chol., 477 mg sodium, 19 g carbo., 4 g fiber, 42 g pro. **Daily Values:** 309% vit. A, 27% vit. C, 7% calcium, 33% iron

Sure to become an autumn favorite, this recipe highlights some of the produce you'll find at farmers' markets during the season.

ROAST WITH TOMATO-WINE GRAVY

PREP:

30 minutes

COOK:

Low 10 hours, High 5 hours

MAKES:

6 servings

SLOW COOKER:

3¹/₂- to 6-quart

1   2- to 2¹/₂-pound beef chuck pot roast

1   tablespoon cooking oil

2   medium turnips, peeled and cut into 1-inch pieces (2 cups)

3   medium carrots, cut into ¹/₂-inch pieces (1¹/₂ cups)

1   15-ounce can tomato sauce

¹/₄   cup dry red wine or beef broth

3   tablespoons quick-cooking tapioca

¹/₄   teaspoon salt

¹/₈   teaspoon ground allspice

¹/₈   teaspoon pepper

1   pound winter squash, peeled, seeded, and cut into thin wedges or 1¹/₂- to 2-inch pieces (2 cups)

1 Trim fat from roast. If necessary, cut roast to fit into slow cooker. In a large skillet brown roast on all sides in hot oil.

2 Meanwhile, in a 3¹/₂- to 6-quart slow cooker place turnips, carrots, tomato sauce, red wine or broth, tapioca, salt, allspice, and pepper; stir together. Place roast to cover vegetables. Place squash on roast. Cover; cook on low-heat setting for 10 to 12 hours or on high-heat setting for 5 to 6 hours.

3 Transfer roast and vegetables to a warm serving platter. Skim fat from gravy. Pass gravy with roast.

Nutrition Facts per serving: 404 cal., 24 g total fat (9 g sat. fat), 87 mg chol., 537 mg sodium, 17 g carbo., 3 g fiber, 26 g pro. **Daily Values:** 183% vit. A, 20% vit. C, 4% calcium, 20% iron

To season meat, some cooks prefer the taste and texture of kosher salt, which has been coarsely ground and contains no additives.

POT ROAST WITH DILL

1   2½- to 3-pound boneless beef chuck pot roast

1   tablespoon cooking oil

½   cup water

1   tablespoon snipped fresh dillweed or 1 teaspoon dried dillweed

½   teaspoon coarse salt (kosher) or ¼ teaspoon regular salt

½   teaspoon pepper

½   cup plain yogurt

2   tablespoons all-purpose flour

3   cups hot cooked noodles

1 If necessary, cut roast to fit into a 3½- to 4-quart slow cooker. In a large skillet brown roast on all sides in hot oil. Transfer roast to cooker and add water. Sprinkle roast with 2 teaspoons of fresh dillweed or ¾ teaspoon of dried dillweed, salt, and pepper.

2 Cover and cook on low-heat setting for 10 to 12 hours or on high-heat setting for 5 to 6 hours or until meat is tender. Transfer roast to a serving platter, reserving juices; cover roast and keep warm. Pour cooking juices into a glass measuring cup; skim off fat. Measure 1 cup reserved juices.

3 For sauce, in a small saucepan stir together yogurt and flour until combined. Stir in the 1 cup reserved cooking juices and remaining dillweed. Cook and stir until thickened and bubbly. Cook and stir for 1 minute more. Serve sauce with meat and noodles.

Nutrition Facts per serving: 435 cal., 19 g total fat (7 g sat. fat), 148 mg chol., 262 mg sodium, 23 g carbo., 1 g fiber, 40 g pro. **Daily Values:** 1% vit. A, 6% calcium, 31% iron

PREP:
20 minutes

COOK:
Low 10 hours, High 5 hours

MAKES:
6 servings

SLOW COOKER:
3½- to 4-quart

With a slow cooker, you can fix this perennial family favorite any day of the week. For mornings on the run, cut the carrots or parsnips and onions the night before.

FAVORITE BEEF POT ROAST

PREP:

30 minutes

COOK:

Low 10 hours, High 5 hours

MAKES:

6 to 8 servings

SLOW COOKER:

3^1/$_2$- to 4-quart

FOR A 5- TO 6-QUART SLOW COOKER

Use a 3- to 3^1/$_2$-pound boneless beef chuck pot roast, 1^1/$_2$ pounds potatoes, 10 carrots or parsnips, and 4 small onions. Use remaining ingredients as directed, except reserve 2^1/$_2$ cups juices (adding water, if necessary) for gravy. To thicken the gravy, combine ^{1}/$_3$ cup all-purpose flour with the ^{1}/$_2$ cup cold water. Makes 10 servings.

1   2- to 2^1/$_2$-pound boneless beef chuck pot roast

1   tablespoon cooking oil

1   pound whole, tiny new potatoes, 3 medium potatoes, or 3 medium sweet potatoes

8   carrots or parsnips, cut into 1-inch pieces

3   small onions, cut into wedges

^{3}/$_4$ cup water

1   tablespoon Worcestershire sauce

2   teaspoons instant beef bouillon granules

1   teaspoon dried basil or oregano, crushed

^{1}/$_2$ cup cold water

^{1}/$_4$ cup all-purpose flour

     Salt and pepper

1 Trim fat from roast. If necessary, cut roast to fit into a 3^1/$_2$- to 4-quart slow cooker. In a large skillet brown meat on all sides in hot oil. Drain off fat.

2 Meanwhile, remove a narrow strip of peel from the center of each new potato, or peel and quarter each medium potato or sweet potato. Place potatoes, carrots or parsnips, and onions in cooker. Place meat over vegetables.

3 In a small bowl combine the ^{3}/$_4$ cup water, Worcestershire sauce, bouillon granules, and basil or oregano. Pour over meat and vegetables.

4 Cover and cook on low-heat setting for 10 to 12 hours or on high-heat setting for 5 to 6 hours.

5 Transfer meat and vegetables to a serving platter, reserving juices; cover meat and keep warm. Pour cooking juices into a glass measuring cup; skim off fat. For gravy, measure 1^1/$_2$ cups juices, adding water, if necessary. Transfer to a saucepan. Combine the ^{1}/$_2$ cup cold water and flour; stir into juices in saucepan. Cook and stir until thickened and bubbly. Cook and stir for 1 minute more. Season gravy to taste with salt and pepper. Serve gravy with meat and vegetables.

Nutrition Facts per serving: 470 cal., 26 g total fat (9 g sat. fat), 98 mg chol., 426 mg sodium, 27 g carbo., 4 g fiber, 32 g pro. **Daily Values:** 30% vit. C, 5% calcium, 26% iron

This German pot roast seems to have several versions, all with layers of earthy tang and spice. Red wine, chopped dill pickles, and hearty mustard set this one apart.

GERMAN-STYLE BEEF ROAST

1	2½- to 3-pound boneless beef chuck pot roast
1	tablespoon cooking oil
2	cups sliced carrots
2	cups chopped onions
1	cup sliced celery
¾	cup chopped kosher-style dill pickles
½	cup dry red wine or beef broth
⅓	cup German-style mustard
½	teaspoon coarse ground black pepper
¼	teaspoon ground cloves
2	bay leaves
2	tablespoons all-purpose flour
2	tablespoons dry red wine or beef broth
	Hot cooked spaetzle or cooked noodles
	Crumbled cooked bacon (optional)

PREP:
25 minutes
COOK:
Low 8 hours, High 4 hours
MAKES:
8 servings
SLOW COOKER:
3½- to 4-quart

1 Trim fat from roast. If necessary, cut roast to fit into a 3½- to 4-quart slow cooker. In a large skillet brown the roast slowly on all sides in hot oil. Drain off fat.

2 Meanwhile, place carrots, onions, celery, and pickles in the slow cooker. Place meat over vegetables. In a small bowl combine the ½ cup red wine or beef broth, mustard, pepper, cloves, and bay leaves. Pour over meat. Cover and cook on low-heat setting for 8 to 10 hours or on high-heat setting for 4 to 5 hours. Transfer meat to a serving platter and cover meat to keep warm.

3 For gravy, transfer vegetables and cooking liquid to a 2-quart saucepan. Skim off fat. Remove bay leaves. Stir together flour and the 2 tablespoons wine or beef broth. Stir into mixture in saucepan. Cook and stir over medium heat until thickened and bubbly. Cook and stir for 1 minute more. Serve meat and vegetables with gravy and hot cooked spaetzle or noodles. If desired, top with bacon.

Nutrition Facts per serving: 372 cal., 25 g total fat (9 g sat. fat), 82 mg chol., 414 mg sodium, 10 g carbo., 2 g fiber, 24 g pro. **Daily Values:** 155% vit. A, 9% vit. C, 5% calcium, 19% iron

Look for couscous, a type of Moroccan pasta, in the pasta and rice section of grocery stores. Follow package directions; it cooks quickly and easily.

CURRIED ROAST & CARROTS

PREP:

15 minutes

COOK:

Low 8 hours, High 4 hours

MAKES:

6 servings

SLOW COOKER:

3^1/$_2$- to 4-quart

5	medium carrots, cut into 2-inch pieces
1	pound boiling onions, peeled, or 2 cups chopped onions
1	1^1/$_2$- to 2-pound boneless beef chuck pot roast
^{1}/$_2$	cup apple juice or water
^{1}/$_3$	cup chutney
2	tablespoons quick-cooking tapioca
2	teaspoons curry powder
^{1}/$_2$	teaspoon ground coriander
^{1}/$_2$	teaspoon dried mint, crushed
3	cups hot cooked couscous or rice

1 Place carrots and onions in a 3^1/$_2$- to 4-quart slow cooker. If necessary, cut roast to fit into the cooker. Place meat on top of the vegetables. In a small bowl combine apple juice or water, chutney, tapioca, curry powder, coriander, and mint. Pour over meat.

2 Cover; cook on low-heat setting for 8 to 10 hours or on high-heat setting for 4 to 5 hours. Transfer meat and vegetables to a platter. Skim fat from juices. Serve meat, vegetables, and juices with couscous or rice.

Nutrition Facts per serving: 588 cal., 27 g total fat (11 g sat. fat), 113 mg chol., 119 mg sodium, 48 g carbo., 7 g fiber, 36 g pro. **Daily Values:** 23% vit. C, 5% calcium, 32% iron

STORING LEFTOVERS

For safety reasons, food should not be left in slow cookers to cool after cooking. Also, don't use slow cookers as storage containers or place them in the refrigerator. To properly store cooked food, remove food from the cooker. (If the food is very hot, transfer it to a large, shallow container to cool.) After it has sufficiently cooled (hold for no longer than 2 hours at room temperature), transfer the food to refrigerator or freezer storage containers. Cover tightly; label and date the containers.

This old-fashioned dinner favorite is seasoned with cinnamon. A quick gravy made with the cooking juices tops the fork-tender meat.

BEEF ROAST WITH SWEET POTATOES

1	2-pound boneless beef chuck pot roast
1	tablespoon cooking oil
1	medium onion, sliced
6	medium sweet potatoes or regular baking potatoes, peeled and quartered (2 pounds)
¾	cup water
1½	teaspoons instant beef bouillon granules
¼	teaspoon celery seeds
¼	teaspoon ground cinnamon
¼	teaspoon pepper
2	tablespoons cornstarch (optional)
2	tablespoons cold water (optional)

PREP:
15 minutes

COOK:
Low 8 hours, High 4 hours

MAKES:
6 servings

SLOW COOKER:
3½- to 4-quart

1 Trim the fat from the pot roast. If necessary, cut roast to fit a 3½- to 4-quart slow cooker. In a large skillet brown roast on all sides in hot oil. Drain well.

2 Place onion and potatoes in cooker. Place meat over vegetables.

3 In a small bowl combine ¾ cup water, bouillon granules, celery seeds, cinnamon, and pepper. Pour over meat and vegetables. Cover; cook on low-heat setting for 8 to 10 hours or on high-heat setting for 4 to 5 hours.

4 Remove meat and vegetables from cooker and place on platter; reserve juices. If desired, for gravy, pour juices into glass measuring cup. Skim off fat. If necessary, add water to equal 2 cups liquid. In a saucepan stir cornstarch into 2 tablespoons cold water; add cooking juices. Cook and stir until thickened and bubbly. Cook and stir 2 minutes more. Serve gravy with roast and vegetables.

Nutrition Facts per serving: 406 cal., 21 g total fat (7 g sat. fat), 61 mg chol., 307 mg sodium, 28 g carbo., 4 g fiber, 26 g pro. **Daily Values:** 393% vit. A, 30% vit. C, 4% calcium, 19% iron

Try a cooked fragrant rice, such as jasmine or basmati, with this tender beef and rich, slightly sweet brown gravy.

JERK ROAST WITH RICE

PREP:

30 minutes

COOK:

Low 8 hours, High 4 hours

MAKES:

6 servings

SLOW COOKER:

3¹/₂- to 4-quart

1   2- to 2¹/₂-pound boneless beef chuck roast

³/₄   cup water

¹/₄   cup raisins

¹/₄   cup steak sauce

3   tablespoons balsamic vinegar

2   tablespoons sugar

2   tablespoons quick-cooking tapioca

1   teaspoon cracked black pepper

1   teaspoon Jamaican jerk seasoning

2   cloves garlic, minced

3   cups hot cooked jasmine or basmati rice

1 Trim fat from meat. If necessary, cut roast to fit a 3¹/₂- to 4-quart slow cooker. Place the beef in the cooker. In a small bowl combine water, raisins, steak sauce, balsamic vinegar, sugar, tapioca, pepper, Jamaican jerk seasoning, and garlic. Pour mixture over roast.

2 Cover; cook on low-heat setting for 8 to 10 hours or on high-heat setting for 4 to 5 hours. Pour cooking-liquid gravy into a bowl. Skim fat from the gravy. Serve beef with rice and gravy.

Nutrition Facts per serving: 359 cal., 7 g total fat (3 g sat. fat), 92 mg chol., 269 mg sodium, 39 g carbo., 1 g fiber, 33 g pro. **Daily Values:** 2% vit. A, 4% vit. C, 3% calcium, 26% iron

Vary the amount of curry powder to suit your taste. Sprinkle with nuts or coconut just before serving for a little crunch.

BEEF CURRY WITH FRUIT

1	2-pound boneless beef chuck pot roast
½	cup chopped onion
1	tablespoon cooking oil
1	15¼-ounce can pineapple chunks (juice pack)
⅔	cup orange juice
2	tablespoons quick-cooking tapioca
1	tablespoon brown sugar
2	to 3 teaspoons curry powder
½	teaspoon salt
¼	teaspoon pepper
½	cup dried figs, coarsely snipped
3	tablespoons currants
1	16-ounce can unpeeled apricot halves (light syrup pack), drained and halved
	Hot cooked rice
½	cup honey-roasted peanuts or cashews, coarsely chopped, and/or flaked coconut

1 Trim fat from meat; cut meat into ¾-inch cubes. In a large skillet brown meat cubes and onion, half at a time, in hot oil. Drain off fat. In a 3½- to 4-quart slow cooker combine undrained pineapple, orange juice, tapioca, brown sugar, curry powder, salt, and pepper. Add meat and onion to cooker.

2 Cover; cook on low-heat setting for 7 to 9 hours or on high-heat setting for 3½ to 4½ hours. Add figs, currants, and apricots. Cover; cook on low- or high-heat setting for 30 minutes more. Serve over rice. Pass nuts and/or coconut to sprinkle over beef.

Nutrition Facts per serving: 679 cal., 29 g total fat (9 g sat. fat), 97 mg chol., 324 mg sodium, 73 g carbo., 6 g fiber, 34 g pro. **Daily Values:** 22% vit. A, 40% vit. C, 7% calcium, 32% iron

PREP:

20 minutes

COOK:

Low 7 hours, High 3½ hours; plus 30 minutes

MAKES:

6 servings

SLOW COOKER:

3½- to 4-quart

FOR A 5- TO 6-QUART SLOW COOKER

Use a 3-pound boneless beef chuck pot roast; ¾ cup chopped onions; 1 tablespoon cooking oil; one 15¼-ounce can pineapple chunks (juice pack); 1 cup orange juice; 3 tablespoons quick-cooking tapioca; 4 teaspoons brown sugar; 3 to 4 teaspoons curry powder; ¾ teaspoon salt; ¼ teaspoon pepper; ⅔ cup figs, coarsely snipped; ¼ cup currants; one 16-ounce can unpeeled apricot halves (light syrup pack), drained; hot cooked rice; and ¾ cup peanuts, chopped, and/or coconut. Prepare as directed. Makes 8 servings.

The slightly spicy ginger-flavored sauce goes equally well over pork or lamb—and it's satisfying with hot cooked rice.

GINGERED BEEF & VEGETABLES

PREP:

20 minutes

COOK:

Low 9 hours, High 4½ hours; plus 20 minutes on High

MAKES:

6 servings

SLOW COOKER:

3½- to 4-quart

1½	pounds boneless beef round steak, cut into 1-inch cubes
4	medium carrots, bias-sliced into ½-inch pieces
½	cup bias-sliced green onions
2	cloves garlic, minced
1½	cups water
2	tablespoons soy sauce
2	teaspoons grated fresh ginger
1½	teaspoons instant beef bouillon granules
¼	teaspoon crushed red pepper
3	tablespoons cornstarch
3	tablespoons cold water
½	cup chopped red sweet pepper
2	cups frozen sugar snap peas, thawed
3	cups hot cooked rice

1 In a 3½- to 4-quart slow cooker combine beef, carrots, green onions, garlic, 1½ cups water, soy sauce, ginger, bouillon granules, and crushed red pepper.

2 Cover; cook on low-heat setting for 9 to 10 hours or on high-heat setting for 4½ to 5 hours.

3 If using low-heat setting, turn to high-heat setting. In a small bowl stir together cornstarch and 3 tablespoons water; stir into meat mixture along with sweet pepper. Cover and cook for 20 to 30 minutes or until thickened, stirring once. Stir in sugar snap peas. Serve over rice.

Nutrition Facts per serving: 350 cal., 10 g total fat (4 g sat. fat), 68 mg chol., 400 mg sodium, 35 g carbo., 3 g fiber, 29 g pro. **Daily Values:** 232% vit. A, 52% vit. C, 6% calcium, 21% iron

Serve this company fare with fresh noodles from the refrigerated section of the grocery store.

ITALIAN ROUND STEAK

1½	pounds boneless beef bottom round steak
2	medium carrots, cut into ½-inch pieces
2	stalks celery, cut into ½-inch pieces
1	cup quartered fresh mushrooms
½	cup sliced green onions
1	14½-ounce can Italian-style stewed tomatoes
1	cup beef broth
½	cup dry red wine, white wine, or beef broth
3	tablespoons quick-cooking tapioca
1	teaspoon dried Italian seasoning, crushed
½	teaspoon salt
¼	teaspoon pepper
1	bay leaf
3	cups hot cooked noodles

1 Trim fat from meat; cut meat into 1-inch cubes.

2 Transfer beef to a 3½- to 4-quart slow cooker. Add carrots, celery, mushrooms, green onions, undrained tomatoes, beef broth, wine, tapioca, Italian seasoning, salt, pepper, and bay leaf.

3 Cover; cook on low-heat setting for 9 to 10 hours or on high-heat setting for 4½ to 5 hours. Discard bay leaf. Serve over hot cooked noodles.

Nutrition Facts per serving: 324 cal., 7 g total fat (2 g sat. fat), 83 mg chol., 552 mg sodium, 33 g carbo., 3 g fiber, 27 g pro. **Daily Values:** 104% vit. A, 7% vit. C, 5% calcium, 25% iron

PREP:
20 minutes

COOK:
Low 9 hours, High 4½ hours

MAKES:
6 servings

SLOW COOKER:
3½- to 4-quart

Use either sweet or hot Hungarian paprika to spice this goulash, depending on how much heat you like.

SLOW COOKER GOULASH

PREP:

25 minutes

COOK:

Low 8 hours, High 3$\frac{1}{2}$ hours; plus 30 minutes on High

MAKES:

6 servings

SLOW COOKER:

3$\frac{1}{2}$- to 4-quart

1$\frac{1}{2}$ pounds beef stew meat

2 medium carrots, bias-sliced into $\frac{1}{2}$-inch pieces

2 medium onions, thinly sliced

3 cloves garlic, minced

1$\frac{1}{4}$ cups beef broth

1 6-ounce can tomato paste

1 tablespoon Hungarian paprika

1 teaspoon finely shredded lemon peel

$\frac{1}{2}$ teaspoon salt

$\frac{1}{2}$ teaspoon caraway seed

$\frac{1}{4}$ teaspoon ground black pepper

1 bay leaf

1 red or green sweet pepper, cut into bite-size strips

3 cups hot cooked noodles

Dairy sour cream or yogurt

1 In a 3$\frac{1}{2}$- to 4-quart slow cooker combine meat, carrots, onions, and garlic. In a small bowl combine beef broth, tomato paste, paprika, lemon peel, salt, caraway seed, black pepper, and bay leaf. Stir into vegetable and meat mixture.

2 Cover; cook on low-heat setting for 8 to 9 hours or on high-heat setting for 3$\frac{1}{2}$ to 4$\frac{1}{2}$ hours.

3 If using low-heat setting, turn to high-heat setting. Stir in sweet pepper strips. Cover and cook 30 minutes more. Discard bay leaf. Serve with hot cooked noodles. Top with sour cream or yogurt.

Nutrition Facts per serving: 356 cal., 11 g total fat (4 g sat. fat), 85 mg chol., 678 mg sodium, 33 g carbo., 4 g fiber, 32 g pro. **Daily Values:** 153% vit. A, 81% vit. C, 6% calcium, 26% iron

Ladle these tender chunks of beef and the richly herbed sauce over noodles or rice. A sprinkling of fresh parsley before serving adds color and freshness.

CLASSIC BEEF STROGANOFF

1½	pounds lean beef stew meat
1	tablespoon cooking oil
2	cups sliced fresh mushrooms
½	cup sliced green onions or ½ cup chopped onion
2	cloves garlic, minced
½	teaspoon dried oregano, crushed
¼	teaspoon salt
¼	teaspoon dried thyme, crushed
¼	teaspoon pepper
1	bay leaf
1½	cups beef broth
⅓	cup dry sherry
1	8-ounce carton dairy sour cream
⅓	cup all-purpose flour
¼	cup water
4	cups hot cooked noodles or rice
	Snipped fresh parsley (optional)

PREP:

30 minutes

COOK:

Low 8 hours, High 4 hours; plus 30 minutes on High

MAKES:

6 servings

SLOW COOKER:

3½- to 4-quart

1 Cut up any large pieces of stew meat. In a large skillet brown beef, half at a time, in hot oil. Drain off fat.

2 In a 3½- to 4-quart slow cooker place mushrooms, onions, garlic, oregano, salt, thyme, pepper, and bay leaf. Add stew meat. Pour beef broth and sherry over all. Cover; cook on low-heat setting for 8 to 10 hours or on high-heat setting for 4 to 5 hours. Discard bay leaf.

3 If using low-heat setting, turn to high-heat setting. In a medium bowl whisk together sour cream, flour, and water until smooth. Stir about 1 cup of the hot liquid into sour cream mixture. Return all to cooker; stir to combine. Cover and cook on high-heat setting for 30 minutes or until thickened and bubbly.

4 Serve over hot cooked noodles or rice. If desired, sprinkle with snipped fresh parsley.

Nutrition Facts per serving: 471 cal., 19 g total fat (8 g sat. fat), 106 mg chol., 402 mg sodium, 37 g carbo., 2 g fiber, 34 g pro. **Daily Values:** 7% vit. A, 3% vit. C, 8% calcium, 27% iron

Brimming with flavors of traditional stir-fry, the sauce for this ever-so-easy beef and veggie dish begins with an envelope of gravy mix.

ORIENTAL BEEF & BROCCOLI

PREP:

20 minutes

COOK:

Low 8 hours, High 4 hours; plus 15 minutes on High

MAKES:

6 servings

SLOW COOKER:

3¹/₂- to 4-quart

6	medium carrots, cut into 1-inch pieces
2	medium onions, cut into wedges
1½	pounds beef round steak, bias-sliced into ½-inch strips
1	tablespoon minced fresh ginger
2	cloves garlic, minced
½	cup water
2	tablespoons reduced-sodium soy sauce
1	¾-ounce envelope beef gravy mix
4	cups broccoli florets
3	cups hot cooked rice

1 In a 3½- to 4-quart slow cooker place carrots, onions, beef strips, ginger, and garlic. Stir together water, soy sauce, and beef gravy mix. Pour over meat and vegetables in cooker.

2 Cover and cook on low-heat setting for 8 to 10 hours or on high-heat setting for 4 to 5 hours.

3 If using low-heat setting, turn to high-heat setting. Stir in broccoli florets. Cover and cook 15 minutes more or until broccoli is crisp-tender. Serve over hot rice.

Nutrition Facts per serving: 327 cal., 6 g total fat (2 g sat. fat), 54 mg chol., 476 mg sodium, 37 g carbo., 4 g fiber, 31 g pro. **Daily Values:** 88% vit. C, 8% calcium, 22% iron

This chili-spiced mixture is hearty and delicious over rice for a one-dish dinner sure to please fans of Mexican food. Use instant rice to keep last-minute preparation to a minimum.

MEXICAN STEAK & BEANS

1½	pounds beef flank steak
1	10-ounce can chopped tomatoes with green chile peppers
1	medium onion, chopped
2	cloves garlic, minced
1	tablespoon snipped fresh oregano or 1 teaspoon dried oregano, crushed
1	teaspoon chili powder
1	teaspoon ground cumin
¼	teaspoon salt
¼	teaspoon black pepper
2	small green, red, and/or yellow sweet peppers, cut into strips
1	15-ounce can pinto beans, rinsed and drained
3	cups hot cooked rice
	Crumbled queso fresco* or feta cheese (optional)
	Snipped fresh oregano (optional)

1 Trim fat from meat. Place meat in a 3½- to 4-quart slow cooker. In a bowl stir together undrained tomatoes, onion, garlic, dried oregano (if using), chili powder, cumin, salt, and black pepper. Pour over meat.

2 Cover and cook on low-heat setting for 7 to 9 hours or on high-heat setting for 3½ to 4½ hours.

3 If using low-heat setting, turn to high-heat setting. Add sweet pepper strips and pinto beans. Cover and cook for 30 minutes more. Remove meat; cool slightly. Shred or thinly slice meat across the grain. If using, stir fresh oregano into bean mixture.

4 To serve, spoon rice into soup bowls. Arrange meat on rice. Spoon bean mixture over meat. If desired, sprinkle with cheese and additional oregano.

Nutrition Facts per serving: 345 cal., 9 g total fat (4 g sat. fat), 53 mg chol., 642 mg sodium, 37 g carbo., 4 g fiber, 28 g pro. **Daily Values:** 30% vit. C, 5% calcium, 33% iron

PREP:

25 minutes

COOK:

Low 7 hours, High 3½ hours; plus 30 minutes on High

MAKES:

6 servings

SLOW COOKER:

3½- to 4-quart

*NOTE
Queso fresco (KAY-so FRESK-o), meaning "fresh cheese" in Spanish, can be found in stores that specialize in Mexican food products.

These delicious steak rolls receive Italian flair from the Parmesan cheese and spaghetti sauce. Serve them with your favorite pasta.

SLOW COOKER STEAK ROLLS

PREP:

30 minutes

COOK:

Low 8 hours, High 4 hours

MAKES:

6 servings

SLOW COOKER:

3¹/₂- to 4-quart

IF YOU CAN'T FIND TENDERIZED ROUND STEAK
Ask a butcher to tenderize 2 pounds boneless beef round steak and cut it into six pieces. Or cut 2 pounds boneless beef round steak into six serving-size pieces. Place the meat between two pieces of plastic wrap and, with a meat mallet, pound each piece to ¹/₄- to ¹/₂-inch thickness.

¹/₂	cup shredded carrot
¹/₃	cup chopped zucchini
¹/₃	cup chopped red or green sweet pepper
¹/₄	cup sliced green onions
2	tablespoons grated Parmesan cheese
1	tablespoon snipped fresh parsley
1	clove garlic, minced
¹/₄	teaspoon ground black pepper
6	tenderized beef round steaks (about 2 pounds)
2	cups meatless spaghetti sauce
6	ounces pasta, cooked and drained

1 In a small bowl combine carrot, zucchini, red or green sweet pepper, green onions, Parmesan cheese, parsley, garlic, and black pepper. Spoon ¹/₄ cup of the vegetable filling on each piece of meat. Roll up meat around the filling and tie each roll with clean kitchen string or secure with wooden toothpicks.

2 Transfer meat rolls to a 3¹/₂- to 4-quart slow cooker. Pour spaghetti sauce over the meat rolls.

3 Cover; cook on low-heat setting for 8 to 10 hours or on high-heat setting for to 4 to 5 hours. Discard string or toothpicks. Serve meat rolls with hot cooked pasta.

Nutrition Facts per serving: 372 cal., 10 g total fat (3 g sat. fat), 89 mg chol., 537 mg sodium, 31 g carbo., 4 g fiber, 39 g pro. **Daily Values:** 54% vit. A, 34% vit. C, 6% calcium, 30% iron

Bottom round steak, less expensive than tip round steak, is a good choice for the slow cooker—the moist-heat cooking tenderizes the meat.

HERBED STEAK & MUSHROOMS

2   pounds beef round steak, cut ¾ inch thick

1   medium onion, sliced

2   cups sliced fresh mushrooms or two 4-ounce jars sliced mushrooms, drained

1   10¾-ounce can condensed cream of mushroom soup

¼   cup dry white wine or beef broth

½   teaspoon dried basil, crushed

¼   teaspoon dried marjoram, crushed

¼   teaspoon pepper

3   cups hot cooked noodles

1 Trim fat from meat. Cut meat into serving-size portions. In a 3½- to 4-quart slow cooker place onion slices and mushrooms. Place beef on top of vegetables.

2 In a small bowl combine soup, wine or broth, basil, marjoram, and pepper; pour over meat. Cover; cook on low-heat setting for 8 to 10 hours or on high-heat setting for 4 to 5 hours. Serve meat and sauce over noodles.

Nutrition Facts per serving: 332 cal., 7 g total fat (2 g sat. fat), 87 mg chol., 442 mg sodium, 26 g carbo., 2 g fiber, 38 g pro. **Daily Values:** 1% vit. A, 1% vit. C, 3% calcium, 25% iron

PREP:
15 minutes

COOK:
Low 8 hours, High 4 hours

MAKES:
6 servings

SLOW COOKER:
3½- to 4-quart

Ladle the wonderfully rich gravy over the tender steak and noodles for a home-style main dish your family will love.

ROUND STEAK WITH HERBS

PREP:

10 minutes

COOK:

Low 10 hours, High 5 hours

MAKES:

6 servings

SLOW COOKER:

3¹/₂- to 4-quart

2   pounds beef round steak, cut ¾ inch thick

1   medium onion, sliced

1   10¾-ounce can condensed cream of celery soup

¹/₂   teaspoon dried oregano, crushed

¹/₄   teaspoon dried thyme, crushed

¹/₄   teaspoon pepper

3   cups hot cooked noodles

1 Trim fat from round steak. Cut meat into serving-size portions. Place onion in a 3¹/₂- to 4-quart slow cooker; place meat over onion. In a small bowl combine soup, oregano, thyme, and pepper; pour over meat.

2 Cover; cook on low-heat setting for 10 to 12 hours or on high-heat setting for 5 to 6 hours. Serve meat and gravy over noodles.

Nutrition Facts per serving: 398 cal., 15 g total fat (5 g sat. fat), 120 mg chol., 456 mg sodium, 25 g carbo., 2 g fiber, 38 g pro. **Daily Values:** 3% vit. A, 1% vit. C, 4% calcium, 26% iron

Lemon peel heightens the flavors of this succulent, savory dish. Try it when you have a house full of guests and want to spend time with them rather than in the kitchen.

SHORT RIBS WITH LEEKS

8	ounces fresh mushrooms, halved
4	medium carrots, cut into 1-inch pieces
4	medium leeks, cut into 1-inch slices
2	pounds boneless beef short ribs
2	teaspoons finely shredded lemon peel
$\frac{1}{2}$	teaspoon pepper
$\frac{1}{2}$	teaspoon dried rosemary, crushed
$\frac{1}{2}$	teaspoon dried thyme, crushed
$\frac{1}{4}$	teaspoon salt
$\frac{3}{4}$	cup beef broth
$\frac{1}{3}$	cup dairy sour cream
1	tablespoon all-purpose flour

PREP:
30 minutes

COOK:
Low 7 hours, High 3$\frac{1}{2}$ hours

MAKES:
6 servings

SLOW COOKER:
3$\frac{1}{2}$- to 4-quart

1 Place mushrooms, carrots, and leeks in a 3$\frac{1}{2}$- to 4-quart slow cooker. Place beef over vegetables. Sprinkle with lemon peel, pepper, rosemary, thyme, and salt. Add broth. Cover; cook on low-heat setting for 7 to 8 hours or on high-heat setting for 3$\frac{1}{2}$ to 4 hours.

2 Use a slotted spoon to transfer meat and vegetables to serving dish. Cover to keep warm.

3 Skim fat from remaining cooking liquid. Measure 1 cup cooking liquid. Place in a saucepan. In a small bowl stir together sour cream and flour. Stir into cooking liquid. Cook and stir over medium heat until slightly thickened and bubbly; cook and stir for 1 minute more. Ladle sauce over meat and vegetables.

Nutrition Facts per serving: 173 cal., 8 g total fat (4 g sat. fat), 33 mg chol., 252 mg sodium, 10 g carbo., 2 g fiber, 15 g pro. **Daily Values:** 208% vit. A, 10% vit. C, 5% calcium, 12% iron

If you need to order veal shanks from the butcher, the rich flavor may well be worth the effort. This recipe is similar to osso buco, a classic Italian dish.

OSSO BUCO-STYLE VEAL

PREP:

25 minutes

COOK:

Low 8 hours, High 4 hours

MAKES:

6 servings

SLOW COOKER:

3¹/₂- to 5-quart

2¹/₂ pounds meaty veal shanks, cut into 2-inch pieces
¹/₂ teaspoon pepper
¹/₄ teaspoon salt
2 tablespoons olive oil or cooking oil
5 medium carrots, cut into 2-inch pieces
2 medium potatoes, cut into eighths
1 cup pearl onions, peeled
1 14¹/₂-ounce can diced tomatoes
³/₄ cup dry red wine or water
¹/₂ cup water
2 teaspoons instant beef bouillon granules
5 cloves garlic, halved
¹/₄ cup all-purpose flour
¹/₄ cup water
¹/₄ cup snipped fresh parsley
1 teaspoon finely shredded lemon peel

1 Sprinkle veal shanks with pepper and salt. In a large skillet brown shanks, a few pieces at a time, in hot oil. Drain off fat.

2 In a 3¹/₂- to 5-quart slow cooker place carrots, potatoes, and onions. Add veal. In a bowl stir together the undrained tomatoes, wine or water, the ¹/₂ cup water, bouillon granules, and garlic. Pour over all.

3 Cover; cook on low-heat setting for 8 to 9 hours or on high-heat setting for 4 to 4¹/₂ hours. Use a slotted spoon to transfer meat and vegetables to a serving platter; keep warm.

4 For gravy, skim fat from juices. Transfer 1¹/₂ cups of the juices to a medium saucepan (discard any remaining juices or save for another use). Combine flour and the ¹/₄ cup water; stir into juices in saucepan. Cook and stir over medium heat until thickened and bubbly. Cook and stir for 1 minute more. Stir together parsley and lemon peel; sprinkle over meat and vegetables. Pass gravy.

Nutrition Facts per serving: 262 cal., 6 g total fat (2 g sat. fat), 61 mg chol., 638 mg sodium, 29 g carbo., 4 g fiber, 20 g pro. **Daily Values:** 41% vit. C, 5% calcium, 9% iron

Marinated corned beef is convenient to have on hand because, when refrigerated, it has a shelf life of several weeks.

ZESTY CORNED BEEF SANDWICHES

1	2- to 3-pound corned beef brisket with spice packet
1	cup water
1/4	cup Dijon-style mustard
1/4	teaspoon finely shredded orange peel (optional)
1/3	cup orange juice
4	teaspoons all-purpose flour
8	kaiser rolls, split
6	ounces sliced Muenster cheese

1 Trim fat from meat. Rub brisket with spices from spice packet. If necessary, cut the brisket to fit into a 3½- to 5-quart slow cooker. Place brisket in cooker. Combine water and mustard; pour over brisket.

2 Cover; cook on low-heat setting for 8 to 10 hours or on high-heat setting for 4 to 5 hours. Remove meat; cover to keep warm. Skim fat from juices. Reserve juices; discard whole spices. In a small saucepan stir together orange peel (if desired), orange juice, and flour. Gradually stir in ¼ cup of the reserved cooking juices. Cook and stir until thickened and bubbly. Cook and stir 1 minute more.

3 Thinly slice meat across the grain. Arrange rolls, cut side up, on the unheated rack of a broiler pan. Broil 3 inches from heat for 1 to 2 minutes or until toasted. Remove roll tops from broiler pan. Place sliced meat on roll bottoms. Drizzle about 1 tablespoon of sauce over meat. Top with cheese. Broil 1 to 2 minutes more or until cheese melts. Cover with roll tops.

Nutrition Facts per serving: 464 cal., 24 g total fat (9 g sat. fat), 99 mg chol., 1,539 mg sodium, 33 g carbo., 0 g fiber, 26 g pro. **Daily Values:** 30% vit. C, 17% calcium, 23% iron

PREP:
30 minutes
COOK:
Low 8 hours, High 4 hours
MAKES:
8 servings
SLOW COOKER:
3½- to 5-quart

Use the low-heat setting for this recipe. Beef brisket needs long, slow cooking to become tender.

SAVORY BRISKET SANDWICHES

PREP:

30 minutes

COOK:

Low 10 hours

MAKES:

10 to 12 servings

SLOW COOKER:

3$\frac{1}{2}$- to 5-quart

1 2$\frac{1}{2}$- to 3-pound fresh beef brisket

1 10-ounce can chopped tomatoes with green chile peppers

1 8-ounce can applesauce

$\frac{1}{2}$ of a 6-ounce can ($\frac{1}{3}$ cup) tomato paste

$\frac{1}{4}$ cup soy sauce

$\frac{1}{4}$ cup packed brown sugar

1 tablespoon Worcestershire sauce

10 to 12 hamburger buns, split and toasted

1 Trim fat from meat. If necessary, cut meat to fit into a 3$\frac{1}{2}$- to 5-quart slow cooker. Place meat in cooker. In a bowl stir together the undrained tomatoes, applesauce, tomato paste, soy sauce, brown sugar, and Worcestershire sauce; pour over meat.

2 Cover; cook on low-heat setting about 10 hours or until meat is tender. Remove meat, reserving juices; cover to keep warm.

3 Pour cooking juices into a large saucepan. Bring to boiling; reduce heat. Boil gently, uncovered, for 15 to 20 minutes or until reduced to desired consistency, stirring frequently. Thinly slice meat across the grain. Place meat on split bun half. Drizzle with cooking juices; top with remaining bun half.

Nutrition Facts per serving: 309 cal., 12 g total fat (4 g sat. fat), 78 mg chol., 661 mg sodium, 23 g carbo., 1 g fiber, 27 g pro. **Daily Values:** 14% vit. C, 3% calcium, 24% iron

Serve open-face steak sandwiches with a culinary twist, like those served in bistros. Focaccia bread is available at many bakeries and large supermarkets.

STEAK SANDWICHES WITH RATATOUILLE

1½	pounds beef flank steak
1	teaspoon dried Italian seasoning, crushed
	Salt
	Ground black pepper
1½	cups sliced fresh mushrooms
1	medium onion, finely chopped
2	cloves garlic, minced
1	14½-ounce can tomatoes, cut up
2	tablespoons red wine vinegar
1	medium yellow summer squash or zucchini, halved lengthwise and cut into ¼-inch slices
1	cup green, red, and/or yellow sweet pepper strips
1	6-ounce jar marinated artichoke hearts, drained and halved
	Focaccia (about a 9-inch round)
⅓	cup finely shredded Asiago or Parmesan cheese

PREP:
20 minutes

COOK:
Low 7 hours, High 3½ hours; plus 30 minutes on High

MAKES:
6 to 8 servings

SLOW COOKER:
3½- to 4-quart

1 Trim fat from meat. Sprinkle both sides of meat with Italian seasoning, salt, and black pepper. If necessary, cut meat to fit into a 3½- to 4-quart slow cooker. Place mushrooms, onion, and garlic in cooker. Add meat. Pour undrained tomatoes and vinegar over all.

2 Cover; cook on low-heat setting for 7 to 9 hours or on high-heat setting for 3½ to 4½ hours. If using low-heat setting, turn to high-heat setting. Add squash or zucchini and sweet peppers to cooker. Cover; cook for 30 minutes more.

3 Remove meat from cooker. Stir in drained artichoke hearts. Thinly slice meat across grain. Arrange meat on the focaccia. Using a slotted spoon, place vegetable mixture over meat. Drizzle with the cooking liquid. Sprinkle with cheese. To serve, cut into wedges.

Nutrition Facts per serving: 440 cal., 15 g total fat (5 g sat. fat), 58 mg chol., 369 mg sodium, 46 g carbo., 4 g fiber, 34 g pro. **Daily Values:** 52% vit. C, 14% calcium, 25% iron

Slow cookers produce unbelievably tender meat for these fajitas. Set out the fajita mixture and the toppers and let guests assemble their own. Mix the margaritas for a real fiesta!

BEEF FAJITAS

PREP:

20 minutes

COOK:

Low 8 hours, High 4 hours

OVEN:

350°

MAKES:

6 servings

SLOW COOKER:

3¹/₂- to 4-quart

1¹/₂	pounds beef flank steak
1	cup chopped onions
1	green sweet pepper, cut into ¹/₂-inch pieces
1	or 2 jalapeño peppers, chopped
1	tablespoon snipped fresh cilantro
2	cloves garlic, minced
1	teaspoon chili powder
1	teaspoon ground cumin
1	teaspoon ground coriander
¹/₄	teaspoon salt
1	14¹/₂-ounce can stewed tomatoes, cut up
12	7-inch flour tortillas
1	tablespoon lime juice
	Shredded co-jack cheese (optional)
	Guacamole (optional)
	Dairy sour cream (optional)
	Salsa (optional)

1 Trim fat from meat. Cut flank steak into 6 portions. In a 3¹/₂- to 4-quart slow cooker combine onions, green sweet pepper, jalapeño pepper(s), cilantro, garlic, chili powder, cumin, coriander, and salt. Place meat in cooker. Add undrained tomatoes.

2 Cover; cook on low-heat setting for 8 to 10 hours or on high-heat setting for 4 to 5 hours.

3 To heat tortillas, wrap them in foil and heat in a 350° oven for 10 to 15 minutes or until softened. Remove meat from cooker and shred using two forks. Return meat to cooker. Stir in lime juice.

4 To serve fajitas, use a slotted spoon to fill the warmed tortillas with the beef mixture. If desired, add shredded cheese, guacamole, sour cream, and salsa. Roll up tortillas.

Nutrition Facts per serving: 476 cal., 19 g total fat (7 g sat. fat), 74 mg chol., 542 mg sodium, 40 g carbo., 3 g fiber, 34 g pro. **Daily Values:** 7% vit. A, 46% vit. C, 10% calcium, 35% iron

These kid-pleasing saucy sandwiches are perfect fare for birthday parties and family-style potlucks. This recipe makes a large batch and requires little attention.

SLOPPY JOES

2½	pounds ground beef
1	medium onion, chopped
3	cloves garlic, minced
1¼	cups catsup
1	medium green sweet pepper, chopped
2	stalks celery, chopped
⅓	cup water
3	tablespoons brown sugar
3	tablespoons prepared mustard
3	tablespoons vinegar
3	tablespoons Worcestershire sauce
1	tablespoon chili powder
16	to 20 hamburger buns, split and toasted

1 In a large skillet cook ground beef, onion, and garlic until meat is brown and onion is tender. Drain off fat.

2 In a 3½- to 4-quart slow cooker combine catsup, sweet pepper, celery, water, brown sugar, mustard, vinegar, Worcestershire sauce, and chili powder. Stir in meat mixture.

3 Cover and cook on low-heat setting for 6 to 8 hours or on high-heat setting for 3 to 4 hours. Spoon into toasted buns.

Nutrition Facts per serving: 298 cal., 12 g total fat (4 g sat. fat), 44 mg chol., 579 mg sodium, 31 g carbo., 2 g fiber, 17 g pro. **Daily Values:** 17% vit. C, 8% calcium, 17% iron

PREP:
25 minutes

COOK:
Low 6 hours, High 3 hours

MAKES:
16 to 20 servings

SLOW COOKER:
3½- to 4-quart

MAKE-AHEAD TIP
Prepare Sloppy Joes, but do not prepare buns. Cool meat mixture. Transfer to four-serving freezer containers; seal, label, and freeze for up to 3 months. Thaw overnight in the refrigerator and reheat in a saucepan over medium heat, stirring frequently. Or place frozen meat mixture in a saucepan and add 2 tablespoons water. Heat, covered, over medium heat until thawed, stirring occasionally to break apart meat. Uncover and cook until heated through and of desired consistency. Serve as directed.

There's nothing ho-hum about this familiar favorite! A couple of sassy ingredients—hot-style tomato juice and jalapeño peppers—lend a lively and interesting twist.

SPICY SLOPPY JOES

PREP:

20 minutes

COOK:

Low 6 hours, High 3 hours

MAKES:

8 servings

SLOW COOKER:

3½- to 4-quart

FOR 5- TO 6-QUART SLOW COOKER
Double all ingredients; prepare as directed. Makes 16 servings.

1½	pounds ground beef
1	large onion, chopped (1 cup)
1	clove garlic, minced
1	6-ounce can hot-style tomato juice or vegetable juice
½	cup catsup
½	cup water
2	tablespoons brown sugar
2	tablespoons chopped canned jalapeño peppers (optional)
1	tablespoon prepared mustard
2	teaspoons chili powder
1	teaspoon Worcestershire sauce
8	hamburger buns
	Shredded cheddar cheese (optional)

1 In a large skillet cook ground beef, onion, and garlic until meat is brown and onion is tender. Drain off fat.

2 Meanwhile, in a 3½- to 4-quart slow cooker combine tomato juice, catsup, water, brown sugar, jalapeño peppers (if desired), mustard, chili powder, and Worcestershire sauce. Stir in meat mixture. Cover; cook on low-heat setting for 6 to 8 hours or on high-heat setting for 3 to 4 hours. Arrange rolls, cut sides up, on an unheated rack of a broiler pan. Broil 3 inches from heat for 1 to 2 minutes or until toasted. Remove roll tops from broiler pan. Spoon meat mixture onto toasted roll bottoms and, if desired, sprinkle with cheese. Add top halves of buns.

Nutrition Facts per serving: 327 cal., 13 g total fat (5 g sat. fat), 53 mg chol., 568 mg sodium, 31 g carbo., 2 g fiber, 21 g pro. **Daily Values:** 11% vit. A, 12% vit. C, 8% calcium, 18% iron

Slow-cooked beef becomes so tender that it shreds easily with a fork. This shredded-beef sandwich is topped with aioli (ay-OH-lee), a garlic-flavored mayonnaise.

BEEF SANDWICHES WITH AIOLI

1   2½- to 3-pound boneless beef chuck pot roast

Salt

Pepper

1   medium onion, finely chopped

½   cup water

3   tablespoons Worcestershire sauce

1   teaspoon dried oregano, crushed

3   cloves garlic, minced

12 to 16 kaiser rolls, split and toasted

1   recipe Avocado Aioli

1   cup shredded lettuce

PREP:
25 minutes

COOK:
Low 8 hours, High 4 hours

MAKES:
12 to 16 servings

SLOW COOKER:
3½- to 4-quart

1 Trim fat from meat. Sprinkle with salt and pepper. If necessary, cut roast to fit into a 3½- to 4-quart slow cooker. Place meat in cooker. Add onion, water, Worcestershire sauce, oregano, and garlic.

2 Cover; cook on low-heat setting for 8 to 10 hours or on high-heat setting for 4 to 5 hours. Remove meat from cooker, reserving juices. Using two forks, shred the meat. Serve meat on rolls with Avocado Aioli and shredded lettuce. If desired, drizzle meat with some of the reserved juices to moisten.

AVOCADO AIOLI: In a small bowl slightly mash 2 seeded and peeled ripe medium avocados with a fork. Stir in ⅔ cup finely chopped radishes; 2 tablespoons mayonnaise or salad dressing; 1 tablespoon lemon juice; 1 clove garlic, minced; 2 teaspoons snipped fresh oregano or ½ teaspoon dried oregano, crushed; and ¼ teaspoon salt. Cover and refrigerate for up to 24 hours. Makes 1¼ cups.

Nutrition Facts per serving: 402 cal., 16 g total fat (4 g sat. fat), 70 mg chol., 498 mg sodium, 34 g carbo., 1 g fiber, 29 g pro. **Daily Values:** 19% vit. C, 6% calcium, 34% iron

Incorporate slow cooking into an informal buffet that stars these sandwiches. Add a tray of fresh vegetables, a dip, and a pitcher of iced tea for a serve-yourself menu.

PEPPERY BEEF SANDWICHES

PREP:

15 minutes

COOK:

Low 10 hours, High 5 hours; plus 30 minutes on High

MAKES:

8 servings

SLOW COOKER:

3¹/₂- to 4-quart

TOTING FOODS SAFELY
Slow-cooked foods—especially sandwiches—are great to take to a picnic or party. After the food is completely cooked, wrap the cooker in heavy foil, several layers of newspapers, or a heavy towel. Place the wrapped cooker in an insulated container. The food should stay hot for up to 2 hours (do not hold for longer than 2 hours). If there is electricity at the picnic or party site, plug in the cooker. The food will stay warm for hours on the low-heat setting.

1	2¹/₂- to 3-pound boneless beef chuck pot roast, cut into 1-inch cubes
1	large onion, chopped
¹/₄	cup Worcestershire sauce
1	tablespoon instant beef bouillon granules
1	teaspoon dried oregano, crushed
¹/₂	teaspoon dried basil, crushed
¹/₂	teaspoon dried thyme, crushed
2	cloves garlic, minced
¹/₂	cup chopped pepperoncini (Italian pickled peppers) or other pickled peppers
8	hoagie buns or kaiser rolls, split and toasted
6	ounces sliced Swiss cheese

1 In a 3¹/₂- to 4-quart slow cooker combine meat, onion, Worcestershire sauce, bouillon granules, oregano, basil, thyme, and garlic.

2 Cover; cook on low-heat setting for 10 hours or on high-heat setting for 5 to 6 hours. Stir to break up meat cubes. Stir in chopped pepperoncini. If using low-heat setting, turn to high-heat setting. Cook, uncovered, for 30 minutes more, stirring often to break up meat.

3 Using a slotted spoon, place meat mixture on the bottom half of buns. Top each sandwich with cheese. Broil sandwiches 4 inches from heat about 1 minute or until cheese melts. Add top half of buns.

Nutrition Facts per serving: 493 cal., 18 g total fat (8 g sat. fat), 122 mg chol., 1,009 mg sodium, 35 g carbo., 2 g fiber, 46 g pro. **Daily Values:** 11% vit. C, 20% calcium, 36% iron

This saucy sandwich is perfect to tote to potlucks. To transport the mixture and keep it warm, wrap the slow cooker in several layers of towels.

BARBECUE BRISKET SANDWICHES

1	3-pound beef brisket
1/2	cup water
3	tablespoons vinegar
2	tablespoons Worcestershire sauce
1	teaspoon ground cumin or chili powder
2	cups bottled barbecue sauce
8	kaiser rolls or hamburger buns, split
	Dill pickle slices (optional)
	Red onion slices (optional)
	Additional barbecue sauce (optional)

PREP:
30 minutes

COOK:
Low 10 hours, High 5 hours; plus 30 minutes on High

MAKES:
8 servings

SLOW COOKER:
3 1/2- to 4-quart

1 Trim fat from brisket. Cut brisket, if necessary, to fit in a 3 1/2- to 4-quart slow cooker. Stir together water, vinegar, Worcestershire sauce, and cumin or chili powder. Pour over meat. Cover and cook on low-heat setting for 10 to 12 hours or on high-heat setting for 5 to 6 hours.

2 Remove the meat from the cooker. Discard cooking liquid. Using two forks to pull, shred meat and return it to the cooker. Stir in barbecue sauce. Cover and cook on high-heat setting for 30 minutes or until heated through. Serve atop split kaiser rolls or hamburger buns with pickles, onion, and/or additional sauce, if desired.

Nutrition Facts per serving: 432 cal., 14 g total fat (4 g sat. fat), 92 mg chol., 910 mg sodium, 39 g carbo., 2 g fiber, 36 g pro. **Daily Values:** 11% vit. A, 8% vit. C, 8% calcium, 30% iron

Apples and dried plums add pleasant sweetness to this pork meal. If you serve this with noodles, choose a short, hollow variety, such as penne, to catch the wonderful sauce.

GINGER PORK WITH DRIED PLUMS

PREP:

20 minutes

COOK:

Low 7 hours, High 3¹/₂ hours

MAKES:

6 servings

SLOW COOKER:

3¹/₂- to 4-quart

1   2-pound boneless pork shoulder roast

3   tablespoons quick-cooking tapioca

2   medium cooking apples, peeled, cored, and cut in ¹/₂-inch slices

4   medium carrots, bias-sliced in ¹/₂-inch pieces

1   medium onion, cut in 1-inch chunks

1   cup pitted dried plums, quartered

1   cup chicken broth

³/₄ cup apple juice

1   tablespoon lemon juice

1   teaspoon ground ginger

¹/₄ teaspoon ground cinnamon

¹/₄ teaspoon pepper

¹/₈ teaspoon ground cloves

6   cups hot cooked couscous or noodles

❶ Trim fat from meat; cut pork into 1-inch cubes. Place pork cubes in a 3¹/₂- to 4-quart slow cooker. Sprinkle tapioca over meat. Add apples, carrots, onion, dried plums, chicken broth, apple juice, lemon juice, ginger, cinnamon, pepper, and cloves. Stir to combine.

❷ Cover; cook on low-heat setting for 7 to 8 hours or on high-heat setting for 3¹/₂ to 4 hours. Serve with hot cooked couscous or noodles.

Nutrition Facts per serving: 505 cal., 12 g total fat (4 g sat. fat), 102 mg chol., 297 mg sodium, 76 g carbo., 7 g fiber, 37 g pro. **Daily Values:** 218% vit. A, 15% vit. C, 8% calcium, 21% iron

Add a tossed salad, peas, and hard rolls for an easy, yet special, guest menu. Purchased brownies topped with your favorite ice cream is an ideal way to round out the meal.

PORK ROAST WITH CURRY

1	2-pound boneless pork shoulder roast
$\frac{1}{4}$	cup quick-cooking tapioca
2	cups water
1	cup chopped onions
$\frac{1}{2}$	cup raisins
2	tablespoons curry powder
1	tablespoon instant chicken bouillon granules
$\frac{1}{2}$	teaspoon paprika
2	medium cooking apples, cored and sliced
	Hot cooked rice

PREP:

15 minutes

COOK:

Low 8$\frac{1}{2}$ hours, High 4 hours; plus 30 minutes

MAKES:

6 servings

SLOW COOKER:

3$\frac{1}{2}$- to 4-quart

1 Trim fat from roast; cut pork into 1-inch cubes. Place pork in a 3$\frac{1}{2}$- to 4-quart slow cooker; sprinkle with tapioca. Add water, onions, raisins, curry, bouillon granules, and paprika.

2 Cover; cook on low-heat setting for 8$\frac{1}{2}$ to 9$\frac{1}{2}$ hours or on high-heat setting for 4 to 4$\frac{1}{2}$ hours. Stir in the apple slices; cover and cook 30 minutes more. Serve over rice.

Nutrition Facts per serving: 470 cal., 14 g total fat (5 g sat. fat), 121 mg chol., 546 mg sodium, 48 g carbo., 3 g fiber, 38 g pro. **Daily Values:** 3% vit. A, 8% vit. C, 4% calcium, 23% iron

Scented with fresh basil and shallots, this one-dish dinner suits weeknight entertaining or weekend celebrations because it frees the cook to visit with the guests.

LEMONY PORK & VEGETABLES

PREP:

30 minutes

COOK:

Low 7 hours, High 3½ hours; plus 5 minutes on High

MAKES:

6 servings

SLOW COOKER:

3½- to 6-quart

2	pounds boneless pork shoulder
¼	cup all-purpose flour
½	teaspoon pepper
2	tablespoons cooking oil
1	16-ounce package peeled baby carrots
8	ounces parsnips, cut into ½-inch slices
2	medium shallots, sliced
1	lemon, quartered
¼	cup thinly sliced fresh basil
1	14½-ounce can chicken broth
1⅓	cups quick-cooking couscous

1 Trim fat from pork. Cut pork into 1-inch pieces. Combine flour and pepper in a plastic bag. Add pork, close bag, and shake to coat pork with flour. In a large skillet brown half of the meat in 1 tablespoon of the oil about 5 minutes, turning to brown evenly. Remove from skillet. Brown remaining pork in remaining 1 tablespoon oil about 5 minutes, turning to brown evenly.

2 In a 3½- to 6-quart slow cooker place carrots, parsnips, shallots, lemon, and basil. Place pork on top of vegetables. Pour broth over all.

3 Cover and cook on low-heat setting for 7 to 8 hours or on high-heat setting for 3½ to 4 hours. Discard lemon pieces.

4 Use a slotted spoon to remove pork and vegetables to a serving dish, reserving juices; cover meat and vegetables to keep warm. Measure 1¾ cups of the cooking juices and return to slow cooker. Discard remaining cooking liquid. If using low-heat setting, turn to high-heat setting. Stir in couscous. Cover and cook for 5 minutes more. Fluff couscous with a fork. Serve pork and vegetables over couscous.

Nutrition Facts per serving: 511 cal., 16 g total fat (4 g sat. fat), 101 mg chol., 368 mg sodium, 53 g carbo., 7 g fiber, 38 g pro. **Daily Values:** 44% vit. C, 8% calcium, 20% iron

Simpler than stir-fry, this Asian-inspired meal may become a regular for weeknight dinners.

GINGERED PORK & PINEAPPLE

2	pounds boneless pork shoulder
2	tablespoons cooking oil
¾	cup chicken broth
3	tablespoons quick-cooking tapioca
3	tablespoons low-sodium soy sauce
3	tablespoons oyster sauce (optional)
1	teaspoon grated fresh ginger
1	15¼-ounce can pineapple chunks (juice pack)
4	medium carrots, cut into ½-inch slices (2 cups)
1	large onion, cut into 1-inch pieces
1	8-ounce can sliced water chestnuts, drained
1½	cups fresh snow pea pods or one 6-ounce package frozen pea pods
3	cups hot cooked rice

1 Trim fat from pork. Cut pork into 1-inch pieces. In a large skillet brown half of the pork at a time in hot oil. Drain off fat.

2 In a 3½- to 4-quart slow cooker combine broth, tapioca, soy sauce, oyster sauce (if desired), and ginger. Drain pineapple, reserving juice. Stir juice into broth mixture; cover and chill pineapple chunks. Add carrots, onion, and water chestnuts to cooker. Add pork.

3 Cover and cook on low-heat setting for 6 to 8 hours or on high-heat setting for 3 to 4 hours.

4 If using low-heat setting, turn to high-heat setting. Stir pineapple chunks and the fresh or frozen snow peas into cooker. Cover and cook 10 to 15 minutes more until peas are crisp-tender. Serve over rice.

Nutrition Facts per serving: 402 cal., 11 g total fat (3 g sat. fat), 62 mg chol., 477 mg sodium, 51 g carbo., 5 g fiber, 23 g pro. **Daily Values:** 33% vit. C, 7% calcium, 17% iron

PREP:
30 minutes

COOK:
Low 6 hours, High 3 hours; plus 10 minutes on High

MAKES:
6 to 8 servings

SLOW COOKER:
3½- to 4-quart

FOR A 5- TO 6-QUART SLOW COOKER
Recipe may be doubled.

Skip the steps of soaking and precooking the beans by using lentils rather than the white beans called for in traditional cassoulets. Unlike dried beans, lentils can be added to the cooker right from the package.

CASSOULET-STYLE PORK

PREP:

20 minutes

COOK:

Low 12 hours, High 4$\frac{1}{2}$ hours

MAKES:

4 servings

SLOW COOKER:

3$\frac{1}{2}$- to 4-quart

12	ounces boneless pork shoulder
1	large onion, cut into wedges
2	cloves garlic, minced
2	teaspoons cooking oil
2$\frac{1}{2}$	cups water
1	14$\frac{1}{2}$-ounce can tomatoes, cut up
4	medium carrots and/or parsnips, cut into $\frac{1}{2}$-inch slices
2	stalks celery, thinly sliced
$\frac{3}{4}$	cup dry lentils, rinsed and drained
1$\frac{1}{2}$	teaspoons dried rosemary, crushed
1	teaspoon instant beef bouillon granules
$\frac{1}{4}$	teaspoon salt
$\frac{1}{4}$	teaspoon pepper
	Fresh rosemary sprigs (optional)

1 Trim fat from pork. Cut meat into $\frac{3}{4}$-inch cubes. In a large nonstick skillet brown pork, onion, and garlic in hot oil. Drain off fat. Transfer mixture to a 3$\frac{1}{2}$- to 4-quart slow cooker. Add the water, undrained tomatoes, carrots and/or parsnips, celery, lentils, rosemary, bouillon granules, salt, and pepper.

2 Cover and cook on low-heat setting for 12 hours or on high-heat setting for 4$\frac{1}{2}$ to 5$\frac{1}{2}$ hours. If desired, garnish with fresh rosemary sprigs.

Nutrition Facts per serving: 354 cal., 12 g total fat (3 g sat. fat), 37 mg chol., 641 mg sodium, 37 g carbo., 5 g fiber, 26 g pro. **Daily Values:** 37% vit. C, 8% calcium, 37% iron

Marengo refers to the battle Napoleon won against Austria in 1800. To celebrate the victory, Napoleon's chef invented a dish similar to this one.

PORK & MUSHROOM MARENGO

1½	pounds boneless pork shoulder, cut into 1-inch cubes
1	tablespoon cooking oil
8	ounces fresh mushrooms, sliced
1	medium onion, chopped
1	14½-ounce can tomatoes, cut up
1	cup water
1	tablespoon snipped fresh marjoram or 1 teaspoon dried marjoram, crushed
1½	teaspoons snipped fresh thyme or ½ teaspoon dried thyme, crushed
1	teaspoon instant chicken bouillon granules
¼	teaspoon salt
	Dash pepper
⅓	cup cold water
3	tablespoons all-purpose flour
2	cups hot cooked rice

1 In a large skillet brown meat, half at a time, in hot oil. Drain off fat. In a 3½- to 5-quart slow cooker place mushrooms, onion, and meat. In a bowl combine undrained tomatoes, 1 cup water, dried marjoram and thyme (if using), bouillon granules, salt, and pepper. Pour over all.

2 Cover; cook on low-heat setting for 8 to 10 hours or on high-heat setting for 4 to 5 hours.

3 If using low-heat setting, turn to high-heat setting. In a bowl stir together the ⅓ cup water and flour. Stir flour mixture into pork mixture in cooker. Cover; cook on high-heat setting for 15 to 20 minutes or until thickened. If using, stir in fresh marjoram and thyme. Serve over hot rice.

Nutrition Facts per serving: 481 cal., 22 g total fat (7 g sat. fat), 112 mg chol., 610 mg sodium, 36 g carbo., 2 g fiber, 35 g pro. **Daily Values:** 32% vit. C, 5% calcium, 32% iron

PREP:

25 minutes

COOK:

Low 8 hours, High 4 hours; plus 15 minutes on High

MAKES:

4 servings

SLOW COOKER:

3½- to 5-quart

Substitute other dried fruits for the cherries, such as coarsely chopped cranberries, apricots, golden raisins, or dried mixed fruit—all work equally well.

CHERRIED PORK ROAST

PREP:

20 minutes

COOK:

Low 7 hours, High 3½ hours

MAKES:

6 to 8 servings

SLOW COOKER:

3½- to 6-quart

1   2- to 2½-pound boneless pork shoulder roast

2   tablespoons cooking oil

1   tablespoon quick-cooking tapioca

1   tablespoon snipped fresh thyme or 1 teaspoon dried thyme, crushed

½   teaspoon pepper

1   medium onion, sliced

1   cup dried cherries

½   cup apple juice or apple cider

3   to 4 cups hot cooked rice or noodles

1 Trim fat from meat. If necessary, cut roast to fit into a 3½- to 6-quart slow cooker. In a large skillet brown meat on all sides in hot oil. Drain off fat.

2 Transfer meat to cooker. Sprinkle tapioca, dried thyme (if using), and pepper over meat. Add onion and dried cherries. Pour apple juice or cider over all.

3 Cover; cook on low-heat setting for 7 to 9 hours or on high-heat setting for 3½ to 4½ hours. Transfer meat to serving platter; cover to keep warm.

4 For sauce, skim fat from cooking juices. If using, stir fresh thyme into juices. Serve meat and cooking juices with hot cooked rice or noodles.

Nutrition Facts per serving: 460 cal., 18 g total fat (6 g sat. fat), 99 mg chol., 80 mg sodium, 43 g carbo., 1 g fiber, 29 g pro. **Daily Values:** 2% vit. C, 1% calcium, 18% iron

Fresh fennel is available from September through April in most areas. Choose firm, smooth bulbs without cracks or brown spots. Use the bright green fennel leaves as garnishes.

PORK ROAST WITH FENNEL

1	2- to 2½-pound boneless pork shoulder roast
1	teaspoon fennel seeds, crushed
½	teaspoon garlic powder
½	teaspoon dried oregano, crushed
¼	teaspoon pepper
2	tablespoons cooking oil
1½	pounds small red potatoes, halved
1	large fennel bulb, trimmed and cut into 1-inch pieces
1½	cups water
2	teaspoons instant chicken bouillon granules
½	cup cold water
¼	cup all-purpose flour
	Salt and pepper

PREP:
25 minutes

COOK:
Low 7 hours, High 3½ hours

MAKES:
6 to 8 servings

SLOW COOKER:
3½- to 4-quart

1 Trim fat from meat. In a small bowl combine crushed fennel seeds, garlic powder, oregano, and pepper. Rub about 1 teaspoon of the seasoning mixture evenly over roast; reserve remainder. In a Dutch oven brown meat on all sides in hot oil. Drain off fat.

2 Place potatoes and fennel in a 3½- to 4-quart slow cooker. Sprinkle with remaining seasoning mixture. Stir together the 1½ cups water and bouillon granules; add to cooker. Cut meat, if necessary, to fit into the cooker. Place roast on vegetables.

3 Cover; cook on low-heat setting for 7 to 8 hours or on high-heat setting for 3½ to 4 hours.

4 For gravy, skim fat from cooking juices. Measure 1½ cups of the juices into a medium saucepan. Stir the ½ cup cold water into the flour; stir into reserved juices in saucepan. Cook and stir until thickened and bubbly. Cook and stir 1 minute more. Season to taste with salt and pepper. Pass gravy with meat.

Nutrition Facts per serving: 360 cal., 14 g total fat (4 g sat. fat), 98 mg chol., 453 mg sodium, 23 g carbo., 8 g fiber, 34 g pro. **Daily Values:** 32% vit. C, 4% calcium, 17% iron

This delicious entrée, made even easier by not browning the chops, is terrific for family and guests. Round out the meal with steamed broccoli.

CRANBERRY-ORANGE PORK CHOPS

PREP:

15 minutes

COOK:

Low 7 hours, High 3¹/₂ hours

STAND:

5 minutes

MAKES:

8 servings

SLOW COOKER:

3¹/₂- to 4-quart

1	16-ounce package peeled baby carrots
8	boneless pork chops, cut about ³/₄ inch thick (about 1³/₄ pounds)
1	12-ounce package purchased cranberry-orange sauce
2	tablespoons quick-cooking tapioca
1	teaspoon finely shredded lemon peel
¹/₄	teaspoon ground cardamom
3	fresh plums and/or apricots, pitted and sliced (about 8 ounces)
4	cups hot cooked couscous or rice

1 Place carrots in a 3¹/₂- to 4-quart slow cooker. Top with pork chops.

2 Combine cranberry-orange sauce, tapioca, lemon peel, and cardamom; pour over meat.

3 Cover; cook on low-heat setting for 7 to 8 hours or on high-heat setting for 3¹/₂ to 4 hours. Stir in sliced fruit. Cover; let stand with cooker turned off for 5 minutes. Serve with hot couscous or rice.

Nutrition Facts per serving: 323 cal., 4 g total fat (1 g sat. fat), 55 mg chol., 73 mg sodium, 47 g carbo., 3 g fiber, 22 g pro. **Daily Values:** 289% vit. A, 12% vit. C, 3% calcium, 8% iron

If you can't find chops ¾ inch thick at the meat counter, ask a butcher to cut a bone-in top loin roast into ¾-inch-thick slices.

DIJON PORK CHOPS

1	10¾-ounce can condensed cream of mushroom soup
¼	cup dry white wine or chicken broth
¼	cup Dijon-style mustard
1	teaspoon dried thyme, crushed
1	clove garlic, minced
¼	teaspoon pepper
5	medium potatoes, cut into ¼-inch slices (1⅔ pounds)
1	medium onion, sliced
4	pork loin chops, cut ¾ inch thick

1 In a large bowl combine soup, wine or chicken broth, mustard, thyme, garlic, and pepper. Add potatoes and onion, stirring to coat. Transfer to a 4- to 5-quart slow cooker. Place chops on potatoes.

2 Cover; cook on low-heat setting for 7 to 8 hours or on high-heat setting for 3½ hours.

Nutrition Facts per serving: 385 cal., 12 g total fat (3 g sat. fat), 48 mg chol., 658 mg sodium, 39 g carbo., 4 g fiber, 26 g pro. **Daily Values:** 2% vit. A, 47% vit. C, 9% calcium, 18% iron

PREP:
20 minutes
COOK:
Low 7 hours, High 3½ hours
MAKES:
4 servings
SLOW COOKER:
4- to 5-quart

Try pork spareribs for a variation of this mouth-watering meal. If you prefer a milder flavor, rinse and drain the sauerkraut.

GERMAN-STYLE PORK CHOPS

PREP:

20 minutes

COOK:

Low 5 hours, High 2¹/₂ hours; plus 30 minutes on high

MAKES:

4 servings

SLOW COOKER:

3¹/₂- to 5-quart

CUTTING VEGETABLES TO SIZE

Vegetables intended for slow cookers are cut into bite-size pieces not only for the convenience in eating, but also for better cooking. Some vegetables take longer to cook than meat in slow cookers. By cutting the vegetables into smaller pieces (about ¹/₂ inch thick), you can be sure they will be tender and ready to eat when the meat is done.

2	medium potatoes, peeled and cut into 1-inch cubes
2	medium carrots, cut into ¹/₂-inch pieces
1	medium onion, thinly sliced
4	pork loin chops, cut ³/₄ inch thick (about 1¹/₂ pounds)
¹/₂	cup apple cider or apple juice
¹/₄	cup catsup
¹/₂	teaspoon caraway seeds
1	16-ounce can sauerkraut, drained
2	small cooking apples, peeled, cored, and cut into ¹/₄-inch slices (1¹/₂ cups)
	Snipped fresh parsley (optional)

1 In a 3¹/₂- to 5-quart slow cooker place potatoes, carrots, and onion; top with pork chops. In a small bowl combine apple cider or apple juice, catsup, and caraway seeds; pour over pork chops.

2 Cover; cook on low-heat setting for 5 to 6 hours or on high-heat setting for 2¹/₂ to 3 hours. If using low-heat setting, turn to high-heat setting. Add sauerkraut and apple slices; cover and cook 30 minutes more. Transfer to a serving dish. Garnish with snipped fresh parsley, if desired.

Nutrition Facts per serving: 340 cal., 8 g total fat (3 g sat. fat), 76 mg chol., 1,005 mg sodium, 35 g carbo., 7 g fiber, 34 g pro. **Daily Values:** 158% vit. A, 55% vit. C, 9% calcium, 21% iron

A splash of apple juice provides a fresh taste to this earthy comfort dish. For dessert, toss some sliced apples in the oven to bake while you eat; serve them warm over ice cream.

MUSHROOM SAUCE PORK CHOPS

4	pork loin chops, cut ¾ inch thick
1	tablespoon cooking oil
1	small onion, thinly sliced
2	tablespoons quick-cooking tapioca
1	10¾-ounce can condensed cream of mushroom soup
½	cup apple juice
1	4-ounce can sliced mushrooms, drained
2	teaspoons Worcestershire sauce
¾	teaspoon dried thyme, crushed
¼	teaspoon garlic powder
	Hot cooked rice or mashed potatoes

1 Trim fat from chops. In a skillet brown chops on both sides in hot oil. Drain off fat. In a 3½- to 4-quart slow cooker place onion; add chops. Grind tapioca with a mortar and pestle. In a bowl combine the tapioca, soup, apple juice, mushrooms, Worcestershire sauce, thyme, and garlic powder; pour over chops.

2 Cover; cook on low-heat setting for 8 to 9 hours or on high-heat setting for 4 to 4½ hours. Serve over rice or mashed potatoes.

Nutrition Facts per serving: 354 cal., 16 g total fat (5 g sat. fat), 77 mg chol., 740 mg sodium, 17 g carbo., 1 g fiber, 33 g pro. **Daily Values:** 1% vit. A, 5% vit. C, 6% calcium, 11% iron

PREP:
15 minutes

COOK:
Low 8 hours, High 4 hours

MAKES:
4 servings

SLOW COOKER:
3½- to 4-quart

FOR A 5- TO 6-QUART SLOW COOKER
Use 6 loin pork chops, cut ¾ inch thick. Leave remaining ingredient amounts the same and prepare as directed. Makes 6 servings.

Orange marmalade and mustard team up in a piquant, glistening sauce to top chops and winter squash slices. Steam green beans or asparagus for a side dish.

ORANGE-MUSTARD PORK CHOPS

PREP:

20 minutes

COOK:

Low 5 hours, High 2¹/₂ hours

MAKES:

6 servings

SLOW COOKER:

5- to 6-quart

2   small or medium acorn squash (1¹/₂ to 2 pounds)

1   large onion, halved and sliced

6   pork chops (with bone), cut ³/₄ inch thick (2¹/₂ to 2³/₄ pounds)

¹/₂   cup chicken broth

¹/₃   cup orange marmalade

1   tablespoon honey mustard or Dijon-style mustard

1   teaspoon dried marjoram or thyme, crushed

¹/₄   teaspoon pepper

2   tablespoons cornstarch

2   tablespoons cold water

1 Cut squash in half lengthwise. Discard seeds and membranes. Cut each half into three wedges. In a 5- to 6-quart slow cooker place squash and onion. Trim fat from chops. Place chops on top of squash and onion.

2 In a bowl stir together broth, marmalade, mustard, marjoram or thyme, and pepper. Pour broth mixture over chops and vegetables.

3 Cover and cook on low-heat setting for 5 to 6 hours or on high-heat setting for 2¹/₂ to 3 hours. Lift chops and vegetables from cooker to platter, reserving juices; cover meat and keep warm.

4 For sauce, strain cooking juices into a glass measuring cup; skim off fat. Measure 1³/₄ cups juices, adding water, if necessary. Pour juices into a medium saucepan. Combine cornstarch and the cold water; stir into juices in saucepan. Cook and stir over medium heat until thickened and bubbly; cook and stir for 2 minutes more. Serve sauce with chops and vegetables.

Nutrition Facts per serving: 265 cal., 8 g total fat (3 g sat. fat), 65 mg chol., 168 mg sodium, 27 g carbo., 3 g fiber, 21 g pro. **Daily Values:** 20% vit. C, 7% calcium, 10% iron

Sweet and spicy describes this pork dish. Raisins, dried apples, and orange juice contribute to the sweetness while a jalapeño pepper supplies the heat.

PORK CHOPS WITH SPICED FRUIT

4	pork sirloin chops, cut ¾ inch thick (about 1½ pounds)
¼	teaspoon salt
¼	teaspoon black pepper
1	tablespoon cooking oil
1	6-ounce package dried apples
1	medium onion, chopped
¼	cup golden raisins
¾	cup orange juice
¾	cup chicken broth
1	small jalapeño pepper, seeded and finely chopped
1	clove garlic, minced
1	teaspoon grated fresh ginger
½	teaspoon apple pie spice
	Chicken broth
¼	cup cold water
2	teaspoons cornstarch
1	recipe Orange-Almond Couscous

PREP:
20 minutes
COOK:
Low 6 hours, High 3 hours
MAKES:
4 servings
SLOW COOKER:
3½- to 4-quart

1 Sprinkle chops with salt and black pepper. In a large skillet cook chops in hot oil until brown, turning once. Transfer chops to a 3½- to 4-quart slow cooker. Sprinkle apples, onion, and raisins over chops.

2 In a bowl stir together orange juice, broth, jalapeño pepper, garlic, fresh ginger, and apple pie spice. Pour over all. Cover; cook on low-heat setting for 6 to 8 hours or on high-heat setting for 3 to 4 hours.

3 Transfer chops and fruit to a platter; keep warm. For sauce, measure juices; skim fat from juices. If necessary, add broth to juices to make 1 cup. Place in a saucepan. Combine the ¼ cup cold water and the cornstarch; stir into juices in pan. Cook and stir until thickened. Cook and stir 2 minutes more. Serve chops and fruit with Orange-Almond Couscous. Pass sauce.

ORANGE-ALMOND COUSCOUS: In a saucepan bring 1 cup water and ¼ teaspoon salt to boiling. Remove from heat. Stir in ⅔ cup quick-cooking couscous and 1 teaspoon finely shredded orange peel. Cover; let stand 5 minutes. Stir in 2 tablespoons slivered almonds, toasted.

Nutrition Facts per serving: 462 cal., 12 g total fat (3 g sat. fat), 48 mg chol., 531 mg sodium, 70 g carbo., 11 g fiber, 22 g pro. **Daily Values:** 55% vit. C, 4% calcium, 15% iron

A creamy peanut sauce spiked with crushed red pepper cloaks these fork-tender chops.
Use unsweetened coconut milk, available in the Asian foods section of the supermarket.

ASIAN-STYLE PORK CHOPS

PREP:

20 minutes

COOK:

Low 6 hours, High 3 hours

MAKES:

8 servings

SLOW COOKER:

3¹/₂- to 4-quart

8	boneless pork chops, cut ¾ inch thick (about 2 pounds)
1	tablespoon cooking oil
2	cups shredded carrots
2	medium onions, chopped (1 cup)
1	14-ounce can light coconut milk
¹/₂	cup chicken broth
¹/₂	cup creamy peanut butter
¹/₂	teaspoon crushed red pepper
6	cups hot cooked basmati rice or shredded Chinese cabbage (napa)

1 In a large skillet brown pork chops, half at a time, on both sides in hot oil. Drain off fat.

2 In a 3¹/₂- to 4-quart slow cooker place carrots and onions. In a bowl combine coconut milk, chicken broth, peanut butter, and red pepper; pour over vegetables. Place browned chops on top of vegetables.

3 Cover and cook on low-heat setting for 6 to 8 hours or on high-heat setting for 3 to 4 hours. Serve with rice or cabbage.

Nutrition Facts per serving: 500 cal., 18 g total fat (6 g sat. fat), 62 mg chol., 212 mg sodium, 47 g carbo., 3 g fiber, 32 g pro. **Daily Values:** 7% vit. C, 6% calcium, 12% iron

TRIMMING AND SKIMMING
Slow cooking requires little fat, thanks to low, moist heat. For low-fat meals, choose lean cuts of meat and trim away as much visible fat as possible. For poultry, remove the skin before cooking. Brown the meat in a nonstick skillet sprayed with nonstick cooking spray. Before serving the meal, use a slotted spoon to transfer the meat and vegetables to a serving platter. Pour the cooking liquid into a glass measuring cup and let it stand for a minute or two. Once the fat rises to the top, skim off any visible fat with a metal spoon.

Sweet and sour pineapple sauce provides the theme for this steak dinner. Sprinkle with macadamia nuts for added flavor and crunch.

HAWAIIAN PORK STEAKS

4	pork shoulder steaks, cut ½ inch thick (2½ to 3 pounds)
1	tablespoon cooking oil
1	8-ounce can crushed pineapple (juice pack)
½	cup chopped green sweet pepper
⅓	cup packed brown sugar
2	tablespoons quick-cooking tapioca
2	tablespoons catsup
1	tablespoon soy sauce
½	teaspoon dry mustard
2	cups hot cooked rice
	Chopped, toasted macadamia nuts (optional)

PREP:
15 minutes

COOK:
Low 7 hours, High 3½ hours

MAKES:
4 servings

SLOW COOKER:
3½- to 4-quart

1 Trim fat from steaks. In a large skillet brown steaks on both sides in hot oil. Drain off fat. Transfer steaks to a 3½- to 4-quart slow cooker. If necessary, cut steaks in half to fit the cooker.

2 In a bowl combine undrained pineapple, sweet pepper, brown sugar, tapioca, catsup, soy sauce, and dry mustard; pour over steaks.

3 Cover; cook on low-heat setting for 7 to 8 hours or on high-heat setting for 3½ to 4 hours. Skim and discard fat from sauce. Serve meat and sauce over hot cooked rice. Sprinkle with macadamia nuts, if desired.

Nutrition Facts per serving: 556 cal., 18 g total fat (6 g sat. fat), 126 mg chol., 459 mg sodium, 57 g carbo., 1 g fiber, 40 g pro. **Daily Values:** 4% vit. A, 36% vit. C, 8% calcium, 22% iron

This no-fuss main dish is an old-fashioned favorite. Use leftover ham or look for diced cooked ham at your local supermarket.

HAM & SCALLOPED POTATOES

PREP:

10 minutes

COOK:

Low 7 hours, High 3¹/₂ hours

MAKES:

6 servings

SLOW COOKER:

3¹/₂-quart

1	28-ounce package loose-pack frozen hash brown potatoes with onion and sweet peppers
2	cups (10 ounces) diced cooked ham
1	2-ounce jar diced pimiento, drained
¹/₄	teaspoon black pepper
1	11-ounce can condensed cheddar cheese soup
³/₄	cup milk
1	tablespoon snipped fresh parsley

1 In a 3¹/₂-quart slow cooker combine frozen hash brown potatoes, ham, pimiento, and black pepper.

2 In a medium bowl combine the soup and milk; pour over the potato mixture. Mix to combine. Cover; cook on low-heat setting for 7 to 9 hours or on high-heat setting for 3¹/₂ to 4 hours. Stir in parsley before serving.

Nutrition Facts per serving: 241 cal., 9 g total fat (3 g sat. fat), 37 mg chol., 1,180 mg sodium, 30 g carbo., 3 g fiber, 16 g pro. **Daily Values:** 20% vit. A, 40% vit. C, 10% calcium, 12% iron

Southerners eat black-eyed peas on New Year's Day to ensure good luck throughout the year. Try them southern-style with warm corn bread.

SMOKED PORK HOCKS

1 1/2	cups dry black-eyed peas
4	small smoked pork hocks (1 1/2 pounds)
4	cups reduced-sodium chicken broth
1	medium green sweet pepper, chopped
1	medium onion, chopped
1	stalk celery, chopped
2	bay leaves
1/4	teaspoon ground red pepper
2	cups sliced okra or one 10-ounce package frozen whole okra, thawed and cut into 1/2-inch slices

1 Rinse black-eyed peas; place in a large saucepan. Add enough water to cover peas by 2 inches. Bring to boiling; reduce heat. Simmer, uncovered, for 10 minutes. Remove from heat. Cover and let stand for 1 hour. Drain and rinse peas.

2 In a 3 1/2- to 5-quart slow cooker combine the black-eyed peas, pork hocks, broth, sweet pepper, onion, celery, bay leaves, and red pepper.

3 Cover; cook on low-heat setting for 8 to 10 hours or on high-heat setting for 4 to 5 hours. Add okra. Cover; let stand for 10 minutes or until okra is tender. Remove pork hocks. When cool enough to handle, cut meat off bones; cut meat into bite-size pieces. Discard bones and bay leaves. To serve, stir meat into black-eyed pea mixture.

Nutrition Facts per serving: 191 cal., 3 g total fat (1 g sat. fat), 14 mg chol., 763 mg sodium, 28 g carbo., 7 g fiber, 15 g pro. **Daily Values:** 32% vit. C, 5% calcium, 20% iron

PREP:
25 minutes
COOK:
Low 8 hours, High 4 hours
STAND:
1 hour, 10 minutes
MAKES:
6 servings
SLOW COOKER:
3 1/2- to 5-quart

Start this spicy blended sauce in the morning and then forget about it until dinner! Serve over spaghetti or your favorite sturdy pasta.

SPAGHETTI SAUCE WITH ITALIAN SAUSAGE

PREP:

15 minutes

COOK:

Low 8 hours, High 4 hours

MAKES:

4 to 5 servings

SLOW COOKER:

3¹/₂- to 4-quart

¹/₂	pound bulk Italian sausage
¹/₄	pound ground beef
¹/₂	cup chopped onion
1	clove garlic, minced
1	16-ounce can tomatoes, cut up
1	8-ounce can tomato sauce
1	4-ounce can sliced mushrooms, drained
¹/₂	cup chopped green sweet pepper
2	tablespoons quick-cooking tapioca
1	bay leaf
1	teaspoon dried Italian seasoning, crushed
¹/₈	teaspoon black pepper
	Dash salt
	Hot cooked spaghetti

1 In a skillet cook sausage, ground beef, onion, and garlic until meat is brown and onion is tender; drain off fat.

2 Meanwhile, in a 3¹/₂- to 4-quart slow cooker combine undrained tomatoes, tomato sauce, mushrooms, green sweet pepper, tapioca, bay leaf, Italian seasoning, black pepper, and salt. Stir in meat mixture.

3 Cover; cook on low-heat setting for 8 to 10 hours or on high-heat setting for 4 to 5 hours. Discard bay leaf. Serve over hot cooked spaghetti.

FOR 5- TO 6-QUART SLOW COOKER: Double all ingredients. Prepare as above. Makes 8 to 10 servings.

FOR 1-QUART SLOW COOKER: Omit bay leaf. Halve remaining ingredients. Prepare as above. Cook for 10 to 12 hours. Makes 2 or 3 servings.

Nutrition Facts per serving: 504 cal., 17 g total fat (7 g sat. fat), 56 mg chol., 897 mg sodium, 60 g carbo., 4 g fiber, 23 g pro. **Daily Values:** 15% vit. A, 51% vit. C, 7% calcium, 23% iron

Fresh crimini mushrooms add a twist to this pasta sauce. Substitute button mushrooms if crimini are not available.

FETTUCCINE WITH SAUSAGE & MUSHROOMS

12	ounces bulk sweet Italian sausage
2	cups sliced fresh crimini and/or button mushrooms
1	28-ounce can crushed tomatoes
1	8-ounce can tomato sauce
1	6-ounce can tomato paste
²/₃	cup water
1	medium onion, chopped
1	tablespoon sugar
1	teaspoon dried rosemary, crushed, or 1 tablespoon snipped fresh rosemary
¼	teaspoon pepper
2	cloves garlic, minced
9	to 12 ounces dried fettuccine, spaghetti, or mafalda
	Freshly shredded or grated Parmesan cheese (optional)

PREP:
15 minutes
COOK:
Low 6 hours, High 3 hours
MAKES:
6 to 8 servings
SLOW COOKER:
3¹/₂- to 4-quart

1 In a large skillet brown sausage. Drain off fat. In a 3½- to 4-quart slow cooker combine mushrooms, tomatoes, tomato sauce, tomato paste, water, onion, sugar, dried rosemary (if using), pepper, and garlic. Stir in sausage.

2 Cover; cook on low-heat setting for 6 to 8 hours or on high-heat setting for 3 to 4 hours.

3 Just before serving, stir in fresh rosemary (if using). Cook pasta according to package directions; drain. Serve sausage mixture over pasta. If desired, sprinkle with Parmesan cheese.

Nutrition Facts per serving: 358 cal., 10 g total fat (3 g sat. fat), 22 mg chol., 938 mg sodium, 54 g carbo., 4 g fiber, 14 g pro. **Daily Values:** 47% vit. C, 4% calcium, 28% iron

Enjoy delicious ribs any time of the year without standing over a hot grill. Shred leftovers to serve on sandwich buns.

BARBECUE PORK RIBS

PREP:

25 minutes

COOK:

Low 10 hours, High 5 hours

MAKES:

4 to 6 servings

SLOW COOKER:

3^1/$_2$- to 4-quart

3 to 3^1/$_2$ pounds pork country-style ribs

1 cup catsup

^{1}/$_2$ cup finely chopped onion

^{1}/$_4$ cup packed brown sugar

1 tablespoon Worcestershire sauce

^{1}/$_2$ teaspoon chili powder

^{1}/$_2$ teaspoon liquid smoke

^{1}/$_4$ teaspoon garlic powder

^{1}/$_4$ teaspoon bottled hot pepper sauce

1 Place ribs in a 3^1/$_2$- to 4-quart slow cooker.

2 In a small bowl combine the remaining ingredients. Pour sauce over ribs, turning to coat. Cover; cook on low-heat setting for 10 to 12 hours or on high-heat setting for 5 to 6 hours.

3 Transfer ribs to a serving platter; cover to keep warm. Skim fat from surface of sauce; pour sauce into a medium saucepan. Bring sauce to boiling; reduce heat slightly. Boil gently, uncovered, until thickened to desired consistency, 5 to 7 minutes (should make about 1 cup). Pass sauce with ribs.

Nutrition Facts per serving: 419 cal., 15 g total fat (5 g sat. fat), 121 mg chol., 891 mg sodium, 33 g carbo., 2 g fiber, 38 g pro. **Daily Values:** 15% vit. A, 20% vit. C, 8% calcium, 16% iron

These pork ribs are fall-off-the-bone tender. Round out this menu with baked beans, coleslaw, and cherry cobbler.

COUNTRY-STYLE PORK RIBS

1	large onion, sliced and separated into rings
2½	to 3 pounds pork country-style ribs
1½	cups vegetable juice cocktail
½	of a 6-ounce can (⅓ cup) tomato paste
¼	cup molasses
3	tablespoons vinegar
1	teaspoon dry mustard
¼	teaspoon salt
¼	teaspoon pepper
⅛	teaspoon dried thyme, crushed
⅛	teaspoon dried rosemary, crushed

1 Place onion rings in a 3½- to 6-quart slow cooker. Place ribs over onions in cooker. In a bowl, combine remaining ingredients. Reserve 1 cup for sauce; cover and refrigerate. Pour remaining mixture over ribs. Cover; cook on low-heat setting for 10 to 12 hours or on high-heat setting for 5 to 6 hours.

2 For sauce, in a small saucepan heat reserved mixture to boiling; reduce heat and simmer, uncovered, for 10 minutes. Drain ribs; discard cooking liquid. Serve sauce with ribs.

Nutrition Facts per serving: 354 cal., 13 g total fat (4 g sat. fat), 101 mg chol., 518 mg sodium, 26 g carbo., 2 g fiber, 33 g pro. **Daily Values:** 22% vit. A, 54% vit. C, 10% calcium, 20% iron

PREP:

15 minutes

COOK:

Low 10 hours, High 5 hours; plus 10 minutes on cooktop

MAKES:

4 to 6 servings

SLOW COOKER:

3½- to 6-quart

Celebrate Oktoberfest anytime with this pork and sauerkraut supper. Rye rolls and ice-cold beer make the meal complete.

APPLE-SAUERKRAUT PORK RIBS

PREP:

30 minutes

COOK:

Low 8 hours, High 4 hours; plus 10 minutes on cooktop

MAKES:

4 servings

SLOW COOKER:

3½- to 4-quart

2½	pounds pork country-style ribs, cut in half crosswise and sliced into 1- to 2-rib portions
1	tablespoon cooking oil
2	medium potatoes, cut into ½-inch slices
2	medium carrots, cut into ¼-inch slices
1	medium onion, thinly sliced
1	8-ounce can sauerkraut, rinsed and drained
½	cup apple cider or apple juice
2	teaspoons caraway or fennel seeds
⅛	teaspoon ground cloves
2	tablespoons cold water
1	tablespoon all-purpose flour
½	of a large apple, cored and thinly sliced
	Salt and black pepper (optional)
1	tablespoon snipped fresh parsley

❶ In a large skillet brown pork ribs on both sides in hot oil over medium-high heat. In a 3½- to 4-quart slow cooker place potatoes, carrots, and onion. Add browned pork ribs and sauerkraut. In a bowl combine apple cider, caraway seeds, and cloves. Pour over sauerkraut.

❷ Cover and cook on low-heat setting for 8 to 10 hours or on high-heat setting for 4 to 5 hours. Transfer meat and vegetables to a serving platter, reserving juices; cover meat and keep warm.

❸ For gravy, strain cooking juices into a glass measuring cup. Skim off fat. Measure 1 cup juices, adding water, if necessary. Pour into a saucepan. Combine cold water and flour until smooth; stir into the juices in saucepan. Cook and stir over medium heat until thickened and bubbly. Stir in the apple. Cook and stir for 1 minute more or until heated through. If desired, season to taste with salt and pepper. Stir in parsley just before serving. Serve gravy with ribs and vegetables.

Nutrition Facts per serving: 431 cal., 20 g total fat (7 g sat. fat), 103 mg chol., 371 mg sodium, 32 g carbo., 4 g fiber, 31 g pro. **Daily Values:** 38% vit. C, 4% calcium, 22% iron

Three kinds of pepper—hot pepper sauce, ground red pepper, and black pepper—provide a flavorful kick to these Asian-style ribs.

PEPPERY ASIAN RIBS

3½	pounds pork country-style ribs
6	green onions, chopped
¼	cup reduced-sodium soy sauce
¼	cup molasses
2	tablespoons hoisin sauce
2	tablespoons brown sugar
2	tablespoons white wine vinegar
2	teaspoons toasted sesame oil
2	teaspoons lemon juice
½	teaspoon bottled hot pepper sauce
½	teaspoon ground ginger
½	teaspoon garlic powder
½	teaspoon chili powder
¼	teaspoon ground red pepper
¼	teaspoon ground black pepper
2	cups hot cooked rice

1 Place ribs in a 3½- to 4-quart slow cooker, cutting as necessary to fit.

2 For sauce, in a small bowl combine green onions, soy sauce, molasses, hoisin sauce, brown sugar, vinegar, toasted sesame oil, lemon juice, hot pepper sauce, ginger, garlic powder, chili powder, ground red pepper, and ground black pepper. Pour sauce over ribs in cooker, turning to coat.

3 Cover and cook on low-heat setting for 8 to 10 hours or on high-heat setting for 4 to 5 hours. Transfer ribs to a serving platter and keep warm. Strain sauce; skim off fat. Serve sauce over ribs and hot cooked rice.

Nutrition Facts per serving: 532 cal., 31 g total fat (11 g sat. fat), 69 mg chol., 511 mg sodium, 32 g carbo., 0 g fiber, 30 g pro. **Daily Values:** 6% vit. C, 3% calcium, 18% iron

SWEET 'N' PEPPERY COUNTRY-STYLE RIB SANDWICHES: Prepare the ribs as directed, except omit the hot cooked rice. Remove the cooked meat from the bones. Using two forks, pull meat apart into shreds. To serve, place meat on split and toasted large sesame buns or kaiser rolls. Serve the strained sauce on the side. Makes 8 to 10 sandwiches.

Nutrition Facts per serving: 560 cal., 28 g total fat (9 g sat. fat), 59 mg chol., 710 mg sodium, 44 g carbo., 2 g fiber, 30 g pro. **Daily Values:** 2% vit. A, 5% vit. C, 10% calcium, 20% iron

PREP:
15 minutes
COOK:
Low 8 hours, High 4 hours
MAKES:
6 servings
SLOW COOKER:
3½- to 4-quart

No bones about it—these boneless pork ribs, cooked in a rich tomato sauce, partner perfectly with a mound of hot noodles. Grab extra napkins!

COUNTRY-STYLE RIBS & SAUCE

PREP:

20 minutes

COOK:

Low 8 hours, High 4 hours

MAKES:

6 servings

SLOW COOKER:

3¹/₂- to 4-quart

1	28-ounce can crushed tomatoes
2	stalks celery, chopped
1	medium green sweet pepper, chopped
1	medium onion, chopped
2	tablespoons quick-cooking tapioca
1¹/₂	teaspoons sugar
1¹/₂	teaspoons snipped fresh basil or ¹/₂ teaspoon dried basil, crushed
¹/₂	teaspoon salt
¹/₄	teaspoon black pepper
¹/₄	teaspoon bottled hot pepper sauce
1	clove garlic, minced
2	pounds boneless pork country-style ribs
3	cups hot cooked noodles

1 For sauce, in a 3¹/₂- to 4-quart slow cooker combine undrained tomatoes, celery, sweet pepper, onion, tapioca, sugar, dried basil (if using), salt, black pepper, hot pepper sauce, and garlic. Add ribs; stir to coat ribs with sauce.

2 Cover; cook on low-heat setting for 8 to 10 hours or on high-heat setting for 4 to 5 hours.

3 Transfer meat to a serving platter. Skim fat from sauce. If using, stir fresh basil into sauce. Spoon some of the sauce over meat. Serve with hot cooked noodles. Pass remaining sauce.

Nutrition Facts per serving: 314 cal., 20 g total fat (8 g sat. fat), 79 mg chol., 477 mg sodium, 12 g carbo., 2 g fiber, 21 g pro. **Daily Values:** 52% vit. C, 6% calcium, 15% iron

For variety, try mesquite- or hickory-flavored barbecue sauce. Complement the pork with coleslaw piled on the sandwiches or served alongside.

BBQ PORK SANDWICHES

2   large green sweet peppers, cut into strips (2½ cups)

1   medium onion, thinly sliced and separated into rings (1 cup)

2   tablespoons quick-cooking tapioca

1   2½- to 3-pound pork shoulder roast

1   cup barbecue sauce

3   to 4 teaspoons chili powder

10   to 12 kaiser rolls, split and toasted

     Coleslaw, drained (optional)

1 In a 3½- to 5-quart slow cooker combine sweet pepper strips and onion rings. Sprinkle tapioca over vegetables. Trim fat from roast. If necessary, cut roast to fit into cooker. Place roast over vegetables.

2 In a medium bowl combine barbecue sauce and chili powder. Pour the sauce over the meat.

3 Cover; cook on low-heat setting for 11 to 12 hours or on high-heat setting for 5½ to 6 hours. Remove roast from cooker; thinly slice or shred the meat. Skim fat from sauce. Return sauce and meat to cooker; cover. Turn cooker to high and cook 15 to 30 minutes more to heat through.

4 Serve on kaiser rolls; top with drained coleslaw, if desired.

Nutrition Facts per serving: 309 cal., 8 g total fat (2 g sat. fat), 47 mg chol., 576 mg sodium, 38 g carbo., 2 g fiber, 20 g pro. **Daily Values:** 13% vit. A, 43% vit. C, 8% calcium, 18% iron

PREP:

20 minutes

COOK:

Low 11 hours, High 5½ hours, plus 15 minutes on High

MAKES:

10 to 12 servings

SLOW COOKER:

3½- to 5-quart

Accompany these spicy pork sandwiches with a mixed fruit salad and mango iced tea. For dessert, serve almond cookies.

ORIENTAL PORK SANDWICHES

PREP:

25 minutes

COOK:

Low 10 hours, High 5$^{1}/_2$ hours

MAKES:

6 to 8 servings

SLOW COOKER:

3$^{1}/_2$- to 4-quart

1	2$^{1}/_2$- to 3-pound pork shoulder roast
1	cup apple juice or apple cider
2	tablespoons soy sauce
2	tablespoons hoisin sauce
1$^{1}/_2$	teaspoons five-spice powder*
6	to 8 kaiser rolls, split and toasted
1$^{1}/_2$	to 2 cups shredded Chinese cabbage (napa) or packaged shredded broccoli (broccoli slaw mix)

1 Trim fat from meat. If necessary, cut roast to fit into a 3$^{1}/_2$- to 4-quart slow cooker. Place meat in cooker. In a small bowl combine apple juice or cider, soy sauce, hoisin sauce, and five-spice powder. Pour over roast.

2 Cover; cook on low-heat setting for 10 to 12 hours or on high-heat setting for 5$^{1}/_2$ to 6 hours.

3 Remove meat from cooker, reserving juices. Remove meat from bone; discard bone. Using two forks, shred meat. Place meat on roll bottoms. Top with shredded Chinese cabbage or broccoli; add roll tops. Skim fat from juices. Serve juices in individual serving bowls for dipping.

Nutrition Facts per serving: 366 cal., 9 g total fat (3 g sat. fat), 73 mg chol., 818 mg sodium, 39 g carbo., 2 g fiber, 29 g pro. **Daily Values:** 5% vit. A, 11% vit. C, 9% calcium, 20% iron

*FIVE·SPICE POWDER
In a blender container combine 3 tablespoons ground cinnamon, 6 star anise or 2 teaspoons anise seeds, 1$^{1}/_2$ teaspoons fennel seeds, 1$^{1}/_2$ teaspoons whole Szechwan pepper or whole black pepper, and $^{3}/_4$ teaspoon ground cloves. Cover and blend to a fine powder. Store in a tightly covered container. Makes $^{1}/_3$ cup.

Mango, onion, and sweet pepper balance the flavor of the jerk seasoning. Serve with sweet potato chips for a change from regular potato chips.

JAMAICAN JERK PORK SANDWICHES

1	1½- to 2-pound boneless pork shoulder roast
1	tablespoon Jamaican jerk seasoning
¼	teaspoon dried thyme, crushed
1	cup water
1	tablespoon lime juice
6	to 8 kaiser rolls, split and toasted
6	to 8 lettuce leaves (optional)
6	thinly sliced red or green sweet pepper rings (optional)
1	medium mango, peeled and thinly sliced (optional)
1	recipe Lime Mayo

1 Trim fat from meat. Rub jerk seasoning evenly over roast. Place meat in a 3½- to 4-quart slow cooker. Sprinkle meat with thyme; pour water into cooker.

2 Cover; cook on low-heat setting for 8 to 10 hours or on high-heat setting for 4 to 5 hours. Remove meat from cooker, reserving juices. Shred meat, discarding any fat. Skim fat from juices. Add enough of the juices to moisten meat (about ½ cup). Stir lime juice into meat.

3 To serve, use a slotted spoon to place pork mixture onto roll bottoms. If desired, layer with lettuce leaves, sweet pepper rings, and mango slices. Spoon Lime Mayo onto each sandwich; cover with roll tops.

LIME MAYO: In a bowl stir together ½ cup light mayonnaise dressing or regular mayonnaise, ¼ cup finely chopped red onion, ¼ teaspoon finely shredded lime peel, 1 tablespoon lime juice, and 1 clove garlic, minced. Cover; chill until ready to serve.

Nutrition Facts per serving: 430 cal., 21 g total fat (6 g sat. fat), 74 mg chol., 609 mg sodium, 34 g carbo., 0 g fiber, 26 g pro. **Daily Values:** 4% vit. C, 6% calcium, 22% iron

PREP:
30 minutes
COOK:
Low 8 hours, High 4 hours
MAKES:
6 to 8 servings
SLOW COOKER:
3½- to 4-quart

Root beer gives these pork sandwiches a rich color and pleasant sweetness. Root beer concentrate, from the spice section of a supermarket, intensifies the flavor.

PULLED PORK BBQ SANDWICHES

PREP:

15 minutes

COOK:

Low 8 hours, High 4 hours; plus 30 minutes on cooktop

MAKES:

8 to 10 sandwiches

SLOW COOKER:

3¹/₂- to 5-quart

*NOTE
Do not substitute diet root beer.

1	**2¹/₂- to 3-pound pork sirloin roast**
¹/₂	teaspoon salt
¹/₂	teaspoon ground black pepper
1	tablespoon cooking oil
2	medium onions, cut into thin wedges
1	cup root beer*
2	tablespoons minced garlic
3	cups root beer (two 12-ounce cans or bottles)*
1	cup bottled chili sauce
¹/₄	teaspoon root beer concentrate (optional)
	Several dashes bottled hot pepper sauce (optional)
8	to 10 hamburger buns, split (and toasted, if desired)
	Lettuce leaves (optional)
	Tomato slices (optional)

1 Trim fat from meat. If necessary, cut roast to fit into a 3¹/₂- to 5-quart slow cooker. Sprinkle meat with the salt and pepper. In a large skillet brown meat on all sides in hot oil. Drain off fat. Transfer meat to cooker. Add onions, the 1 cup root beer, and garlic.

2 Cover and cook on low-heat setting for 8 to 10 hours or on high-heat setting for 4 to 5 hours.

3 Meanwhile, for sauce, in a medium saucepan combine the 3 cups root beer and the chili sauce. Bring to boiling; reduce heat. Boil gently, uncovered, stirring occasionally, about 30 minutes or until mixture is reduced to 2 cups. If desired, add root beer concentrate and bottled hot pepper sauce.

4 Transfer roast to a cutting board or serving platter. Using a slotted spoon, remove onions from cooking juices and place on serving platter. Discard juices. Using two forks, pull meat apart into shreds. To serve, line buns with lettuce leaves and tomato slices, if desired. Add meat and onions; spoon on sauce.

Nutrition Facts per serving: 356 cal., 10 g total fat (3 g sat. fat), 59 mg chol., 786 mg sodium, 44 g carbo., 1 g fiber, 22 g pro. **Daily Values:** 9% vit. C, 4% calcium, 13% iron

These southern-style barbecue sandwiches carry just the right amount of heat. Serve with coleslaw and corn on the cob.

SHREDDED PORK SANDWICHES

1	2½- to 3-pound pork sirloin roast
½	teaspoon garlic powder
½	teaspoon ground ginger
½	teaspoon dried thyme, crushed
1	cup chicken broth
½	cup vinegar
½	teaspoon ground red pepper
8	to 10 hamburger buns, split and toasted

PREP:
15 minutes

COOK:
Low 8 hours, High 4 hours

MAKES:
8 to 10 servings

SLOW COOKER:
3½- to 4-quart

1 Remove string from meat, if present. Trim fat from pork roast. If necessary, cut roast to fit into slow cooker. In a small bowl combine garlic powder, ginger, and thyme. Sprinkle mixture over meat and rub in with fingers.

2 Transfer meat to a 3½- to 4-quart slow cooker. Pour broth over roast. Cover; cook on low-heat setting for 8 to 10 hours or on high-heat setting for 4 to 5 hours.

3 Remove meat from cooker, reserving cooking liquid. Skim off fat from juices. Using two forks, shred meat and place in a large bowl. Add 1 cup of the cooking liquid, the vinegar, and red pepper to meat in bowl; toss to combine. Serve on buns.

Nutrition Facts per serving: 292 cal., 7 g total fat (2 g sat. fat), 79 mg chol., 402 mg sodium, 23 g carbo., 1 g fiber, 31 g pro. **Daily Values:** 1% vit. A, 2% vit. C, 8% calcium, 15% iron

Perfect for a casual weekend (or weeknight) dinner, these mildly spicy sandwiches will satisfy everyone. Set out some bowls of potato chips and cold drinks—dinner is done!

SAUCY SAUSAGE SANDWICHES

PREP:
20 minutes

COOK:
Low 8 hours, High 4 hours

MAKES:
8 servings

SLOW COOKER:
3$\frac{1}{2}$- to 4-quart

**FOR 5- TO 6-QUART
SLOW COOKER**
Double all ingredients. Prepare as directed. Makes 16 servings.

1   pound bulk Italian sausage
$\frac{1}{2}$ pound ground beef
1   cup chopped onion
1   14$\frac{1}{2}$-ounce can diced tomatoes, drained
1   8-ounce can tomato sauce
1   4$\frac{1}{2}$-ounce jar sliced mushrooms, drained
$\frac{1}{2}$ cup sliced pitted ripe olives
4   teaspoons quick-cooking tapioca
1   teaspoon sugar
1   teaspoon dried oregano, crushed
$\frac{1}{8}$ teaspoon ground black pepper
    Dash garlic powder
8   French rolls, split
6   ounces sliced mozzarella cheese

1 In a large skillet cook sausage, ground beef, and onion until meat is brown and onion is tender. Drain off fat.

2 Meanwhile, in a 3$\frac{1}{2}$- to 4-quart slow cooker combine the drained tomatoes, tomato sauce, mushrooms, olives, tapioca, sugar, oregano, pepper, and garlic powder. Stir in meat mixture. Cover; cook on low-heat setting for 8 to 10 hours or on high-heat setting for 4 to 5 hours.

3 Using a fork, hollow out bottom halves of rolls, leaving $\frac{1}{4}$-inch shells (reserve bread pieces for another use). Place cheese in bottom halves, trimming as necessary to fit. Spoon meat mixture into rolls. Cut any remaining cheese into strips and place over meat mixture. Cover with bun tops.

Nutrition Facts per serving: 425 cal., 22 g total fat (9 g sat. fat), 68 mg chol., 1,029 mg sodium, 29 g carbo., 3 g fiber, 23 g pro. **Daily Values:** 3% vit. A, 9% vit. C, 20% calcium, 16% iron

Take these spicy sandwiches to your next block party. Tortilla chips, guacamole, and pasta salad are simple accompaniments.

SPICY CHORIZO SANDWICHES

1	pound chorizo sausage or bulk Italian sausage
2	pounds ground raw turkey or lean ground beef
2	cups chopped onions
1	15-ounce can tomato sauce
1	14½-ounce can diced tomatoes
2	tablespoons quick-cooking tapioca
2	tablespoons finely chopped, seeded jalapeño peppers
2	teaspoons sugar
2	teaspoons dried oregano, crushed
16	French-style rolls, split lengthwise
	Sliced, pitted ripe olives; shredded Monterey Jack cheese; and/or sliced mild cherry peppers (optional)

PREP:
25 minutes
COOK:
Low 8 hours, High 4 hours
MAKES:
16 servings
SLOW COOKER:
5- to 6-quart

1 Remove casing from chorizo (if using). In a large skillet cook sausage and ground turkey or beef, half at a time, until meat is no longer pink. Drain off fat. In a 5- to 6-quart slow cooker combine onions, tomato sauce, undrained tomatoes, tapioca, jalapeño peppers, sugar, and oregano. Stir in the meat.

2 Cover; cook on low-heat setting for 8 to 10 hours or on high-heat setting for 4 to 5 hours. Using a fork, hollow out bottom halves of rolls, leaving ¼-inch shells. Spoon meat mixture into roll cavity and cover with top half of roll. If desired, serve with sliced olives, shredded cheese, and/or cherry peppers.

Nutrition Facts per serving: 253 cal., 8 g total fat (2 g sat. fat), 21 mg chol., 593 mg sodium, 35 g carbo., 1 g fiber, 14 g pro. **Daily Values:** 15% vit. C, 6% calcium, 17% iron

Boneless ribs are easy to prepare and eat. Present these pork sandwiches family-style—on a platter. Or serve the ribs over a bed of buttered egg noodles tossed with poppy seeds.

SPICED RIB SANDWICHES

PREP:

25 minutes

COOK:

Low 8 hours, High 4 hours

MAKES:

8 servings

SLOW COOKER:

3¹/₂- to 4-quart

RECIPE ADAPTATIONS
Follow these tips to prepare your favorite entrées in a slow cooker: Use recipes that call for less tender cuts of meat, which benefit from long cooking times. Find a recipe in this book that is similar to a favorite of yours to get a sense of appropriate quantities and liquid levels. Cut vegetables into similar-size pieces to those in your recipe; place them in the bottom of the cooker. Trim and brown the meat (if desired), then place on top of vegetables. Reduce the liquids called for in your recipe by about half (except dishes that contain long grain rice). Follow the suggested cooking times for the recipe listed in this book.

2 to 2½ pounds boneless pork country-style ribs

1 medium onion, sliced

½ cup catsup

¼ cup plum sauce

¼ cup chili sauce

¼ cup water

2 tablespoons brown sugar

½ teaspoon ground cinnamon or Five-Spice Powder (see recipe, page 216)

8 French rolls, split and toasted

1 Place ribs in a 3½- to 4-quart slow cooker. Top with onion. Combine catsup, plum sauce, chili sauce, water, brown sugar, and cinnamon. Pour over ribs.

2 Cover; cook on low-heat setting for 8 to 10 hours or on high-heat setting for 4 to 5 hours. Remove meat from cooker, reserving juices. Using two forks, shred meat. Skim fat from juices; pour juices into a medium saucepan. Simmer for 5 to 10 minutes or until slightly thickened. Place meat on roll bottoms; cover with roll tops. Serve juices in bowls for dipping.

Nutrition Facts per serving: 362 cal., 17 g total fat (6 g sat. fat), 60 mg chol., 612 mg sodium, 34 g carbo., 1 g fiber, 19 g pro. **Daily Values:** 7% vit. C, 6% calcium, 15% iron

With cocktail wieners and wagon wheel pasta, this dish is delightful for a children's party. Fill out the menu with fruit salad, chips, and brownies.

SAUCY PASTA FRANKS

2   15-ounce cans tomato sauce with chunky tomatoes

1   14½-ounce can Mexican-style stewed tomatoes

1   15-ounce can red kidney beans, rinsed and drained

½   cup water

1   medium onion, chopped

½   cup chopped green sweet pepper

2   teaspoons chili powder

1   clove garlic, minced

1   5.3-ounce package (16) cocktail wieners

8   ounces dried wagon wheel pasta

     Shredded cheddar or Monterey Jack cheese (optional)

     Dairy sour cream (optional)

1 In a 3½- to 4-quart slow cooker combine tomato sauce, undrained stewed tomatoes, beans, water, onion, sweet pepper, chili powder, and garlic. Stir in wieners.

2 Cover; cook on low-heat setting for 7 to 9 hours or on high-heat setting for 3 to 4 hours.

3 Just before serving, cook pasta according to package directions; drain. Stir cooked pasta into wiener mixture. Spoon into bowls. If desired, serve with shredded cheese and sour cream.

Nutrition Facts per serving: 350 cal., 8 g total fat (3 g sat. fat), 13 mg chol., 1,489 mg sodium, 57 g carbo., 7 g fiber, 15 g pro. **Daily Values:** 74% vit. C, 5% calcium, 29% iron

PREP:

15 minutes

COOK:

Low 7 hours, High 3 hours

MAKES:

6 servings

SLOW COOKER:

3½- to 4-quart

Ask the butcher for lamb foreshanks, which are smaller than hindshanks. On the side, mashed potatoes are a good alternative to the polenta.

LAMB SHANKS WITH POLENTA

PREP:

15 minutes

COOK:

Low 11 hours, High 5$\frac{1}{2}$ hours

MAKES:

4 to 6 servings

SLOW COOKER:

5- to 6-quart

1	pound boiling onions, peeled
$\frac{1}{2}$	cup pitted Greek black olives
4	meaty lamb foreshanks (about 4 pounds) or meaty veal shank crosscuts (about 3 pounds)
4	cloves garlic, minced
2	teaspoons dried rosemary, crushed
$\frac{1}{2}$	teaspoon salt
$\frac{1}{4}$	teaspoon pepper
1	cup chicken broth
1$\frac{1}{4}$	cups quick-cooking polenta mix
	Snipped fresh flat-leaf parsley (optional)

1 Place onions and olives in a 5- to 6-quart slow cooker. Arrange lamb in cooker. Sprinkle with garlic, rosemary, salt, and pepper. Pour chicken broth over all. Cover; cook on low-heat setting for 11 to 12 hours or on high-heat setting for 5$\frac{1}{2}$ to 6 hours.

2 Meanwhile, prepare polenta according to package directions; set aside. With a slotted spoon, remove lamb, onions, and olives from broth mixture to a serving dish. Skim fat from cooking liquid. Serve meat, onions, and olives with polenta. Strain broth mixture, if desired; pass with meat. If desired, garnish with fresh parsley.

Nutrition Facts per serving: 701 cal., 21 g total fat (7 g sat. fat), 136 mg chol., 768 mg sodium, 79 g carbo., 12 g fiber, 46 g pro. **Daily Values:** 11% vit. C, 8% calcium, 24% iron

Perfect for a simple Sunday supper, the lamb shanks cook while you hike in the woods, play a game of flag football, or snuggle in to watch a favorite movie.

BARLEY LAMB SHANKS

3	to 3½ pounds lamb shanks or beef shank crosscuts
1	tablespoon cooking oil
1	cup regular barley
1	medium onion, chopped
4	carrots, cut into ½-inch slices (2 cups)
3	stalks celery, cut into ½-inch slices (1½ cups)
1	14-ounce can chicken broth
1	14½-ounce can diced tomatoes
⅓	cup water
½	teaspoon pepper
2	tablespoons balsamic vinegar (optional)

1 In a large skillet brown the lamb shanks in hot oil over medium heat. Drain off fat.

2 In a 5- to 6-quart slow cooker combine barley, onion, carrots, celery, broth, undrained tomatoes, water, and pepper. Add lamb shanks.

3 Cover and cook on low-heat setting for 7 to 9 hours or until lamb pulls easily from bones and barley is tender. Transfer meat to a serving platter. Skim off fat from vegetable-barley mixture. Stir in balsamic vinegar, if desired. Serve with lamb.

Nutrition Facts per serving: 370 cal., 8 g total fat (2 g sat. fat), 99 mg chol., 529 mg sodium, 36 g carbo., 7 g fiber, 37 g pro. **Daily Values:** 24% vit. C, 7% calcium, 24% iron

PREP:
20 minutes

COOK:
Low 7 hours

MAKES:
6 to 8 servings

SLOW COOKER:
5- to 6-quart

KEEPING MEAT WARM
Few things are more satisfying than a piping-hot meal. To ensure that the meat and vegetables stay warm while thickening the gravy or making a sauce, warm the platter or serving dish by running it under hot water and drying it quickly with a towel. Arrange the meat and vegetables on the platter and cover it with foil while making the sauce.

Spoon golden gravy flavored with mustard and lemon over this tender lamb and roasted vegetables.

LEMON-MUSTARD LAMB ROAST

PREP:

25 minutes

COOK:

Low 8 hours, High 4 hours; plus 30 minutes on High

MAKES:

4 servings

SLOW COOKER:

3¹/₂- to 4-quart

1	2- to 2¹/₂-pound boneless lamb shoulder roast
¹/₂	teaspoon lemon-pepper seasoning
¹/₂	teaspoon dry mustard
1	tablespoon cooking oil
4	medium potatoes, quartered
1¹/₂	cups whole, tiny carrots
1	cup chicken broth
¹/₄	cup Dijon-style mustard
2	tablespoons quick-cooking tapioca
1	tablespoon lemon juice
¹/₂	teaspoon dried rosemary, crushed
¹/₄	teaspoon finely shredded lemon peel
¹/₄	teaspoon black pepper
2	cloves garlic, minced
1	9-ounce package frozen artichoke hearts, thawed

1 Trim fat from lamb roast. If necessary, cut roast to fit into a 3¹/₂- to 4-quart slow cooker. In a small bowl combine lemon-pepper seasoning and dry mustard. Sprinkle evenly over sides of lamb roast; rub lightly with fingers. In a large skillet brown the roast on all sides in hot oil. Drain off fat.

2 Meanwhile, place potatoes and carrots in cooker. Place meat on vegetables. In a bowl combine broth, Dijon-style mustard, tapioca, lemon juice, rosemary, lemon peel, black pepper, and garlic; pour over all in cooker.

3 Cover; cook on low-heat setting for 8 to 10 hours or on high-heat setting for 4 to 5 hours.

4 If using low-heat setting, turn to high-heat setting. Add artichoke hearts. Cover and cook 30 minutes longer. Remove roast from cooker and remove string or netting if present. Skim fat from gravy and serve with sliced roast and vegetables.

Nutrition Facts per serving: 539 cal., 19 g total fat (5 g sat. fat), 148 mg chol., 694 mg sodium, 40 g carbo., 8 g fiber, 51 g pro. **Daily Values:** 232% vit. A, 45% vit. C, 12% calcium, 32% iron

The combination of spices and flavors adds exotic richness to this roast. For convenience and extra vitamins, leave the skins on the potatoes.

SAUCY LAMB & VEGETABLES

1½	pounds tiny new potatoes or 5 medium potatoes
2	cups packaged, peeled baby carrots
2	small onions, cut into wedges
1	tablespoon honey
1	tablespoon grated fresh ginger or ¾ teaspoon ground ginger
½	teaspoon salt
½	teaspoon anise seeds or ¼ teaspoon ground allspice
½	teaspoon ground cinnamon
⅛	to ¼ teaspoon ground red pepper
1	2½- to 3-pound boneless lamb shoulder roast
1¼	cups beef broth
½	cup cold water
¼	cup all-purpose flour
1	teaspoon finely shredded orange peel

PREP:

15 minutes

COOK:

Low 10 hours, High 5 hours; plus 10 minutes on cooktop

MAKES:

6 to 8 servings

SLOW COOKER:

3½- to 5-quart

1 Remove a narrow strip of peel from the center of each new potato, or peel (if desired) and quarter each medium potato. In a 3½- to 5-quart slow cooker place potatoes, carrots, and onions. Drizzle with honey and sprinkle with ginger, salt, anise seeds or allspice, cinnamon, and red pepper.

2 Trim the fat from the lamb roast. If necessary, cut roast to fit into slow cooker. Place meat over vegetables. Pour broth over meat and vegetables. Cover; cook on low-heat setting for 10 to 12 hours or on high-heat setting for 5 to 6 hours.

3 Remove meat and vegetables with slotted spoon; keep warm. For gravy, skim fat from juices; measure 1½ cups juices. In a small saucepan, combine cold water, flour, and orange peel. Stir in the reserved 1½ cups juices. Cook and stir until thickened and bubbly. Cook and stir 1 minute more. Season to taste. Pass gravy with the meat and vegetables.

Nutrition Facts per serving: 408 cal., 12 g total fat (4 g sat. fat), 123 mg chol., 519 mg sodium, 34 g carbo., 4 g fiber, 41 g pro. **Daily Values:** 205% vit. A, 33% vit. C, 6% calcium, 26% iron

Mediterranean flavors contribute to this robust dish, which has chunks of lamb combined with spinach, orzo, and feta cheese.

LAMB WITH SPINACH & ORZO

PREP:

20 minutes

COOK:

Low 8 hours, High 4 hours

MAKES:

8 servings

SLOW COOKER:

3¹/₂- to 6-quart

1	3- to 3¹/₂-pound lamb shoulder roast (bone-in)
1	tablespoon dried oregano, crushed
1	tablespoon finely shredded lemon peel
4	cloves garlic, minced
¹/₄	teaspoon salt
¹/₄	cup lemon juice
1	10-ounce bag prewashed fresh spinach, chopped
5	cups cooked orzo
4	ounces crumbled feta cheese

1 Trim fat from roast. If necessary, cut roast to fit into a 3¹/₂- to 6-quart slow cooker. In a small bowl combine oregano, lemon peel, garlic, and salt. Sprinkle evenly over sides of lamb roast; rub lightly with fingers. Place lamb in cooker. Sprinkle lamb with lemon juice.

2 Cover and cook on low-heat setting for 8 to 10 hours or on high-heat setting for 4 to 5 hours.

3 Remove lamb from cooker. Remove meat from bones; discard bones and fat. Chop meat; set aside. Skim fat from juices. Add spinach to cooking juices in cooker, stirring until spinach is wilted. Add cooked orzo, feta, and lamb; stir to combine.

Nutrition Facts per serving: 409 cal., 16 g total fat (7 g sat. fat), 120 mg chol., 338 mg sodium, 25 g carbo., 5 g fiber, 38 g pro. **Daily Values:** 38% vit. A, 17% vit. C, 14% calcium, 34% iron

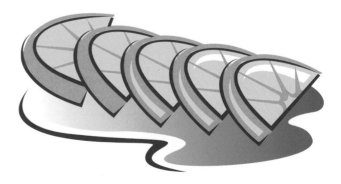

Curry adds intrigue to this colorful main dish. On the side, try a fresh spinach, cucumber, and tomato salad.

BROWN RICE RISOTTO WITH LAMB

1	2- to 2½-pound boneless lamb shoulder roast
1	tablespoon cooking oil
2½	cups hot-style vegetable juice
1	cup regular brown rice
1	teaspoon curry powder
¼	teaspoon salt
2	medium carrots, diced
1	medium green sweet pepper, diced

1 Trim fat from lamb roast. In a large skillet brown roast on all sides in hot oil. Drain off fat.

2 Meanwhile, in a 3½- to 4-quart slow cooker combine vegetable juice, uncooked rice, curry powder, and salt. Add carrots. Place meat over carrots. Cover; cook on low-heat setting for 8 to 9 hours or on high-heat setting for 4 to 4½ hours.

3 Add the green sweet pepper to the cooker. Cover and let stand 5 to 10 minutes.

Nutrition Facts per serving: 299 cal., 12 g total fat (3 g sat. fat), 99 mg chol., 537 mg sodium, 15 g carbo., 2 g fiber, 32 g pro. **Daily Values:** 122% vit. A, 53% vit. C, 4% calcium, 18% iron

PREP:
15 minutes

COOK:
Low 8 hours, High 4 hours

STAND:
5 minutes

MAKES:
6 servings

SLOW COOKER:
3½- to 4-quart

Classic French cassoulet is a garlic-flavored bean stew that features sausage, poultry, and various other types of meat, depending on the version. This dish goes well with a simple vinaigrette-dressed salad.

CASSOULET WITH LAMB & SAUSAGE

PREP:

25 minutes

COOK:

Low 8 hours, High 4 hours; plus 30 minutes on High

STAND:

1 hour

MAKES:

6 servings

SLOW COOKER:

3^1/$_2$- to 5-quart

1	cup dry Great Northern beans or dry navy beans
12	ounces lamb stew meat, cut into 1-inch cubes
1	tablespoon cooking oil
2	cups beef broth
8	ounces cooked kielbasa, cut into ^{1}/$_4$-inch slices
1	tablespoon snipped fresh thyme or 1 teaspoon dried thyme, crushed
3	cloves garlic, minced
^{1}/$_4$	teaspoon whole black peppercorns
1	bay leaf
1	small eggplant, peeled and chopped
1	large green or red sweet pepper, coarsely chopped
1	6-ounce can tomato paste
	Salt and black pepper
3	cups hot cooked couscous

1 Rinse beans; place in a large saucepan. Add enough water to cover beans by 2 inches. Bring to boiling; reduce heat. Simmer, uncovered, for 10 minutes. Remove from heat. Cover and let stand for 1 hour. (Or place beans in a large saucepan, cover with water, and let soak in a cool place overnight.) Drain and rinse beans.

2 Meanwhile, in a large skillet brown lamb in hot oil. Drain off fat. In a 3^1/$_2$- to 5-quart slow cooker combine the beans, lamb, broth, kielbasa, dried thyme (if using), garlic, peppercorns, and bay leaf. Cover; cook on low-heat setting for 8 to 10 hours or on high-heat setting for 4 to 5 hours.

3 If using low-heat setting, turn to high-heat setting. Stir in the eggplant, sweet pepper, and tomato paste. Cover and cook for 30 minutes more. Discard bay leaf. If using, stir in fresh thyme. Season to taste with salt and black pepper. Serve over hot couscous.

Nutrition Facts per serving: 405 cal., 19 g total fat (2 g sat. fat), 33 mg chol., 959 mg sodium, 37 g carbo., 7 g fiber, 23 g pro. **Daily Values:** 45% vit. C, 4% calcium, 21% iron

Reminiscent of gyros, these much simpler lamb sandwiches offer a distinct change. They're great with fresh melon wedges.

LEMONY LAMB SANDWICHES

1	1½- to 2-pound boneless lamb shoulder roast
½	teaspoon lemon-pepper seasoning
½	teaspoon dry mustard
½	cup chicken broth
¼	teaspoon finely shredded lemon peel
1	tablespoon lemon juice
1	teaspoon snipped fresh rosemary or ¼ teaspoon dried rosemary, crushed
2	cloves garlic, minced
½	cup plain yogurt
¼	cup chopped, seeded cucumber
¼	teaspoon lemon-pepper seasoning
6	lettuce leaves
3	large pita bread rounds, halved crosswise
1	small tomato, seeded and chopped

PREP:
20 minutes
COOK:
Low 8 hours, High 4 hours
MAKES:
6 servings
SLOW COOKER:
3½- to 4-quart

1 Trim fat from meat. In a small bowl combine the ½ teaspoon lemon-pepper seasoning and the dry mustard. Sprinkle evenly over the roast; rub lightly over the meat with your fingers. Place meat in a 3½- to 4-quart slow cooker. In a bowl combine broth, lemon peel, lemon juice, rosemary, and garlic. Pour over meat.

2 Cover; cook on low-heat setting for 8 to 10 hours or on high-heat setting for 4 to 5 hours.

3 In a bowl stir together yogurt, cucumber, and the ¼ teaspoon lemon-pepper seasoning. Set aside. Remove meat from cooker. Cool slightly. Using two forks, shred meat. Place a lettuce leaf in each pita half. Spoon lamb into pita halves. Top each with yogurt mixture and chopped tomato.

Nutrition Facts per serving: 264 cal., 9 g total fat (3 g sat. fat), 68 mg chol., 430 mg sodium, 20 g carbo., 0 g fiber, 24 g pro. **Daily Values:** 9% vit. C, 7% calcium, 18% iron

An exotic mix of garlic, wine, allspice, mint, and yogurt flavors the lamb that is layered in pitas and topped with lettuce, tomato, and cumin-spiked yogurt.

MEDITERRANEAN PITAS

PREP:

25 minutes

COOK:

Low 8 hours, High 4 hours; plus 15 minutes

MAKES:

12 servings

SLOW COOKER:

3¹/₂- to 4-quart

1	2-pound portion boneless lamb leg roast
1	tablespoon olive oil
1	15-ounce can garbanzo beans, rinsed and drained
³/₄	cup dry red wine
¹/₂	of a 6-ounce can (¹/₃ cup) tomato paste
¹/₄	cup water
1	cup chopped onion
4	cloves garlic, minced
¹/₂	teaspoon ground allspice
¹/₂	teaspoon dried mint, crushed
¹/₄	teaspoon salt
¹/₄	teaspoon black pepper
6	large pita bread rounds, halved crosswise
	Lettuce leaves and/or thinly sliced cucumber
1	8-ounce carton plain yogurt
¹/₄	teaspoon ground cumin
1	medium tomato, chopped

1 Trim the fat from the lamb roast. If necessary, cut roast to fit into a 3¹/₂- to 4-quart slow cooker. In a large skillet brown lamb on all sides in hot oil. Drain off fat.

2 Meanwhile, combine drained garbanzo beans, wine, tomato paste, water, onion, garlic, allspice, mint, salt, and pepper in cooker. Place meat over bean mixture. Cover; cook on low-heat setting for 8 to 10 hours or on high-heat setting for 4 to 5 hours.

3 Remove meat from cooker; shred the meat and return to cooker. Cover and cook 15 minutes more. Remove meat and beans with a slotted spoon.

4 To serve, open pita bread halves to form a large pocket. Line pitas with lettuce and/or cucumber. Combine yogurt and ground cumin. Spoon meat mixture, then yogurt mixture, into pitas. Sprinkle with chopped tomato.

Nutrition Facts per serving: 255 cal., 6 g total fat (2 g sat. fat), 51 mg chol., 434 mg sodium, 27 g carbo., 3 g fiber, 21 g pro. **Daily Values:** 6% vit. A, 11% vit. C, 8% calcium, 16% iron

POULTRY

5

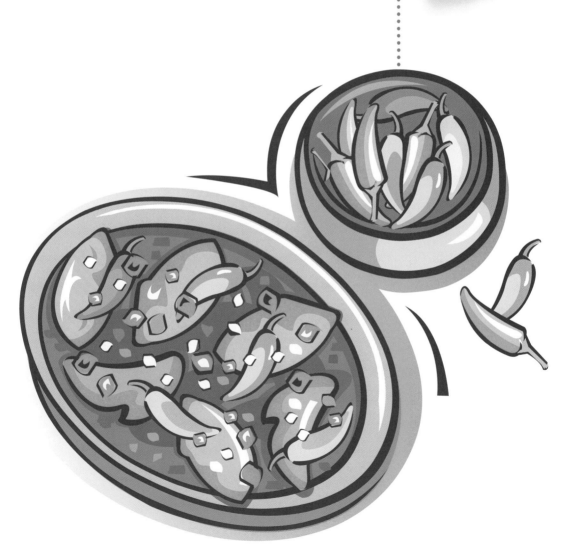

An easy-to-make family dinner, this chicken dish goes together quickly. Pair with a green salad and bread and butter, and finish with vanilla ice cream drizzled with hot fudge sauce.

EASY ITALIAN CHICKEN

PREP:

10 minutes

COOK:

Low 6 hours, High 3 hours

MAKES:

4 to 6 servings

SLOW COOKER:

3¹/₂- to 6-quart

½ of a medium head of cabbage, cut into wedges (about 12 ounces)

1 medium onion, sliced and separated into rings (½ cup)

1 4½-ounce jar sliced mushrooms, drained

2 tablespoons quick-cooking tapioca

2 to 2½ pounds meaty chicken pieces, skinned

2 cups meatless spaghetti sauce

Grated Parmesan cheese

1 In a 3½- to 6-quart slow cooker place cabbage wedges, onion, and mushrooms. Sprinkle tapioca over vegetables. Place chicken pieces on vegetables. Pour spaghetti sauce over chicken.

2 Cover; cook on low-heat setting for 6 to 7 hours or on high-heat setting for 3 to 3½ hours. Transfer to a serving platter. Sprinkle with Parmesan cheese.

Nutrition Facts per serving: 300 cal., 9 g total fat (3 g sat. fat), 94 mg chol., 662 mg sodium, 24 g carbo., 4 g fiber, 35 g pro. **Daily Values:** 7% vit. A, 62% vit. C, 11% calcium, 18% iron

Olé, olé, mole (MO-lay)! This spicy sauce, traditionally made with chiles and chocolate, is a treat for the taste buds. For a more traditional garnish, sprinkle with toasted pepitas (pumpkin seeds) instead of almonds.

MOLE WITH CHICKEN & RICE

1	14$\frac{1}{2}$-ounce can diced tomatoes
$\frac{1}{2}$	cup chopped onion
$\frac{1}{4}$	cup slivered almonds, toasted
3	cloves garlic, quartered
2	canned jalapeño peppers, drained
3	tablespoons unsweetened cocoa powder
3	tablespoons raisins
1	tablespoon sesame seeds
1	teaspoon sugar
$\frac{1}{4}$	teaspoon salt
$\frac{1}{4}$	teaspoon ground cinnamon
$\frac{1}{8}$	teaspoon ground nutmeg
$\frac{1}{8}$	teaspoon ground coriander
2	tablespoons quick-cooking tapioca
1	2$\frac{1}{2}$- to 3-pound broiler-fryer chicken, cut up and skinned
2	tablespoons slivered almonds, toasted
	Hot cooked rice

PREP:

25 minutes

COOK:

Low 9 hours, High 4$\frac{1}{2}$ hours

MAKES:

4 to 6 servings

SLOW COOKER:

3$\frac{1}{2}$- to 4-quart

1 For mole sauce, in a blender container or food processor bowl combine undrained tomatoes, onion, the $\frac{1}{4}$ cup almonds, garlic, jalapeño peppers, cocoa powder, raisins, sesame seeds, sugar, salt, and spices. Cover and blend or process until mixture is a coarse puree.

2 In a 3$\frac{1}{2}$- to 4-quart slow cooker place tapioca. Add chicken and then sauce. Cover; cook on low-heat setting for 9 to 11 hours or on high-heat setting for 4$\frac{1}{2}$ to 5$\frac{1}{2}$ hours.

3 Remove chicken from cooker and arrange on a serving platter. Stir sauce; pour sauce over chicken. Sprinkle with remaining almonds. Serve with rice.

Nutrition Facts per serving: 448 cal., 23 g total fat (5 g sat. fat), 99 mg chol., 586 mg sodium, 24 g carbo., 4 g fiber, 36 g pro. **Daily Values:** 3% vit. A, 17% vit. C, 12% calcium, 18% iron

Lemon, pineapple, and orange provide a pleasant tang to this chicken dish. You could substitute hot cooked basmati rice for the couscous.

SPICY CITRUS CHICKEN

PREP:

20 minutes

COOK:

Low 8 hours, High 4 hours

MAKES:

4 servings

SLOW COOKER:

3¹/₂- to 4-quart

1	6-ounce can frozen pineapple-orange juice concentrate, thawed (³⁄₄ cup)
¹/₂	cup catsup
2	tablespoons lemon juice
¹/₄	teaspoon ground red pepper
2	tablespoons quick-cooking tapioca
2	inches stick cinnamon
8	whole allspice
4	whole cloves
2¹/₂	to 3 pounds meaty chicken pieces (breast halves, thighs, and drumsticks), skinned
	Hot cooked couscous

1 For sauce, in a small bowl combine juice concentrate, catsup, lemon juice, and ground red pepper. Pour about half of the sauce into a 3¹/₂- to 4-quart slow cooker. Add tapioca to the cooker; stir. For spice bag, place cinnamon, allspice, and cloves in 100-percent-cotton cheesecloth and tie closed with clean kitchen string. Add bag to cooker. Place chicken pieces in cooker. Pour remaining sauce over chicken.

2 Cover; cook on low-heat setting for 8 to 9 hours or on high-heat setting for 4 to 4¹/₂ hours. Transfer chicken to a serving platter, reserving sauce. Discard spice bag. Strain sauce and skim off fat. Serve sauce and hot couscous with the chicken.

Nutrition Facts per serving: 471 cal., 9 g total fat (3 g sat. fat), 115 mg chol., 479 mg sodium, 54 g carbo., 2 g fiber, 41 g pro. **Daily Values:** 7% vit. A, 164% vit. C, 4% calcium, 11% iron

To peel pearl onions, submerge them in boiling water for about 3 minutes. Cut off the root ends. Gently press the onions and the skins will slip off.

CHICKEN & VEGETABLES WITH HERBS

8	ounces mushrooms, halved
16	pearl onions (about 1 cup plus 3 ounces), peeled
½	cup chicken broth
¼	cup dry red wine
2	tablespoons tomato paste
½	teaspoon garlic salt
½	teaspoon dried rosemary, crushed
½	teaspoon dried thyme, crushed
¼	teaspoon black pepper
1	bay leaf
4	small chicken legs (drumstick-thigh portion; 2 to 2½ pounds), skinned
¼	cup chicken broth
2	tablespoons all-purpose flour
2	cups hot cooked mashed potatoes (optional)
	Snipped fresh parsley (optional)

PREP:

25 minutes

COOK:

Low 7 hours, High 3½ hours; plus 10 minutes on cooktop

MAKES:

4 servings

SLOW COOKER:

5½- to 6-quart

1 In a 5½- to 6-quart slow cooker place mushrooms and onions. Stir in the ½ cup broth, wine, tomato paste, garlic salt, rosemary, thyme, pepper, and bay leaf. Add the chicken.

2 Cover and cook on low-heat setting for 7 to 8 hours or on high-heat setting for 3½ to 4 hours.

3 Transfer chicken and vegetables to a serving platter using a slotted spoon; remove and discard bay leaf. Cover chicken and vegetables to keep warm.

4 For sauce, skim fat from cooking liquid. Measure 2 cups cooking liquid, adding additional chicken broth, if necessary, to equal 2 cups. Transfer liquid to a medium saucepan. In a small bowl stir the ¼ cup broth into the flour; stir into mixture in saucepan. Cook and stir until thickened and bubbly; cook and stir for 1 minute more. Spoon some of the sauce over chicken. Pass remaining sauce. If desired, serve with mashed potatoes and sprinkle with parsley.

Nutrition Facts per serving: 304 cal., 9 g total fat (2 g sat. fat), 159 mg chol., 548 mg sodium, 9 g carbo., 1 g fiber, 43 g pro. **Daily Values:** 7% vit. A, 19% vit. C, 4% calcium, 17% iron

The slow cooker version of this popular casserole makes it possible to serve a family-pleasing supper any day of the week.

SLOW COOKER CHICKEN & NOODLES

PREP:

25 minutes

COOK:

Low 8 hours, High 4 hours

MAKES:

6 servings

SLOW COOKER:

3½- to 4-quart

2	cups sliced carrots
1½	cups chopped onions
1	cup sliced celery
2	tablespoons snipped fresh parsley
1	bay leaf
3	medium chicken legs (drumstick-thigh portion; about 2 pounds), skinned
2	10¾-ounce cans reduced-fat and reduced-sodium condensed cream of chicken soup
½	cup water
1	teaspoon dried thyme, crushed
¼	teaspoon black pepper
10	ounces wide noodles (about 5 cups)
1	cup frozen peas
	Salt and pepper (optional)

1 In a 3½- to 4-quart slow cooker place carrots, onions, celery, parsley, and bay leaf. Place chicken on top of vegetables. In a bowl stir together soup, water, thyme, and pepper. Pour over chicken and vegetables.

2 Cover and cook on low-heat setting for 8 to 9 hours or on high-heat setting for 4 to 4½ hours. Remove chicken from cooker; cool slightly. Remove and discard bay leaf.

3 Meanwhile, cook noodles according to package directions; drain. Stir peas into mixture in cooker. Remove chicken from bones; discard bones. Cut meat into bite-size pieces; stir into cooker. To serve, pour chicken mixture over noodles; toss gently to combine. Season to taste with salt and pepper, if desired.

Nutrition Facts per serving: 406 cal., 7 g total fat (2 g sat. fat), 122 mg chol., 532 mg sodium, 56 g carbo., 5 g fiber, 28 g pro. **Daily Values:** 60% vit. C, 6% calcium, 19% iron

Serve this familiar Italian classic with plenty of pasta to support all the sauce. Similar to the traditional dish, this one brims with onions, mushrooms, and perfectly herbed tomatoes.

CACCIATORE-STYLE CHICKEN

2	cups sliced fresh mushrooms
1	cup sliced celery
1	cup chopped carrot
2	medium onions, cut into wedges
1	green, yellow, or red sweet pepper, cut into strips
4	cloves garlic, minced
12	chicken drumsticks, skinned (about 3½ pounds)
½	cup chicken broth
¼	cup dry white wine
2	tablespoons quick-cooking tapioca
2	bay leaves
1	teaspoon dried oregano, crushed
1	teaspoon sugar
½	teaspoon salt
¼	teaspoon black pepper
1	14½-ounce can diced tomatoes
⅓	cup tomato paste
	Hot cooked pasta or rice

PREP:

25 minutes

COOK:

Low 6 hours, High 3 hours; plus 15 minutes on High

MAKES:

6 servings

SLOW COOKER:

5- to 6-quart

1 In a 5- to 6-quart slow cooker combine mushrooms, celery, carrot, onions, sweet pepper, and garlic. Cover vegetables with the chicken. Add broth, wine, tapioca, bay leaves, oregano, sugar, salt, and black pepper.

2 Cover and cook on low-heat setting for 6 to 7 hours or on high-heat setting for 3 to 3½ hours.

3 Remove chicken and keep warm. Remove bay leaves and discard. If using low-heat setting, turn to high-heat setting. Stir in undrained tomatoes and tomato paste. Cover and cook 15 minutes longer on high-heat setting. To serve, spoon vegetable mixture over chicken and pasta.

Nutrition Facts per serving: 345 cal., 7 g total fat (2 g sat. fat), 81 mg chol., 606 mg sodium, 37 g carbo., 4 g fiber, 32 g pro. **Daily Values:** 114% vit. A, 57% vit. C, 8% calcium, 20% iron

Saffron, although expensive, provides a unique flavor and color to this dish. For an economical and equally delicious alternative, substitute turmeric.

CHICKEN, SAUSAGE, & RICE SKILLET

PREP:

30 minutes

COOK:

Low 7 hours, High 3½ hours

STAND:

5 minutes

MAKES:

6 servings

SLOW COOKER:

3½- to 5-quart

2½	to 3 pounds meaty chicken pieces (breasts, thighs, and drumsticks), skinned
1	tablespoon cooking oil
8	ounces cooked smoked turkey sausage, halved lengthwise and sliced
1	large onion, sliced
3	cloves garlic, sliced
2	tablespoons snipped fresh thyme or 2 teaspoons dried thyme, crushed
¼	teaspoon black pepper
⅛	thread saffron or ¼ teaspoon ground turmeric
1	14½-ounce can reduced-sodium chicken broth
½	cup water
2	cups chopped tomatoes
2	yellow or green sweet peppers, cut into very thin bite-size strips
1	cup frozen peas
3	cups hot cooked rice

1 In a large skillet brown chicken pieces, half at a time, in hot oil. Drain off fat. In a 3½- to 5-quart slow cooker place chicken pieces, turkey sausage, and onion. Sprinkle with garlic, dried thyme (if using), black pepper, and saffron or turmeric. Pour broth and water over all.

2 Cover and cook on low-heat setting for 7 to 8 hours or on high-heat setting for 3½ to 4 hours. Add the tomatoes, sweet peppers, peas, and fresh thyme (if using) to the cooker. Cover and let stand for 5 minutes. Serve over the hot rice.

Nutrition Facts per serving: 397 cal., 12 g total fat (3 g sat. fat), 101 mg chol., 608 mg sodium, 35 g carbo., 2 g fiber, 36 g pro. **Daily Values:** 109% vit. C, 6% calcium, 22% iron

Although 12 cloves may seem a bit much, the garlic mellows as it slowly envelops the chicken in a delightful flavor.

CHICKEN WITH GARLIC, PEPPERS, & ARTICHOKES

12	cloves garlic, minced
1	medium onion, chopped
1	tablespoon olive or cooking oil
1	8- or 9-ounce package frozen artichoke hearts
1	red sweet pepper, cut into strips
½	cup chicken broth
1	tablespoon quick-cooking tapioca
2	teaspoons dried rosemary, crushed
1	teaspoon finely shredded lemon peel
½	teaspoon ground black pepper
1½	pounds skinless, boneless chicken breast halves or thighs
4	cups hot cooked brown rice

1 In a small skillet cook garlic and onion in hot oil over medium heat, stirring occasionally, 5 minutes or until tender.

2 In a 3½- to 4-quart slow cooker combine the frozen artichoke hearts, garlic mixture, sweet pepper, chicken broth, tapioca, rosemary, lemon peel, and black pepper. Add chicken; spoon some of the garlic mixture over chicken.

3 Cover and cook on low-heat setting for 6 to 7 hours or on high-heat setting for 3 to 3½ hours. Serve with rice.

Nutrition Facts per serving: 341 cal., 6 g total fat (1 g sat. fat), 66 mg chol., 159 mg sodium, 39 g carbo., 6 g fiber, 32 g pro. **Daily Values:** 62% vit. C, 7% calcium, 10% iron

PREP:
20 minutes
COOK:
Low 6 hours, High 3 hours
MAKES:
6 servings
SLOW COOKER:
3½- to 4-quart

FRIENDS FOR DINNER
Looking for an easy dinner to share with friends after attending a game or other activity away from home? For such occasions, pull out the slow cooker to make recipes that include both meat and vegetables, such as pot roasts, thick soups, or hearty stews. Before leaving for the event, clean the greens and cut up vegetables for a salad to toss together when you return. To keep dessert simple, plan for ice cream and cookies.

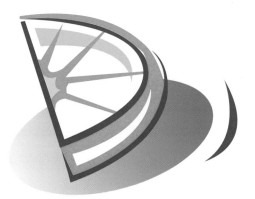

This fuss-free dinner is ideal for casual entertaining. Rent some videos or arrange to play games, then invite friends for dinner and entertainment.

HERBED CHICKEN & MUSHROOMS

PREP:

25 minutes

COOK:

Low 7 hours, High 3¹/2 hours

MAKES:

6 servings

SLOW COOKER:

4- to 5-quart

5	cups sliced assorted fresh mushrooms, such as shiitake, button, crimini, and oyster
1	medium onion, chopped
¹/2	cup chopped carrot
¹/4	cup dried tomato pieces (not oil-packed)
³/4	cup chicken broth
¹/4	cup dry white wine or chicken broth
3	tablespoons quick-cooking tapioca
1	teaspoon dried thyme, crushed
¹/2	teaspoon dried basil, crushed
¹/2	teaspoon garlic salt
¹/4	to ¹/2 teaspoon pepper
3	pounds chicken thighs or drumsticks (with bone), skinned
4¹/2	cups hot cooked plain and/or spinach linguine or fettuccine, or hot cooked rice

1 In a 4- to 5-quart slow cooker combine mushrooms, onion, carrot, and dried tomato pieces. Pour chicken broth and wine over all. Sprinkle with tapioca, thyme, basil, garlic salt, and pepper. Place chicken pieces on vegetables in cooker.

2 Cover and cook on low-heat setting for 7 to 8 hours or on high-heat setting for 3¹/2 to 4 hours. To serve, arrange chicken and vegetables over pasta or rice; spoon over the juices.

Nutrition Facts per serving: 360 cal., 7 g total fat (2 g sat. fat), 107 mg chol., 350 mg sodium, 39 g carbo., 3 g fiber, 34 g pro. **Daily Values:** 54% vit. A, 9% vit. C, 3% calcium, 20% iron

If you think you've prepared chicken in every way imaginable, try this recipe. The flavors of artichokes, olives, and thyme lend a Mediterranean accent that you'll love.

CHICKEN with ARTICHOKES & OLIVES

2	cups sliced fresh mushrooms
1	14½-ounce can diced tomatoes
1	8- or 9-ounce package frozen artichoke hearts
1	cup chicken broth
1	medium onion, chopped
½	cup sliced, pitted ripe olives or ¼ cup capers, drained
¼	cup dry white wine or chicken broth
3	tablespoons quick-cooking tapioca
2	to 3 teaspoons curry powder
¾	teaspoon dried thyme, crushed
¼	teaspoon salt
¼	teaspoon pepper
1½	pounds skinless, boneless chicken breast halves and/or thighs
4	cups hot cooked couscous

1 In a 3½- to 4-quart slow cooker combine the mushrooms, undrained tomatoes, frozen artichoke hearts, chicken broth, onion, olives or capers, and wine or broth. Stir in tapioca, curry powder, thyme, salt, and pepper. Add chicken; spoon some of the tomato mixture over the chicken.

2 Cover; cook on low-heat setting for 7 to 8 hours or on high-heat setting for 3½ to 4 hours. Serve with hot cooked couscous.

Nutrition Facts per serving: 345 cal., 6 g total fat (1 g sat. fat), 60 mg chol., 531 mg sodium, 43 g carbo., 9 g fiber, 30 g pro. **Daily Values:** 27% vit. C, 6% calcium, 21% iron

PREP:

20 minutes

COOK:

Low 7 hours, High 3½ hours

MAKES:

6 servings

SLOW COOKER:

3½- to 4-quart

FROZEN FOOD TIMELINE
Once a food is frozen, it will not keep forever. Label frozen items with a date so you can enjoy them at their best. Freeze soups, stews, and meat dishes with gravy for up to 3 months. Meats with vegetables and pasta can be frozen for up to 1 month. To prevent freezer burn, store food in freezer containers with tightly fitting lids or wrap food tightly in freezer packaging material.

To ensure proper doneness, place ingredients in the slow cooker in the order listed in the recipe. Often, vegetables are added first and the meat last.

CHICKEN & MUSHROOMS IN WINE SAUCE

PREP:

25 minutes

COOK:

Low 7 hours, High 3 1/2 hours

MAKES:

4 to 6 servings

SLOW COOKER:

3 1/2- to 5-quart

3	cups sliced fresh mushrooms
1	large onion, chopped
2	cloves garlic, minced
2 1/2	to 3 pounds meaty chicken pieces (breasts, thighs, and drumsticks), skinned
3/4	cup chicken broth
1	6-ounce can tomato paste
1/4	cup dry red wine (such as Merlot) or chicken broth
2	tablespoons quick-cooking tapioca
2	tablespoons snipped fresh basil or 1 1/2 teaspoons dried basil, crushed
2	teaspoons sugar
1/4	teaspoon salt
1/4	teaspoon pepper
2	cups hot cooked noodles
2	tablespoons finely shredded Parmesan cheese

1 In a 3 1/2- to 5-quart slow cooker place mushrooms, onion, and garlic. Place chicken pieces on top of the vegetables. In a bowl combine broth, tomato paste, wine or chicken broth, tapioca, dried basil (if using), sugar, salt, and pepper. Pour over chicken.

2 Cover; cook on low-heat setting for 7 to 8 hours or on high-heat setting for 3 1/2 to 4 hours. If using, stir in fresh basil. To serve, spoon chicken, mushrooms, and sauce over hot cooked noodles. Sprinkle with Parmesan cheese.

Nutrition Facts per serving: 469 cal., 12 g total fat (3 g sat. fat), 144 mg chol., 468 mg sodium, 41 g carbo., 5 g fiber, 46 g pro. **Daily Values:** 37% vit. C, 7% calcium, 35% iron

Juniper berries, native to Europe and America, add an intriguing flavor to this dish. Popular in marinades and sauces, the berries are also used in making gin.

OLD WORLD CHICKEN

2	slices bacon
1	teaspoon whole juniper berries
3	medium carrots, cut into ½-inch pieces
¼	cup chopped shallots or onion
¼	cup coarsely chopped celery
2½	to 3 pounds meaty chicken pieces (breasts, thighs, and drumsticks), skinned
½	cup chicken broth
¼	cup dry red wine or port
2	tablespoons quick-cooking tapioca
1½	teaspoons snipped fresh thyme or ½ teaspoon dried thyme, crushed
1	teaspoon snipped fresh rosemary or ¼ teaspoon dried rosemary, crushed
¼	teaspoon salt
⅛	teaspoon pepper
1	cup frozen peas
2	tablespoons currant jelly
2	cups hot cooked rice

PREP:
30 minutes

COOK:
Low 6 hours, High 3 hours; plus 5 minutes on High

MAKES:
4 servings

SLOW COOKER:
3½- to 5-quart

1 In a small skillet cook bacon until crisp; drain on paper towels. Crumble bacon; set aside. For spice bag, place juniper berries on a double-thick, 6-inch square of 100-percent-cotton cheesecloth. Bring corners together and tie with clean kitchen string.

2 In a 3½- to 5-quart slow cooker place carrots, shallots or onion, celery, and spice bag. Add chicken. Sprinkle with bacon. In a small bowl combine broth, wine or port, tapioca, dried thyme and rosemary (if using), salt, and pepper. Pour over all.

3 Cover; cook on low-heat setting for 6 to 7 hours or on high-heat setting for 3 to 3½ hours or until chicken is tender. Using a slotted spoon, transfer chicken and carrots to a serving platter; keep warm. If using low-heat setting, turn to high-heat setting. Stir in the peas and, if using, the fresh thyme and rosemary. Cook for 5 minutes more. Remove spice bag. Skim fat. Add currant jelly; stir until smooth. Pour over chicken mixture. Serve with hot cooked rice.

Nutrition Facts per serving: 474 cal., 11 g total fat (3 g sat. fat), 118 mg chol., 500 mg sodium, 45 g carbo., 3 g fiber, 43 g pro. **Daily Values:** 11% vit. C, 5% calcium, 25% iron

Feta cheese and olives add Greek flair to this meal. For the ultimate Greek touch, use kalamata olives, which are salty, rich, and fruity.

OREGANO CHICKEN WITH ORZO

PREP:

25 minutes

COOK:

Low 5 hours, High 2 1/2 hours

MAKES:

4 servings

SLOW COOKER:

3 1/2- to 4-quart

4	medium chicken breast halves (about 1 1/2 pounds)
2	tablespoons cooking oil
1	medium fennel bulb, cut into 1/2-inch pieces (2 cups)
1	medium onion, cut into wedges
2	cloves garlic, minced
2	cups water
2	tablespoons white balsamic vinegar
2	teaspoons instant chicken bouillon granules
1	tablespoon snipped fresh oregano or 1 teaspoon dried oregano, crushed
1/4	teaspoon crushed red pepper
1 1/3	cups orzo (rosamarina)
1	medium tomato, chopped
1/4	cup crumbled feta cheese (1 ounce)
1/4	cup chopped, pitted ripe olives
1	tablespoon snipped fresh oregano

1 Skin chicken. In a large skillet brown chicken breasts in hot oil. Drain off fat. In a 3 1/2- to 4-quart slow cooker combine fennel, onion, and garlic. Add the chicken breasts. In a bowl stir together water, balsamic vinegar, bouillon granules, dried oregano (if using), and red pepper. Pour over all.

2 Cover; cook on low-heat setting for 5 to 6 hours or on high-heat setting for 2 1/2 to 3 hours. If using, stir in the 1 tablespoon fresh oregano.

3 Cook the orzo according to package directions; drain. Stir tomato, cheese, olives, and the remaining 1 tablespoon fresh oregano into orzo. Using a slotted spoon, remove chicken and vegetables from cooker. Serve with orzo mixture.

Nutrition Facts per serving: 439 cal., 12 g total fat (3 g sat. fat), 58 mg chol., 626 mg sodium, 53 g carbo., 13 g fiber, 28 g pro. **Daily Values:** 22% vit. C, 8% calcium, 24% iron

This is a delicious, easy-to-prepare version of a classic French cassoulet that is traditionally made with beans and various meats; ingredient combinations vary by region.

CASSOULET-STYLE CHICKEN & SAUSAGE

3	medium carrots, cut into ½-inch pieces (1½ cups)
1	medium onion, chopped (½ cup)
1	6-ounce can tomato paste
½	cup dry red wine or water
⅓	cup water
1	teaspoon garlic powder
½	teaspoon dried thyme, crushed
¼	teaspoon salt
⅛	teaspoon ground cloves
2	bay leaves
2	15-ounce cans navy beans, rinsed and drained
1	pound skinless, boneless chicken breast thighs or halves
8	ounces fully cooked Polish sausage, cut into ¼-inch slices

PREP:

15 minutes

COOK:

Low 5 hours, High 2½ hours

MAKES:

4 servings

SLOW COOKER:

3½- to 4-quart

1 In a 3½- to 4-quart slow cooker combine carrots, onion, tomato paste, wine, the ⅓ cup water, garlic powder, thyme, salt, cloves, and bay leaves. Add beans. Place chicken on bean mixture. Place sausage on chicken.

2 Cover; cook on low-heat setting for 5 to 7 hours or on high-heat setting for 2½ to 3½ hours. Before serving, discard bay leaves and skim off fat.

Nutrition Facts per serving: 651 cal., 22 g total fat (7 g sat. fat), 132 mg chol., 2,051 mg sodium, 61 g carbo., 14 g fiber, 48 g pro. **Daily Values:** 254% vit. A, 65% vit. C, 17% calcium, 40% iron

Substitutions are encouraged in this recipe: Try spinach or red pepper instead of plain fettuccine, or use regular frozen green beans in place of Italian-style.

ITALIAN CHICKEN & PASTA

PREP:

15 minutes

COOK:

Low 5 hours, High 2 1/2 hours

MAKES:

4 servings

SLOW COOKER:

3 1/2- to 4-quart

12	ounces skinless, boneless chicken thighs
1	9-ounce package frozen Italian-style green beans
1	cup fresh mushrooms, quartered
1	small onion, sliced 1/4 inch thick
1	14 1/2-ounce can Italian-style stewed tomatoes
1	6-ounce can Italian-style tomato paste
1	teaspoon dried Italian seasoning, crushed
2	cloves garlic, minced
6	ounces fettuccine, cooked and drained
3	tablespoons finely shredded or grated Parmesan cheese

1 Cut chicken into 1-inch pieces; set aside.

2 In a 3 1/2- to 4-quart slow cooker place green beans, mushrooms, and onion. Place chicken on vegetables.

3 In a small bowl combine undrained tomatoes, tomato paste, Italian seasoning, and garlic. Pour over chicken.

4 Cover; cook on low-heat setting for 5 to 6 hours or on high-heat setting for 2 1/2 to 3 hours. Serve over hot cooked fettuccine. Sprinkle with Parmesan cheese.

Nutrition Facts per serving: 405 cal., 7 g total fat (2 g sat. fat), 75 mg chol., 728 mg sodium, 55 g carbo., 4 g fiber, 28 g pro. **Daily Values:** 7% vit. A, 46% vit. C, 15% calcium, 26% iron

This orange sauce is sweet and full of flavor. Use orange sections or slices to garnish the meal. For variety and to pack in extra nutrition, serve with hot cooked brown rice.

TERIYAKI CHICKEN WITH ORANGE SAUCE

1	pound skinless, boneless chicken breast halves or thighs
1	16-ounce package loose-pack frozen broccoli, baby carrots, and water chestnuts
2	tablespoons quick-cooking tapioca
¾	cup chicken broth
3	tablespoons orange marmalade
2	tablespoons teriyaki sauce
1	teaspoon dry mustard
½	teaspoon ground ginger
2	cups hot cooked rice

1 Cut chicken into 1-inch pieces; set aside.

2 In a 3½- to 4-quart slow cooker place frozen vegetables. Sprinkle tapioca over vegetables. Stir to combine. Place chicken pieces on vegetable mixture.

3 For sauce, in a small bowl combine chicken broth, marmalade, teriyaki sauce, mustard, and ginger. Pour sauce over chicken pieces.

4 Cover; cook on low-heat setting for 4 to 5 hours or on high-heat setting for 2 to 2½ hours. Serve with hot cooked rice.

Nutrition Facts per serving: 375 cal., 4 g total fat (1 g sat. fat), 79 mg chol., 790 mg sodium, 52 g carbo., 4 g fiber, 30 g pro. **Daily Values:** 40% vit. A, 16% vit. C, 3% calcium, 17% iron

PREP:
15 minutes

COOK:
Low 4 hours, High 2 hours

MAKES:
4 servings

SLOW COOKER:
3½- to 4-quart

A superb balance of tomato, ginger, garlic, and crushed red pepper makes this dish a favorite. Serve over hot cooked couscous or rice.

ZESTY GINGER-TOMATO CHICKEN

PREP:

20 minutes

COOK:

Low 6 hours, High 3 hours

MAKES:

6 servings

SLOW COOKER:

3¹/₂- to 4-quart

12	chicken drumsticks and/or thighs, skinned (2¹/₂ to 3 pounds)
2	14¹/₂-ounce cans tomatoes
2	tablespoons quick-cooking tapioca
1	tablespoon grated fresh ginger
1	tablespoon snipped fresh cilantro or parsley
4	cloves garlic, minced
2	teaspoons brown sugar
¹/₂	teaspoon crushed red pepper
¹/₂	teaspoon salt
3	cups hot cooked couscous or rice

1 Place chicken pieces in a 3¹/₂- to 4-quart slow cooker.

2 Drain 1 can of tomatoes; chop tomatoes from both cans. For sauce, in a medium bowl combine chopped tomatoes and the juice from one can, tapioca, ginger, cilantro, garlic, brown sugar, red pepper, and salt. Pour sauce over chicken.

3 Cover; cook on low-heat setting for 6 to 7 hours or on high-heat setting for 3 to 3¹/₂ hours. Skim fat from sauce. Serve sauce with chicken in shallow bowls with couscous or rice.

Nutrition Facts per serving: 378 cal., 7 g total fat (2 g sat. fat), 157 mg chol., 615 mg sodium, 30 g carbo., 3 g fiber, 46 g pro. **Daily Values:** 3% vit. A, 27% vit. C, 5% calcium, 14% iron

Jalapeño pepper jelly, nutty cumin, and citrus provide the zing in this piquant dish. Set out remaining pepper jelly with cream cheese and crackers for an appetizer.

SAVORY BARBECUE CHICKEN

½ cup tomato sauce

2 tablespoons jalapeño pepper jelly

2 tablespoons lime or lemon juice

2 tablespoons quick-cooking tapioca

1 teaspoon brown sugar

1 teaspoon ground cumin

¼ to ½ teaspoon crushed red pepper

8 to 10 chicken thighs and/or drumsticks, skinned (2 to 2½ pounds)

   Flour tortillas

PREP:
15 minutes

COOK:
Low 6 hours, High 3 hours

MAKES:
4 to 5 servings

SLOW COOKER:
3½- to 4-quart

1 In a 3½- to 4-quart slow cooker combine tomato sauce, jelly, lime or lemon juice, tapioca, brown sugar, cumin, and red pepper. Place chicken pieces, meaty side down, on sauce mixture.

2 Cover; cook on low-heat setting for 6 to 7 hours or on high-heat setting for 3 to 3½ hours. Serve with flour tortillas.

Nutrition Facts per serving: 405 cal., 10 g total fat (3 g sat. fat), 115 mg chol., 548 mg sodium, 44 g carbo., 2 g fiber, 32 g pro. **Daily Values:** 8% vit. A, 18% vit. C, 9% calcium, 21% iron

Tender chicken pieces and chunks of vegetables make up this Mediterranean-flavored meal that is perfectly suited to pasta.

MEDITERRANEAN CHICKEN

PREP:

30 minutes

COOK:

Low 7 hours, High 3 1/2 hours

MAKES:

4 to 6 servings

SLOW COOKER:

3 1/2- to 4-quart

2   cups sliced fresh mushrooms

1   14 1/2-ounce can whole tomatoes, drained and cut up

1   6-ounce jar marinated artichoke hearts

1   2 1/2-ounce can sliced, pitted ripe olives, drained

3   tablespoons quick-cooking tapioca

2   to 2 1/2 pounds chicken thighs and/or drumsticks, skinned

1   tablespoon dried Italian seasoning, crushed

1/2   teaspoon salt

3/4   cup chicken broth

1/4   cup dry white wine or chicken broth

6   ounces linguine, cooked and drained

1 In a 3 1/2- to 4-quart slow cooker combine the mushrooms, tomatoes, undrained artichoke hearts (cut up large pieces), and olives. Sprinkle with tapioca. Place the chicken pieces over the vegetables. Sprinkle with Italian seasoning and salt. Add chicken broth and white wine.

2 Cover; cook on low-heat setting for 7 to 8 hours or on high-heat setting for 3 1/2 to 4 hours. Serve with hot cooked linguine.

Nutrition Facts per serving: 447 cal., 11 g total fat (2 g sat. fat), 107 mg chol., 968 mg sodium, 51 g carbo., 3 g fiber, 36 g pro. **Daily Values:** 15% vit. A, 47% vit. C, 10% calcium, 27% iron

Chicken and hearty vegetables are simmered in a delicately wine-flavored sauce. Dark meat chicken—legs, thighs, or drumsticks—has an ideal taste and texture for this dish.

CHICKEN & VEGETABLES IN WINE SAUCE

4	medium red-skinned potatoes, quartered
4	medium carrots, cut into ½-inch pieces
2	stalks celery, cut into 1-inch pieces
1	small onion, sliced
3	pounds chicken thighs or drumsticks, skinned
1	tablespoon snipped fresh parsley
½	teaspoon salt
½	teaspoon dried rosemary, crushed
½	teaspoon dried thyme, crushed
¼	teaspoon pepper
1	clove garlic, minced
1	cup chicken broth
½	cup dry white wine
3	tablespoons butter
3	tablespoons all-purpose flour

PREP:

20 minutes

COOK:

Low 8 hours, High 4 hours; plus 10 minutes on cooktop

MAKES:

6 servings

SLOW COOKER:

5- to 6-quart

1 Place potatoes, carrots, celery, and onion in a 5- to 6-quart slow cooker. Place chicken pieces on vegetables. Sprinkle with parsley, salt, rosemary, thyme, pepper, and garlic; add chicken broth and wine.

2 Cover; cook on low-heat setting for 8 to 9 hours or on high-heat setting for 4 to 4½ hours.

3 Using a slotted spoon, transfer chicken and vegetables to a warm platter. Cover to keep chicken and vegetables warm.

4 For gravy, skim and discard fat from cooking juices; strain juices. In a large saucepan, melt butter. Stir in flour and cook for one minute. Add cooking juices. Cook and stir until thickened and bubbly. Cook and stir 2 minutes more. Pass the gravy with the chicken and vegetables.

Nutrition Facts per serving: 328 cal., 11 g total fat (5 g sat. fat), 124 mg chol., 544 mg sodium, 24 g carbo., 3 g fiber, 29 g pro. **Daily Values:** 213% vit. A, 33% vit. C, 5% calcium, 14% iron

Serve this festive dish with a salad of baby greens and a white wine, such as Gewürztraminer. Finish the delicious meal with a fresh fruit tart.

CHICKEN & SHRIMP WITH VEGETABLES

PREP:

15 minutes

COOK:

Low 6 hours, High 3 hours; plus 5 minutes on High

MAKES:

4 to 5 servings

SLOW COOKER:

3^1/$_2$- to 5-quart

12	ounces skinless, boneless chicken thighs
1	large onion, chopped
3	cloves garlic, minced
1	14^1/$_2$-ounce can diced tomatoes with basil, garlic, and oregano, or diced tomatoes with onion and garlic
2	tablespoons tomato paste
^{1}/$_2$	cup port wine or chicken broth
2	tablespoons lemon juice
2	bay leaves
^{1}/$_2$	teaspoon salt
^{1}/$_4$	teaspoon crushed red pepper
1	8-ounce package frozen peeled, cooked shrimp, thawed and drained
1	9-ounce package frozen artichoke hearts, thawed and coarsely chopped
2	cups hot cooked orzo (rosamarina)
^{1}/$_2$	cup crumbled feta cheese (2 ounces)

1 Rinse chicken; pat dry. Cut chicken thighs into quarters. In a 3^1/$_2$- to 5-quart slow cooker place the onion and garlic. Top with chicken pieces. In a bowl combine the undrained tomatoes, tomato paste, wine or broth, lemon juice, bay leaves, salt, and red pepper. Pour over all.

2 Cover; cook on low-heat setting for 6 to 7 hours or on high-heat setting for 3 to 3^1/$_2$ hours.

3 If using low-heat setting, turn to high-heat setting. Remove bay leaves. Stir in shrimp and artichoke hearts. Cover; cook for 5 minutes more. Serve chicken and shrimp mixture over hot cooked orzo. Sprinkle with feta cheese.

Nutrition Facts per serving: 615 cal., 21 g total fat (9 g sat. fat), 187 mg chol., 1,203 mg sodium, 56 g carbo., 4 g fiber, 46 g pro. **Daily Values:** 267% vit. C, 23% calcium, 40% iron

An intriguing blend of spices makes this slow-simmer chicken and potato dish sizzle with flavors typical of Indian cuisine.

INDIAN CURRY WITH CHICKEN

5 medium white potatoes, peeled (1½ pounds)

1 medium green sweet pepper, cut into 1-inch pieces (¾ cup)

1 medium onion, sliced

1 pound skinless, boneless chicken breast halves or thighs, cut into 1-inch pieces

1½ cups chopped tomatoes

1 tablespoon ground coriander

1½ teaspoons paprika

1 teaspoon grated fresh ginger or ¼ teaspoon ground ginger

¾ teaspoon salt

¼ to ½ teaspoon crushed red pepper

½ teaspoon ground turmeric

¼ teaspoon ground cinnamon

⅛ teaspoon ground cloves

1 cup chicken broth

2 tablespoons cold water

4 teaspoons cornstarch

PREP:

30 minutes

COOK:

Low 8 hours, High 4 hours; plus 15 minutes on High

MAKES:

5 servings

SLOW COOKER:

3½- to 6-quart

1 In a 3½- to 6-quart slow cooker place potatoes, sweet pepper, and onion. Place chicken on top of vegetables.

2 In a medium bowl combine tomatoes and spices; stir in chicken broth. Pour over chicken pieces.

3 Cover and cook on low-heat setting for 8 to 10 hours or on high-heat setting for 4 to 5 hours.

4 If using low-heat setting, turn to high-heat setting. Combine cold water and cornstarch; stir into mixture in cooker. Cover and cook 15 to 20 minutes more or until slightly thickened and bubbly.

Nutrition Facts per serving: 246 cal., 2 g total fat (0 g sat. fat), 53 mg chol., 609 mg sodium, 31 g carbo., 5 g fiber, 26 g pro. **Daily Values:** 90% vit. C, 3% calcium, 14% iron

If you like spicy Cajun food, use the Homemade Cajun Seasoning. The Cajun seasoning blend from the supermarket is less peppery than this three-pepper combination.

JAMBALAYA-STYLE CHICKEN & SHRIMP

PREP:

20 minutes

COOK:

Low 5 hours, High 2½ hours

STAND:

10 minutes

MAKES:

6 servings

SLOW COOKER:

3½- to 4-quart

1	cup sliced celery
1	large onion, chopped
1	14½-ounce can low-sodium tomatoes, cut up
1	14-ounce can reduced-sodium chicken broth
½	of a 6-ounce can (⅓ cup) tomato paste
1	tablespoon Worcestershire sauce
1½	teaspoons Cajun seasoning or 1 recipe Homemade Cajun Seasoning
1	pound skinless, boneless chicken breast halves or thighs, cut into ¾-inch pieces
1½	cups instant rice
8	ounces cooked peeled, deveined shrimp
¾	cup chopped green sweet pepper

❶ In a 3½- to 4-quart slow cooker combine celery, onion, undrained tomatoes, broth, tomato paste, Worcestershire sauce, and Cajun seasoning. Stir in chicken.

❷ Cover and cook on low-heat setting for 5 to 6 hours or on high-heat setting for 2½ to 3 hours. Stir in rice, shrimp, and sweet pepper. Cover and let stand 10 to 15 minutes or until most of the liquid is absorbed and rice is tender.

HOMEMADE CAJUN SEASONING: In a small bowl combine ¼ teaspoon white pepper, ¼ teaspoon garlic powder, ¼ teaspoon onion powder, ⅛ to ¼ teaspoon ground red pepper, ¼ teaspoon paprika, and ¼ teaspoon black pepper.

Nutrition Facts per serving: 261 cal., 2 g total fat (0 g sat. fat), 118 mg chol., 391 mg sodium, 30 g carbo., 2 g fiber, 30 g pro. **Daily Values:** 54% vit. C, 6% calcium, 22% iron

Wrap this zippy chicken and rice filling in a colorful assortment of green spinach, orange chile, and plain flour tortillas.

SPICY CHICKEN BURRITOS

1	medium zucchini, halved lengthwise and cut into ¾-inch slices
1	large green sweet pepper, cubed
1	medium onion, coarsely chopped
½	cup coarsely chopped celery
1½	pounds skinless, boneless chicken breast halves, cut into ½-inch strips
1	8-ounce bottle green taco sauce
1	teaspoon instant chicken bouillon granules
½	teaspoon ground cumin
1	cup instant rice
6	to 8 nine- to ten-inch spinach, chile, or plain flour tortillas
¾	cup shredded Monterey Jack cheese with jalapeño peppers (3 ounces)
2	small tomatoes, chopped
2	green onions, sliced

PREP:

25 minutes

COOK:

Low 6 hours, High 3 hours

STAND:

5 minutes

MAKES:

6 to 8 servings

SLOW COOKER:

3½- to 4-quart

1 In a 3½- to 4-quart slow cooker combine zucchini, sweet pepper, onion, and celery. Top with chicken strips. In a small bowl combine taco sauce, bouillon granules, and cumin. Pour over chicken.

2 Cover and cook on low-heat setting for 6 to 7 hours or on high-heat setting for 3 to 3½ hours. Stir in rice. Cover and let stand for 5 minutes.

3 Warm tortillas according to package directions. Divide chicken mixture evenly among warmed tortillas. Top with shredded cheese, tomatoes, and green onions. Fold up bottom edge of each tortilla over filling. Fold in opposite sides just until they meet. Roll up from the bottom. Secure with wooden toothpicks, if necessary.

Nutrition Facts per serving: 408 cal., 10 g total fat (4 g sat. fat), 81 mg chol., 735 mg sodium, 43 g carbo., 3 g fiber, 35 g pro. **Daily Values:** 25% vit. A, 58% vit. C, 18% calcium, 19% iron

Who needs a grill for barbecue? And who says slow cooking means mush? These shapely, saucy thighs hold their form nicely in slow heat.

TURKEY THIGHS IN BARBECUE SAUCE

PREP:

15 minutes

COOK:

Low 10 hours, High 5 hours

MAKES:

4 to 6 servings

SLOW COOKER:

3^1/$_2$- to 4-quart

FOR 5- TO 6-QUART SLOW COOKER: Use ^{3}/$_4$ cup catsup, 3 tablespoons brown sugar, 4 teaspoons quick-cooking tapioca, 4 teaspoons vinegar, 2 teaspoons Worcestershire sauce, ^{1}/$_4$ teaspoon ground cinnamon, ^{1}/$_4$ teaspoon crushed red pepper, and 3 to 3^1/$_2$ pounds turkey thighs or meaty chicken pieces, skinned. Prepare as directed. Makes 6 to 8 servings.

^{1}/$_2$	cup catsup
2	tablespoons brown sugar
1	tablespoon quick-cooking tapioca
1	tablespoon vinegar
1	teaspoon Worcestershire sauce
^{1}/$_4$	teaspoon ground cinnamon
^{1}/$_4$	teaspoon crushed red pepper
2	to 2^1/$_2$ pounds turkey thighs (about 2 thighs) or meaty chicken pieces (breasts, thighs, and drumsticks), skinned
	Hot cooked rice or noodles (optional)

1 In a 3^1/$_2$- to 4-quart slow cooker combine catsup, brown sugar, tapioca, vinegar, Worcestershire sauce, cinnamon, and red pepper. Place turkey thighs or chicken pieces, meaty side down, on catsup mixture.

2 Cover; cook on low-heat setting for 10 to 12 hours or on high-heat setting for 5 to 6 hours. Transfer turkey or chicken to a serving dish. Place cooking liquid in a small bowl or glass measuring cup and skim off fat. If desired, serve turkey or chicken and sauce with rice or noodles.

Nutrition Facts per serving: 239 cal., 6 g total fat (2 g sat. fat), 100 mg chol., 449 mg sodium, 16 g carbo., 1 g fiber, 30 g pro. **Daily Values:** 6% vit. A, 8% vit. C, 3% calcium, 16% iron

The delicious combination of dried apricots and plums, red wine, garlic, honey, and thyme makes these turkey thighs scrumptiously unique.

TURKEY THIGHS IN RED WINE SAUCE

3	pounds turkey thighs
1	tablespoon cooking oil
½	cup pitted dried plums
½	cup dried apricot halves
½	cup orange juice
¼	cup dry red wine
4	cloves garlic, minced
1	tablespoon honey
1	tablespoon finely shredded lemon peel
2	teaspoons dried thyme, crushed
½	teaspoon salt
1	tablespoon cornstarch
1	tablespoon cold water
	Hot cooked rice

PREP:
30 minutes

COOK:
Low 6 hours, High 3 hours

MAKES:
4 or 5 servings

SLOW COOKER:
3½- to 4-quart

1 Remove skin from turkey thighs. In a large skillet brown turkey in hot oil. Transfer turkey to a 3½- to 4-quart slow cooker. Place plums and apricots on turkey.

2 Stir together orange juice, wine, garlic, honey, lemon peel, thyme, and salt. Pour orange juice mixture over turkey.

3 Cover and cook on low-heat setting for 6 to 7 hours or on high-heat setting for 3 to 3½ hours.

4 Using a slotted spoon, transfer turkey and fruit to a serving platter; cover turkey and keep warm. Pour cooking juices into a glass measuring cup; skim off fat. For sauce, measure 1¼ cups juices. Transfer to a saucepan. Combine the cornstarch and cold water; stir into juices in saucepan. Cook and stir over medium heat until thickened and bubbly. Cook and stir for 2 minutes more. Spoon sauce over turkey and hot cooked rice.

Nutrition Facts per serving: 531 cal., 14 g total fat (4 g sat. fat), 156 mg chol., 406 mg sodium, 49 g carbo., 3 g fiber, 47 g pro. **Daily Values:** 26% vit. C, 9% calcium, 36% iron

It's economical to use turkey portions in your favorite dishes; in this recipe, two thighs serve six people.

ZESTY TURKEY THIGHS

PREP:

15 minutes

COOK:

Low 5 hours, High 2½ hours

MAKES:

6 servings

SLOW COOKER:

3½- to 4-quart

2 turkey thighs (2½ to 2¾ pounds), skinned
⅔ cup chopped onion
¾ cup cranberry juice cocktail
¼ cup Dijon-style mustard
¼ teaspoon ground red pepper
½ cup dried cranberries or cherries
1 tablespoon water
2 teaspoons cornstarch
3 cups hot cooked barley
1 medium nectarine or pear, cored and chopped

1 Rinse turkey thighs. Place turkey thighs in the bottom of a 3½- to 4-quart slow cooker. Add onion. In a bowl combine cranberry juice cocktail, mustard, and red pepper. Pour over all.

2 Cover; cook on low-heat setting for 5 to 6 hours or on high-heat setting for 2½ to 3 hours. Remove turkey; cover to keep warm.

3 For sauce, strain cooking juices. Measure juices; if necessary, add water to make 1½ cups. In a small saucepan combine juices and cranberries or cherries. Stir together cornstarch and 1 tablespoon water; add to mixture in saucepan. Cook and stir over medium heat until thickened and bubbly. Cook and stir for 2 minutes more. To serve, toss hot cooked barley with nectarine or pear. Serve turkey and sauce over barley mixture.

Nutrition Facts per serving: 436 cal., 11 g total fat (3 g sat. fat), 116 mg chol., 365 mg sodium, 41 g carbo., 6 g fiber, 42 g pro. **Daily Values:** 22% vit. C, 5% calcium, 29% iron

Spoon some of the gravy over the turkey. Pass the rest and serve with mashed potatoes, if desired.

TURKEY CHABLIS

$^3/_4$ cup dry white wine

$^1/_2$ cup chopped onion

1   clove garlic, minced

1   bay leaf

1    $3^1/_2$- to 4-pound frozen boneless turkey, thawed

1   teaspoon dried rosemary, crushed

$^1/_4$ teaspoon pepper

$^1/_3$ cup half-and-half, light cream, or milk

2   tablespoons cornstarch

1 In a $3^1/_2$- to 6-quart slow cooker combine white wine, onion, garlic, and bay leaf. If turkey is wrapped in netting, remove netting and discard. If gravy packet is present, remove and refrigerate for another use. Combine rosemary and pepper. Rub turkey with rosemary mixture. Place turkey in cooker.

2 Cover; cook on low-heat setting for 9 to 10 hours or on high-heat setting for $4^1/_2$ to 5 hours. Remove turkey and keep warm. For gravy, strain cooking juices; discard solids. Skim fat from juices. Measure $1^1/_3$ cups juices into a small saucepan. Combine half-and-half and cornstarch; stir into juices. Cook and stir until thickened and bubbly. Cook and stir 2 minutes more.

3 Slice turkey. Spoon some gravy over turkey. Pass remaining gravy with turkey.

Nutrition Facts per serving: 365 cal., 9 g total fat (3 g sat. fat), 176 mg chol., 193 mg sodium, 5 g carbo., .4 g fiber, 58 g pro. **Daily Values:** 2% vit. C, 6% calcium, 23% iron

PREP:

15 minutes

COOK:

Low 9 hours, High $4^1/_2$ hours

MAKES:

6 to 8 servings

SLOW COOKER:

$3^1/_2$- to 6-quart

No one will believe this rich-tasting gravy starts with a mix. If you're pressed for time, substitute fully cooked frozen turkey meatballs, thawed.

SLOW-COOKED MEATBALLS WITH GRAVY

PREP:

30 minutes

COOK:

Low 6 hours, High 3 hours

MAKES:

8 servings

SLOW COOKER:

3$^{1}/_{2}$- to 4-quart

2	beaten eggs
$^{3}/_{4}$	cup fine, dry, seasoned bread crumbs
$^{1}/_{2}$	cup finely chopped onion
$^{1}/_{2}$	cup finely chopped celery
2	tablespoons snipped fresh parsley
$^{1}/_{4}$	teaspoon pepper
$^{1}/_{8}$	teaspoon garlic powder
2	pounds ground raw turkey
1$^{1}/_{2}$	teaspoons cooking oil
1	10$^{3}/_{4}$-ounce can reduced-sodium condensed cream of mushroom soup
1	cup water
1	15- or 16-ounce envelope turkey gravy mix
$^{1}/_{2}$	teaspoon finely shredded lemon peel
$^{1}/_{2}$	teaspoon dried thyme, crushed
1	bay leaf
	Hot cooked mashed potatoes or buttered noodles
	Snipped fresh parsley (optional)

1 In a large bowl combine eggs, bread crumbs, onion, celery, 2 tablespoons parsley, pepper, and garlic powder. Add ground turkey and mix well. Shape into 1$^{1}/_{2}$-inch balls.

2 In a large skillet brown meatballs, half at a time, in hot oil. If necessary add additional oil. Drain meatballs. Transfer to a 3$^{1}/_{2}$- to 4-quart slow cooker.

3 In a bowl combine soup, water, gravy mix, lemon peel, thyme, and bay leaf. Pour over meatballs.

4 Cover; cook on low-heat setting for 6 to 8 hours or on high-heat setting for 3 to 4 hours. Discard bay leaf. Serve with mashed potatoes or noodles. Sprinkle with additional snipped fresh parsley.

Nutrition Facts per serving: 314 cal., 14 g total fat (3 g sat. fat), 98 mg chol., 916 mg sodium, 25 g carbo., 21 g pro. **Daily Values:** 8% vit. A, 40% vit. C, 10% calcium, 15% iron

For a less spicy pasta sauce, use ground turkey in place of the hot Italian turkey sausage. Freeze any leftover sauce for another meal.

TURKEY SAUSAGE WITH PEPPER SAUCE

1½   pounds uncooked turkey Italian sausage

4   cups chopped, peeled tomatoes (6 large) or two 14½-ounce cans tomatoes, cut up

2   medium green and/or yellow sweet peppers, cut into strips

2   cups sliced fresh mushrooms

1   large onion, chopped

2   6-ounce cans Italian-style tomato paste

2   cloves garlic, minced

1   teaspoon sugar

½   teaspoon black pepper

1   bay leaf

12   to 16 ounces dried penne, rigatoni, or other pasta

     Finely shredded Parmesan cheese (optional)

PREP:

15 minutes

COOK:

Low 8 hours, High 4 hours

MAKES:

6 to 8 servings

SLOW COOKER:

3½- to 5-quart

1 Remove casings from sausage, if present. In a large skillet cook turkey sausage until brown. Drain off fat. Transfer cooked sausage to a 3½- to 5-quart slow cooker. Stir in fresh or undrained canned tomatoes, sweet peppers, mushrooms, onion, tomato paste, garlic, sugar, black pepper, and bay leaf.

2 Cover and cook on low-heat setting for 8 to 10 hours or on high-heat setting for 4 to 5 hours.

3 Cook pasta according to package directions; drain. Remove and discard bay leaf from sauce. Serve sauce over pasta. Sprinkle with Parmesan cheese, if desired.

Nutrition Facts per serving: 517 cal., 14 g total fat (4 g sat. fat), 60 mg chol., 1,394 mg sodium, 69 g carbo., 6 g fiber, 30 g pro. **Daily Values:** 106% vit. C, 6% calcium, 37% iron

Let the salsa—mild, medium, or hot—determine the spiciness of this bean and sausage dinner. Accompany the meal with a pan of corn bread.

SPICY SAUSAGE & BEANS

PREP:

15 minutes

COOK:

Low 6 hours, High 3 hours

MAKES:

6 servings

SLOW COOKER:

3^1/$_2$- to 4-quart

1	cup chopped green sweet pepper
1	large onion, chopped
3	cloves garlic, minced
1	15-ounce can white kidney beans (cannellini), rinsed and drained
1	15-ounce can black beans, rinsed and drained
1	15-ounce can red kidney beans, rinsed and drained
1^1/$_2$	cups frozen whole kernel corn
1^1/$_2$	cups bottled salsa
1	teaspoon ground cumin
1	pound smoked turkey sausage, sliced

❶ Combine all ingredients in a 3^1/$_2$- to 4-quart slow cooker. Cover and cook on low-heat setting for 6 to 7 hours or on high-heat setting for 3 to 3^1/$_2$ hours.

Nutrition Facts per serving: 307 cal., 8 g total fat (2 g sat. fat), 47 mg chol., 1,213 mg sodium, 47 g carbo., 12 g fiber, 28 g pro. **Daily Values:** 44% vit. C, 8% calcium, 21% iron

BEANS ON ICE
Canned beans are rich in fiber and protein and easy to use, but they also contain a hefty dose of sodium. Home-cooked dried beans offer all the nutrients of canned without all the sodium, and they are available in many more varieties. When you have time, cook dried beans and freeze them in 2-cup portions. Whenever a recipe calls for a 15-ounce can of beans, thaw a container of cooked beans to use instead.

With the addition of kielbasa, German-style potato salad becomes an easy main dish.
Serve slices of pumpernickel bread alongside.

GERMAN POTATO SALAD WITH KIELBASA

10	to 12 whole, tiny new potatoes
1	pound cooked turkey kielbasa or smoked sausage, cut into 1-inch pieces
1	large onion, chopped
1	cup chopped celery
1	cup water
2/3	cup cider vinegar
1/4	cup sugar
2	tablespoons quick-cooking tapioca
3/4	teaspoon celery seeds
1/4	teaspoon salt
1/4	teaspoon pepper
6	cups torn fresh spinach

PREP:
25 minutes

COOK:
High 4 hours

MAKES:
4 servings

SLOW COOKER:
3 1/2- to 4-quart

1 Scrub potatoes thoroughly with a stiff brush. Cut potatoes into halves or quarters. Place in a 3 1/2- to 4-quart slow cooker. Add sausage, onion, and celery. In a bowl stir together water, vinegar, sugar, tapioca, celery seeds, salt, and pepper. Pour over vegetables and sausage.

2 Cover and cook on high-heat setting for 4 to 4 1/2 hours.

3 To serve, divide spinach among 4 salad plates. Drizzle about 2 tablespoons of the cooking juices over the spinach on each plate. Using a slotted spoon, remove potatoes and sausage from cooker; arrange on spinach. Serve immediately.

Nutrition Facts per serving: 339 cal., 10 g total fat (3 g sat. fat), 70 mg chol., 1,227 mg sodium, 43 g carbo., 7 g fiber, 23 g pro. **Daily Values:** 50% vit. C, 7% calcium, 34% iron

Four varieties of canned beans make this a colorful dish. Top each serving with sour cream or yogurt, if desired.

FOUR-BEAN & SAUSAGE DINNER

PREP:

15 minutes

COOK:

Low 8 hours, High 4 hours

MAKES:

8 servings

SLOW COOKER:

3¹/₂- to 4-quart

1   15-ounce can red kidney beans, rinsed and drained

1   15-ounce can black beans, rinsed and drained

1   15-ounce can Great Northern beans, rinsed and drained

1   15-ounce can butter beans, rinsed and drained

1   pound cooked smoked turkey sausage, halved lengthwise and cut into ¹/₂-inch slices

1   8-ounce can tomato sauce

¹/₂   cup catsup

1   medium green sweet pepper, chopped

¹/₂   cup chopped onion

¹/₄   cup packed brown sugar

2   teaspoons Worcestershire sauce

1   teaspoon dry mustard

¹/₂   teaspoon bottled hot pepper sauce

1 In a 3¹/₂- to 4-quart slow cooker combine all ingredients. Stir ingredients together.

2 Cover; cook on low-heat setting for 8 to 10 hours or on high-heat setting for 4 to 5 hours.

Nutrition Facts per serving: 324 cal., 5 g total fat (1 g sat. fat), 38 mg chol., 1,243 mg sodium, 50 g carbo., 11 g fiber, 24 g pro. **Daily Values:** 5% vit. A, 24% vit. C, 10% calcium, 22% iron

MEATLESS
MAIN
DISHES

Armed with a package of ready-made tortellini, you'll find this satisfying meal-in-a-bowl is super simple. The salad is mixed into the soup, and don't count on leftovers to scrape from the cooker.

CREAMY TORTELLINI SOUP

PREP:

20 minutes

COOK:

Low 5 hours, High 2¹/₂ hours; plus 1 hour on Low, 45 minutes on High

MAKES:

4 servings

SLOW COOKER:

3¹/₂- to 4-quart

1	1.8-ounce envelope white sauce mix
4	cups water
1	14-ounce can vegetable broth
1¹/₂	cups sliced fresh mushrooms
¹/₂	cup chopped onion
3	cloves garlic, minced
¹/₂	teaspoon dried basil, crushed
¹/₄	teaspoon salt
¹/₄	teaspoon dried oregano, crushed
¹/₈	teaspoon ground red pepper
1	7- to 8-ounce package dried cheese tortellini (about 2 cups)
1	12-ounce can evaporated milk
6	cups fresh baby spinach leaves or torn spinach
	Finely shredded Parmesan cheese

1 In a 3¹/₂- to 4-quart slow cooker place the white sauce mix. Gradually stir water into white sauce mix until mixture is smooth. Stir in broth, mushrooms, onion, garlic, basil, salt, oregano, and red pepper.

2 Cover; cook on low-heat setting for 5 to 6 hours or on high-heat setting for 2¹/₂ to 3 hours. Stir in tortellini. Cover; cook on low-heat setting for 1 hour or on high-heat setting for 45 minutes. Stir in milk and fresh spinach. Ladle into bowls. Sprinkle each serving with finely shredded Parmesan cheese.

Nutrition Facts per serving: 450 cal., 18 g total fat (7 g sat. fat), 34 mg chol., 1,710 mg sodium, 53 g carbo., 2 g fiber, 22 g pro. **Daily Values:** 66% vit. A, 24% vit. C, 53% calcium, 13% iron

Cubes of potatoes melt into broth and mingle with cheese, cream, and a spoonful of roasted garlic to yield a rich, creamy-chunky soup.

SMASHED POTATO SOUP

3½	pounds potatoes, peeled and cut into ¾-inch cubes
½	cup chopped yellow or red sweet pepper
1½	teaspoons bottled roasted garlic
½	teaspoon black pepper
4½	cups chicken broth
½	cup whipping cream, half-and-half, or light cream
1	cup shredded cheddar cheese (4 ounces)
½	cup thinly sliced green onions
	Dairy sour cream
	Shredded cheddar cheese

1 In a 4- to 6-quart slow cooker combine potatoes, sweet pepper, garlic, and black pepper. Pour broth over all.

2 Cover; cook on low-heat setting for 8 to 10 hours or on high-heat setting for 4 to 5 hours.

3 Mash potatoes slightly with a potato masher. Stir in whipping cream, the 1 cup shredded cheddar, and green onions. To serve, ladle soup into serving bowls. Top with sour cream and additional cheddar cheese.

Nutrition Facts per serving: 311 cal., 16 g total fat (10 g sat. fat), 48 mg chol., 590 mg sodium, 30 g carbo., 3 g fiber, 12 g pro. **Daily Values:** 12% vit. A, 78% vit. C, 20% calcium, 10% iron

PREP:
25 minutes
COOK:
Low 8 hours, High 4 hours
MAKES:
8 servings
SLOW COOKER:
4- to 6-quart

Garam masala makes this soup! Find it in your supermarket or at an Indian market. The blend of spices can include cinnamon, nutmeg, cloves, coriander, cumin, cardamom, pepper, chiles, fennel, and mace.

SPICED BUTTERNUT SQUASH & LENTIL SOUP

PREP:

25 minutes

COOK:

Low 8 hours, High 4 hours

MAKES:

5 or 6 servings

SLOW COOKER:

3$\frac{1}{2}$- to 4-quart

1	cup dry lentils
2$\frac{1}{2}$	cups peeled butternut squash, cut into $\frac{3}{4}$-inch pieces
$\frac{1}{2}$	cup chopped onion (1 medium)
$\frac{1}{2}$	cup chopped carrot (1 medium)
$\frac{1}{2}$	cup chopped celery (1 stalk)
2	cloves garlic, minced
1	teaspoon garam masala
4	cups chicken broth or vegetable broth

1 Rinse and drain lentils. In a 3$\frac{1}{2}$- to 4-quart slow cooker place lentils, squash, onion, carrot, and celery. Sprinkle garlic and garam masala over vegetables. Pour broth over all.

2 Cover and cook on low-heat setting for 8 to 9 hours or on high-heat setting for 4 to 4$\frac{1}{2}$ hours. Ladle into bowls.

Nutrition Facts per serving: 199 cal., 2 g total fat (0 g sat. fat), 0 mg chol., 639 mg sodium, 31 g carbo., 13 g fiber, 16 g pro. **Daily Values:** 107% vit. A, 17% vit. C, 6% calcium, 22% iron

Need a new party stew? This one is festive and great for a group. Set the chowder on a buffet table next to bowls, spoons, and toppings.

CHEESE ENCHILADA CHOWDER

1	15-ounce can black beans, rinsed and drained
1	14½-ounce can diced tomatoes, drained
1	10-ounce package frozen whole kernel corn
½	cup chopped onion
½	cup chopped yellow, green, or red sweet pepper
1	small jalapeño pepper, seeded, if desired, and finely chopped
2	10-ounce cans enchilada sauce
1	10¾-ounce can condensed cream of chicken soup
2	cups milk
1	cup shredded Monterey Jack cheese (4 ounces)
1	cup shredded cheddar cheese (4 ounces)
	Dairy sour cream (optional)
	Guacamole (optional)
	Tortilla chips, coarsely broken (optional)

PREP:
25 minutes

COOK:
Low 6 hours, High 3 hours

MAKES:
6 servings

SLOW COOKER:
3½- to 5-quart

1 In a 3½- to 5-quart slow cooker combine black beans, tomatoes, frozen corn, onion, sweet pepper, and jalapeño pepper. In a large mixing bowl whisk together enchilada sauce and soup. Gradually whisk in milk until smooth. Pour sauce mixture over ingredients in cooker.

2 Cover; cook on low-heat setting for 6 to 8 hours or on high-heat setting for 3 to 4 hours. Stir in Monterey Jack and cheddar cheese until melted. Ladle into bowls. If desired, top each serving with sour cream, guacamole, and tortilla chips.

Nutrition Facts per serving: 374 cal., 18 g total fat (10 g sat. fat), 47 mg chol., 1,536 mg sodium, 37 g carbo., 6 g fiber, 21 g pro. **Daily Values:** 21% vit. A, 81% vit. C, 46% calcium, 14% iron

Steak sauce and a topper of shredded cheese are a pleasing twist to this very easy, beloved basic dish.

VEGETABLE STEW

PREP:

15 minutes

COOK:

Low 9 hours, High 4¹/₂ hours

MAKES:

5 servings

SLOW COOKER:

3¹/₂- to 4-quart

1   pound potatoes, cut into 1-inch cubes

1   large onion, chopped

2   medium carrots, sliced

1   15-ounce can red kidney beans, rinsed and drained

1   15-ounce can tomato sauce

1   14¹/₂-ounce can diced tomatoes with basil, garlic, and oregano

1   10-ounce package frozen whole kernel corn

2   teaspoons steak sauce

²/₃ cup shredded cheddar cheese

1 In a 3¹/₂- to 4-quart slow cooker combine potatoes, onion, carrots, beans, tomato sauce, undrained tomatoes, corn, and steak sauce.

2 Cover and cook on low-heat setting for 9 to 11 hours or on high-heat setting for 4¹/₂ to 5¹/₂ hours. To serve, sprinkle cheese over soup.

Nutrition Facts per serving: 325 cal., 6 g total fat (3 g sat. fat), 16 mg chol., 1,219 mg sodium, 60 g carbo., 10 g fiber, 16 g pro. **Daily Values:** 154% vit. A, 59% vit. C, 22% calcium, 25% iron

Garbanzo beans and chickpeas are the same food. Usually they are stocked along with canned beans or in the Mexican foods section of grocery stores.

EGGPLANT-TOMATO STEW WITH GARBANZOS

1	medium eggplant, peeled, if desired, and cut into ½-inch cubes
2	cups chopped tomatoes
1½	cups sliced carrots
1	15-ounce can garbanzo beans, rinsed and drained
1	15-ounce can red kidney beans, rinsed and drained
1	cup chopped onion
1	cup sliced celery
3	cloves garlic, minced
3	cups vegetable broth or chicken broth
1	6-ounce can Italian-style tomato paste
½	teaspoon dried oregano, crushed
½	teaspoon dried basil, crushed
¼	teaspoon salt
¼	teaspoon black pepper
¼	teaspoon crushed red pepper
1	bay leaf

PREP:
25 minutes

COOK:
Low 8 hours, High 4 hours

MAKES:
6 servings

SLOW COOKER:
5- to 6-quart

1 In a 5- to 6-quart slow cooker combine all ingredients.

2 Cover; cook on low-heat setting for 8 to 9 hours or on high-heat setting for 4 to 4½ hours. Discard bay leaf.

Nutrition Facts per serving: 227 cal., 3 g total fat (0 g sat. fat), 0 mg chol., 1,231 mg sodium, 44 g carbo., 12 g fiber, 13 g pro. **Daily Values:** 176% vit. A, 38% vit. C, 8% calcium, 18% iron

Watch the dumplings through the transparent cooker lid; lifting the lid during cooking causes the dumplings to cook too slowly.

VEGETABLE STEW WITH CORNMEAL DUMPLINGS

PREP:

25 minutes

COOK:

Low 8 hours, High 4 hours; plus 50 minutes on High

MAKES:

6 servings

SLOW COOKER:

3¹/₂- to 4-quart

3   cups peeled butternut or acorn squash, cut into ¹/₂-inch cubes

2   cups sliced fresh mushrooms

2   14¹/₂-ounce cans diced tomatoes

1   15-ounce can Great Northern beans, rinsed and drained

1   cup water

4   cloves garlic, minced

1   teaspoon dried Italian seasoning, crushed

¹/₄   teaspoon pepper

¹/₂   cup all-purpose flour

¹/₃   cup cornmeal

2   tablespoons grated Parmesan cheese

1   tablespoon snipped fresh parsley

1   teaspoon baking powder

¹/₄   teaspoon salt

1   beaten egg

2   tablespoons milk

2   tablespoons cooking oil

1   9-ounce package frozen Italian-style green beans or frozen cut green beans

     Paprika

1 In a 3¹/₂- to 4-quart slow cooker combine squash, mushrooms, undrained tomatoes, Great Northern beans, water, garlic, Italian seasoning, and pepper.

2 Cover; cook on low-heat setting for 8 to 10 hours or on high-heat setting for 4 to 5 hours.

3 Meanwhile, for dumplings, in a medium bowl stir together flour, cornmeal, grated Parmesan cheese, parsley, baking powder, and salt. Combine egg, milk, and oil. Add to the flour mixture; stir with a fork just until combined.

4 If using low-heat setting, turn to high-heat setting. Stir green beans into stew. Drop the dumpling mixture by tablespoons onto stew to make 6 dumplings. Sprinkle with paprika. Cover and cook 50 minutes more on high-heat setting, leaving the cover on during the entire cooking time.

Nutrition Facts per serving: 288 cal., 7 g total fat (2 g sat. fat), 37 mg chol., 442 mg sodium, 45 g carbo., 7 g fiber, 12 g pro. **Daily Values:** 51% vit. A, 50% vit. C, 21% calcium, 21% iron

Finely chopping the onion ensures that it is fully cooked by the time this family-style supper is ready to serve.

VEGETARIAN CHILI WITH PASTA

1	15-ounce can garbanzo beans, rinsed and drained
1	15-ounce can red kidney beans, rinsed and drained
2	14½-ounce cans diced tomatoes
1	8-ounce can tomato sauce
1	large onion, finely chopped (1 cup)
½	cup chopped green or yellow sweet pepper
2	cloves garlic, minced
2	to 3 teaspoons chili powder
½	teaspoon dried oregano, crushed
⅛	teaspoon ground red pepper (optional)
1	cup wagon wheel pasta or elbow macaroni
	Shredded cheddar cheese (optional)

PREP:
20 minutes

COOK:
Low 4 hours, High 2 hours

MAKES:
5 servings

SLOW COOKER:
3½- to 4-quart

1 In a 3½- to 4-quart slow cooker combine beans, undrained tomatoes, tomato sauce, onion, sweet pepper, garlic, chili powder, oregano, and red pepper, if desired.

2 Cover; cook on low-heat setting for 4 to 5 hours or on high-heat setting for 2 to 2½ hours.

3 Cook pasta according to package directions; drain. Stir cooked pasta into bean mixture. Serve in bowls and, if desired, sprinkle with cheddar cheese.

Nutrition Facts per serving: 273 cal., 2 g total fat (0 g sat. fat), 0 mg chol., 868 mg sodium, 53 g carbo., 10 g fiber, 14 g pro. **Daily Values:** 57% vit. C, 13% calcium, 22% iron

Toasting the cumin seeds for this chili is more than worth the effort. Low heat intensifies the flavor, gives a nutty taste, and makes your house smell so very good!

WHITE BEAN & TOASTED CUMIN CHILI

PREP:

20 minutes

COOK:

Low 9 hours, High 4$\frac{1}{2}$ hours

MAKES:

4 servings

SLOW COOKER:

3$\frac{1}{2}$- to 4-quart

*NOTE
To toast cumin seeds, place them in a dry skillet over low heat. Cook, stirring often, for 8 minutes or until fragrant. Remove from heat; allow to cool before grinding with a food mill or a mortar and pestle.

1	cup chopped onion
3	cloves garlic, minced
2	14$\frac{1}{2}$-ounce cans tomatoes, cut up
1	12-ounce can beer or nonalcoholic beer
1	chipotle chile pepper in adobo sauce, chopped
1	tablespoon cumin seeds, toasted* and crushed
1	teaspoon sugar
$\frac{1}{2}$	teaspoon salt
2	19-ounce cans cannellini beans, rinsed and drained
1$\frac{1}{2}$	cups coarsely chopped, seeded, and peeled Golden Nugget or acorn squash (about 12 ounces)
$\frac{1}{2}$	cup dairy sour cream
2	tablespoons lime juice
1	tablespoon snipped fresh chives
	Whole fresh chives (optional)
	Lime wedges (optional)

1 In a 3$\frac{1}{2}$- to 4-quart slow cooker stir together the onion, garlic, undrained tomatoes, beer, chipotle pepper, cumin, sugar, and salt. Stir in beans and squash.

2 Cover; cook on low-heat setting for 9 to 10 hours or on high-heat setting for 4$\frac{1}{2}$ to 5 hours. Meanwhile, combine sour cream, lime juice, and snipped chives. Chill until ready to use.

3 To serve, ladle chili into bowls. Top with sour cream mixture. If desired, garnish with whole fresh chives and small lime wedges.

Nutrition Facts per serving: 327 cal., 7 g total fat (3 g sat. fat), 11 mg chol., 1,070 mg sodium, 60 g carbo., 16 g fiber, 20 g pro. **Daily Values:** 63% vit. A, 66% vit. C, 20% calcium, 30% iron

For your next breakfast buffet, instead of an egg and sausage casserole, try this savory alternative that's loaded with vegetables too.

BRUNCH CASSEROLE

Nonstick cooking spray

1 8- to 10-ounce package meatless breakfast links

1 $10\frac{3}{4}$-ounce can condensed cream of potato soup

$\frac{2}{3}$ cup milk

2 teaspoons Worcestershire or steak sauce

$\frac{1}{4}$ teaspoon freshly ground black pepper

1 28-ounce package frozen loose-pack diced hash brown potatoes with onion and peppers, thawed

1 10-ounce package frozen broccoli, cauliflower, and carrots in cheese sauce, thawed

$\frac{1}{2}$ cup shredded cheddar cheese (2 ounces)

1 Lightly coat a $3\frac{1}{2}$- to 4-quart slow cooker with cooking spray. Brown sausage according to package directions; cool slightly. Slice links into $\frac{1}{2}$-inch pieces.

2 In slow cooker combine soup, milk, Worcestershire or steak sauce, and pepper. Stir in potatoes, vegetables with cheese sauce, and sausage pieces.

3 Cover and cook on low-heat setting for 5 to 6 hours or on high-heat setting for $2\frac{1}{2}$ to 3 hours. Turn off cooker. Sprinkle mixture with cheese. Cover and let stand 15 minutes before serving.

Nutrition Facts per serving: 290 cal., 8 g total fat (3 g sat. fat), 15 mg chol., 1,075 mg sodium, 40 g carbo., 6 g fiber, 18 g pro. **Daily Values:** 29% vit. A, 35% vit. C, 20% calcium, 17% iron

PREP:
15 minutes

COOK:
Low 5 hours, High $2\frac{1}{2}$ hours

STAND:
15 minutes

MAKES:
6 to 8 servings

SLOW COOKER:
$3\frac{1}{2}$- to 4-quart

For variety, use a tube of polenta with wild mushrooms or even Italian-style polenta. Look for the tubes in the produce section of your supermarket.

SWEET BEANS & LENTILS OVER POLENTA

PREP:

20 minutes

COOK:

Low 7 hours, High 3^1/$_2$ hours

MAKES:

6 servings

SLOW COOKER:

3^1/$_2$- to 4-quart

1   14-ounce can vegetable broth

^{1}/$_2$ cup water

1   cup dry lentils

1   12-ounce package frozen soybeans

1   medium red sweet pepper, chopped

1   teaspoon dried oregano, crushed

2   cloves garlic, minced

^{1}/$_2$ teaspoon salt

2   medium tomatoes, chopped

1   16-ounce tube refrigerated polenta

1 In a 3^1/$_2$- to 4-quart slow cooker combine broth, water, lentils, soybeans, sweet pepper, oregano, garlic, and salt.

2 Cover and cook on low-heat setting for 7 to 8 hours or on high-heat setting for 3^1/$_2$ to 4 hours. Stir in chopped tomatoes.

3 Meanwhile, prepare polenta according to package directions. Serve lentil mixture over polenta.

Nutrition Facts per serving: 280 cal., 5 g total fat (1 g sat. fat), 0 mg chol., 794 mg sodium, 43 g carbo., 15 g fiber, 19 g pro. **Daily Values:** 30% vit. A, 85% vit. C, 12% calcium, 26% iron

Thick, rich, and well-seasoned, a ragout is typically a stew of meat and vegetables. With the earthy mushrooms, crunchy fennel, and beans in this full-flavored version, you'll never miss the meat.

MUSHROOM & FENNEL RAGOUT

1	large fennel bulb, trimmed and coarsely chopped (1¾ cups)
8	ounces mushrooms, quartered
1	19-ounce can fava beans, rinsed and drained
8	plum tomatoes, coarsely chopped (3½ cups)
¼	cup vegetable broth
1	tablespoon quick-cooking tapioca
1	teaspoon dried Italian seasoning, crushed
½	teaspoon salt
¼	teaspoon freshly ground pepper
6	ounces dried penne pasta
2	tablespoons pine nuts, toasted

PREP:
20 minutes

COOK:
Low 8 hours, High 4 hours

MAKES:
4 servings

SLOW COOKER:
3½- to 4-quart

1 In a 3½- to 4- quart slow cooker combine fennel, mushrooms, fava beans, plum tomatoes, and broth. Sprinkle with tapioca, Italian seasoning, salt, and pepper; stir to combine.

2 Cover and cook on low-heat setting for 8 to 9 hours or on high-heat setting for 4 to 4½ hours.

3 Cook pasta according to package directions; drain. Toss pasta with vegetable mixture. Sprinkle with toasted pine nuts.

Nutrition Facts per serving: 347 cal., 5 g total fat (1 g sat. fat), 0 mg chol., 811 mg sodium, 62 g carbo., 25 g fiber, 18 g pro. **Daily Values:** 20% vit. A, 66% vit. C, 9% calcium, 16% iron

A curry is an Indian or Far Eastern dish that features foods seasoned with curry powder, which is a blend of 16 to 20 ground spices.

VEGETABLE CURRY

PREP:

20 minutes

COOK:

Low 7 hours, High 3^1/$_2$ hours

STAND:

5 minutes

MAKES:

4 servings

SLOW COOKER:

3^1/$_2$- to 5-quart

4	medium carrots, sliced (2 cups)
2	medium potatoes, cut into ^{1}/$_2$-inch cubes (2 cups)
1	15-ounce can garbanzo beans, rinsed and drained
8	ounces green beans, cut into 1-inch pieces (1^3/$_4$ cups)
1	cup coarsely chopped onion
3	cloves garlic, minced
2	tablespoons quick-cooking tapioca
2	teaspoons curry powder
1	teaspoon ground coriander
^{1}/$_4$	to ^{1}/$_2$ teaspoon crushed red pepper
^{1}/$_4$	teaspoon salt
^{1}/$_8$	teaspoon ground cinnamon
1	14-ounce can vegetable broth or chicken broth
1	14^1/$_2$-ounce can diced tomatoes
2	cups hot cooked rice

1 In a 3^1/$_2$- to 5-quart slow cooker combine carrots, potatoes, garbanzo beans, green beans, onion, garlic, tapioca, curry powder, coriander, red pepper, salt, and cinnamon. Pour broth over all.

2 Cover; cook on low-heat setting for 7 to 9 hours or on high-heat setting for 3^1/$_2$ to 4^1/$_2$ hours. Stir in undrained tomatoes. Cover; let stand 5 minutes. Serve with cooked rice.

Nutrition Facts per serving: 407 cal., 3 g total fat (0 g sat. fat), 0 mg chol., 1,068 mg sodium, 87 g carbo., 12 g fiber, 13 g pro. **Daily Values:** 392% vit. A, 71% vit. C, 15% calcium, 28% iron

Prepare this mélange of vegetables and barley in summer when zucchini and tomatoes are at their peak. A slow cooker makes the meal without heating up the kitchen—perfect when it's hot outside!

VEGETABLE-BARLEY MEDLEY

1	15-ounce can black beans, rinsed and drained
1	14-ounce can vegetable broth or chicken broth
1	10-ounce package frozen whole kernel corn
1	large onion, chopped
½	cup regular barley
1	medium green sweet pepper, chopped (¾ cup)
1	medium carrot, thinly sliced (½ cup)
2	cloves garlic, minced
2	tablespoons snipped fresh parsley
1	teaspoon dried basil or oregano, crushed
½	teaspoon salt
¼	teaspoon ground black pepper
1	medium zucchini, halved lengthwise and thinly sliced (1¼ cups)
2	medium tomatoes, coarsely chopped (1½ cups)
1	tablespoon lemon juice

1 In a 3½- to 5-quart slow cooker combine drained beans, broth, corn, onion, barley, sweet pepper, carrot, garlic, parsley, basil or oregano, salt, and black pepper.

2 Cover and cook on low-heat setting for 7 to 8 hours or on high-heat setting for 3½ to 4 hours.

3 If using low-heat setting, turn to high-heat setting. Stir in the zucchini, tomatoes, and lemon juice. Cover and cook 30 minutes more on high-heat setting.

Nutrition Facts per serving: 278 cal., 2 g total fat (0 g sat. fat), 0 mg chol., 1,001 mg sodium, 62 g carbo., 13 g fiber, 14 g pro. **Daily Values:** 80% vit. C, 8% calcium, 17% iron

PREP:

20 minutes

COOK:

Low 7 hours, High 3½ hours; plus 30 minutes on High

MAKES:

4 servings

SLOW COOKER:

3½- to 5-quart

A healthy dose of cumin gives this bean and rice dish a kick. For the carnivore at your table, serve some Cajun-spiced sausages alongside.

BEANS & RICE WITH CUMIN

PREP:

20 minutes

COOK:

High 4 hours; plus 15 minutes

STAND:

1 hour

MAKES:

5 servings

SLOW COOKER:

3$\frac{1}{2}$- to 4-quart

2$\frac{1}{4}$ cups dry black beans (about 1 pound)

3 cups chopped onions

4$\frac{1}{2}$ cups water

3 to 4 chopped jalapeño peppers

6 to 8 garlic cloves

4 bay leaves

1 tablespoon ground cumin

2 teaspoons salt

$\frac{1}{2}$ teaspoon black pepper

2 cups instant brown rice

Fresh cilantro (optional)

Jalapeño pepper slices (optional)

Lemon wedges (optional)

1 Rinse beans; place in a large saucepan. Add enough water to cover beans by 2 inches. Bring to boiling; reduce heat. Simmer, uncovered, for 10 minutes. Remove from heat. Cover; let stand for 1 hour. (Or place beans in water in a large saucepan. Cover; let soak in a cool place overnight.) Drain and rinse beans.

2 In a 3$\frac{1}{2}$- to 4-quart slow cooker combine the beans, onions, water, chopped jalapeños, garlic, bay leaves, cumin, salt, and pepper.

3 Cover; cook on high-heat setting for 4 to 5 hours. Remove and discard bay leaves. Stir in instant brown rice. Cover and cook 15 minutes more.

4 Ladle soup into bowls. If desired, garnish with cilantro and serve with jalapeños and lemon wedges.

Nutrition Facts per serving: 542 cal., 3 g total fat (0 g sat. fat), 0 mg chol., 1,189 mg sodium, 105 g carbo., 21 g fiber, 28 g pro. **Daily Values:** 20% vit. C, 18% calcium, 36% iron

A variety of textures and flavors makes this an exotic main dish. Look for chutney in the condiment aisle of the supermarket.

CURRIED VEGETABLES & RICE

3	medium potatoes, cut into ½-inch chunks (3 cups)
4	medium carrots, cut into ¼-inch slices (2 cups)
1	large red onion, cut into strips (1 cup)
1¼	cups apple juice
2	tablespoons quick-cooking tapioca
2	teaspoons curry powder
1	teaspoon grated fresh ginger
½	teaspoon salt
½	teaspoon ground cardamom
1	cup uncooked regular brown rice
1	12.3-ounce package extra-firm tofu, drained and cut into ¾-inch cubes
1	medium zucchini, halved lengthwise and cut into ½-inch slices
1	cup frozen peas
⅓	cup golden raisins
	Chutney (optional)

1 In a 3½- to 4-quart slow cooker combine potatoes, carrots, red onion, apple juice, tapioca, curry powder, ginger, salt, and cardamom.

2 Cover; cook on low-heat setting for 8 to 10 hours or on high-heat setting for 4 to 5 hours.

3 Cook rice according to package directions.

4 If using low-heat setting, turn to high-heat setting. Add tofu, zucchini, peas, and raisins to cooker. Cover and cook for 30 minutes more. Serve vegetable mixture over hot cooked rice. If desired, serve with chutney.

Nutrition Facts per serving: 326 cal., 3 g total fat (0 g sat. fat), 0 mg chol., 262 mg sodium, 65 g carbo., 7 g fiber, 11 g pro. **Daily Values:** 33% vit. C, 7% calcium, 17% iron

PREP:

15 minutes

COOK:

Low 8 hours, High 4 hours; plus 30 minutes on High

MAKES:

6 servings

SLOW COOKER:

3½- to 4-quart

Spoon these beans over a bed of nutty-tasting brown rice, the least-processed form of rice. Chewy, tan-colored layers of bran on the rice kernels provide flavor and nutrition.

SAVORY BEANS & RICE

PREP:

20 minutes

COOK:

Low 9 hours, High 4 hours; plus 30 minutes

STAND:

1 hour

MAKES:

5 servings

SLOW COOKER:

3¹/₂- to 4-quart

1¹/₄ cups dry red beans or dry red kidney beans

  1 large onion, chopped (1 cup)

  ³/₄ cup sliced celery

  2 cloves garlic, minced

  ¹/₂ of a vegetable bouillon cube

  1 teaspoon dried basil, crushed

  1 bay leaf

1¹/₄ cups water

1¹/₄ cups uncooked brown rice

  1 14¹/₂-ounce can stewed tomatoes

  1 4-ounce can diced green chile peppers, drained

    Few dashes bottled hot pepper sauce

1 Rinse beans; place in a large saucepan. Add enough water to cover beans by 2 inches. Bring to boiling; reduce heat. Simmer for 10 minutes. Remove from heat. Cover and let stand for 1 hour. (Or place beans in water in a large saucepan. Cover; let soak in a cool place overnight.) Drain and rinse beans.

2 In a 3¹/₂- to 4-quart slow cooker combine beans, onion, celery, garlic, bouillon, basil, and bay leaf. Pour the 1¹/₄ cups water over all.

3 Cover and cook on low-heat setting for 9 to 10 hours or on high-heat setting for 4 to 5 hours.

4 Cook brown rice according to package directions; keep warm. Remove bay leaf from bean mixture; discard bay leaf. Stir undrained stewed tomatoes, chile peppers, and hot pepper sauce into cooked beans. Cook 30 minutes more. Serve bean mixture over hot cooked rice.

Nutrition Facts per serving: 383 cal., 3 g total fat (0 g sat. fat), 0 mg chol., 406 mg sodium, 74 g carbo., 10 g fiber, 16 g pro. **Daily Values:** 22% vit. C, 11% calcium, 21% iron

BREAD IDEAS
One thing to love about slow cooker meals is that you need only bread and a salad or a fresh fruit or vegetable plate to complete a meal. Keep a supply of various baking mixes on hand so you can quickly bake a batch of muffins or biscuits to serve with dinner. For variety, stir canned diced chile peppers into corn muffin batter or mix a little grated Parmesan cheese into biscuit mix.

As an option, try such pepper varieties as serrano, Anaheim (banana), or small poblano peppers. Leave the seeds in the peppers for a hotter dish.

SPICY BLACK BEANS & RICE

2	cups dry black beans
1	cup chopped onion
1	cup chopped celery
1	cup chopped carrot
1	medium yellow or green sweet pepper, chopped
2	jalapeño peppers, chopped
4	cloves garlic, minced
1½	teaspoons ground cumin
1½	teaspoons ground coriander
1	teaspoon dried thyme, crushed
1	teaspoon salt
½	teaspoon black pepper
2	bay leaves
2	14-ounce cans chicken broth (3½ cups)
2	tablespoons butter, softened
2	tablespoons all-purpose flour
4	cups hot cooked rice

PREP:

30 minutes

COOK:

Low 10 hours, High 5 hours; plus 30 minutes on High

STAND:

1 hour

MAKES:

8 servings

SLOW COOKER:

3½- to 4-quart

1 Rinse beans; place in a large saucepan. Add enough water to cover beans by 2 inches. Bring to boiling; reduce heat. Simmer for 10 minutes. Remove from heat. Cover and let stand for 1 hour. (Or place beans in cold water in a large saucepan. Cover; let soak overnight.) Drain beans.

2 In a 3½- to 4-quart slow cooker combine drained beans, onion, celery, carrot, sweet pepper, jalapeño peppers, garlic, cumin, coriander, thyme, salt, black pepper, and bay leaves. Pour chicken broth over all.

3 Cover; cook on low-heat setting for 10 to 11 hours or on high-heat setting for 5 to 5½ hours. If using low-heat setting, turn to high-heat setting. Stir together butter and flour to make a paste. Whisk into bean mixture. Cover and cook 30 minutes longer. Discard bay leaves. Serve with hot rice.

Nutrition Facts per serving: 341 cal., 5 g total fat (2 g sat. fat), 8 mg chol., 783 mg sodium, 60 g carbo., 9 g fiber, 14 g pro. **Daily Values:** 82% vit. A, 69% vit. C, 9% calcium, 21% iron

Beans and rice are popular in many countries. Tonight, why not get your palate ready for a lively treat and try them Cuban-style?

CUBAN-STYLE BLACK BEANS & RICE

PREP:

20 minutes

COOK:

Low 10 hours, High 5 hours

STAND:

1 hour

MAKES:

5 servings

SLOW COOKER:

3¹/₂- to 4-quart

*NOTE
Protect your hands from pungent oils while preparing fresh chile peppers. Wear plastic gloves or put sandwich bags over your hands to prevent skin contact with the peppers. Always wash your hands and nails with hot, soapy water after handling chile peppers.

1¹/₂	cups dry black beans
2	14-ounce cans reduced-sodium chicken broth (3¹/₂ cups)
1	cup chopped onion
2	bay leaves
1	to 2 fresh jalapeño peppers, seeded and finely chopped*
4	cloves garlic, minced
2	teaspoons ground cumin
2	teaspoons finely shredded lime peel
³/₄	teaspoon salt
¹/₄	teaspoon black pepper
3	cups hot cooked brown rice
	Fresh cilantro sprigs (optional)
	Fresh jalapeño pepper slices (optional)
	Lime wedges (optional)

1 Rinse beans. In a large saucepan combine beans and 4 cups water. Bring to boiling; reduce heat. Simmer for 10 minutes. Remove from heat. Cover and let stand for 1 hour. Drain and rinse beans.

2 Place beans in a 3¹/₂- to 4-quart slow cooker. Add broth, onion, bay leaves, jalapeño peppers, garlic, cumin, lime peel, salt, and black pepper. Cover; cook on low-heat setting for 10 to 12 hours or on high-heat setting for 5 to 6 hours. Remove bay leaves. Mash beans slightly.

3 Serve beans with hot cooked rice. If desired, garnish with cilantro and serve with jalapeño pepper slices and lime wedges.

Nutrition Facts per serving: 353 cal., 2 g total fat (0 g sat. fat), 0 mg chol., 795 mg sodium, 67 g carbo., 12 g fiber, 18 g pro. **Daily Values:** 8% vit. C, 10% calcium, 19% iron

Cheese, chili beans, and rice come straight from the cooker neatly packaged in sweet peppers. Use a mix of red, orange, and yellow peppers for a festive table.

BEAN-AND-RICE-STUFFED PEPPERS

4 small to medium green, red, or yellow sweet peppers

1 cup cooked converted rice

1 15-ounce can chili beans with chili gravy

4 ounces Monterey Jack cheese, shredded (1 cup)

1 15-ounce can chunky tomato sauce with onion, celery, and green pepper

1 Remove tops, membranes, and seeds from sweet peppers. Stir together rice, beans, and ½ cup of the cheese; spoon into peppers. Pour tomato sauce into a 5- to 6-quart slow cooker. Place peppers, filled side up, in cooker.

2 Cover and cook on low-heat setting for 6 to 6½ hours or on high-heat setting for 3 to 3½ hours. Transfer sweet peppers to serving platter. Spoon tomato sauce over peppers and sprinkle with remaining cheese.

Nutrition Facts per serving: 323 cal., 11 g total fat (5 g sat. fat), 25 mg chol., 918 mg sodium, 41 g carbo., 9 g fiber, 16 g pro. **Daily Values:** 86% vit. A, 206% vit. C, 34% calcium, 16% iron

PREP:

15 minutes

COOK:

Low 6 hours, High 3 hours

MAKES:

4 servings

SLOW COOKER:

5- to 6-quart

Raisins and brown sugar sweeten ready-to-use marinara sauce, while a splash of lemon juice adds pleasing tartness. The result is a tangy-sweet sauce that complements these cabbage rolls filled with beans and rice.

SWEET & SOUR CABBAGE ROLLS

PREP:

1 hour

COOK:

Low 7 hours, High 3¹/₂ hours

MAKES:

4 servings

SLOW COOKER:

3¹/₂- to 6-quart

1	large head green cabbage
1	15-ounce can black beans or red kidney beans, rinsed and drained
1	cup cooked brown rice
¹/₂	cup chopped carrot
¹/₂	cup chopped celery
1	medium onion, chopped
1	clove garlic, minced
3¹/₂	cups marinara sauce or meatless spaghetti sauce
¹/₃	cup raisins
3	tablespoons lemon juice
1	tablespoon brown sugar

1 Remove 8 large outer leaves from the cabbage. In a Dutch oven cook cabbage leaves in boiling water for 4 to 5 minutes or just until leaves are limp. Drain cabbage leaves. Trim the thick rib from the center of each leaf. Set leaves aside. Shred 4 cups of the remaining cabbage; place shredded cabbage in a 3¹/₂- to 6-quart slow cooker.

2 In a medium bowl combine beans, cooked rice, carrot, celery, onion, garlic, and ¹/₂ cup of the marinara sauce. Evenly divide the bean mixture among the 8 cabbage leaves, using about ¹/₃ cup per leaf. Fold sides of leaf over filling and roll up.

3 Combine remaining marinara sauce, raisins, lemon juice, and brown sugar. Pour about half of the sauce mixture over shredded cabbage in cooker. Stir to mix. Place cabbage rolls on the shredded cabbage, flap side down. Top with remaining sauce.

4 Cover and cook on low-heat setting for 7 to 9 hours or on high-heat setting for 3¹/₂ to 4¹/₂ hours. Carefully remove the cooked cabbage rolls and serve with the shredded cabbage.

Nutrition Facts per serving: 406 cal., 12 g total fat (3 g sat. fat), 0 mg chol., 1,476 mg sodium, 69 g carbo., 15 g fiber, 14 g pro. **Daily Values:** 116% vit. C, 18% calcium, 21% iron

Eggplant, with its mild flavor and spongy texture, soaks up flavors from other foods. In this recipe, chunks of eggplant (a low-calorie alternative to ground beef or sausage) cook in a traditional spaghetti sauce.

PASTA WITH EGGPLANT SAUCE

1	medium eggplant
1	medium onion, chopped
1	28-ounce can Italian-style tomatoes, cut up
1	6-ounce can Italian-style tomato paste
1	4-ounce can sliced mushrooms, drained
2	cloves garlic, minced
1/4	cup dry red wine
1/4	cup water
1 1/2	teaspoons dried oregano, crushed
1/2	cup pitted kalamata olives or pitted ripe olives, sliced
2	tablespoons snipped fresh parsley
	Salt and pepper
4	cups hot cooked penne pasta
1/3	cup grated or shredded Parmesan cheese
2	tablespoons pine nuts, toasted (optional)

PREP:
20 minutes

COOK:
Low 7 hours, High 3 1/2 hours

MAKES:
6 servings

SLOW COOKER:
3 1/2- to 5 1/2-quart

1 Peel eggplant, if desired; cut eggplant into 1-inch cubes. In a 3 1/2- to 5 1/2-quart slow cooker combine eggplant, onion, undrained tomatoes, tomato paste, mushrooms, garlic, wine, water, and oregano.

2 Cover and cook on low-heat setting for 7 to 8 hours or on high-heat setting for 3 1/2 to 4 hours. Stir in olives and parsley. Season to taste with salt and pepper. Serve over pasta; sprinkle with Parmesan cheese. If desired, garnish with toasted pine nuts.

Nutrition Facts per serving: 259 cal., 6 g total fat (1 g sat. fat), 4 mg chol., 804 mg sodium, 42 g carbo., 7 g fiber, 10 g pro. **Daily Values:** 37% vit. C, 13% calcium, 20% iron

For a heartier main dish, brown ground beef in a skillet, drain the fat, and add the browned meat to the tomato mixture before cooking.

HERBED MUSHROOM-TOMATO SAUCE

PREP:

25 minutes

COOK:

Low 8 hours, High 4 hours

MAKES:

6 servings

SLOW COOKER:

3¹/₂- to 4-quart

2   14¹/₂-ounce cans whole tomatoes, cut up
3   cups sliced fresh mushrooms
1   6-ounce can tomato paste
¹/₂   cup chopped onion
2   cloves garlic, minced
2   tablespoons grated Parmesan cheese
2   teaspoons dried oregano, crushed
2   teaspoons brown sugar
1¹/₂   teaspoons dried basil, crushed
¹/₂   teaspoon salt
¹/₂   teaspoon fennel seeds, crushed
¹/₄   teaspoon crushed red pepper (optional)
1   bay leaf
12   ounces spaghetti, linguine, or other pasta, cooked and drained
    Grated Parmesan cheese (optional)

1 In a 3¹/₂- to 4-quart slow cooker combine undrained tomatoes, mushrooms, tomato paste, onion, garlic, 2 tablespoons grated Parmesan cheese, oregano, brown sugar, basil, salt, fennel seeds, red pepper (if desired), and bay leaf.

2 Cover; cook on low-heat setting for 8 to 10 hours or on high-heat setting for 4 to 5 hours.

3 Discard bay leaf. Serve sauce over hot cooked pasta. Top with grated Parmesan cheese, if desired.

Nutrition Facts per serving: 302 cal., 2 g total fat (1 g sat. fat), 1 mg chol., 679 mg sodium, 59 g carbo., 4 g fiber, 11 g pro. **Daily Values:** 15% vit. A, 50% vit. C, 12% calcium, 20% iron

In the same way slow drying in the sun intensifies the flavor of tomatoes, plenty of time over a low flame blends flavors for a sauce that tastes greater than the sum of its parts.

PASTA WITH SUN-DRIED TOMATO SAUCE

2   15-ounce cans tomato sauce

1   14^1/$_2$-ounce can chunky Italian-style tomatoes

1   cup sliced fresh mushrooms

^{1}/$_2$ cup oil-packed sun-dried tomatoes, drained and chopped

^{1}/$_2$ cup chopped onion

^{1}/$_2$ cup chopped red or green sweet pepper

^{1}/$_4$ cup chopped carrot

2   bay leaves

3   cloves garlic, minced

2   teaspoons Italian seasoning

1   teaspoon sugar

^{1}/$_4$ teaspoon salt

^{1}/$_8$ teaspoon crushed red pepper

1^1/$_2$ cups water

12   ounces dried linguine or farfalle (bow tie) pasta

      Finely shredded Romano or Parmesan cheese (optional)

1 In a 3^1/$_2$- to 4-quart slow cooker combine tomato sauce, undrained Italian-style tomatoes, mushrooms, sun-dried tomatoes, onion, sweet pepper, carrot, bay leaves, garlic, Italian seasoning, sugar, salt, and red pepper. Pour water over all.

2 Cover; cook on low-heat setting for 9 to 10 hours or on high-heat setting for 4^1/$_2$ to 5 hours. Meanwhile, cook pasta according to package directions; drain.

3 Remove bay leaves from sauce before serving. Serve sauce over hot cooked pasta. Sprinkle each serving with Romano or Parmesan cheese, if desired.

Nutrition Facts per serving: 311 cal., 3 g total fat (0 g sat. fat), 0 mg chol., 1,079 mg sodium, 62 g carbo., 5 g fiber, 10 g pro. **Daily Values:** 42% vit. A, 56% vit. C, 4% calcium, 18% iron

PREP:

30 minutes

COOK:

Low 9 hours, High 4^1/$_2$ hours

MAKES:

6 servings

SLOW COOKER:

3^1/$_2$- to 4-quart

Instead of sandwiches, try serving the vegetable mixture on tostada shells with shredded lettuce, chopped tomato, and shredded cheese for a taco-style salad.

SLOPPY VEGGIE SANDWICHES

PREP:

30 minutes

COOK:

High 3^1/$_2$ hours (do not cook on Low)

MAKES:

8 servings

SLOW COOKER:

3^1/$_2$- to 4-quart

1	cup chopped carrots
1	cup chopped celery
^{2}/$_3$	cup dry lentils, rinsed and drained
^{2}/$_3$	cup regular brown rice
^{1}/$_2$	cup chopped onion
1	clove garlic, minced
2	tablespoons brown sugar
2	tablespoons prepared mustard
^{1}/$_2$	teaspoon salt
^{1}/$_8$	to ^{1}/$_4$ teaspoon ground red pepper
2	14-ounce cans vegetable broth or chicken broth
1	15-ounce can tomato sauce
2	tablespoons apple cider vinegar
8	whole wheat buns or French rolls, split and toasted

1 In a 3^1/$_2$- to 4-quart slow cooker combine carrots, celery, dry lentils, uncooked brown rice, onion, garlic, brown sugar, mustard, salt, and red pepper. Stir in broth.

2 Cover; cook on high-heat setting for 3 to 3^1/$_2$ hours or until rice and lentils are done. Stir in tomato sauce and vinegar; cover and cook 30 minutes more.

3 To serve, spoon mixture onto toasted buns or rolls.

Nutrition Facts per serving: 261 cal., 4 g total fat (1 g sat. fat), 0 mg chol., 1,036 mg sodium, 50 g carbo., 8 g fiber, 11 g pro. **Daily Values:** 78% vit. A, 5% vit. C, 7% calcium, 21% iron

FIVE INGREDIENTS

If desired, top this family-pleasing chili with corn chips, sour cream, and sliced green onions.

TACO CHILI

PREP:

10 minutes

COOK:

Low 2 hours, High 4 hours

MAKES:

4 to 6 servings

SLOW COOKER:

3¹/₂- to 4-quart

1	pound ground beef
1	1.2-ounce package taco seasoning mix
2	15-ounce cans chunky Mexican-style tomatoes
1	15-ounce can red kidney beans
1	15-ounce can whole kernel corn

1 In a large skillet cook ground beef until brown. Drain fat.

2 In a 3¹/₂- to 4-quart slow cooker combine the cooked ground beef, taco seasoning mix, undrained tomatoes, undrained beans, and undrained corn. Cover and cook on low-heat setting for 4 to 6 hours or on high-heat setting for 2 to 3 hours.

Nutrition Facts per serving: 464 cal., 17 g total fat (6 g sat. fat), 71 mg chol., 2,317 mg sodium, 50 g carbo., 9 g fiber, 33 g pro. **Daily Values:** 60% vit. C, 6% calcium, 22% iron

This beef stew takes on a whole new dimension with the addition of sweet and sour sauce. For starters, serve purchased egg rolls.

SWEET & SOUR BEEF STEW

1½	pounds beef stew meat, cut into ¾- to 1-inch cubes
1	16-ounce package loose-pack frozen stew vegetables (3 cups)
2	10¾-ounce cans condensed beefy mushroom soup
½	cup bottled sweet and sour sauce
⅛	to ¼ teaspoon ground red pepper

1 In a 3½- to 4-quart slow cooker place stew meat and frozen vegetables. Stir in ½ cup water, soup, sweet and sour sauce, and ground red pepper.

2 Cover; cook on low-heat setting for 10 to 11 hours or on high-heat setting for 5 to 5½ hours.

Nutrition Facts per serving: 291 cal., 9 g total fat (3 g sat. fat), 62 mg chol., 1,019 mg sodium, 19 g carbo., 2 g fiber, 30 g pro. **Daily Values:** 74% vit. A, 4% vit. C, 1% calcium, 16% iron

PREP:
10 minutes

COOK:
Low 10 hours, High 5 hours

MAKES:
6 to 8 servings

SLOW COOKER:
3½- to 4-quart

Serve this spicy stew with warm flour tortillas and cool lime wedges. Sour cream makes a tasty topper.

TEXAS TWO-STEP STEW

PREP:

20 minutes

COOK:

*Low 4 hours, High 2 hours;
plus 1 hour on Low or
45 minutes on High*

MAKES:

6 servings

SLOW COOKER:

3¹/₂- to 4-quart

8   ounces uncooked chorizo sausage

1   medium onion, chopped (¹/₂ cup)

1   15-ounce can Mexican-style or Tex-Mex-style chili beans

1   15-ounce can hominy or one 11-ounce can whole kernel corn
    with sweet peppers, drained

1   6-ounce package regular Spanish-style rice mix

1 Remove casings from sausage, if present. In a medium skillet cook
sausage and onion over medium heat until sausage is no longer pink.
Drain fat. Transfer sausage mixture to a 3¹/₂- to 4-quart slow cooker. Stir in
undrained chili beans, hominy, and the seasoning packet contents from
the rice mix, if present (set aside remaining rice mix). Pour 6 cups water
over all.

2 Cover; cook on low-heat setting for 4 to 6 hours or on high-heat
setting for 2 to 3 hours. Stir in remaining rice mix. Cover; cook on low-
heat setting for 1 hour more or on high-heat setting for 45 minutes more.

Nutrition Facts per serving: 383 cal., 16 g total fat (6 g sat. fat), 33 mg chol., 1,385 mg sodium,
44 g carbo., 6 g fiber, 16 g pro. **Daily Values:** 4% vit. A, 9% vit. C, 5% calcium, 16% iron

This easy fix-up will please the entire family. For a change of pace, substitute 10 ounces frozen broccoli for the mixed vegetables.

CREAMY CHICKEN NOODLE SOUP

2   10¾-ounce cans condensed creamy chicken mushroom soup

2   cups chopped cooked chicken

1   9- to 10-ounce package frozen mixed vegetables (cut green beans, corn, diced carrots, peas)

1   teaspoon seasoned pepper or garlic-pepper seasoning

1½   cups dried egg noodles

1 In a 3½- to 4-quart slow cooker gradually stir 5 cups water into the soup. Stir or whisk until smooth. Stir in chicken, vegetables, and seasoned pepper.

2 Cover; cook on low-heat setting for 6 to 8 hours or on high-heat setting for 3 to 4 hours.

3 If using low-heat setting, turn to high-heat setting. Stir in noodles. Cover and cook for 20 to 30 minutes more or until noodles are just tender.

Nutrition Facts per serving: 262 cal., 12 g total fat (3 g sat. fat), 63 mg chol., 908 mg sodium, 21 g carbo., 3 g fiber, 19 g pro. **Daily Values:** 54% vit. A, 6% vit. C, 4% calcium, 9% iron

PREP:
15 minutes

COOK:
Low 6 hours, High 3 hours; plus 20 minutes on High

MAKES:
6 to 8 servings

SLOW COOKER:
3½- to 4-quart

Ladle this delicious soup into bowls and serve with a loaf of crusty bread, or serve small portions in cups with a sandwich or salad.

SAUSAGE-CORN CHOWDER

PREP:

15 minutes

COOK:

Low 8 hours, High 4 hours

MAKES:

6 servings

SLOW COOKER:

3½- to 5-quart

1 pound cooked smoked turkey sausage, halved lengthwise and cut into ½-inch slices

3 cups frozen loose-pack diced hash brown potatoes with onion and peppers

2 medium carrots, coarsely chopped

1 15- to 16½-ounce can cream-style corn

1 10¾-ounce can condensed golden mushroom soup

Snipped fresh chives or parsley (optional)

1 Place sausage, potatoes, and carrots in a 3½- to 5-quart slow cooker. In a medium bowl combine 2½ cups water, corn, and soup. Add to cooker.

2 Cover and cook on low-heat setting for 8 to 10 hours or on high-heat setting for 4 to 5 hours. Ladle into bowls. If desired, sprinkle with snipped fresh chives or parsley.

Nutrition Facts per serving: 238 cal., 8 g total fat (2 g sat. fat), 53 mg chol., 1,280 mg sodium, 28 g carbo., 2 g fiber, 15 g pro. **Daily Values:** 38% vit. C, 2% calcium, 8% iron

So easy and so delicious—take these to your next potluck dinner and you'll come home with an empty bowl.

CREAMY RANCH POTATOES

2½ pounds small red potatoes, quartered

1 8-ounce container dairy sour cream

1 0.4-ounce package buttermilk ranch dry salad dressing mix

1 10¾-ounce can condensed cream of mushroom soup

1 In a 3½- to 4-quart slow cooker place potatoes. In a small bowl combine remaining ingredients. Spoon mixture over potatoes; stir.

2 Cover; cook on low-heat setting for 7 to 8 hours or on high-heat setting for 3½ to 4 hours. Stir gently before serving.

Nutrition Facts per serving: 245 cal., 12 g total fat (6 g sat. fat), 17 mg chol., 517 mg sodium, 30 g carbo., 2 g fiber, 5 g pro. **Daily Values:** 6% vit. A, 31% vit. C, 7% calcium, 12% iron

PREP:

15 minutes

COOK:

Low 7 hours, High 3½ hours

MAKES:

6 servings

SLOW COOKER:

3½- to 4-quart

Cook a package of frozen mashed potatoes to serve with this saucy round steak. For extra flavor, stir snipped fresh basil or grated Parmesan cheese into the cooked potatoes.

STEAK WITH MUSHROOMS

PREP:

10 minutes

COOK:

Low 8 hours, High 4 hours

MAKES:

4 servings

SLOW COOKER:

3^1/$_2$- to 4-quart

FOR A 5- TO 6-QUART SLOW COOKER
Recipe may be doubled.

1	pound boneless beef round steak, cut 1 inch thick
2	medium onions, sliced
2	4^1/$_2$-ounce jars whole mushrooms, drained
1	12-ounce jar beef gravy
^{1}/$_4$	cup dry red wine or apple juice

1 Trim fat from meat. Cut meat into 4 serving-size pieces. In a 3^1/$_2$- to 4-quart slow cooker place onion slices. Arrange mushrooms over onions; add beef. Stir together gravy and wine or apple juice. Pour over beef.

2 Cover and cook on low-heat setting for 8 to 10 hours or on high-heat setting for 4 to 5 hours.

Nutrition Facts per serving: 220 cal., 4 g total fat (2 g sat. fat), 51 mg chol., 814 mg sodium, 11 g carbo., 3 g fiber, 31 g pro. **Daily Values:** 3% vit. A, 3% calcium, 20% iron

Serve this fruited roast with hot cooked couscous or rice to soak up the flavorful sauce. You can vary the amount of chipotle peppers depending on how much heat you like.

POT ROAST WITH CHIPOTLE-FRUIT SAUCE

1	3-pound boneless beef chuck pot roast
2	teaspoons garlic-pepper seasoning
1	7-ounce package dried mixed fruit
1	tablespoon finely chopped chipotle peppers in adobo sauce
2	teaspoons cornstarch

1 Sprinkle both sides of meat with garlic-pepper seasoning. If necessary, cut meat to fit a 3½- to 4-quart slow cooker. Place meat in cooker. Add fruit, peppers, and ½ cup water.

2 Cover; cook on low-heat setting for 10 to 11 hours or on high-heat setting for 5 to 5½ hours. Transfer meat and fruit to a serving platter. Cover and keep warm.

3 Transfer cooking liquid to a bowl or measuring cup; skim off fat. In a medium saucepan combine cornstarch and 1 tablespoon water; add cooking liquid. Cook and stir until thickened and bubbly; cook and stir 2 minutes more. Thinly slice meat. To serve, spoon sauce over sliced meat and fruit.

Nutrition Facts per serving: 576 cal., 19 g total fat (7 g sat. fat), 229 mg chol., 502 mg sodium, 23 g carbo., 1 g fiber, 76 g pro. **Daily Values:** 2% vit. C, 3% calcium, 53% iron

PREP:
15 minutes
COOK:
Low 10 hours, High 5 hours
MAKES:
6 to 8 servings
SLOW COOKER:
3½- to 4-quart

The number of frozen meatballs in a package varies by brand. Although this recipe calls for a package of 16, you could substitute a package of 35 smaller meatballs.

PLUM GOOD SAUSAGE & MEATBALLS

PREP:

10 minutes

COOK:

Low 5 hours, High 2¹/₂ hours

MAKES:

16 appetizers

SLOW COOKER:

3¹/₂- to 4-quart

1 10- or 12-ounce jar plum jam or preserves

1 18-ounce bottle barbecue sauce (1²/₃ cups)

1 16-ounce link cooked jalapeño smoked sausage or smoked sausage, sliced into bite-size pieces

1 16- to 18-ounce package Italian-style or original flavor frozen cooked meatballs (16), thawed

❶ In a 3¹/₂- to 4-quart slow cooker combine the jam and barbecue sauce. Add the sausage and thawed meatballs. Cover and cook on low-heat setting for 5 to 6 hours or on high-heat setting for 2¹/₂ to 3 hours. Use decorative picks to serve.

❷ To serve at a buffet, keep warm at low-heat setting.

Nutrition Facts per serving: 267 cal., 16 g total fat (6 g sat. fat), 38 mg chol., 898 mg sodium, 19 g carbo., 2 g fiber, 12 g pro. **Daily Values:** 6% vit. A, 7% vit. C, 3% calcium, 7% iron

Pass the mustard-spiked apricot sauce along with slices of succulent pork roast. Serve rice as a side dish.

PORK ROAST WITH APRICOT GLAZE

1   3- to 3½-pound boneless pork shoulder roast

1   18-ounce jar apricot preserves

¼   cup chicken broth

2   tablespoons Dijon-style mustard

1   large onion, chopped

1 Trim fat from roast. If necessary, cut roast to fit into a 3½- to 6-quart slow cooker. Place meat in cooker. Combine preserves, broth, mustard, and onion; pour over meat.

2 Cover and cook on low-heat setting for 10 to 12 hours or on high-heat setting for 5 to 6 hours. Transfer meat to a serving platter. Skim fat from the sauce. Spoon some of the sauce over the meat.

Nutrition Facts per serving: 456 cal., 10 g total fat (3 g sat. fat), 93 mg chol., 184 mg sodium, 61 g carbo., 2 g fiber, 29 g pro. **Daily Values:** 17% vit. C, 5% calcium, 13% iron

PREP:

15 minutes

COOK:

Low 10 hours, High 5 hours

MAKES:

6 to 8 servings

SLOW COOKER:

3½- to 6-quart

Take 15 minutes in the morning to brown the roast, chop the potatoes, and layer the ingredients in a slow cooker. In the evening, gather the family for a pot roast complete with meat, potatoes, carrots, and gravy.

POT ROAST WITH MUSHROOM SAUCE

PREP:

15 minutes

COOK:

Low 10 hours, High 5 hours

MAKES:

5 servings

SLOW COOKER:

3¹/₂- to 4-quart

1	1¹/₂-pound boneless beef eye of round roast or round rump roast
4	medium potatoes, quartered
1	16-ounce package peeled baby carrots
1	10³/₄-ounce can condensed golden mushroom soup
¹/₂	teaspoon dried tarragon or basil, crushed

1 Trim fat from roast. Lightly coat an unheated large skillet with nonstick cooking spray. Heat over medium heat. Add meat to skillet and brown on all sides.

2 Place potatoes and carrots in a 3¹/₂- to 4-quart slow cooker. Place browned meat on top of vegetables. In a small bowl stir together soup and tarragon or basil; pour over meat in cooker.

3 Cover and cook on low-heat setting for 10 to 12 hours or on high-heat setting for 5 to 6 hours. To serve, transfer meat and vegetables to a serving platter. Stir sauce; spoon over meat and vegetables.

Nutrition Facts per serving: 391 cal., 13 g total fat (5 g sat. fat), 79 mg chol., 567 mg sodium, 33 g carbo., 5 g fiber, 33 g pro. **Daily Values:** 38% vit. C, 4% calcium, 19% iron

STOCKING UP
Keeping a freezer and pantry stocked with standbys helps last-minute meal preparations go more smoothly and prevents unnecessary trips to the grocery store. In the freezer, keep a variety of frozen vegetables (to add to recipes or serve on the side), frozen fruit, and brown-and-serve rolls. In the pantry, stock up on packaged rice and noodle mixes, salad dressings, and muffin mixes to round out your meals.

Dried thyme, mustard, and orange season the boneless pork chops in this dinner. Serve with steamed broccoli and rice pilaf.

PORK CHOPS WITH ORANGE-DIJON SAUCE

6	boneless pork sirloin chops, cut 1 inch thick
	Salt and pepper
½	teaspoon dried thyme, crushed
1	cup orange marmalade
⅓	cup Dijon-style mustard

1 Sprinkle both sides of chops lightly with salt and pepper. Sprinkle chops with thyme. Place chops in a 3½- to 4-quart slow cooker. In a bowl combine orange marmalade and mustard. Remove 2 tablespoons of the mixture; cover and refrigerate. Combine remaining mixture and ¼ cup water. Pour over chops.

2 Cover; cook on low-heat setting for 6 to 7 hours or on high-heat setting for 3 to 3½ hours. Transfer chops to a serving platter; discard cooking liquid. Spread reserved marmalade mixture over chops.

Nutrition Facts per serving: 409 cal., 15 g total fat (5 g sat. fat), 165 mg chol., 212 mg sodium, 9 g carbo., 1 g fiber, 56 g pro. **Daily Values:** 1% vit. A, 5% vit. C, 5% calcium, 14% iron

PREP:

15 minutes.

COOK:

Low 6 hours, High 3 hours

MAKES:

6 servings

SLOW COOKER:

3½- to 4-quart

Vary the hotness of this recipe with different styles of barbecue sauce, or substitute 1½-inch slices of frankfurters or Polish sausages for the cocktail wieners.

CRANBERRY-SAUCED FRANKS

PREP:

10 minutes

COOK:

Low 4 hours, High 2 hours

MAKES:

32 appetizers

SLOW COOKER:

3½- to 4-quart

1   cup bottled barbecue sauce

1   16-ounce can jellied cranberry sauce

2   1-pound packages cocktail wieners and/or small cooked smoked sausage links

❶ In a 3½- to 4-quart slow cooker stir together the barbecue sauce and cranberry sauce until combined. Stir in the wieners and/or sausages.

❷ Cover; cook on low-heat setting for 4 to 5 hours or on high-heat setting for 2 to 2½ hours. Serve immediately or keep warm on low-heat setting for up to 2 hours. Serve with a slotted spoon or toothpicks.

Nutrition Facts per serving: 118 cal., 8 g total fat (4 g sat. fat), 15 mg chol., 275 mg sodium, 8 g carbo., 0 g fiber, 3 g pro. **Daily Values:** 1% vit. A, 1% vit. C, 1% iron

Party hearty with these ribs, which are perfect for an open-house gathering. Keep the ribs warm in the honey-sweetened picante sauce—no one will leave hungry.

SPICY SPARERIBS

3½   to 4 pounds pork baby back ribs, cut into 1-rib portions
2   cups bottled picante sauce or salsa
½   cup honey
1   tablespoon quick-cooking tapioca
1   teaspoon ground ginger

1 Preheat broiler. Place ribs on the unheated rack of a broiler pan. Broil 6 inches from the heat about 10 minutes or until brown, turning once. Transfer ribs to a 3½- to 6-quart slow cooker.

2 In a medium bowl combine picante sauce or salsa, honey, tapioca, and ginger. Pour sauce over ribs.

3 Cover and cook on low-heat setting for 6 to 7 hours or on high-heat setting for 3 to 3½ hours. Skim fat from sauce. Serve sauce with ribs.

Nutrition Facts per serving: 215 cal., 6 g total fat (2 g sat. fat), 43 mg chol., 246 mg sodium, 18 g carbo., 0 g fiber, 20 g pro. **Daily Values:** 7% vit. C, 1% calcium, 4% iron

PREP:
20 minutes

COOK:
Low 6 hours, High 3 hours

MAKES:
10 to 12 appetizers

SLOW COOKER:
3½- to 6-quart

PARTY TIME
Looking for an easy way to entertain? Host an appetizer buffet with the help of a slow cooker. Start with one or two of the appetizer recipes in this section and borrow another cooker, if necessary. Complement the slow cooker recipes with purchased dips, chips, crackers, cheese, fresh fruit or vegetables, and a selection of beverages.

Vary the flavor of this starter with your favorite barbecue sauce. Have plenty of napkins on hand!

CHICKEN WINGS WITH BBQ SAUCE

PREP:

15 minutes

COOK:

Low 3 hours, High 1½ hours

BROIL:

15 minutes

MAKES:

28 to 32 appetizers

SLOW COOKER:

3½- to 4-quart

3	pounds chicken wings (about 14 to 16)
1½	cups bottled barbecue sauce
¼	cup honey
2	teaspoons prepared mustard
1½	teaspoons Worcestershire sauce

1 Cut off and discard wing tips. Cut each wing at joint to make two sections.

2 Place chicken on the unheated rack of a broiler pan. Broil 4 to 5 inches from the heat for 15 to 20 minutes or until chicken is brown, turning once. Transfer chicken to a 3½- to 4-quart slow cooker.

3 For sauce, combine barbecue sauce, honey, mustard, and Worcestershire sauce; pour over chicken wings. Cover; cook on low-heat setting for 3 to 4 hours or on high-heat setting for 1½ to 2 hours.

Nutrition Facts per serving: 83 cal., 4 g total fat (1 g sat. fat), 20 mg chol., 197 mg sodium, 6 g carbo., 0 g fiber, 5 g pro. **Daily Values:** 1% vit. A, 1% iron

Need an appetizer for a houseful of guests? This favorite is great for almost any get-together.

BUFFALO WINGS WITH BLUE CHEESE DIP

16 chicken wings (about 3 pounds)

1½ cups bottled chili sauce

3 to 4 tablespoons bottled hot pepper sauce

1 recipe Blue Cheese Dip or bottled ranch salad dressing

1 Cut off and discard wing tips. Cut each wing into two sections. Rinse chicken; pat dry. Place chicken on the unheated rack of a broiler pan. Broil 4 to 5 inches from the heat about 10 minutes or until chicken is brown, turning once. Transfer chicken to a 3½- to 4-quart slow cooker. Combine chili sauce and hot pepper sauce; pour over chicken wings.

2 Cover; cook on low-heat setting for 4 to 5 hours or on high-heat setting for 2 to 2½ hours. Serve chicken wings with Blue Cheese Dip or ranch salad dressing.

BLUE CHEESE DIP: In a blender container combine one 8-ounce carton dairy sour cream; ½ cup mayonnaise or salad dressing; ½ cup crumbled blue cheese (2 ounces); 1 clove garlic, minced; and 1 tablespoon white wine vinegar or white vinegar. Cover and blend until smooth. Store dip, covered, in the refrigerator for up to 2 weeks. If desired, top dip with additional crumbled blue cheese before serving.

Nutrition Facts per serving: 108 cal., 8 g total fat (3 g sat. fat), 21 mg chol., 217 mg sodium, 3 g carbo., 0 g fiber, 6 g pro. **Daily Values:** 3% vit. C, 1% calcium, 2% iron

PREP:
30 minutes

COOK:
Low 4 hours, High 2 hours

BROIL:
10 minutes

MAKES:
32 appetizers

SLOW COOKER:
3½- to 4-quart

This fruity dish has a lovely blend of spices. It is especially satisfying served over hot cooked couscous or rice.

CHERRIED CHICKEN

PREP:

20 minutes

COOK:

Low 5 hours, High 2^1/$_2$ hours

MAKES:

4 servings

SLOW COOKER:

3^1/$_2$- to 4-quart

2^1/$_2$ to 3 pounds chicken drumsticks, skinned

1   teaspoon herb-pepper seasoning

1   15- to 17-ounce can pitted dark sweet cherries, drained

1   12-ounce bottle chili sauce

^{1}/$_2$ cup packed brown sugar

1 Sprinkle chicken evenly with herb-pepper seasoning. Place chicken in a 3^1/$_2$- to 4-quart slow cooker. In a mixing bowl combine cherries, chili sauce, and brown sugar. Pour over chicken.

2 Cover; cook on low-heat setting for 5 to 6 hours or on high-heat setting for 2^1/$_2$ to 3 hours. Remove chicken to a serving platter. Skim fat from sauce. Spoon some sauce over chicken; pass remaining sauce.

Nutrition Facts per serving: 410 cal., 5 g total fat (1 g sat. fat), 105 mg chol., 1,539 mg sodium, 63 g carbo., 7 g fiber, 31 g pro. **Daily Values:** 15% vit. A, 33% vit. C, 7% calcium, 17% iron

Thyme, garlic, a little orange juice, and a splash of balsamic vinegar flavor these moist, fork-tender chicken breasts.

CHICKEN WITH THYME & GARLIC SAUCE

6	cloves garlic, minced
1½	teaspoons dried thyme, crushed
3	to 4 pounds whole chicken breasts (with bone), halved and skinned
¼	cup orange juice
1	tablespoon balsamic vinegar

1 Sprinkle garlic and thyme over chicken. Place chicken pieces in a 3½- to 4-quart slow cooker. Pour orange juice and vinegar over chicken.

2 Cover and cook on low-heat setting for 5 to 6 hours or on high-heat setting for 2½ to 3 hours.

3 Remove chicken from cooker; cover and keep warm. Skim off fat from cooking juices. Strain juices into a saucepan. Bring to boiling; reduce heat. Boil gently, uncovered, for 10 minutes or until reduced to 1 cup. Pass juices to spoon over chicken.

Nutrition Facts per serving: 178 cal., 2 g total fat (0 g sat. fat), 85 mg chol., 78 mg sodium, 3 g carbo., 0 g fiber, 34 g pro. **Daily Values:** 13% vit. C, 3% calcium, 7% iron

PREP:

15 minutes

COOK:

Low 5 hours, High 2½ hours; plus 15 minutes on cooktop

MAKES:

6 to 8 servings

SLOW COOKER:

3½- to 4-quart

Preparing this dinner may be less hassle than ordering takeout. Along with this tasty one-dish dinner, bake frozen egg roll appetizers and serve fortune cookies and sherbet for dessert.

SWEET & SOUR CHICKEN

PREP:

15 minutes

COOK:

Low 5 hours, High 2¹/₂ hours

MAKES:

4 servings

SLOW COOKER:

3¹/₂- to 4-quart

1	pound skinless, boneless chicken breast halves
2	9-ounce jars sweet and sour sauce
1	16-ounce package loose-pack frozen broccoli, carrots, and water chestnuts
2¹/₂	cups hot cooked rice
¹/₄	cup chopped almonds, toasted

1 Cut chicken into 1-inch pieces. In a 3¹/₂- to 4-quart slow cooker combine chicken, sweet and sour sauce, and frozen vegetables.

2 Cover and cook on low-heat setting for 5 to 5¹/₂ hours or on high-heat setting for 2¹/₂ to 2³/₄ hours. Serve with hot cooked rice. Sprinkle with almonds.

Nutrition Facts per serving: 340 cal., 10 g total fat (1 g sat. fat), 66 mg chol., 785 mg sodium, 68 g carbo., 5 g fiber, 33 g pro. **Daily Values:** 40% vit. C, 7% calcium, 17% iron

Use leftover chicken, thaw a package of frozen diced cooked chicken, or cut up a roast chicken from the deli to make this family-pleasing meal.

HOME STYLE CHICKEN & STUFFING

1	10¾-ounce can reduced-fat and reduced-sodium condensed cream of chicken soup or cream of mushroom soup
¼	cup margarine or butter, melted
1	16-ounce package loose-pack frozen broccoli, corn, and red peppers
2½	cups cubed cooked chicken
1	8-ounce package cornbread stuffing mix

1 In a very large bowl stir together soup, melted margarine, and ¼ cup water. Add vegetables, chicken, and stuffing mix; stir until combined. Transfer mixture to a 3½- to 4-quart slow cooker.

2 Cover and cook on low-heat setting for 5 to 6 hours or on high-heat setting for 2½ to 3 hours.

Nutrition Facts per serving: 387 cal., 14 g total fat (2 g sat. fat), 56 mg chol., 795 mg sodium, 41 g carbo., 2 g fiber, 23 g pro. **Daily Values:** 52% vit. C, 3% calcium, 13% iron

PREP:
15 minutes

COOK:
Low 5 hours, High 2½ hours

MAKES:
6 servings

SLOW COOKER:
3½- to 4-quart

Turkey is year-round good nutrition. Complement this easy-to-prepare meal with steamed green beans.

TURKEY THIGHS WITH MAPLE-MUSTARD SAUCE

PREP:

20 minutes.

COOK:

Low 6 hours, High 3 hours

MAKES:

4 servings

SLOW COOKER:

3¹/₂- to 4-quart

1   pound new potatoes, quartered

2   to 2¹/₂ pounds turkey thighs (about 2 thighs), skinned

¹/₃   cup coarse-grain brown mustard

¹/₄   cup maple syrup or maple-flavored syrup

1   tablespoon quick-cooking tapioca

1 In a 3¹/₂- to 4-quart slow cooker place potatoes. Place turkey thighs on potatoes.

2 In a small bowl stir together mustard, syrup, and tapioca. Pour over turkey. Cover; cook on low-heat setting for 6 to 7 hours or on high-heat setting for to 3 to 3¹/₂ hours.

Nutrition Facts per serving: 377 cal., 10 g total fat (3 g sat. fat), 93 mg chol., 369 mg sodium, 36 g carbo., 2 g fiber, 36 g pro. **Daily Values:** 24% vit. C, 9% calcium, 26% iron

You can adjust the heat level with the number of jalapeños you use. For even more heat, don't seed the peppers. Next time, use this shredded meat as a filling for quesadillas.

HOT PEPPER PORK SANDWICHES

1   2½- to 3-pound boneless pork shoulder roast

2   teaspoons fajita seasoning

1   or 2 jalapeño peppers, seeded (if desired) and finely chopped, or 1 large green or red sweet pepper, seeded and cut into bite-size strips

2   10-ounce cans enchilada sauce

8   kaiser rolls, split and toasted

PREP:

20 minutes

COOK:

Low 11 hours, High 5½ hours

MAKES:

8 servings

SLOW COOKER:

3½- to 5-quart

1 Trim fat from meat. If necessary, cut roast to fit into a 3½- to 5-quart slow cooker. Place meat in cooker. Sprinkle meat with the fajita seasoning. Add jalapeño or sweet pepper and enchilada sauce.

2 Cover; cook on low-heat setting for 11 to 12 hours or on high-heat setting for 5½ to 6 hours. Transfer roast to a cutting board. Using two forks, pull meat apart into shreds. Stir shredded meat into sauce mixture in slow cooker. Using a slotted spoon, spoon shredded meat mixture into toasted buns.

Nutrition Facts per serving: 316 cal., 9 g total fat (2 g sat. fat), 58 mg chol., 891 mg sodium, 34 g carbo., 2 g fiber, 23 g pro. **Daily Values:** 4% vit. A, 6% vit. C, 8% calcium, 19% iron

Slices of meaty portobello mushrooms add savory dimension to French dip sandwiches. Pour the seasoned broth into bowls just large enough to dunk a corner of the sandwich.

FRENCH DIPS WITH MUSHROOMS

PREP:

25 minutes

COOK:

Low 8 hours, High 4 hours

STAND:

10 minutes

MAKES:

8 sandwiches

SLOW COOKER:

3¹/₂- to 6-quart

1   3- to 3¹/₂-pound beef bottom round or rump roast

4   portobello mushrooms (3 to 4 inches in diameter)

1   14-ounce can beef broth seasoned with onion

8   hoagie buns, split and toasted

1   large red onion, cut into ¹/₂-inch slices

1 Trim fat from roast. If necessary, cut roast to fit into a 3¹/₂- to 6-quart slow cooker. In a large skillet brown meat on all sides in hot oil. Drain off fat. Transfer meat to cooker.

2 Clean mushrooms; remove and discard stems. Cut mushrooms into ¹/₄-inch slices. Add to cooker. Pour broth over meat and mushrooms.

3 Cover and cook on low-heat setting for 8 to 9 hours or on high-heat setting for 4 to 4¹/₂ hours. Remove meat from cooker; cover and let stand for 10 minutes.

4 Meanwhile, using a slotted spoon, remove mushrooms and set aside. Thinly slice meat. Arrange meat, mushroom slices, and onion slices on toasted buns. Pour cooking juices into a measuring cup; skim off fat. Drizzle a little of the juices onto each sandwich and pour the remaining juices into bowls to serve with sandwiches for dipping.

Nutrition Facts per serving: 780 cal., 33 g total fat (11 g sat. fat), 106 mg chol., 955 mg sodium, 73 g carbo., 4 g fiber, 47 g pro. **Daily Values:** 11% calcium, 42% iron

Kids will love this peanut-buttery cocoa that can be made in a snap using smooth or creamy peanut butter. Don't use crunchy-style for this recipe.

PEANUT BUTTER COCOA

1	cup instant milk chocolate or chocolate fudge cocoa mix
8	cups hot water
¾	cup chocolate-flavored syrup
¼	cup smooth peanut butter
1½	teaspoons vanilla

1 Place cocoa mix in a 3½- to 4-quart slow cooker. Carefully stir in hot water. Stir in chocolate syrup. Cover; cook on low-heat setting for 3 to 4 hours or on high-heat setting for 1½ to 2 hours. Whisk in peanut butter and vanilla until smooth.

Nutrition Facts per serving: 176 cal., 4 g total fat (1 g sat. fat), 1 mg chol., 115 mg sodium, 32 g carbo., 1 g fiber, 3 g pro. **Daily Values:** 3% calcium, 2% iron

PREP:
10 minutes

COOK:
Low 3 hours, High 1½ hours

MAKES:
9 (8-ounce) servings

SLOW COOKER:
3½- to 4-quart

Sweeten this warm drink with honey or brown sugar. Cinnamon sticks make handy, and tasty, stirrers.

HONEY-MULLED APPLE CIDER

PREP:

10 minutes

COOK:

Low 5 hours, High 2¹/₂ hours

MAKES:

10 (8-ounce) servings

SLOW COOKER:

3¹/₂- to 5-quart

6   inches stick cinnamon, broken

1   teaspoon whole allspice

1   teaspoon whole cloves

10   cups pasteurized apple cider or apple juice (2¹/₂ quarts)

¹/₃   cup honey or packed light brown sugar

     Cinnamon sticks (optional)

1 Cut a 6-inch square from a double thickness of 100-percent-cotton cheesecloth. Place broken stick cinnamon, allspice, and cloves in the center of the cloth. Bring the corners together and tie closed with clean kitchen string. In a 3¹/₂- to 5-quart slow cooker combine spice bag, apple cider or juice, and honey or brown sugar.

2 Cover; cook on low-heat setting for 5 to 6 hours or on high-heat setting for 2¹/₂ to 3 hours.

3 Remove spice bag and discard. If desired, serve in mugs with a cinnamon stick stirrer.

Nutrition Facts per serving: 150 cal., 0 g total fat (0 g sat. fat), 0 mg chol., 8 mg sodium, 38 g carbo., 0 g fiber, 0 g pro. **Daily Values:** 4% vit. C, 2% calcium, 5% iron

ONE-DISH DINNERS

8

It's amazing that just seven ingredients and only 15 minutes of prep time bring such flavorful variety to a meal.

ROUND STEAK WITH WINTER SQUASH

PREP:

15 minutes

COOK:

1 hour 15 minutes

MAKES:

4 servings

1 pound boneless beef round steak

3 slices bacon

1/2 teaspoon seasoned salt

1 14 1/2-ounce can diced tomatoes with green peppers and onion

1 medium onion, halved and sliced

1 teaspoon dried marjoram, crushed

1 medium butternut squash (about 1 1/2 pounds), peeled, halved, seeded, and cut into 1 1/2-inch pieces

1 Trim fat from beef. Cut beef into four serving-size pieces; set aside. In a large skillet cook bacon until crisp. Remove bacon, reserving 2 tablespoons drippings in skillet; drain bacon on paper towels, crumble, and set aside in the refrigerator.

2 Sprinkle beef with seasoned salt. Brown beef on both sides in reserved drippings over medium heat. Add undrained tomatoes, onion, and marjoram to skillet. Bring to boiling; reduce heat. Simmer, covered, for 20 minutes. Add squash to skillet. Simmer, covered, for 55 minutes more or until beef and squash are tender. To serve, sprinkle bacon over top.

Nutrition Facts per serving: 337 cal., 14 g total fat (5 g sat. fat), 82 mg chol., 684 mg sodium, 22 g carbo., 4 g fiber, 31 g pro. **Daily Values:** 90% vit. A, 46% vit. C, 6% calcium, 24% iron

To speed up this already quick-to-make dinner, purchase prewashed spinach and shredded carrots.

BEEF WITH ASIAN NOODLES

2	3-ounce packages ramen noodles
12	ounces beef flank steak or beef top round steak
2	teaspoons chile oil or 2 teaspoons cooking oil plus $\frac{1}{8}$ to $\frac{1}{4}$ teaspoon ground red pepper
1	teaspoon grated fresh ginger
2	cloves garlic, minced
1	cup beef broth
1	tablespoon soy sauce
2	cups torn fresh spinach
1	cup shredded carrots
$\frac{1}{4}$	cup snipped fresh mint or cilantro
	Chopped peanuts (optional)

START TO FINISH:

30 minutes

MAKES:

4 servings

1 In a large saucepan bring 4 cups of water to boiling. If desired, break up noodles; drop noodles into the boiling water. (Do not use the flavor packets.) Return to boiling; boil for 2 to 3 minutes or just until noodles are tender but firm, stirring occasionally. Drain noodles.

2 Cut beef into bite-size strips. In a wok or large skillet heat chile oil over medium-high heat. Cook and stir beef, ginger, and garlic in hot oil for 2 to 3 minutes or to desired doneness. Push beef from center of wok. Add broth and soy sauce. Bring to boiling; reduce heat. Stir meat into broth mixture. Cook and stir 1 to 2 minutes more or until heated through.

3 Add noodles, spinach, carrots, and mint to mixture in wok; toss to combine. Ladle mixture into soup bowls. If desired, sprinkle with chopped peanuts.

Nutrition Facts per serving: 211 cal., 10 g total fat (3 g sat. fat), 47 mg chol., 690 mg sodium, 11 g carbo., 2 g fiber, 20 g pro. **Daily Values:** 101% vit. A, 23% vit. C, 4% calcium, 26% iron

A LITTLE DAB WILL DO
Much loved in Chinese cookery, chile oil adds plenty of heat with just a small dose. Made by steeping spicy chiles in vegetable oil, this fiery concoction can be found wherever Asian foods are sold. Store it in the refrigerator.

Prepare this recipe in 30 minutes for casual get-togethers. Spoon the mixture over pasta and serve with crusty bread or corn bread and wedges of melon. For dessert, serve refreshing sorbet and sugar cookies.

STEAK-VEGETABLE RAGOUT

START TO FINISH:

30 minutes

MAKES:

4 servings

DON'T CONFUSE THE PEAS, PLEASE

Sugar snap peas (also called sugar peas), those wonderfully sweet peas encased in an edible pod, should not be confused with snow peas. Although both have edible pods, the peas in the snow pea pod are tiny and the pod is almost translucent; the peas in the sugar snap pod are larger. Each legume yields different flavors and textures.

12	ounces beef tenderloin
1	tablespoon olive oil or cooking oil
1½	cups sliced fresh shiitake or button mushrooms (4 ounces)
½	cup chopped onion
2	cloves garlic, minced
3	tablespoons all-purpose flour
½	teaspoon salt
¼	teaspoon pepper
1	14-ounce can beef broth
¼	cup port wine or dry sherry
2	cups sugar snap peas or one 10-ounce package frozen sugar snap peas, thawed
1	cup cherry tomatoes, halved
	Cooked pasta (optional)

1 Cut beef into ¾-inch pieces. In a large nonstick skillet heat oil. Cook and stir meat in hot oil for 2 to 3 minutes or to desired doneness. Remove meat; set aside. In the same skillet cook mushrooms, onion, and garlic until tender.

2 Stir in flour, salt, and pepper. Add broth and wine. Cook and stir until thickened and bubbly. Stir in sugar snap peas; cook and stir for 2 to 3 minutes more or until peas are tender. Stir in meat and tomatoes; heat through. If desired, serve the meat and vegetable mixture over hot cooked pasta or wide noodles.

Nutrition Facts per serving: 252 cal., 9 g total fat (3 g sat. fat), 48 mg chol., 647 mg sodium, 17 g carbo., 3 g fiber, 21 g pro. **Daily Values:** 4% vit. A, 74% vit. C, 4% calcium, 32% iron

This version of the classic Szechwan recipe is a bit less pungent than one you might find at Chinese restaurants. The spinach and water chestnuts add color and crunch.

ORANGE-BEEF STIR-FRY

12	ounces beef top round steak
1	teaspoon finely shredded orange peel
½	cup orange juice
1	tablespoon cornstarch
1	tablespoon soy sauce
1	teaspoon sugar
1	teaspoon instant beef bouillon granules
2	tablespoons cooking oil
4	green onions, bias-sliced into 1-inch pieces
1	clove garlic, minced
5	cups coarsely shredded fresh spinach (5 to 6 ounces)
½	of an 8-ounce can sliced water chestnuts, drained
3	cups hot cooked rice
	Slivered orange peel (optional)
	Green onions (optional)

PREP:
30 minutes
COOK:
6 minutes
MAKES:
4 servings

1 Trim fat from beef. Partially freeze beef. Thinly slice across the grain into bite-size strips; set aside. For sauce, in a small bowl stir together orange peel, orange juice, cornstarch, soy sauce, sugar, and bouillon granules. Set aside.

2 In a wok or large skillet heat 1 tablespoon of the oil over medium-high heat. Add green onions and garlic; cook and stir in hot oil for 1 minute. Remove onion mixture from wok using a slotted spoon. Add remaining 1 tablespoon oil to wok. Add beef to hot wok. (Add more oil as necessary during cooking.) Cook and stir for 2 to 3 minutes or to desired doneness. Push beef from center of wok.

3 Stir sauce. Add sauce to center of wok. Cook and stir until thickened and bubbly. Return green onion mixture to wok. Add spinach and water chestnuts. Stir all ingredients together to coat with sauce. Cover and cook for 1 minute more or until heated through. Serve immediately over hot cooked rice. If desired, garnish with slivered orange peel and additional green onions.

Nutrition Facts per serving: 366 cal., 9 g total fat (2 g sat. fat), 37 mg chol., 527 mg sodium, 45 g carbo., 3 g fiber, 25 g pro. **Daily Values:** 25% vit. A, 38% vit. C, 8% calcium, 26% iron

Corned beef got its name before refrigeration, when meat was preserved with coarse grains of salt, called "corn." Today beef is corned with spices for flavor, not for preservation. The meat must be refrigerated.

CORNED BEEF & CABBAGE

PREP:

20 minutes

COOK:

2 hours 30 minutes

MAKES:

6 servings

*NOTE
If the brisket has an additional packet of spices, add it rather than the pepper and bay leaves called for in the ingredients list.

1   2- to 2½-pound corned beef brisket*

2   bay leaves

1   teaspoon whole black pepper

3   medium carrots, quartered lengthwise

2   medium parsnips or 1 medium rutabaga, peeled and cut into chunks

2   medium red onions, cut into wedges

10   to 12 whole, tiny new potatoes

1   small cabbage, cut into 6 wedges (1 pound)

1 Trim fat from meat. Place in a 4- to 6-quart Dutch oven; add juices and spices from package of beef, if available. Add enough water to cover meat. Add bay leaves and pepper (if using). Bring to boiling; reduce heat. Simmer, covered, about 2 hours or until meat is almost tender.

2 Add carrots, parsnips, and onions to meat. Return to boiling; reduce heat. Simmer, covered, for 10 minutes. Scrub potatoes; halve or quarter. Add potatoes and cabbage to Dutch oven. Cover and cook about 20 minutes more or until vegetables and meat are tender. Discard bay leaves. Remove meat from Dutch oven.

3 To serve, slice the meat across the grain.

Nutrition Facts per serving: 319 cal., 15 g total fat (5 g sat. fat), 74 mg chol., 895 mg sodium, 30 g carbo., 6 g fiber, 17 g pro. **Daily Values:** 57% vit. A, 74% vit. C, 5% calcium, 22% iron

Cinnamon and currants add hints of aromatic spices and fruity sweetness to the meat. Serve with warm pita bread and a green salad garnished with onions, kalamata olives, tomatoes, and feta cheese.

GREEK POT ROAST

1	2- to 2½-pound boneless beef chuck pot roast
2	tablespoons cooking oil
½	cup beef broth
3	cloves garlic, minced
¼	teaspoon ground cinnamon
¼	teaspoon cracked black pepper
8	carrots, peeled and bias-cut into 2-inch pieces
2	large onions, cut into wedges
¼	cup dried currants
1	14½-ounce can diced tomatoes
2	tablespoons tomato paste
3	to 4 cups hot cooked fettuccine

PREP:
15 minutes

COOK:
2 hours 10 minutes

MAKES:
6 to 8 servings

1 Trim fat from meat. In a 4- to 6-quart Dutch oven heat oil. Brown meat on all sides in hot oil. Drain off fat. Combine broth, garlic, cinnamon, and pepper. Carefully pour over meat. Bring to boiling; reduce heat. Simmer, covered, for 1¼ hours.

2 Add carrots, onions, and currants to Dutch oven. Return to boiling; reduce heat. Simmer, covered, for 50 to 60 minutes or until meat and vegetables are tender. Transfer meat and vegetables to a serving platter, reserving cooking liquid in pan. Cover meat and vegetables with foil to keep warm.

3 For sauce, stir undrained tomatoes and tomato paste into mixture in pan. Bring to boiling; reduce heat. Simmer, uncovered, about 5 minutes or until slightly thickened. Pour some of the sauce over meat and vegetables. Serve with fettuccine. Pass remaining sauce.

Nutrition Facts per serving: 586 cal., 30 g total fat (11 g sat. fat), 129 mg chol., 308 mg sodium, 43 g carbo., 5 g fiber, 35 g pro. **Daily Values:** 197% vit. A, 31% vit. C, 9% calcium, 32% iron

Wrap your favorite Italian flavors in this meat loaf. Serve it with hot pasta, tossed with butter and herbs, and a spinach salad.

SICILIAN-STYLE MEAT ROLL

PREP:
20 minutes

BAKE:
1 hour 20 minutes

OVEN:
325°

MAKES:
8 to 10 servings

2	slightly beaten eggs
¾	cup soft bread crumbs (1 slice)
½	cup tomato juice
2	tablespoons snipped fresh parsley
½	teaspoon dried oregano, crushed
¼	teaspoon salt
¼	teaspoon pepper
1	small clove garlic, minced
2	pounds lean ground beef
6	1-ounce thin slices cooked ham
1¾	cups shredded mozzarella cheese (7 ounces)

1 In a large bowl combine the eggs, bread crumbs, tomato juice, parsley, oregano, salt, pepper, and garlic. Stir in the ground beef, mixing well.

2 On foil, pat meat mixture into a 12×10-inch rectangle. Arrange the ham slices on the meat, leaving a ¾-inch border around all edges. Sprinkle 1½ cups of the shredded mozzarella cheese over the ham. Starting from a short end, carefully roll up meat, using foil to lift; seal edges and ends. Place roll, seam side down, in a 13×9×2-inch baking pan.

3 Bake in 350° oven about 1¼ hours or until temperature registers 170° and juices run clear. (Center of meat roll will be pink because of ham.) Sprinkle the remaining shredded mozzarella over roll. Return to oven about 5 minutes or until cheese melts.

Nutrition Facts per serving: 323 cal., 19 g total fat (8 g sat. fat), 152 mg chol., 604 mg sodium, 4 g carbo., 33 g pro. **Daily Values:** 8% vit. A, 14% vit. C, 16% calcium, 18% iron

These pinwheels are a take on brasciole, an Italian vegetable-stuffed meat roll. Transform the Continental classic into an American one-dish meal by roasting potatoes and onions with the meat.

BEEF PINWHEELS WITH HERBS

1	1- to 1¼-pound beef flank steak
2	tablespoons olive oil or cooking oil
2	medium leeks, sliced (⅔ cup)
2	cloves garlic, minced
3	tablespoons snipped fresh basil
¼	teaspoon salt
⅛	teaspoon pepper
2	Yukon gold potatoes, cut into eighths
1	large onion, cut into thin wedges
1	14½-ounce can diced tomatoes with basil, oregano, and garlic

1 Score meat by making shallow diagonal cuts at 1-inch intervals, making diamond patterns on both sides. Place between two pieces of plastic wrap. Working from center to edges, use flat side of meat mallet to pound steak into a 12×8-inch rectangle. Remove wrap; set aside.

2 In a large skillet heat 1 tablespoon of the oil over medium-high heat. Add leeks and garlic. Cook 3 to 5 minutes or until leeks are tender. Stir in basil, salt, and pepper. Remove from heat. Spread leek mixture evenly on one side of steak. Starting at a short end, tightly roll meat into a spiral. Tie four evenly spaced pieces of kitchen string around steak. In same large skillet heat remaining oil over medium-high heat. Brown meat on all sides in the hot oil. Transfer meat to a 2-quart rectangular baking dish.

3 Arrange potatoes and onion wedges around meat in dish. Pour undrained tomatoes over beef and vegetables. Bake, uncovered, in a 350° oven for 1¼ to 1½ hours or until beef is tender. Transfer meat to a cutting board. Cut into serving-size pieces. Remove string. Serve with vegetables.

Nutrition Facts per serving: 355 cal., 15 g total fat (4 g sat. fat), 53 mg chol., 722 mg sodium, 30 g carbo., 4 g fiber, 25 g pro. **Daily Values:** 7% vit. A, 49% vit. C, 6% calcium, 27% iron

PREP:
25 minutes
COOK:
1 hour 15 minutes
OVEN:
350°
MAKES:
4 servings

MAKE-AHEAD TIP
Score and pound meat. Prepare leek filling and spread on meat. Roll up and tie, but do not brown meat before refrigerating. Wrap tightly and place in the refrigerator for up to 24 hours. To cook, brown meat roll in hot oil in a large skillet; transfer meat to baking dish with vegetables and bake as directed.

Reminiscent of a French braised meat dish, pot-au-feu (pot on the fire), this is a cross between a Sunday roast and the Continental classic. The pan juices meld with sour cream for a creamy finish.

BEEF WITH MUSTARD-MUSHROOM SAUCE

PREP:

10 minutes

COOK:

1 hour 45 minutes

MAKES:

6 to 8 servings

1	2- to 2½-pound boneless beef round rump roast
2	tablespoons cooking oil
¾	cup beef broth
½	teaspoon dried thyme, crushed
¼	teaspoon dried marjoram, crushed
¼	teaspoon pepper
4	cups halved fresh mushrooms
12	ounces packaged, peeled baby carrots
2	cups frozen small, whole onions
1	8-ounce carton dairy sour cream
¼	cup Dijon-style mustard
¼	cup all-purpose flour
3	to 4 cups hot cooked noodles

1 Trim fat from meat. In a 4- to 6-quart Dutch oven heat oil. Brown meat on all sides in hot oil. Drain off fat. Combine broth, thyme, marjoram, and pepper. Carefully pour over meat. Bring to boiling; reduce heat. Simmer, covered, for 1¼ hours.

2 Add mushrooms, carrots, and onions to meat. Return to boiling; reduce heat. Cover and simmer for 30 to 40 minutes or until vegetables are tender. Transfer meat and vegetables to a serving platter. Cover with foil to keep warm.

3 For sauce, skim fat from pan juices. If necessary, add enough water to equal 1⅓ cups liquid. Return to Dutch oven. Stir together sour cream, mustard, and flour. Stir into juices in Dutch oven. Cook and stir over medium heat until thickened and bubbly. Cook and stir 1 minute more. Serve sauce with meat, vegetables, and noodles.

Nutrition Facts per serving: 455 cal., 18 g total fat (7 g sat. fat), 115 mg chol., 465 mg sodium, 38 g carbo., 5 g fiber, 36 g pro. **Daily Values:** 137% vit. A, 9% vit. C, 7% calcium, 35% iron

Adapt this recipe, based on a popular Romanian dish that celebrates spring, to your favorite fresh vegetables available at the market.

POT ROAST WITH GARDEN VEGETABLES

1	3-pound beef bottom round roast
1/2	to 1 teaspoon cracked black pepper
1/4	teaspoon salt
1	tablespoon cooking oil
1	cup beef broth
2	tablespoons tomato paste
1/2	cup coarsely chopped onion
2	cloves garlic, minced
1/2	teaspoon dried marjoram, crushed
1/2	teaspoon dried thyme, crushed
1/3	cup golden raisins
3	cups vegetables (such as whole green beans, or peeled and cut-up winter squash, parsnips, celery, broccoli, and/or cauliflower)
1	cup sugar snap peas
1	tablespoon cornstarch

PREP:
30 minutes
COOK:
2 1/2 hours
MAKES:
6 servings plus leftover meat

1 Trim fat from meat. Sprinkle with cracked pepper and salt. In a 4- to 6-quart Dutch oven heat oil. Brown meat on all sides in hot oil about 5 minutes. Drain off fat. Combine broth and tomato paste. Carefully pour over meat. Add onion, garlic, marjoram, and thyme. Bring to boiling; reduce heat. Simmer, covered, for 2 hours or until meat is tender.

2 Add raisins and (if using) green beans, squash, or parsnips. Return to boiling; reduce heat. Simmer, covered, for 10 to 15 minutes more or until vegetables are just tender. Stir in sugar snap peas and (if using) celery, broccoli, or cauliflower. Cook 3 to 4 minutes more or until vegetables are crisp-tender. Transfer meat and vegetables to a serving platter; reserve cooking liquid in pan. Cover platter with foil to keep warm.

3 For gravy, strain juices into a glass measuring cup. Skim fat from juices; return 1 1/4 cups juices to Dutch oven (discard remaining juices). In a small bowl stir cornstarch into 2 tablespoons cold water until smooth (or shake together in a screw-top jar). Stir into juices in Dutch oven. Cook and stir until thickened and bubbly. Cook and stir 2 minutes more. Slice meat. Spoon some of the gravy over meat and vegetables. Pass remaining gravy.

Nutrition Facts per serving: 303 cal., 10 g total fat (3 g sat. fat), 82 mg chol., 277 mg sodium, 23 g carbo., 4 g fiber, 30 g pro. **Daily Values:** 20% vit. A, 30% vit. C, 5% calcium, 29% iron

Try this decidedly different version of meat loaf. Salsa, raisins, spices, and almonds give it pizzazz.

SOUTHWESTERN-STYLE MEAT LOAF

PREP:

15 minutes

BAKE:

1 hour 5 minutes

STAND:

10 minutes

OVEN:

350°

MAKES:

6 servings

1	slightly beaten egg
¾	cup soft bread crumbs (1 slice bread)
¾	cup salsa
⅓	cup raisins
¼	cup finely chopped almonds, toasted
¼	cup finely chopped onion
½	teaspoon sugar
½	teaspoon salt
¼	teaspoon ground cinnamon
⅛	teaspoon ground cloves
1½	pounds lean ground beef
¼	cup salsa
	Additional salsa (optional)

1 In a large bowl stir together the egg, bread crumbs, the ¾ cup salsa, raisins, almonds, onion, sugar, salt, cinnamon, and cloves. Add ground beef; mix well. In a shallow baking pan pat meat mixture into an 8×4×2-inch oval loaf. (Or pat meat mixture into an 8×4×2-inch loaf pan.) Bake in a 350° oven for 1 hour.

2 Drain off fat. Insert a meat thermometer into center of loaf. Spoon the ¼ cup salsa over meat loaf. Bake for 5 to 10 minutes more or until thermometer registers 160°. Transfer meat loaf to a serving platter. Let stand 10 minutes before serving.

3 To serve, slice meat loaf with a thin-bladed, serrated knife. If desired, serve meat loaf with additional salsa.

Nutrition Facts per serving: 312 cal., 18 g total fat (6 g sat. fat), 107 mg chol., 426 mg sodium, 14 g carbo., 1 g fiber, 25 g pro. **Daily Values:** 6% vit. A, 21% vit. C, 3% calcium, 20% iron

Serve a simple salad to complete this hearty main dish. Mashed potatoes are the surprise ingredient in the crust.

TWO-CRUST PIZZA CASSEROLE

<table>
<tr><td>3</td><td>cups all-purpose flour</td></tr>
<tr><td>3</td><td>cups packaged instant mashed potatoes</td></tr>
<tr><td>2</td><td>cups milk</td></tr>
<tr><td>½</td><td>cup butter or margarine, melted</td></tr>
<tr><td>1</td><td>pound lean ground beef</td></tr>
<tr><td>¾</td><td>pound bulk Italian sausage</td></tr>
<tr><td>1</td><td>large onion, coarsely chopped (1 cup)</td></tr>
<tr><td>1</td><td>8-ounce can tomato sauce</td></tr>
<tr><td>1</td><td>6-ounce can Italian-style tomato paste</td></tr>
<tr><td>½</td><td>of a 1.3- to 1.5-ounce package sloppy joe seasoning mix (about 2 tablespoons)</td></tr>
<tr><td>1</td><td>2¼-ounce can sliced ripe olives, drained (optional)</td></tr>
<tr><td>1</td><td>cup shredded mozzarella cheese (4 ounces)</td></tr>
<tr><td>1</td><td>tablespoon cornmeal</td></tr>
</table>

PREP:
25 minutes

BAKE:
35 minutes

STAND:
5 minutes

OVEN:
425°

MAKES:
12 servings

1 For crust, combine flour, potatoes, milk, and butter or margarine; set aside. (Mixture stiffens slightly as it stands.)

2 For filling, in a 12-inch skillet or a Dutch oven cook beef, sausage, and onion until meat is no longer pink. Drain off fat. Stir in tomato sauce, tomato paste, seasoning mix, and, if desired, olives.

3 Using floured fingers, press half of the dough into the bottom and about 1½ inches up the sides of a 13×9×2-inch baking pan or a 3-quart rectangular baking dish. Spread filling over crust; sprinkle with mozzarella cheese. Between two large sheets of waxed paper, roll remaining crust to a 15×11-inch rectangle; remove top sheet and invert over filling. Remove paper. Trim edges as necessary. Turn edges of top crust under and seal to bottom crust. Sprinkle with cornmeal. Bake in a 425° oven about 35 minutes or until heated through and crust is golden brown. Let stand for 5 minutes before serving.

Nutrition Facts per serving: 428 cal., 20 g total fat (10 g sat. fat), 69 mg chol., 715 mg sodium, 41 g carbo., 2 g fiber, 20 g pro. **Daily Values:** 15% vit. A, 27% vit. C, 13% calcium, 16% iron

Enjoy the bold Italian flavors of sausage and tomato sauce bubbling under a mashed potato crust. Use homemade mashed potatoes or timesaving refrigerated mashed potatoes for the savory topping.

TRADITIONAL HAMBURGER PIE

PREP:

25 minutes

BAKE:

30 minutes

STAND:

5 minutes

OVEN:

375°

MAKES:

6 servings

3/4 cup shredded pizza cheese or Italian-blend cheeses (3 ounces)

2 cups mashed potatoes* or refrigerated mashed potatoes

4 ounces sweet Italian sausage

8 ounces lean ground beef

1/2 cup chopped onion

2 cups sliced zucchini or yellow summer squash

1 14 1/2-ounce can chunky pasta-style tomatoes

1/2 of a 6-ounce can (1/3 cup) tomato paste

1/4 teaspoon pepper

Paprika

Snipped fresh flat-leaf parsley (optional)

1 Stir 1/2 cup of the cheese into the potatoes; set aside. Remove casing from sausage, if present. In a large skillet cook sausage, ground beef, and onion until meat is no longer pink and onion is tender. Drain off fat. Stir in squash, undrained tomatoes, tomato paste, and pepper. Bring to boiling. Transfer mixture to a 2-quart casserole.

2 Spoon mashed potato mixture into a large pastry bag fitted with a large round tip. Starting at one end, fill in the center of the casserole with rows of the mashed potato mixture until the meat mixture is covered. (Or spoon mashed potato mixture in mounds on top of hot mixture.) Sprinkle with remaining cheese and paprika.

3 Bake in a 375° oven for 30 minutes or until mashed potato top is golden brown. Let stand 5 minutes before serving. If desired, sprinkle with fresh flat-leaf parsley.

Nutrition Facts per serving: 254 cal., 12 g total fat (3 g sat. fat), 39 mg chol., 644 mg sodium, 21 g carbo., 3 g fiber, 16 g pro. **Daily Values:** 8% vit. A, 47% vit. C, 2% calcium, 11% iron

*NOTE

To make mashed potatoes, wash and peel 1 pound of potatoes. Cut into quarters or cubes. Cover and cook in a small amount of boiling salted water for 20 to 25 minutes or until tender. Mash potatoes until lumps are gone. If desired, add a little milk.

MAKE-AHEAD TIP

After bringing meat filling mixture to a boil, divide evenly among six 10-ounce casserole dishes. Top with potatoes. Cover with plastic wrap; chill for up to 48 hours. To bake, remove plastic wrap. Place casseroles in a 15×10×1-inch baking pan. Cover with foil. Bake, covered, in a 375° oven for 35 minutes. Remove foil. Bake, uncovered, 5 minutes more. Let stand 5 minutes before serving.

With six cloves of garlic in this fresh and simple sauce, you know it's going to be flavorful. When buying garlic, choose plump heads and store them in a cool, dry place.

PASTA WITH BEEF & SPICY GARLIC SAUCE

1	9-ounce package refrigerated tomato or red sweet pepper linguine or fettuccine
1	small yellow summer squash or zucchini, halved lengthwise and sliced
1	medium green sweet pepper, cut into bite-size strips
1/2	teaspoon coarsely ground black pepper
8	ounces beef top loin steak, cut 3/4 inch thick
1	tablespoon olive oil or cooking oil
1/2	cup chicken broth
1/4	cup dry white wine
6	cloves garlic, minced

START TO FINISH:
25 minutes
MAKES:
4 servings

1 Cook pasta according to package directions, adding summer squash and sweet pepper the last 2 minutes of cooking; drain. Return pasta and vegetables to saucepan.

2 Meanwhile, rub black pepper onto both sides of steak. In a large skillet heat oil. Cook steak in hot oil over medium heat to desired doneness, turning once. (Allow 10 to 12 minutes for medium doneness.) Remove meat from skillet.

3 For sauce, stir broth, wine, and garlic into skillet. Bring to boiling; reduce heat. Simmer, uncovered, for 2 minutes. Remove skillet from heat. Cut steak into thin bite-size strips. Pour sauce over pasta mixture; add steak slices. Toss gently to combine. Transfer pasta-meat mixture to a warm serving platter.

Nutrition Facts per serving: 247 cal., 13 g total fat (4 g sat. fat), 49 mg chol., 238 mg sodium, 13 g carbo., 1 g fiber, 18 g pro. **Daily Values:** 5% vit. A, 36% vit. C, 6% calcium, 16% iron

Look for canned chipotle peppers in adobo sauce in the Mexican food section of supermarkets or at Mexican grocery stores.

SOUTHWESTERN PAN-BROILED STEAK

START TO FINISH:

25 minutes

MAKES:

4 servings

1 teaspoon garlic salt

1 teaspoon ground cumin

1 teaspoon dried oregano, crushed

2 tablespoons olive oil

1 medium red sweet pepper, cut into thin bite-size strips (1 cup)

1 medium onion, chopped ($\frac{1}{2}$ cup)

1 to 2 chipotle peppers in adobo sauce, drained and chopped

1 pound boneless beef top loin steak, cut $\frac{3}{4}$ inch thick

1 medium tomato, seeded and chopped ($\frac{1}{2}$ cup)

Flour tortillas, warmed

Purchased guacamole

Snipped fresh cilantro (optional)

1 In a small bowl combine garlic salt, cumin, and oregano. In a large skillet heat 1 tablespoon of the oil over medium-high heat. Add 2 teaspoons of the garlic salt mixture, sweet pepper, onion, and chipotle peppers. Cook and stir for 2 to 3 minutes or just until vegetables are tender. Using a slotted spoon, remove vegetables from skillet; cover and keep warm.

2 Add remaining oil, remaining garlic salt mixture, and meat to same skillet. Cook meat over medium-high heat about 4 minutes on each side or until meat is slightly pink in the center. Transfer meat to a serving platter, reserving drippings in skillet. Thinly slice meat; cover and keep warm.

3 Return vegetables to skillet. Stir in tomato; heat through. Spoon vegetables over meat. To serve, fill tortillas with meat-vegetable mixture; roll up. Serve with guacamole. Garnish with fresh cilantro, if desired.

Nutrition Facts per serving: 341 cal., 15 g total fat (3 g sat. fat), 65 mg chol., 772 mg sodium, 25 g carbo., 1 g fiber, 26 g pro. **Daily Values:** 20% vit. A, 62% vit. C, 6% calcium, 31% iron

Sweet hoisin sauce makes the mu shu easy. Made from fermented soybeans, molasses, vinegar, mustard, sesame seeds, garlic, and chiles, hoisin brings wonderful flavors to the dish.

MU SHU-STYLE BEEF & CABBAGE WRAPS

8	8-inch flour tortillas
12	ounces lean ground beef
½	cup chopped red onion or green onions
2	cups packaged shredded cabbage with carrots (coleslaw mix)
1	cup fresh cut or frozen whole kernel corn
¼	cup hoisin sauce
1	teaspoon toasted sesame oil
	Additional hoisin sauce (optional)

START TO FINISH:

20 minutes

OVEN:

350°

MAKES:

4 servings

1 Stack tortillas; wrap in foil. Heat in a 350° oven for 10 minutes to soften. Meanwhile, for filling, in a large skillet cook beef and onion until meat is brown. Drain off fat. Stir in coleslaw mix and corn. Cover and cook about 4 minutes or until vegetables are tender, stirring once. Stir in hoisin sauce and sesame oil. Cook and stir until heated through.

2 Spoon ½ cup filling onto each tortilla just below center. Fold bottom edge up and over filling. Fold in opposite sides just until they meet. Roll up from bottom. If desired, serve with additional hoisin sauce.

Nutrition Facts per serving: 431 cal., 14 g total fat (5 g sat. fat), 54 mg chol., 604 mg sodium, 52 g carbo., 4 g fiber, 21 g pro. **Daily Values:** 20% vit. A, 37% vit. C, 7% calcium, 25% iron

Drive past the long line at a drive-through restaurant and head home to a fresh, colorful Mexican dish that is ready in 20 minutes.

FLANK STEAK & PEPPER FAJITAS

PREP:

10 minutes

COOK:

10 minutes

OVEN:

350°

MAKES:

8 fajitas

12	ounces beef flank steak or boneless beef sirloin steak
8	8-inch plain or flavored flour tortillas
1	tablespoon cooking oil
2	cloves garlic, minced
1	large onion, cut into thin wedges
1	small red sweet pepper, cut into bite-size strips
1	small green or yellow sweet pepper, cut into bite-size strips
1	cup packaged shredded cabbage with carrot (coleslaw mix)
⅓	cup bottled stir-fry sauce

1 Slice steak across grain into thin, bite-size strips; set aside. Stack tortillas; wrap in foil. Heat in a 350° oven for 10 minutes to soften, or heat according to package directions.

2 Meanwhile, in a large skillet heat oil over medium-high heat. Add beef and garlic. Cook and stir for 2 minutes. Add onion and sweet pepper; cook and stir for 4 to 5 minutes more or until vegetables are crisp-tender. Stir in cabbage and stir-fry sauce; heat through.

3 To serve, use tongs or a slotted spoon to fill warm tortillas with the beef-vegetable mixture. Roll up tortillas.

Nutrition Facts per serving: 197 cal., 7 g total fat (2 g sat. fat), 17 mg chol., 499 mg sodium, 21 g carbo., 2 g fiber, 12 g pro. **Daily Values:** 19% vit. A, 50% vit. C, 5% calcium, 10% iron

Combine fresh vegetables from the grocery store with convenience items such as herb-pepper seasoning, bottled roasted red sweet peppers, and quick-cooking brown rice for a speedy, seasonal dish.

PEPPERY PORK CHOPS WITH PILAF

4	3-ounce boneless pork loin chops, cut ¾ inch thick
2	teaspoons herb-pepper seasoning
1	tablespoon olive oil
2	cups cut-up salad bar vegetables, such as broccoli, carrots, mushrooms, onions, and/or sweet peppers
1	14-ounce can chicken broth
2	cups uncooked instant brown rice
¼	cup roasted red sweet pepper strips

START TO FINISH:

25 minutes

MAKES:

4 servings

1 Sprinkle both sides of meat with the herb-pepper seasoning. In a large skillet heat oil. Cook chops in hot oil for 5 minutes. Turn chops. Cook for 5 to 7 minutes more or until juices run clear. Remove chops from skillet; cover and keep warm.

2 Meanwhile, cut vegetables into bite-size pieces. Add vegetables, broth, and uncooked rice to skillet. Bring to boiling; reduce heat. Simmer, covered, for 5 to 7 minutes or until rice is done and vegetables are crisp-tender. Return pork chops to skillet; cover and heat through. Garnish with roasted red pepper strips.

Nutrition Facts per serving: 390 cal., 17 g total fat (5 g sat. fat), 70 mg chol., 492 mg sodium, 33 g carbo., 3 g fiber, 29 g pro. **Daily Values:** 49% vit. A, 65% vit. C, 4% calcium, 7% iron

Move over, pepper steak! Pork chops lend themselves equally well to the treatment of colorful sweet peppers and sweet onions. Serve with slices of hearty bread to get even more of the flavorful juices.

PORK CHOPS WITH PEPPERS & ONIONS

START TO FINISH:

25 minutes

MAKES:

4 servings

1	tablespoon olive oil
4	pork loin or rib chops, cut ½ to ¾ inch thick (1¼ pounds)
1	red sweet pepper, cut into strips
1	green sweet pepper, cut into strips
1	yellow sweet pepper, cut into strips
1	large sweet onion, thinly sliced
¼	cup water
¼	cup dry white wine or chicken broth
1	teaspoon snipped fresh rosemary or ½ teaspoon dried rosemary, crushed
¼	teaspoon salt
4	slices crusty bread

1 In a large skillet heat oil. Brown chops in hot oil over medium-high heat for 4 to 5 minutes, turning once. Remove chops from skillet; set aside. Add sweet peppers and onion to skillet. Cook, stirring frequently, about 10 minutes or until vegetables are tender.

2 Return chops to skillet; add water, wine, rosemary, and salt. Bring to boiling; reduce heat. Simmer, covered, for 5 to 6 minutes or until pork is no longer pink and juices run clear. Serve chops and vegetables with bread.

Nutrition Facts per serving: 273 cal., 12 g total fat (3 g sat. fat), 51 mg chol., 328 mg sodium, 20 g carbo., 1 g fiber, 19 g pro. **Daily Values:** 15% vit. A, 135% vit. C, 3% calcium, 10% iron

A potato skillet dinner usually means peeling and chopping. Forget that! To keep cooking simple, this recipe calls for frozen hash brown potatoes and frozen carrots and peas.

PORK & POTATO DINNER

4	4-ounce boneless pork loin chops
½	teaspoon seasoned salt
2	tablespoons cooking oil
1	leek, halved and sliced, or ⅓ cup chopped onion
1	medium red sweet pepper, cut into ¾-inch pieces
3	cups frozen diced hash brown potatoes
2	cups frozen peas and carrots
1	teaspoon dried thyme, crushed
¼	teaspoon seasoned salt

PREP:
10 minutes
COOK:
21 minutes
MAKES:
4 servings

1 Sprinkle both sides of meat evenly with the ½ teaspoon seasoned salt. In a large skillet heat 1 tablespoon of the oil over medium-high heat. Cook chops in hot oil for 3 minutes. Turn chops. Cook for 3 minutes more or until brown. Remove chops from skillet.

2 Carefully add remaining 1 tablespoon oil to skillet. Add leek and sweet pepper; cook 1 minute. Add potatoes, peas and carrots, thyme, and the ¼ teaspoon seasoned salt; mix well. Cook 7 minutes, stirring frequently.

3 Place chops on potatoes in skillet; cover. Reduce heat to medium. Cook 7 to 9 minutes more or until pork chops are no longer pink and potatoes are brown.

Nutrition Facts per serving: 374 cal., 16 g total fat (4 g sat. fat), 51 mg chol., 363 mg sodium, 39 g carbo., 7 g fiber, 22 g pro. **Daily Values:** 68% vit. A, 85% vit. C, 4% calcium, 23% iron

Satisfy a craving for breaded pork tenderloin with this distinctive version. Dijon-style mustard and ground red pepper provide a pleasant spiciness; ground pecans add crunch to the bread-crumb coating.

SPICY PORK WITH PECANS

PREP:

15 minutes

COOK:

6 minutes

MAKES:

4 servings

1   12-ounce boneless pork loin

1   egg

1   egg white

2   to 3 tablespoons Dijon-style mustard

½   teaspoon ground red pepper

½   cup fine, dry bread crumbs

½   cup ground pecans, toasted

⅓   cup all-purpose flour

2   tablespoons cooking oil

Sliced fresh chile peppers (optional)*

1 Cut pork loin crosswise into four equal slices. Place a meat slice between two sheets of plastic wrap; pound with the flat side of a meat mallet to ¼-inch thickness. Repeat with remaining meat slices. In a shallow dish beat together egg, egg white, mustard, and ground red pepper just until combined. In another dish stir together bread crumbs and pecans; place flour in a third dish.

2 Coat each pork slice with flour; dip in egg mixture and finally in crumb mixture.

3 In a 12-inch skillet heat oil over medium-high heat. Add pork slices. Cook for 6 to 8 minutes or until tender and just slightly pink, turning once. (If necessary, reduce heat to medium to avoid burning.) If desired, top each serving with sliced chile peppers.

Nutrition Facts per serving: 375 cal., 23 g total fat (4 g sat. fat), 103 mg chol., 374 mg sodium, 18 g carbo., 2 g fiber, 24 g pro. **Daily Values:** 4% vit. A, 2% vit. C, 6% calcium, 13% iron

***NOTE**
Because chile peppers contain volatile oils that can burn your skin and eyes, avoid direct contact. Wear plastic or latex gloves to handle the peppers. If your bare hands touch the chile peppers, wash your hands and fingernails well with soap and water.

Fennel brings a delicate licorice flavor to the luscious roast. Choose fennel bulbs that are smooth and firm, without cracks or brown spots. Stalks should be crisp, and leaves should be bright green and fresh.

ITALIAN PORK ROAST

2	tablespoons fennel seeds, crushed
2	tablespoons dried parsley, crushed
4	teaspoons dried Italian seasoning, crushed
1½	teaspoons garlic salt
1	teaspoon pepper
1	3- to 4-pound boneless pork shoulder roast
1	tablespoon cooking oil
5	carrots, quartered
6	small potatoes, peeled
1	large fennel bulb, trimmed and cut into wedges
¼	cup instant-type flour

PREP:
25 minutes

ROAST:
2 hours 20 minutes

STAND:
15 minutes

OVEN:
325°

MAKES:
6 to 8 servings

1 Combine fennel seeds, parsley, Italian seasoning, garlic salt, and pepper; set aside. Untie pork roast and unroll. Trim fat from meat. Rub meat with seasoning mixture. Retie roast with heavy kitchen string. In an ovenproof 4- to 6-quart Dutch oven heat oil. Brown pork slowly on all sides. Drain off fat.

2 Carefully pour ¾ cup water over meat. Cover and roast in a 325° oven for 1½ hours. Arrange carrots, potatoes, and fennel around roast in Dutch oven. Cover and roast 50 to 60 minutes more or until vegetables and meat are tender, adding water if necessary. Transfer meat to a serving platter and cover with foil to keep warm; let stand 15 minutes. Remove strings and carve meat. Using a slotted spoon, transfer vegetables to a serving bowl; cover and keep warm.

3 For gravy, strain juices into a glass measuring cup. Skim fat from juices; measure juices. If necessary, add enough water to equal 1½ cups. Return to Dutch oven. Cook over medium-high heat until bubbly. Combine ½ cup cold water and flour, stirring until smooth. Gradually add to hot pan juices; whisk until smooth and bubbly. Cook and stir 1 minute more. Serve gravy with roast and vegetables.

Nutrition Facts per serving: 552 cal., 26 g total fat (8 g sat. fat), 149 mg chol., 686 mg sodium, 35 g carbo., 4 g fiber, 43 g pro. **Daily Values:** 143% vit. A, 21% vit. C, 7% calcium, 30% iron

Chorizo, a spicy sausage made from ground pork, can be found in Mexican markets. Use the Mexican version of the sausage, made from fresh pork, for this recipe. Spanish chorizo is made from smoked pork.

MEXICAN SAUSAGE SKILLET

START TO FINISH:

25 minutes

STAND:

2 minutes

MAKES:

6 servings

12	ounces chorizo or pork sausage
2	cups frozen whole kernel corn
1	14$\frac{1}{2}$-ounce can diced tomatoes
1	cup uncooked instant rice
$\frac{1}{2}$	cup water
2	teaspoons chili powder
$\frac{1}{2}$	teaspoon ground cumin
1	15-ounce can pinto beans, rinsed and drained
$\frac{3}{4}$	cup shredded Mexican-blend cheeses or co-jack cheese (3 ounces)

1 Remove casing from sausage, if present. In a large skillet cook sausage over medium heat for 10 to 15 minutes or until brown. Drain off fat; set aside.

2 Add corn, undrained tomatoes, uncooked rice, water, chili powder, and cumin to skillet. Bring to boiling; reduce heat. Simmer, covered, for 5 minutes or until liquid is absorbed and rice is tender. Stir in beans and cooked sausage; heat through. Sprinkle with cheese; cover and let stand for 2 to 3 minutes until cheese is slightly melted.

Nutrition Facts per serving: 230 cal., 27 g total fat (11 g sat. fat), 13 mg chol., 585 mg sodium, 38 g carbo., 5 g fiber, 23 g pro. **Daily Values:** 9% vit. A, 22% vit. C, 11% calcium, 18% iron

This is a traditional lasagna in most respects, except for the colorful addition of spinach. Serve a salad of cooked and chilled green beans tossed with a vinaigrette.

FLORENTINE LASAGNA

12	ounces Italian sausage or uncooked turkey Italian sausage
½	cup chopped onion
1	8-ounce can tomato sauce
1	7½-ounce can tomatoes, cut up
2	teaspoons dried Italian seasoning, crushed
6	dried lasagna noodles
1	slightly beaten egg
1	15-ounce container ricotta cheese or 2 cups cream-style cottage cheese, drained
⅓	cup grated Parmesan cheese
¼	teaspoon coarsely ground pepper
½	of a 10-ounce package frozen chopped spinach, thawed and well drained
8	ounces sliced mozzarella cheese

PREP:
25 minutes

BAKE:
30 minutes

STAND:
10 minutes

OVEN:
375°

MAKES:
8 servings

1 Remove casings from sausage, if present. For meat sauce, in a medium saucepan cook sausage and onion until sausage is no longer pink and onion is tender. Drain off fat. Stir in tomato sauce, undrained tomatoes, and Italian seasoning. Bring to boiling; reduce heat. Simmer, uncovered, for 15 to 20 minutes or until desired consistency.

2 Meanwhile, cook noodles in boiling, lightly salted water for 10 to 12 minutes or until tender, but still firm. Drain. Rinse with cold water; drain well. For filling, in a bowl stir together egg, ricotta cheese, ¼ cup of the Parmesan cheese, and the coarsely ground pepper. Fold in spinach. In a 2-quart rectangular baking dish layer half of the cooked noodles. Spread with half of the filling. Top with half of the meat sauce and half of the mozzarella cheese. Repeat layers. Sprinkle with remaining Parmesan cheese.

3 Bake, uncovered, in a 375° oven for about 30 minutes or until heated through. Let stand for 10 minutes before serving.

Nutrition Facts per serving: 343 cal., 19 g total fat (9 g sat. fat), 87 mg chol., 796 mg sodium, 19 g carbo., 2 g fiber, 24 g pro. **Daily Values:** 27% vit. A, 13% vit. C, 36% calcium, 14% iron

MAKE·AHEAD TIP
Prepare through Step 2. Cover; refrigerate for up to 24 hours. Bake, covered, in a 375° oven for 40 minutes. Uncover; bake about 20 minutes more or until hot.

TO TOTE
Prepare lasagna just before leaving home. Cover with foil and wrap in several layers of newspapers. Place in an insulated container. Do not hold for longer than 2 hours.

Windy City winters demand hearty, filling foods. It's apparent why Chicago invented deep-dish pizza pie. This recipe sticks to traditional toppings, but feel free to tailor the toppings to your tastes.

DEEP-DISH SAUSAGE PIZZA

PREP:

25 minutes

RISE:

30 minutes

BAKE:

25 minutes

OVEN:

425°

MAKES:

6 servings

1	tablespoon olive oil
1	16-ounce loaf frozen white-bread dough, thawed
8	ounces Italian sausage
1½	cups shredded mozzarella cheese (6 ounces)
3	to 4 roma tomatoes, thinly sliced
⅓	cup thinly sliced onion*
⅓	cup short, thin green sweet pepper strips*
1	teaspoon dried Italian seasoning, crushed
½	cup finely shredded Parmesan cheese

1 For crust, with oiled fingers stretch and pat thawed dough in the bottom of a lightly greased 13×9×2-inch baking pan. Brush dough with remaining oil. Cover and let rise in a warm place until nearly doubled (30 to 45 minutes). Bake in a 425° oven for 10 minutes or until crust is light brown.

2 Meanwhile, remove casings from sausage, if present. In a skillet cook sausage until no longer pink, breaking up the sausage. *(If desired, cook onion and sweet pepper strips with sausage until vegetables are desired doneness.) Drain off fat. Remove crust from oven. If necessary, carefully push down the bubble of dough in the center of pan with a spatula. Sprinkle with mozzarella cheese. Top with sausage, tomatoes, onion, and sweet pepper strips. Sprinkle with Italian seasoning and Parmesan cheese.

3 Return pizza to oven and bake 15 to 20 minutes more or until crust is golden and topping is bubbly.

Nutrition Facts per serving: 410 cal., 16 g total fat (6 g sat. fat), 44 mg chol., 496 mg sodium, 37 g carbo., 1 g fiber, 22 g pro. **Daily Values:** 8% vit. A, 29% vit. C, 28% calcium, 6% iron

For this colorful dish, use rotini or rotelle—either adds kid-pleasing design to this flavorful skillet meal.

KIELBASA SKILLET WITH ROTINI

2	cups dried rotini or rotelle pasta (about 6 ounces)
1	tablespoon olive oil
1	medium onion, cut into wedges
2	cloves garlic, minced
1	pound cooked kielbasa, halved lengthwise and sliced diagonally
1	small zucchini, cut into matchstick-size strips
1	yellow or orange sweet pepper, cut into small strips
1	teaspoon dried Italian seasoning, crushed
1/8	teaspoon ground red pepper
8	roma tomatoes, cored and chopped (about 1 pound)
	Fresh herbs (optional)

START TO FINISH:
35 minutes
MAKES:
6 servings

1 Cook pasta according to package directions; drain. Meanwhile, in a very large skillet heat oil over medium-high heat. Add onion and garlic and cook for 1 minute. Add kielbasa; cook until onion is tender, stirring frequently.

2 Add zucchini, sweet pepper, Italian seasoning, and ground red pepper; cook and stir for 5 minutes. Stir in tomatoes and cooked pasta. Heat through, stirring occasionally. If desired, garnish with fresh herbs.

Nutrition Facts per serving: 410 cal., 26 g total fat (0 g sat. fat), 0 mg chol., 714 mg sodium, 31 g carbo., 2 g fiber, 14 g pro. **Daily Values:** 5% vit. A, 65% vit. C, 1% calcium, 10% iron

MEATS TO KEEP ON HAND
Preserved meats store longer than others, making them good choices for hectic, ever-changing schedules. If you don't cook them on the day you planned, they'll usually keep until you can get to them. Next time you shop, check the "sell by" and "use by" dates of meats such as pepperoni, kielbasa, and packaged corned beef. Notice that these selections usually have a longer shelf life when refrigerated, making them good choices to keep on hand.

When you crave pizza but don't have time to make it yourself—or to wait for delivery—use your noodle! Try this quick pasta dish filled with the flavors of traditional pizza.

PEPPERONI PASTA PRONTO

START TO FINISH:

30 minutes

MAKES:

4 servings

6 ounces dried spaghetti, broken in half

3 cups sliced fresh mushrooms (8 ounces)

²/₃ cup cubed pepperoni (3 ounces)

1 tablespoon margarine or butter

6 cups lightly packed, torn fresh spinach

¼ cup grated Parmesan cheese

2 tablespoons snipped fresh basil

1 teaspoon lemon juice

Breadsticks (optional)

1 Prepare pasta according to package directions. Meanwhile, in a very large skillet cook mushrooms and pepperoni in margarine over medium heat for 5 minutes or until mushrooms are just tender. Drain fat. Stir in spinach. Cook and stir for 1 minute or until spinach begins to wilt. Remove from heat.

2 Drain cooked pasta. In a large bowl combine pasta, pepperoni mixture, 3 tablespoons of the Parmesan cheese, the basil, and lemon juice. Toss to combine. Sprinkle with remaining Parmesan cheese. If desired, serve with breadsticks.

Nutrition Facts per serving: 344 cal., 14 g total fat (5 g sat. fat), 32 mg chol., 604 mg sodium, 39 g carbo., 2 g fiber, 15 g pro. **Daily Values:** 35% vit. A, 15% vit. C, 12% calcium, 29% iron

Three favorite Jamaican ingredients—pork, sweet potatoes, and jerk seasoning—create one satisfying dish. To make it easy, slice the quartered potato and green onions in a food processor fitted with a thin slicing blade.

JERK PORK & SWEET POTATO STIR-FRY

1½	cups uncooked instant rice
¼	cup thinly sliced green onions
1	large sweet potato (about 12 ounces)
1	medium tart apple (such as Granny Smith), cored
12	ounces lean boneless pork strips for stir-frying or pork tenderloin cut into thin strips
2	to 3 teaspoons purchased Jamaican jerk seasoning or Homemade Jamaican Jerk Seasoning
1	tablespoon cooking oil
⅓	cup apple juice or water
	Green onions (optional)

START TO FINISH:

20 minutes

MAKES:

4 servings

1 Prepare rice according to package directions. Stir half of the green onions into cooked rice; keep warm.

2 Meanwhile, peel sweet potato. Cut into quarters lengthwise, then thinly slice crosswise. Place sweet potato slices in a microwave-safe shallow dish. Cover with vented plastic wrap. Microwave on 100 percent power (high) for 3 to 4 minutes or until tender, stirring once. Cut apple into 16 wedges. Sprinkle pork strips with Jamaican jerk seasoning; toss to coat evenly.

3 In a wok or large skillet heat oil over medium-high heat. (Add more oil, if necessary, during cooking.) Cook and stir seasoned pork in hot oil for 2 minutes. Add apple and remaining green onions; cook and stir for 1 to 2 minutes or until pork is no longer pink. Stir in sweet potato and apple juice. Bring to boiling; reduce heat. Simmer, uncovered, for 1 minute more. Serve over rice mixture. If desired, garnish with green onions.

HOMEMADE JAMAICAN JERK SEASONING: In a small bowl combine 1 teaspoon crushed red pepper; ½ teaspoon ground allspice; ¼ teaspoon curry powder; ¼ teaspoon coarsely ground black pepper; ⅛ teaspoon dried thyme, crushed; ⅛ teaspoon ground red pepper; and ⅛ teaspoon ground ginger.

Nutrition Facts per serving: 365 cal., 9 g total fat (2 g sat. fat), 38 mg chol., 131 mg sodium, 54 g carbo., 3 g fiber, 16 g pro. **Daily Values:** 150% vit. A, 32% vit. C, 3% calcium, 17% iron

Bok choy lends a crisp green color and mandarin oranges add brightness. This beautiful and tasty dish is ready in a few minutes. Serve with hot jasmine or oolong tea and fortune cookies.

PORK LO MEIN SHANGHAI-STYLE

START TO FINISH:

20 minutes

MAKES:

4 servings

6	ounces dried somen* or fine egg noodles or angel hair pasta
2	teaspoons cooking oil
8	ounces pork tenderloin, halved lengthwise and sliced ¼ inch thick
2	cups sliced bok choy
¾	cup reduced-sodium chicken broth
¼	cup orange juice
3	tablespoons reduced-sodium soy sauce
2	teaspoons toasted sesame oil
¼	to ½ teaspoon crushed red pepper
1	11-ounce can mandarin orange sections, drained, or 2 large oranges, peeled, sectioned, and seeded

1 Cook noodles according to package directions; drain. Meanwhile, in a wok or large skillet heat oil. Cook and stir pork in hot oil for 3 minutes, adding more oil if necessary. Add bok choy; cook and stir about 2 minutes more or until the pork is no longer pink and the bok choy is crisp-tender.

2 Add chicken broth, orange juice, soy sauce, sesame oil, and red pepper to wok; bring to boiling. Stir in cooked noodles. Cook for 1 minute, stirring occasionally. Stir in the orange sections.

Nutrition Facts per serving: 323 cal., 7 g total fat (1 g sat. fat), 40 mg chol., 1,337 mg sodium, 45 g carbo., 1 g fiber, 20 g pro. **Daily Values:** 5% vit. A, 30% vit. C, 3% calcium, 11% iron

*SOMEN NOODLES
With very fine texture similar to angel hair pasta, dried Japanese somen noodles are made from wheat flour and are most often white. Look for them wherever Asian foods are sold, wrapped in bundles in such variations as plain, green tea (cha somen), egg yolk (tmago somen), or plum (ume somen).

This bistro-style dish calls for celeriac (sometimes called celery root). When selecting it in the produce section, choose small, firm bulbs. Large bulbs tend to be woody and tough.

BRAISED LAMB SHANKS & VEGETABLES

2	tablespoons all-purpose flour
4	meaty lamb shanks (about 4 pounds)
	Salt and pepper
6	leeks, sliced (2 cups)
2	tablespoons cooking oil
1	14-ounce can reduced-sodium chicken broth
1	14½-ounce can stewed tomatoes
8	cloves garlic, crushed
2	teaspoons dried rosemary, crushed
8	ounces celeriac, peeled and cut into 1-inch pieces
8	ounces turnips, peeled and cut into 1-inch pieces
8	ounces small whole carrots, peeled, or packaged, peeled baby carrots
	Fresh snipped parsley (optional)

PREP:
30 minutes
COOK:
2 hours
MAKES:
4 servings

1 Place flour in a large plastic food bag. Add lamb shanks, one or two at a time, shaking to coat. Season lamb with salt and pepper; set aside.

2 In a 4-quart Dutch oven cook leeks in hot oil until tender, but not brown. Remove from Dutch oven. Brown shanks on all sides, two at a time, in hot oil in Dutch oven. Return all shanks and leeks to Dutch oven.

3 Add broth, undrained tomatoes, garlic, and rosemary. Bring to boiling; reduce heat. Simmer, covered, for 1½ hours. Add celeriac, turnips, and carrots. Simmer, covered, for 15 to 20 minutes more or until the vegetables and lamb are tender. Transfer lamb to a serving platter. Using a slotted spoon, transfer vegetables to platter; cover to keep warm.

4 For sauce, skim fat from pan juices; measure juices. If necessary, add enough water to equal 2½ cups. Return mixture to Dutch oven. Bring juices to boiling; reduce heat. Simmer, uncovered, for 15 minutes or until sauce is reduced by half. Season to taste with salt and pepper. To serve, spoon sauce over vegetables and lamb. If desired, sprinkle with parsley.

Nutrition Facts per serving: 449 cal., 15 g total fat (4 g sat. fat), 119 mg chol., 892 mg sodium, 40 g carbo., 10 g fiber, 41 g pro. **Daily Values:** 132% vit. A, 46% vit. C, 12% calcium, 40% iron

The essence of fresh and simple Tuscan-style cooking—rosemary and garlic flavor white kidney beans topped with lamb chops. Serve with Italian bread and a salad of mixed baby greens.

TUSCAN LAMB WITH BEANS

START TO FINISH:

20 minutes

MAKES:

4 servings

8	lamb rib chops, cut 1 inch thick (1½ pounds)
2	teaspoons olive oil
3	cloves garlic, minced
1	19-ounce can white kidney (cannellini) beans, rinsed and drained
1	8-ounce can Italian-style stewed tomatoes
1	tablespoon balsamic vinegar
2	teaspoons snipped fresh rosemary
	Fresh rosemary sprigs (optional)

1 Trim fat from chops. In a large skillet heat oil. Cook chops in hot oil over medium heat about 8 minutes for medium doneness, turning once. Transfer to a plate; keep warm.

2 Stir garlic into drippings in skillet. Cook and stir for 1 minute. Stir in beans, undrained tomatoes, vinegar, and snipped rosemary. Bring to boiling; reduce heat. Simmer, uncovered, for 3 minutes.

3 Spoon bean mixture onto 4 dinner plates; arrange 2 chops on each serving. If desired, garnish with fresh rosemary sprigs.

Nutrition Facts per serving: 272 cal., 9 g total fat (3 g sat. fat), 67 mg chol., 466 mg sodium, 24 g carbo., 6 g fiber, 30 g pro. **Daily Values:** 4% vit. A, 13% vit. C, 4% calcium, 21% iron

When you're in a hurry for a fancy feast, impress your guests with this entrée. The peppercorn blend, which can be found in the spice or gourmet sections of supermarkets, provides plenty of flavor.

PEPPERED LAMB CHOPS

8	lamb rib or loin chops, cut 1 inch thick (about 2 pounds)
1½	to 2 teaspoons dried, whole mixed peppercorns
3	tablespoons coarse-grain brown mustard
1	tablespoon snipped fresh rosemary or ½ teaspoon dried rosemary, crushed
1	clove garlic, minced
⅓	cup soft bread crumbs
	Fresh rosemary sprigs (optional)

PREP:
15 minutes
BROIL:
10 minutes
MAKES:
4 servings

1 Trim fat from meat. Using a sharp knife, cut a pocket in the fatty side of the meat, cutting almost to the bone.

2 Crush peppercorns with a mortar and pestle. (Or place in a plastic bag, seal, and crush peppercorns with the flat side of a meat mallet.) In a small bowl combine crushed peppercorns, brown mustard, rosemary, and garlic. Spread about ½ teaspoon of the mixture in the pocket of each chop. Reserve remaining mustard mixture.

3 Place lamb chops on the unheated rack of a broiler pan. Broil 3 to 4 inches from heat for 5 minutes.

4 Meanwhile, stir bread crumbs into remaining mustard mixture. Turn chops. Broil 2 minutes more. Spread some of the crumb mixture evenly over each chop. Broil for 3 to 4 minutes more for medium doneness. If desired, garnish with rosemary sprigs.

Nutrition Facts per serving: 291 cal., 16 g total fat (5 g sat. fat), 103 mg chol., 267 mg sodium, 3 g carbo., 0 g fiber, 33 g pro. **Daily Values:** 20% vit. C, 3% calcium, 20% iron

With chunky vegetables, a small amount of ground lamb, and garlic-flavored tomatoes, this sauce takes on a Mediterranean style.

MOSTACCIOLI WITH LAMB & EGGPLANT

START TO FINISH:

30 minutes

MAKES:

4 servings

6   ounces dried mostaccioli or gemelli

½   of a medium eggplant, cubed (about 3 cups)

2   cups sliced zucchini

8   ounces ground lamb or ground beef

2   14½-ounce cans diced tomatoes with basil, oregano, and garlic

½   cup raisins

¼   cup snipped fresh basil

½   teaspoon ground cinnamon

2   tablespoons balsamic vinegar

    Feta cheese, crumbled (optional)

1 Cook pasta according to package directions, adding eggplant and zucchini the last 2 minutes of cooking. Drain; keep warm.

2 Meanwhile, for sauce, in a large skillet cook meat until brown; drain off fat. Stir in undrained tomatoes, raisins, basil, and cinnamon. Bring to boiling; reduce heat. Simmer, covered, for 5 minutes, stirring once or twice. Remove from heat; stir in vinegar.

3 Transfer pasta mixture to a warm serving platter. Spoon sauce over pasta mixture. If desired, sprinkle with crumbled feta cheese.

Nutrition Facts per serving: 432 cal., 8 g total fat (3 g sat. fat), 38 mg chol., 939 mg sodium, 72 g carbo., 7 g fiber, 18 g pro. **Daily Values:** 14% vit. A, 48% vit. C, 5% calcium, 25% iron

To make perfect use of refrigerated polenta, try this easy—yet impressive—recipe. Baked in small casserole dishes and inverted onto serving plates, this layered dish makes a striking presentation.

BAKED LAMB & POLENTA

12	ounces ground lamb
1	medium onion, chopped
1	small fennel bulb, chopped
4	cloves garlic, minced
1	tablespoon snipped fresh oregano or 1 teaspoon dried oregano, crushed
½	teaspoon coarsely ground pepper
1	14½-ounce can whole Italian-style tomatoes, undrained and cut up
1	16-ounce package cooked polenta
1	cup crumbled feta or garlic-and-herb feta cheese
1	cup Italian-style tomato sauce
	Cherry tomatoes, quartered (optional)
	Fresh parsley sprigs (optional)

PREP:
35 minutes
BAKE:
30 minutes
STAND:
10 minutes
OVEN:
375°
MAKES:
4 servings

1 In a large skillet cook lamb, onion, fennel, garlic, oregano, and pepper until lamb is brown and onion is tender. Drain. Add undrained tomatoes to mixture in skillet. Bring to boiling; reduce heat. Simmer, uncovered, for 10 to 15 minutes or until most of the liquid is evaporated, stirring occasionally.

2 Meanwhile, slice polenta about ½ inch thick. Press or crumble half of the slices into the bottom of four 10- to 12-ounce greased casseroles or soufflé dishes, overlapping slices as necessary.

3 Divide lamb mixture among casseroles on top of the polenta. Sprinkle cheese over lamb mixture, reserving ¼ cup cheese. Firmly press or crumble remaining polenta on top. Bake in a 375° oven about 30 minutes or until heated through. Let stand 10 minutes.

4 Meanwhile, in a saucepan heat tomato sauce just until boiling. Loosen edges of casseroles and invert onto serving plates; gently remove dishes. Spoon sauce around casseroles. Sprinkle with remaining cheese. If desired, garnish with cherry tomato quarters and parsley sprigs.

Nutrition Facts per serving: 414 cal., 18 g total fat (9 g sat. fat), 82 mg chol., 1,551 mg sodium, 39 g carbo., 13 g fiber, 24 g pro. **Daily Values:** 19% vit. A, 43% vit. C, 17% calcium, 15% iron

MAKE-AHEAD TIP:
Prepare casseroles as directed, except do not bake. Cover and freeze for up to 3 months. Thaw casseroles overnight in refrigerator. To serve, bake, covered with foil, in a 350° oven for 45 to 50 minutes or until heated through, uncovering the last 10 minutes of baking. Let stand 10 minutes before loosening edges and inverting onto plates.

Take the simplicity of a macaroni skillet supper and combine it with wonderfully complex Greek-style flavors—lamb, cinnamon, and feta cheese—for worldly results that are easy.

GREEK-STYLE LAMB & VEGETABLES

PREP:

20 minutes

COOK:

15 minutes

MAKES:

4 servings

8	ounces lean ground lamb or ground beef
¾	cup chopped onion
2	cloves garlic, minced
1	14-ounce can beef broth
1½	cups dried medium shell macaroni
2	cups frozen mixed vegetables
1	14½-ounce can tomatoes, cut up
2	tablespoons tomato paste
2	teaspoons snipped fresh marjoram or 1 teaspoon dried marjoram, crushed
⅛	teaspoon ground cinnamon
⅛	teaspoon ground nutmeg
½	cup crumbled feta cheese (2 ounces)
1	teaspoon snipped fresh marjoram

1 In a large skillet cook meat, onion, and garlic over medium heat until meat is brown and onion is tender. Drain off fat. Stir in broth and macaroni. Bring to boiling; reduce heat. Simmer, covered, for 10 minutes.

2 Stir in vegetables, undrained tomatoes, tomato paste, dried marjoram (if using), cinnamon, and nutmeg. Return to boiling; reduce heat. Simmer, uncovered, for 5 to 10 minutes more or until vegetables are tender. Stir in the 2 teaspoons fresh marjoram, if using. Sprinkle with feta cheese and the 1 teaspoon fresh marjoram.

Nutrition Facts per serving: 400 cal., 12 g total fat (6 g sat. fat), 50 mg chol., 783 mg sodium, 51 g carbo., 3 g fiber, 22 g pro. **Daily Values:** 39% vit. A, 38% vit. C, 12% calcium, 28% iron

To make preparation even easier, skip peeling the ginger before grating it. Basmati or jasmine rice makes a good accompaniment to this dish.

CHICKEN IN CITRUS SAUCE

2	to 2½ pounds meaty chicken pieces (breasts, thighs, and drumsticks)
¼	cup all-purpose flour
¾	teaspoon salt
¼	teaspoon pepper
2	tablespoons cooking oil
1	cup chopped onion
½	cup chopped celery
2	cups water
1	cup uncooked long grain rice
1	tablespoon grated fresh ginger or 1 teaspoon ground ginger
½	teaspoon salt
¼	teaspoon ground allspice
¼	teaspoon ground turmeric
1	lemon, cut into thick slices
3	tablespoons snipped fresh flat-leaf parsley

PREP:
20 minutes

COOK:
45 minutes

MAKES:
4 servings

1 Remove skin from chicken. In a shallow dish combine flour, the ¾ teaspoon salt, and pepper. Coat chicken with flour mixture. Discard any remaining flour mixture.

2 In a 12-inch skillet brown chicken in hot oil over medium heat for 20 minutes, turning occasionally. Remove from skillet; reserve drippings. Set chicken aside. Add onion and celery to drippings in skillet. Cook and stir 3 to 4 minutes or until vegetables are just tender.

3 Carefully stir water, rice, ginger, the ½ teaspoon salt, allspice, and turmeric into vegetables in skillet. Bring to boiling; add chicken pieces. Reduce heat. Simmer, covered, for 20 to 25 minutes or until rice is tender and chicken is no longer pink. Top with lemon slices the last 5 minutes of cooking.

4 Just before serving, sprinkle parsley over chicken mixture. Squeeze warm lemon juice from the slices over the chicken in the pan for additional citrus flavor.

Nutrition Facts per serving: 470 cal., 15 g total fat (3 g sat. fat), 92 mg chol., 832 mg sodium, 48 g carbo., 2 g fiber, 34 g pro. **Daily Values:** 3% vit. A, 18% vit. C, 5% calcium, 21% iron

You don't have to think ahead to enjoy flavor-soaked chicken. Most meat departments stock chicken breasts in several marinades; they're ready to cook as soon as you get them home.

CHEESY MARINATED CHICKEN BREASTS

START TO FINISH:

30 minutes

MAKES:

4 servings

1   6-ounce package long grain and wild rice pilaf mix

¼   cup thinly sliced green onions (2)

1   cup broccoli florets

4   Italian-style or butter-garlic-marinated boneless chicken breast halves

2   teaspoons olive oil

1   medium tomato, halved and thinly sliced

2   slices part-skim mozzarella cheese, halved (3 ounces)

1 Prepare rice according to package directions, adding green onions the last 5 minutes of cooking. In a saucepan bring ½ cup water to boiling; add broccoli. Cook, covered, for 3 minutes or until crisp-tender; drain and set aside.

2 In a large cast-iron skillet cook chicken breasts in hot oil over medium heat 8 to 10 minutes or until no longer pink, turning once. Overlap halved tomato slices on chicken breasts. Spoon cooked broccoli over tomato slices; cover each with a half slice of cheese. Broil chicken 3 to 4 inches from heat 1 minute or until cheese is melted and bubbly. Serve over hot rice.

Nutrition Facts per serving: 377 cal., 12 g total fat (4 g sat. fat), 22 mg chol., 1,532 mg sodium, 38 g carbo., 2 g fiber, 31 g pro. **Daily Values:** 14% vit. A, 60% vit. C, 16% calcium, 8% iron

Don't let the 15 to 20 garlic cloves scare you. During cooking, the garlic mellows sweetly.

GARLICKY CHICKEN OVER PASTA

2	pounds meaty chicken pieces
1/3	cup all-purpose flour
1	tablespoon olive oil
15	to 20 garlic cloves, peeled
1 1/4	cups rosé wine or chicken broth
3/4	cup water
1	teaspoon paprika
1/2	teaspoon poultry seasoning
1/4	teaspoon pepper
1/4	teaspoon salt
1/4	cup water
2	tablespoons all-purpose flour
1	tablespoon snipped fresh basil or 1 teaspoon dried basil, crushed
	Hot cooked penne pasta
	Fresh basil (optional)

PREP:
25 minutes
COOK:
45 minutes
MAKES:
6 servings

1 Skin chicken, if desired. Rinse chicken; pat dry. Place the 1/3 cup flour in a plastic bag. Add a few chicken pieces at a time to the flour, shaking to coat.

2 In a 12-inch nonstick skillet heat olive oil. Add chicken and garlic cloves to skillet. Cook, uncovered, over medium heat for 10 minutes, turning to brown evenly. Reduce heat; carefully add the wine, 3/4 cup water, paprika, poultry seasoning, pepper, and salt. Bring to boiling; reduce heat. Simmer, covered, about 30 minutes or until chicken is tender and no longer pink. Remove chicken; keep warm.

3 Skim fat from drippings. Crush garlic with the tines of a fork. Stir together the 1/4 cup water, the 2 tablespoons flour, and basil; stir into pan drippings. Cook and stir until thickened and bubbly. Cook and stir for 1 minute more. Serve chicken and sauce over hot cooked pasta. If desired, garnish with additional fresh basil.

Nutrition Facts per serving: 419 cal., 12 g total fat (3 g sat. fat), 69 mg chol., 156 mg sodium, 40 g carbo., 2 g fiber, 29 g pro. **Daily Values:** 4% vit. A, 4% vit. C, 3% calcium, 22% iron

This lovely herb-infused version of roast chicken and vegetables calls for the chicken to be cut up to save roasting time. With a recipe this good and quick, you'll even find time to prepare it during the week.

ROAST HERBED CHICKEN & VEGGIES

PREP:

15 minutes

ROAST:

35 minutes

OVEN:

425°

MAKES:

6 servings

TO TOTE

Prepare roast chicken and vegetables as directed just before leaving home. Cover roasting pan tightly with foil; wrap in several layers of newspapers or a heavy towel. Place the wrapped pan in an insulated container. Do not hold longer than 2 hours.

3   tablespoons olive oil or cooking oil

2   teaspoons dried basil, crushed

2   teaspoons dried marjoram, crushed

1   teaspoon dried rosemary, crushed

2   cloves garlic, minced

½   teaspoon salt

¼   teaspoon pepper

4   medium carrots, peeled and cut into 1½-inch pieces

1   large onion, cut into wedges

1   3- to 3½-pound broiler-fryer chicken, cut up

1 In a small bowl combine oil, basil, marjoram, rosemary, garlic, salt, and pepper. In a shallow roasting pan combine carrots and onion. Drizzle half of the oil mixture over the vegetables; toss to combine and push to edges of pan. Brush the remaining oil mixture on the chicken pieces. Place chicken in the prepared pan.

2 Roast, uncovered, in a 425° oven for 35 to 45 minutes or until chicken is no longer pink and vegetables are tender.

Nutrition Facts per serving: 308 cal., 19 g total fat (4 g sat. fat), 79 mg chol., 283 mg sodium, 8 g carbo., 2 g fiber, 25 g pro. **Daily Values:** 119% vit. A, 4% vit. C, 3% calcium, 12% iron

Using beer to flavor cooking is increasingly popular because of the brew pubs around the country. This dish cooks quickly; start the water boiling for the fettuccine before you put the chicken on to cook.

CHICKEN IN ALE SAUCE

4	teaspoons cooking oil
6	skinless, boneless chicken breast halves (about 1½ pounds)
⅓	cup chopped onion
2½	cups chopped mixed mushrooms (such as white, chanterelle, crimini, and/or shiitake)
1¼	cups chicken broth
⅓	cup brown ale or beer or amber nonalcoholic beer
4	teaspoons white wine Worcestershire sauce
1	tablespoon snipped fresh thyme or ½ teaspoon dried thyme, crushed
¼	teaspoon salt
¼	teaspoon black pepper
12	ounces dried fettuccine
3	tablespoons all-purpose flour
	Fresh thyme sprigs (optional)

1 In a large skillet heat oil. Brown chicken and onion in hot oil over medium-high heat, turning chicken once to brown both sides (about 2 minutes per side). Add mushrooms, ¾ cup of the broth, the ale, Worcestershire sauce, thyme, salt, and pepper. Bring to boiling; reduce heat. Cover; cook about 5 minutes or until chicken is no longer pink.

2 Meanwhile, cook fettuccine according to package directions. Drain well. Set aside and keep warm. Remove chicken breasts to serving platter; cover with foil and keep warm. In a screw-top jar shake together flour and remaining broth; add to skillet. Cook and stir until thickened and bubbly. Cook and stir for 1 minute more. Serve chicken and sauce over fettuccine. If desired, garnish with sprigs of fresh thyme.

Nutrition Facts per serving: 413 cal., 8 g total fat (2 g sat. fat), 60 mg chol., 336 mg sodium, 52 g carbo., 1 g fiber, 32 g pro. **Daily Values:** 3% vit. C, 2% calcium, 26% iron

START TO FINISH:

35 minutes

MAKES:

6 servings

TALK TURKEY (AND CHICKEN TOO!)

Next time a question about cooking or handling meat or poultry has you stumped, contact the U.S. Department of Agriculture Meat and Poultry Hotline. Recorded messages cover a variety of topics, including safe cooking methods; safe use of cooking equipment; information on preparing meat and poultry products; food storage, refrigeration, and freezing; handling and serving food; foodborne bacteria and illnesses; recalls and advisories; problems related to power failure or natural disasters; and labeling and nutrition of meat and poultry products. The toll-free number is 800-535-4555

When was the last time you had a wonderfully comforting meal of chicken and dumplings? Try this up-to-date version with shortcuts that include condensed soup and ready-to-bake buttermilk biscuits.

CREAMY CHICKEN & DUMPLINGS

PREP:

15 minutes

COOK:

32 minutes

MAKES:

4 servings

1	tablespoon all-purpose flour
12	ounces skinless, boneless chicken breast halves or thighs, cut into 1-inch pieces
2	tablespoons margarine or butter
1	stalk celery, sliced
1	medium carrot, chopped
1	onion, cut into wedges
1¼	cups chicken broth
1	10¾-ounce can condensed cream of chicken with herbs soup
⅛	teaspoon pepper
1	4.5-ounce package (6) refrigerated buttermilk biscuits*
1	cup frozen peas

1 Place flour in a plastic bag. Add chicken pieces and shake until coated. In large saucepan cook chicken, celery, carrot, and onion in hot margarine for 2 to 3 minutes or until chicken is brown. Stir in broth, condensed soup, and pepper. Bring to boiling; reduce heat. Simmer, covered, about 20 minutes or until chicken and vegetables are tender.

2 Meanwhile, separate biscuits. Cut each biscuit into quarters. Stir peas into chicken mixture; return to boiling. Place biscuit pieces on top of chicken mixture. Simmer, covered, over medium-low heat 10 to 15 minutes or until a toothpick inserted in center of biscuit comes out clean. Serve in bowls.

Nutrition Facts per serving: 338 cal., 11 g total fat (2 g sat. fat), 56 mg chol., 1,194 mg sodium, 31 g carbo., 4 g fiber, 28 g pro. **Daily Values:** 53% vit. A, 13% vit. C, 5% calcium, 15% iron

*NOTE
As an option, substitute drop biscuits for refrigerated biscuits. To prepare biscuits, in a medium mixing bowl combine 1 cup packaged biscuit mix and 1/3 cup milk. Drop mixture by teaspoonfuls into 8 dumplings on top of hot chicken mixture. Cook, covered, as directed.

Crush cumin seeds and caraway seeds before using to add exciting bursts of flavor to a recipe.

SPICED CHICKEN & SWEET POTATOES

1	tablespoon caraway seeds, crushed
2	teaspoons dried oregano, crushed
1	teaspoon cumin seeds, crushed
1	teaspoon ground turmeric
$\frac{1}{2}$	teaspoon salt
$\frac{1}{4}$	teaspoon garlic powder
$\frac{1}{8}$	to $\frac{1}{4}$ teaspoon ground red pepper
1	2$\frac{1}{2}$- to 3-pound whole broiler-fryer chicken
3	tablespoons olive oil
4	medium sweet potatoes, peeled and sliced
1	cup apple juice

PREP:
15 minutes
ROAST:
1 hour
STAND:
10 minutes
OVEN:
375°
MAKES:
6 servings

1 In a small bowl combine caraway seeds, oregano, cumin seeds, turmeric, salt, garlic powder, and red pepper. Skewer neck skin of chicken to back; tie legs to tail and twist wings under back. Place chicken, breast side up, on a rack in a shallow roasting pan. Brush chicken with 2 tablespoons of the olive oil.

2 Set aside 2 teaspoons of the spice mixture. Rub chicken with remaining spice mixture. Insert a meat thermometer into center of an inside thigh muscle. Do not allow thermometer bulb to touch bone. Roast, uncovered, in a 375° oven for 20 minutes.

3 Meanwhile, toss sweet potatoes with remaining 1 tablespoon olive oil and the reserved spice mixture. Pour apple juice into roasting pan around chicken. Add potatoes. Continue roasting for 40 to 55 minutes or until meat thermometer registers 180° to 185°, drumsticks move easily in their sockets, and potatoes are tender. Remove from oven. Let chicken stand, covered, for 10 minutes before carving. Spoon potatoes into a serving bowl.

Nutrition Facts per serving: 346 cal., 17 g total fat (4 g sat. fat), 66 mg chol., 249 mg sodium, 25 g carbo., 3 g fiber, 22 g pro. **Daily Values:** 175% vit. A, 33% vit. C, 4% calcium, 14% iron

TO TOTE
Prepare roast chicken and sweet potatoes as directed just before leaving home. Cover roasting pan tightly with foil; wrap in several layers of newspapers or a heavy towel. Place the wrapped pan in an insulated container. Do not hold for longer than 2 hours.

Balsamic vinegar lends its sharp, sweet flavor and rich mahogany hue to this dish, while rosemary and thyme bring the delightful aromas of sunny Provence.

ROSEMARY CHICKEN & POTATOES

PREP:

10 minutes

COOK:

50 minutes

MAKES:

4 servings

1   3- to 3½-pound broiler-fryer chicken, cut up

2   tablespoons olive oil

½   cup chicken broth

3   tablespoons balsamic vinegar or dry white wine

2   medium shallots, chopped

1   tablespoon snipped fresh rosemary

1   teaspoon snipped fresh thyme

1   clove garlic, minced

¼   teaspoon salt

¼   teaspoon pepper

1   pound tiny new potatoes, halved

2   cups packaged, peeled baby carrots

2   teaspoons cornstarch

1 If desired, remove skin from chicken. In a very large skillet heat oil. Cook chicken in hot oil over medium heat about 10 minutes or until chicken is lightly brown, turning to brown evenly. Drain off fat. Add broth, vinegar, shallots, rosemary, thyme, garlic, salt, and pepper to skillet. Add potatoes and carrots. Bring to boiling; reduce heat. Simmer, covered, for 35 to 40 minutes or until chicken is no longer pink and vegetables are tender. Remove chicken and vegetables to a serving platter; cover and keep warm. Reserve pan juices.

2 For sauce, skim fat from juices; measure juices. If necessary, add water to equal 1 cup. Return juices to skillet. In a bowl combine 1 tablespoon cold water and cornstarch; add to juices in skillet. Cook and stir until bubbly. Cook 2 minutes more. Spoon over all.

Nutrition Facts per serving: 550 cal., 26 g total fat (6 g sat. fat), 119 mg chol., 397 mg sodium, 38 g carbo., 4 g fiber, 41 g pro. **Daily Values:** 184% vit. A, 31% vit. C, 5% calcium, 31% iron

Recipes from the Caribbean tend to be international in nature. This dish, for example, resembles Spain's paella—a classic seafood dish, minus the seafood.

CHICKEN & RICE CARIBBEAN

2	tablespoons cooking oil
4	skinless, boneless chicken thighs (about 12 ounces)
½	cup chopped onion
1	medium green sweet pepper, seeded and chopped
1	10-ounce package Spanish yellow rice mix
2½	cups water
1	cup frozen peas
½	cup diced cooked ham
½	cup sliced, pimiento-stuffed green olives (optional)
2	tablespoons snipped fresh cilantro

1 In a large skillet heat oil. Brown chicken in hot oil over medium-high heat about 5 minutes, turning once. Remove chicken from skillet. Add the onion and sweet pepper to drippings in skillet. Cook and stir for 3 to 5 minutes or until tender. Stir in the rice mix and 2½ cups water (or according to package directions); bring to boiling. Carefully transfer mixture to a 2-quart casserole. Arrange chicken on top.

2 Bake, covered, in a 350° oven about 25 minutes or until most of the liquid is absorbed. Remove from oven and stir in the peas, ham, and, if desired, olives. Bake, covered, 10 minutes more. Sprinkle cilantro over the top.

Nutrition Facts per serving: 442 cal., 13 g total fat (3 g sat. fat), 50 mg chol., 1,443 mg sodium, 59 g carbo., 4 g fiber, 24 g pro. **Daily Values:** 5% vit. A, 43% vit. C, 6% calcium, 11% iron

PREP:
25 minutes
BAKE:
35 minutes
OVEN:
350°
MAKES:
4 servings

KEEPING HOT FOODS HOT
One-dish meals make great potluck fare. For food safety, keep hot foods hot:
• Keep hot food in the oven until just before leaving home.
• If desired, transfer hot food (such as baked beans, soups, and casseroles) to an electric slow cooker for extra insulation.
• Wrap the covered dish, container, or cooker in heavy foil, several layers of newspapers, or a heavy towel. Place the wrapped container in an insulated container to tote.
• Food should stay hot for up to 2 hours. If electricity is available at the dining site and you have a slow cooker, food will stay warm for hours on low-heat setting (add additional liquid as needed).

This 20-minute dish calls on three convenience products—frozen stir-fry vegetables, refrigerated pasta sauce, and uncooked instant rice—to give the phrase "easy does it" delicious meaning.

ALFREDO CHICKEN & VEGETABLES WITH RICE

START TO FINISH:

20 minutes

MAKES:

4 servings

1	tablespoon margarine or butter
12	ounces skinless, boneless chicken breasts or thighs
1	clove garlic, minced
2½	cups frozen stir-fry vegetables (such as broccoli, carrots, onion, and red sweet pepper)
1	10-ounce container refrigerated light Alfredo sauce
1	cup milk
1⅓	cups uncooked instant rice
2	tablespoons finely shredded Parmesan cheese (optional)

1 In a large skillet melt margarine over medium heat; add chicken and garlic. Cook for 3 to 4 minutes per side or until chicken is brown. Remove chicken from skillet.

2 Add frozen vegetables, Alfredo sauce, milk, and uncooked rice to skillet. Bring to boiling, stirring occasionally; reduce heat. Top with chicken. Cover and cook over medium-low heat for 6 to 8 minutes or until chicken is no longer pink, stirring mixture once or twice. If desired, sprinkle with finely shredded Parmesan cheese.

Nutrition Facts per serving: 599 cal., 16 g total fat (8 g sat. fat), 85 mg chol., 732 mg sodium, 77 g carbo., 2 g fiber, 35 g pro. **Daily Values:** 20% vit. A, 51% vit. C, 31% calcium, 11% iron

PASTA PRONTO

Prepared pasta sauces in cans, jars, and refrigerated packages provide a boon to time-pressed cooks. Because most have a long shelf life, you can stock up for last-minute meal preparation. Dress them up with these ingredients:
• Cooked ham pieces and frozen peas added to light Alfredo sauce and heated through. Serve over rotini or other pasta.
• Grilled vegetables and prepared pesto sauce tossed with bowtie pasta.
• Cooked Italian sausages and grilled red sweet peppers added to chunky marinara sauce and served over linguine. Sprinkle snipped fresh basil over all.

Thirty minutes to hot homemade stir-fry beats takeout any day, especially when the results are seasoned with hoisin sauce and sesame oil—two super-easy ways to bring complex, aromatic flavors to a dish.

CHICKEN & BROCCOLI STIR-FRY

½ cup water

2 tablespoons soy sauce

2 tablespoons hoisin sauce

2 teaspoons cornstarch

1 teaspoon grated fresh ginger

1 teaspoon toasted sesame oil

1 pound broccoli

1 yellow sweet pepper

2 tablespoons cooking oil

12 ounces skinless, boneless chicken, cut into bite-size pieces

2 cups chow mein noodles or hot cooked rice

Sesame seeds, toasted (optional)

Additional hoisin sauce (optional)

START TO FINISH:

30 minutes

MAKES:

4 servings

❶ For sauce, in a small bowl stir together water, soy sauce, hoisin sauce, cornstarch, ginger, and sesame oil. Set aside.

❷ Cut florets from broccoli stems and separate florets into small pieces. Cut broccoli stems crosswise into ¼-inch slices. Cut sweet pepper into short, thin strips.

❸ In a wok or large skillet heat 1 tablespoon of the cooking oil over medium-high heat. Cook and stir broccoli stems in hot oil for 1 minute. Add broccoli florets and sweet pepper; cook and stir for 3 to 4 minutes or until crisp-tender. Remove from wok; set aside.

❹ Add remaining oil to wok or skillet. Add chicken; cook and stir for 2 to 3 minutes or until no longer pink. Push chicken from center of wok. Stir sauce; pour into center of wok. Cook and stir until thickened and bubbly. Return cooked vegetables to wok. Stir together to coat. Cook and stir 1 minute more or until heated through. Serve over chow mein noodles or rice. If desired, garnish with toasted sesame seeds and serve with additional hoisin sauce.

Nutrition Facts per serving: 378 cal., 16 g total fat (3 g sat. fat), 49 mg chol., 877 mg sodium, 31 g carbo., 6 g fiber, 29 g pro. **Daily Values:** 18% vit. A, 272% vit. C, 8% calcium, 13% iron

If lemon-pepper pasta is not available, use 2 cups plain cooked pasta and add ¼ teaspoon black pepper and ¼ teaspoon finely shredded lemon peel just before tossing with the chicken.

CHICKEN WITH LEMON-PEPPER PASTA

START TO FINISH:

20 minutes

MAKES:

4 servings

8	ounces dried lemon-pepper linguine or penne pasta
1	cup shelled fresh or frozen baby peas
3	tablespoons olive oil
12	ounces skinless, boneless chicken breast halves, cut into thin, bite-size strips
1	medium red onion, cut into thin wedges
1	tablespoon snipped fresh marjoram or 1 teaspoon dried marjoram, crushed
4	cloves garlic, sliced
½	teaspoon salt
1	tablespoon lemon juice

1 Prepare pasta according to package directions, adding peas during the last minute of cooking. Drain pasta mixture; toss with 1 tablespoon of the olive oil. Set aside.

2 Meanwhile, in a large skillet heat remaining olive oil over medium heat. Cook chicken, onion, dried marjoram (if using), garlic, and salt in hot oil for 3 to 4 minutes or until chicken is no longer pink, stirring often. Stir in lemon juice. Cook and stir for 1 minute more, scraping up brown bits. Gently toss pasta with chicken mixture and fresh marjoram (if using). Serve immediately.

Nutrition Facts per serving: 446 cal., 14 g total fat (2 g sat. fat), 45 mg chol., 311 mg sodium, 54 g carbo., 4 g fiber, 26 g pro. **Daily Values:** 2% vit. A, 14% vit. C, 3% calcium, 23% iron

THE LIMITS OF LEFTOVERS
Frozen leftovers will keep for a long time—but not forever! Be sure to label items with the date they were placed in the freezer. To prevent freezer burn, store food in freezer containers with tight-fitting lids, or wrap food tightly in freezer packaging material. Store soups and stews in the freezer for up to 3 months and cooked meat casseroles for up to 6 months.

There's something undeniably delightful about being served a personal-size casserole. Make this recipe and freeze it in baking dishes for up to two months to enjoy homemade dinner in just moments.

CHICKEN TORTILLA CASSEROLES

Nonstick cooking spray

6   6-inch corn tortillas, each cut into six wedges

2   cups cubed cooked chicken

1   cup frozen whole kernel corn

1   16-ounce jar salsa verde

3   tablespoons light dairy sour cream

3   tablespoons snipped fresh cilantro

1   tablespoon all-purpose flour

1   cup crumbled Mexican Chihuahua cheese or farmer cheese (4 ounces)

Dairy sour cream (optional)

Thinly sliced fresh jalapeño pepper (optional)

Snipped fresh cilantro (optional)

Chopped tomato (optional)

PREP:
25 minutes
BAKE:
35 minutes
OVEN:
350°
MAKES:
4 servings

1 Lightly coat four 10- to 12-ounce baking dishes with nonstick spray. Place five tortilla wedges in the bottom of each dish. Place remaining tortilla pieces on a baking sheet. Bake in a 350° oven about 10 minutes or until crisp and golden.

2 Meanwhile, combine chicken, corn, salsa verde, sour cream, cilantro, and flour. Divide mixture evenly among dishes.

3 Bake, uncovered, in a 350° oven for 20 minutes. Arrange baked tortilla pieces on top of casseroles. Top with crumbled cheese; bake for 5 to 10 minutes more or until heated through. If desired, garnish with additional dairy sour cream, thinly sliced fresh jalapeño pepper, snipped fresh cilantro, and chopped tomato.

Nutrition Facts per serving: 479 cal., 21 g total fat (3 g sat. fat), 98 mg chol., 1,247 mg sodium, 45 g carbo., 7 g fiber, 34 g pro. **Daily Values:** 22% vit. A, 73% vit. C, 27% calcium, 11% iron

MAKE-AHEAD TIP
Assemble casseroles as directed through Step 2. Place baked tortilla pieces in a moisture- and vapor-proof plastic bag. Freeze wrapped and labeled casseroles and baked tortilla pieces for up to two months. To bake frozen casseroles, cover and bake in a 350° oven for 25 minutes. Uncover and bake about 20 minutes more or until heated through. Top with tortilla pieces and cheese; bake for 5 to 10 minutes more or until heated through. If desired, garnish as above.

Thanks to precooked turkey breast, this curry-flavored dish comes together quickly—so put the rice on to boil before you stir up the sauce or slice the turkey breast.

THAI-STYLE TURKEY

START TO FINISH:

30 minutes

MAKES:

4 servings

2 tablespoons soy sauce

1 tablespoon honey

2 teaspoons toasted sesame oil

2 teaspoons curry powder

1 teaspoon cornstarch

⅛ to ¼ teaspoon crushed red pepper

Nonstick cooking spray

1 small onion, cut into thin wedges

1 red sweet pepper, cut into thin strips

12 ounces cooked turkey, cut into bite-size strips (about 3 cups)

1 clove garlic, minced

2 cups hot cooked rice

Sliced serrano peppers (optional)

1 For sauce, in a small bowl combine ⅔ cup water, the soy sauce, honey, sesame oil, curry powder, cornstarch, and crushed red pepper; set aside.

2 Coat a large skillet or wok with nonstick cooking spray. Cook and stir onion and sweet pepper over medium heat until tender. Stir in the turkey and garlic. Stir in sauce. Cook and stir until thickened and bubbly. Cook and stir for 2 minutes more. Serve over rice. If desired, garnish with sliced serrano peppers.

Nutrition Facts per serving: 335 cal., 11 g total fat (3 g sat. fat), 81 mg chol., 576 mg sodium, 31 g carbo., 1 g fiber, 27 g pro. **Daily Values:** 20% vit. A, 53% vit. C, 3% calcium, 21% iron

MICROWAVING LEFTOVER RICE

Next time you cook rice, cook extra to refrigerate in an airtight container for up to one week. To reheat the chilled cooked rice, place rice in a microwave-safe container and cover with vented plastic wrap. For 2 cups chilled rice, add 1 tablespoon water and microwave on 100% power (high) for 2 to 3 minutes or until heated through, stirring once. For 3 cups chilled cooked rice, add 2 tablespoons water and microwave on high for 3 to 4 minutes or until heated through, stirring once. After the rice is heated, fluff gently with a fork.

Simmer all the ingredients for this apple-studded pilaf in a single skillet. Served warm, the flavors are perfect for a brisk fall day; for warmer temperatures, chill it overnight and serve it cold on lettuce leaves.

WILD RICE PILAF with SMOKED TURKEY

1	tablespoon margarine or butter
1	cup sliced celery
¼	cup chopped onion
⅓	cup uncooked wild rice, rinsed and drained
1	14-ounce can reduced-sodium chicken broth
⅓	cup uncooked long grain rice
12	ounces cooked smoked turkey, cubed
2	medium red-skinned apples, chopped
1	large carrot, peeled and cut into matchstick-size strips
2	tablespoons snipped fresh parsley

PREP:

15 minutes

COOK:

56 minutes

MAKES:

4 servings

❶ In a large skillet melt margarine. Add celery and onion and cook about 10 minutes or until tender. Add uncooked wild rice; cook and stir for 3 minutes. Add broth. Bring to boiling; reduce heat. Simmer, covered, for 20 minutes. Stir in long grain rice. Return to boiling; reduce heat. Simmer, covered, about 20 minutes more or until wild rice and long grain rice are tender and most of the liquid is absorbed.

❷ Stir in turkey, apples, and carrot. Cook, uncovered, for 3 to 4 minutes more or until heated through and liquid is absorbed. Stir in parsley.

Nutrition Facts per serving: 289 cal., 7 g total fat (2 g sat. fat), 44 mg chol., 1,231 mg sodium, 37 g carbo., 3 g fiber, 21 g pro. **Daily Values:** 65% vit. A, 14% vit. C, 3% calcium, 12% iron

TO TOTE

Prepare the dish as directed. Cool slightly and transfer to a storage container. Cover and chill thoroughly for up to 24 hours. Just before leaving home, place in an insulated container. Do not hold for longer than 2 hours.

Lasagna gets with today's program with a profile lighter in fat and calories and a no-fuss cooktop method. Never fear—all the traditional flavors of this family favorite are still delightfully present.

SKILLET LASAGNA

START TO FINISH:

40 minutes

STAND:

10 minutes

MAKES:

6 servings

8	ounces uncooked ground turkey sausage
½	cup chopped onion
2	cups light spaghetti sauce
1	cup water
1½	cups coarsely chopped zucchini
2	cups dried wide noodles
½	cup fat-free ricotta cheese
2	tablespoons grated Parmesan or Romano cheese
1	tablespoon snipped fresh parsley
½	cup shredded reduced-fat mozzarella cheese (2 ounces)

1 Remove casing from sausage, if present. In a large skillet cook sausage and onion until meat is brown, breaking up meat during cooking. Drain off fat. Stir in spaghetti sauce and water. Bring to boiling. Stir in zucchini and uncooked noodles. Return to boiling; reduce heat. Simmer, covered, for 12 minutes or until pasta is tender, stirring occasionally.

2 Meanwhile, in a small bowl stir together ricotta cheese, Parmesan cheese, and parsley. Drop cheese mixture by spoonfuls into six mounds over the sausage-pasta mixture in the skillet. Sprinkle each mound with mozzarella. Cover and cook over low heat for 4 to 5 minutes or until cheese mixture is heated through. Let stand 10 minutes before serving.

Nutrition Facts per serving: 235 cal., 8 g total fat (2 g sat. fat), 38 mg chol., 418 mg sodium, 26 g carbo., 2 g fiber, 18 g pro. **Daily Values:** 9% vit. A, 16% vit. C, 7% calcium, 13% iron

KNOW WHAT YOU BUY
Although ground turkey and ground chicken may seem to be leaner alternatives to ground beef, beware! Some products contain dark meat and/or skin, which are less lean than breast meat. When a recipe calls for ground chicken or turkey, look for the leanest meat you can find. If you can't find packages that are specifically labeled as breast meat only, ask the butcher to skin, bone, and grind chicken or turkey breasts for you, or grind it yourself using a coarse blade in a food grinder.

Polenta is served soft, like mashed potatoes, or chilled and shaped, as in this recipe. Prepare homemade polenta unless you're short on time; if so, follow the recipe variation that calls for prepared refrigerated polenta.

TURKEY-POLENTA CASSEROLE

Nonstick cooking spray

1 cup yellow cornmeal

1 tablespoon snipped fresh basil or ¾ teaspoon dried basil, crushed

½ teaspoon salt

¼ cup finely shredded Parmesan cheese

8 ounces Italian sausage or uncooked turkey Italian sausage

½ cup chopped carrot

1⅓ cups tomato and herb pasta sauce

1 cup shredded provolone or mozzarella cheese (4 ounces)

¼ cup grated or shredded Parmesan cheese

Celery leaves (optional)

PREP:
35 minutes

BAKE:
30 minutes

STAND:
10 minutes

CHILL:
2 hours

OVEN:
400°

MAKES:
6 servings

1 Coat a 2-quart rectangular baking dish with cooking spray; set aside. For polenta, in a saucepan bring 2¾ cups water to boiling. Meanwhile, in a mixing bowl combine cornmeal, 1 cup cold water, basil, and salt. Slowly add the cornmeal mixture to the boiling water, stirring constantly. Cook and stir until the mixture returns to boiling. Reduce heat to low. Cook, uncovered, for 10 to 15 minutes or until mixture is very thick, stirring constantly. Stir in the ¼ cup Parmesan cheese, stirring until melted. Spread polenta in prepared baking dish. Cover and chill for 2 hours or overnight.

2 Remove casing from sausage, if present. In a medium saucepan cook sausage and carrots until sausage is no longer pink. Drain off fat. Reserve ¾ cup of the pasta sauce; cover and refrigerate. Stir remaining sauce into sausage mixture. Cool slightly; cover and chill. To assemble, remove polenta from baking dish; cut into 24 triangles or squares. Spread reserved ¾ cup sauce in bottom of same rectangular baking dish. Arrange polenta on top of sauce. Spoon chilled sausage mixture over polenta. Sprinkle with provolone.

3 Cover dish with foil. Bake in a 400° oven for 25 minutes. Remove foil. Sprinkle ¼ cup Parmesan cheese over top. Bake, uncovered, 5 to 10 minutes more or until cheese is bubbly and begins to brown. Let stand for 10 minutes. If desired, garnish with celery leaves.

EASY LAYERED POLENTA CASSEROLE: Substitute one and one-half 16-ounce tubes refrigerated herb-flavored or plain cooked polenta for the water, cornmeal, basil, and salt. Cut polenta into ½-inch slices; arrange on the ¾ cup sauce spread in baking dish. Spoon sausage mixture over polenta. Sprinkle with provolone cheese. Continue with Step 3.

Nutrition Facts per serving: 340 cal., 16 g total fat (6 g sat. fat), 42 mg chol., 932 mg sodium, 31 g carbo., 2 g fiber, 17 g pro. **Daily Values:** 44% vit. A, 21% vit. C, 21% calcium, 14% iron.

Combine your favorite frozen vegetables in this skillet recipe. Cooking time is about the same for all varieties of vegetables.

VEGETABLE-PASTA SUPPER

START TO FINISH:

50 minutes

OVEN:

400°

MAKES:

6 servings

2	tablespoons olive oil
2	cloves garlic, minced
8	½-inch-thick slices baguette-style French bread
2¼	cups water
1	14-ounce jar chunky-style spaghetti sauce with mushrooms (about 1½ cups)
8	ounces rotelle pasta (about 2½ cups)
3	cups loose-pack frozen vegetables, such as white boiling onions, sugar snap peas, and cauliflower
2	teaspoons olive oil
½	cup ricotta cheese
2	tablespoons milk
½	teaspoon dried oregano, crushed
¼	teaspoon pepper
½	cup shredded mozzarella cheese (2 ounces)
¼	cup grated Parmesan cheese
¼	cup shredded mozzarella cheese (1 ounce)

1 Combine the 2 tablespoons olive oil and garlic. Brush both sides of bread with mixture. Place on a baking sheet; bake in a 400° oven for 4 minutes. Turn; bake for 4 to 5 minutes more or until toasted. Set aside.

2 In a 10-inch skillet bring water and spaghetti sauce to boiling; stir in pasta. Return to boiling; reduce heat. Cover and simmer 12 minutes, stirring pasta occasionally.

3 Meanwhile, place vegetables in a colander; run cool water over vegetables to thaw. Press with spatula to remove excess liquid. Transfer vegetables to a large bowl. Add the 2 teaspoons olive oil, ¼ teaspoon salt, and ⅛ teaspoon pepper; toss mixture gently to coat. Set aside. In a small bowl stir together ricotta cheese, milk, dried oregano, and ¼ teaspoon pepper. Stir in the ½ cup mozzarella cheese and the Parmesan cheese.

4 Spoon cheese mixture into center of skillet over pasta mixture, spreading slightly to make a 4- to 5-inch circle. Spoon vegetables evenly around edge of skillet over pasta mixture (do not cover cheese in center). Simmer, covered, 10 minutes or until vegetables are crisp-tender. Just before serving, sprinkle the ¼ cup mozzarella over vegetables and cheese mixture, and arrange bread slices on cheese mixture.

Nutrition Facts per serving: 483 cal., 17 g total fat (6 g sat. fat), 22 mg chol., 845 mg sodium, 65 g carbo., 5 g fiber, 18 g pro. **Daily Values:** 24% vit. A, 35% vit. C, 28% calcium, 18% iron

To cook as one dish rather than as portions, spoon mixture into a greased 2-quart casserole and bake for 15 to 20 minutes or until bubbly.

VEGETARIAN SHEPHERD'S PIE

1	14-ounce can vegetable broth or chicken broth
¼	cup water
1	cup dry lentils, rinsed and drained
6	purple boiling onions, halved, or 2 medium red onions, quartered
3	cloves garlic, minced
1½	pounds parsnips, peeled and cut into 1-inch slices (about 4 cups)
1	14½-ounce can diced tomatoes with Italian herbs
2	tablespoons tomato paste
3	cups water
1	cup quick-cooking polenta mix
1	tablespoon snipped fresh thyme or ½ teaspoon dried thyme, crushed
½	teaspoon salt
1	cup shredded Monterey Jack cheese with jalapeño peppers or Monterey Jack cheese (4 ounces)

PREP:
20 minutes

BAKE:
15 minutes

COOK:
30 minutes

STAND:
10 minutes

OVEN:
350°

MAKES:
6 servings

1 In a large saucepan combine vegetable broth, the ¼ cup water, lentils, onions, and garlic. Bring to boiling; reduce heat. Simmer, covered, for 20 minutes. Add parsnips. Return to boiling; reduce heat. Simmer, covered, for 10 to 15 minutes more or until vegetables and lentils are just tender. Remove from heat. Stir in tomatoes and tomato paste.

2 Meanwhile, preheat oven to 350°. In a 2-quart saucepan bring the 3 cups water to boiling. Stir in polenta mix, thyme, and salt. Cook and stir over low heat about 5 minutes or until thick. Remove from heat. Stir in ¾ cup of the cheese until melted.

3 Spoon lentil mixture into six 12- to 15-ounce au gratin dishes. Spoon polenta mixture over lentil mixture. Sprinkle with remaining cheese. Place on a large, shallow baking pan. Bake, uncovered, 15 to 20 minutes or until bubbly. Let stand 10 minutes.

Nutrition Facts per serving: 460 cal., 7 g total fat (4 g sat. fat), 20 mg chol., 790 mg sodium, 80 g carbo., 20 g fiber, 21 g pro. **Daily Values:** 10% vit. A, 40% vit. C, 22% calcium, 22% iron

Buttery-soft Brie cheese oozes between layers of crisp-tender zucchini and crusty bread in a casserole that will please family or guests.

BRIE STRATA WITH DILL

PREP:

25 minutes

CHILL:

4 hours

BAKE:

55 minutes

STAND:

10 minutes

OVEN:

325°

MAKES:

8 servings

2   small zucchini, cut crosswise into ¼-inch slices (about 2 cups)

    Nonstick cooking spray

6   ½-inch-thick slices crusty sourdough bread (6 ounces)

8   ounces Brie cheese, cut into ½-inch cubes

2   roma tomatoes, cut lengthwise into ¼-inch slices

6   to 8 cherry tomatoes

1   cup refrigerated or frozen egg product, thawed

⅔   cup evaporated skim milk

⅓   cup finely chopped onion

3   tablespoons snipped fresh dillweed

½   teaspoon salt

⅛   teaspoon black pepper

1 Cook zucchini, covered, in a small amount of lightly salted boiling water for 2 to 3 minutes or just until tender. Drain zucchini and set aside.

2 Meanwhile, coat a 2-quart rectangular baking dish with nonstick cooking spray. Arrange bread slices in the prepared baking dish, cutting as necessary to fit. Sprinkle half of the Brie evenly on top. Arrange zucchini and tomatoes on bread. Sprinkle with the remaining cheese.

3 In a medium bowl combine egg product, evaporated skim milk, onion, dill, salt, and pepper. Pour evenly over vegetables and cheese. Lightly press down vegetables with back of spoon to saturate ingredients with egg mixture. Cover with plastic wrap and refrigerate for 4 to 24 hours.

4 Preheat oven to 325°. Remove plastic wrap from strata; cover with foil. Bake 30 minutes. Uncover and bake 25 to 30 minutes more or until a knife inserted near center comes out clean. Let stand 10 minutes before serving.

Nutrition Facts per serving: 198 cal., 8 g total fat (5 g sat. fat), 29 mg chol., 525 mg sodium, 18 g carbo., 1 g fiber, 13 g pro. **Daily Values:** 13% vit. A, 13% vit. C, 13% calcium, 9% iron

Some like it hot, and others don't! No problem here—adjust the spice in this layered, low-fat casserole by choosing mild, medium, or hot salsa.

BEAN-RICE-TORTILLA BAKE

1½	cups water
⅔	cup uncooked long grain rice
6	6-inch corn tortillas
¾	cup fat-free dairy sour cream
1	tablespoon all-purpose flour
1	tablespoon skim milk
1	14½-ounce can Mexican-style stewed tomatoes
1	8-ounce jar salsa
1	15-ounce can kidney beans or small red beans, rinsed and drained
	Nonstick cooking spray
	Jalapeño slices (optional)
	Shredded reduced-fat Monterey Jack cheese (optional)

PREP:
30 minutes

BAKE:
25 minutes

OVEN:
350°

MAKES:
6 servings

1 In a medium saucepan bring water to boiling. Add rice and return to boiling; reduce heat. Simmer, covered, for 20 minutes or until rice is tender. Meanwhile, stack tortillas; wrap in foil. Heat in a 350° oven for 10 minutes to soften.

2 In a bowl stir together the sour cream, flour, and milk; set aside. In a medium bowl combine the tomatoes and salsa. Stir drained beans into cooked rice.

3 Coat a 2-quart casserole or baking dish with nonstick cooking spray. Cut softened tortillas into quarters and arrange half of them in the bottom of the casserole. Layer half of the rice-bean mixture over tortillas, then half of the tomato mixture and half of the sour cream mixture. Repeat layers.

4 Bake, covered, in a 350° oven for 25 to 30 minutes or until heated through. If desired, garnish with jalapeño slices and shredded reduced-fat Monterey Jack cheese.

Nutrition Facts per serving: 269 cal., 1 g total fat (0 g sat. fat), 0 mg chol., 540 mg sodium, 56 g carbo., 6 g fiber, 11 g pro. **Daily Values:** 11% vit. A, 26% vit. C, 12% calcium, 21% iron

TO TOTE
Prepare casserole as directed just before leaving home. Omit the optional garnishes. Cover tightly; wrap in several layers of newspapers or a heavy towel. Place the wrapped casserole in an insulated container. Hold no longer than 2 hours.

Rather than playing a supporting role, mushrooms star in this recipe. The meaty texture and rich flavor make portobellos a good substitute for meat. Before slicing the mushrooms, discard the tough stems.

STROGANOFF WITH PORTOBELLO MUSHROOMS

START TO FINISH:

35 minutes

MAKES:

4 servings

8	ounces dried fettuccine
1	8-ounce carton light dairy sour cream
2	tablespoons all-purpose flour
¾	cup water
1	teaspoon instant vegetable bouillon granules
¼	teaspoon pepper
12	ounces portobello mushrooms
	Nonstick cooking spray
1	tablespoon margarine or butter
2	medium onions, cut into thin wedges
1	clove garlic, minced
	Snipped fresh parsley

1 Cook fettuccine according to package directions, except omit oil or salt. Drain and keep warm. In a small bowl stir together the sour cream and flour. Stir in the water, bouillon granules, and pepper. Set aside. Remove stems from mushrooms; quarter and thinly slice mushroom tops and set aside.

2 Coat an unheated large skillet with nonstick spray. Add margarine and heat over medium-high heat until melted. Add the mushrooms, onions, and garlic. Cook and stir until the vegetables are tender. Stir the sour cream mixture into skillet. Cook and stir until thickened and bubbly. Cook and stir for 1 minute more. Pour the mushroom mixture over the hot cooked fettuccine, tossing gently to coat. Sprinkle with parsley.

Nutrition Facts per serving: 376 cal., 8 g total fat (3 g sat. fat), 0 mg chol., 320 mg sodium, 63 g carbo., 2 g fiber, 14 g pro. **Daily Values:** 9% vit. A, 10% vit. C, 7% calcium, 26% iron

With a sophisticated medley of cheeses, a selection of colorful vegetables, and a little red pepper kick, this casserole transcends memories of school cafeteria fare and gives the baked Italian classic its due.

SPICY MAC & CHEESE WITH TOMATO

1½	cups dried elbow macaroni
2	cups broccoli florets
⅓	cup dried tomatoes (not oil-packed)
⅓	cup sliced green onions
2	tablespoons margarine or butter
2	tablespoons all-purpose flour
1½	teaspoons dried basil, crushed
¼	teaspoon ground red pepper
⅛	teaspoon salt
1¾	cups milk
¾	cup shredded sharp cheddar cheese (3 ounces)
¾	cup shredded Gruyère cheese (3 ounces)
¾	cup shredded Gouda cheese (3 ounces)

PREP:
30 minutes
COOK:
30 minutes
STAND:
10 minutes
OVEN:
350°
MAKES:
5 servings

1 In a large saucepan cook pasta in lightly salted boiling water for 10 minutes or until tender but firm. Add broccoli. Drain well. Meanwhile, snip dried tomatoes. Place in a small bowl; add enough warm water to cover. Let stand 10 minutes or until softened; drain well.

2 In a medium saucepan cook onions in margarine until tender. Stir in flour, basil, red pepper, and salt. Stir in milk. Cook and stir until slightly thickened and bubbly. Add three cheeses, a little at a time, stirring constantly until melted after each addition. Stir in macaroni-broccoli mixture and softened tomatoes; transfer to a 1½-quart casserole.

3 Bake, uncovered, in a 350° oven about 30 minutes or until hot and bubbly. Let stand 10 minutes before serving.

Nutrition Facts per serving: 445 cal., 23 g total fat (12 g sat. fat), 62 mg chol., 539 mg sodium, 37 g carbo., 3 g fiber, 23 g pro. **Daily Values:** 32% vit. A, 49% vit. C, 46% calcium, 14% iron

COOKING AL DENTE
Cook pasta as the Italians do—just to the al dente stage. Meaning "to the tooth," al dente describes the stage at which the cooked pasta offers just a slight resistance when bitten. Cooking pasta to this stage allows it to soak up sauce. To achieve this toothsome effect, taste the pasta often near the end of the cooking time.

For a flavorful meatless dish, prepare this two-bean casserole that features garbanzo beans and red beans in a sauce between layers of thinly sliced potatoes.

BEAN & POTATO PIE

PREP:

25 minutes

BAKE:

45 minutes

OVEN:

350°

MAKES:

5 servings

MAKE-AHEAD TIP
Prepare as directed through Step 1. Cover tightly and chill overnight. To serve, bake, covered, in a 350° oven about 1 hour or until heated through. Uncover and sprinkle with the cheese. Bake, uncovered, 5 minutes more or until cheese melts.

1	pound small red potatoes
1	tablespoon cooking oil
1	cup chopped onion
2	stalks celery, sliced
4	cloves garlic, minced
¼	teaspoon cracked black pepper
1	15-ounce can garbanzo beans, rinsed and drained
1	15-ounce can small red beans, rinsed and drained
1	cup frozen peas
1	cup chopped green sweet pepper
1	10¾-ounce can condensed cream of potato soup
¼	cup skim milk
½	teaspoon ground cumin
½	teaspoon ground coriander
½	cup shredded reduced-fat Monterey Jack cheese (2 ounces)

1 Scrub potatoes; thinly slice. Cook, covered, in enough boiling water to cover for 4 to 5 minutes or until nearly tender. Drain. Run cold water over potatoes in colander. Drain; set aside. In a large saucepan heat oil. Add onion, celery, garlic, and black pepper; cook for 5 minutes or until vegetables are tender. Mash ½ cup of the garbanzo beans; add to vegetable mixture along with remaining garbanzo beans, red beans, peas, sweet pepper, soup, milk, cumin, and coriander. Gently stir to combine. Grease a 2-quart casserole dish. Place a single layer of potato slices in casserole. Spoon bean mixture on top and cover with remaining potato slices in layers, overlapping if necessary.

2 Bake, covered, in a 350° oven for 35 minutes. Uncover and sprinkle with cheese. Bake about 10 minutes more or until cheese melts.

Nutrition Facts per serving: 376 cal., 8 g total fat (2 g sat. fat), 11 mg chol., 1,073 mg sodium, 63 g carbo., 12 g fiber, 19 g pro. **Daily Values:** 6% vit. A, 41% vit. C, 16% calcium, 35% iron

DESSERTS

This delicious fruit sauce can be as versatile as you like. Choose several types of fruit or just one. Serve over ice cream, angel food cake, or pound cake.

GINGER-SPICED FRUIT SAUCE

PREP:

25 minutes

COOK:

Low 4 hours, High 2 hours

STAND:

10 minutes

MAKES:

8 servings

SLOW COOKER:

3¹/₂- to 4-quart

6 cups assorted thinly sliced fruit, such as peeled mangoes, apricots, peaches, pears, apples, and/or unpeeled nectarines

³/₄ cup apricot nectar or orange juice

¹/₄ cup packed brown sugar

1 tablespoon quick-cooking tapioca

1 teaspoon finely shredded orange peel

1 teaspoon grated fresh ginger

¹/₂ cup dried cherries

Vanilla ice cream (optional)

Slivered almonds, toasted (optional)

1 In a 3¹/₂- to 4-quart slow cooker combine desired fruit, apricot nectar or orange juice, brown sugar, tapioca, orange peel, and fresh ginger.

2 Cover; cook on low-heat setting for 4 to 5 hours or on high-heat setting for 2 to 3 hours. Add cherries; let stand, covered, for 10 minutes. If desired, serve over ice cream and sprinkle with slivered almonds.

Nutrition Facts per serving: 134 cal., 0 g total fat (0 g sat. fat), 0 mg chol., 4 mg sodium, 34 g carbo., 3 g fiber, 1 g pro. **Daily Values:** 45% vit. C, 1% calcium, 3% iron

THE MULTI-USE COOKER

During the holidays, oven and cooktop space fills up quickly. Use your slow cooker to make the festive desserts in this book. Slow cookers provide a handy way to bake breads and cook vegetable side dishes. Also use slow cookers for potlucks. Carry side dishes and desserts in a cooker to the party; then plug it in to keep food warm.

This dessert is a real treat when rhubarb and strawberries are in season, yet wonderful made with frozen fruit. Serve over ice cream or frozen yogurt.

STRAWBERRY-RHUBARB SAUCE

6   cups fresh rhubarb, cut into 1-inch pieces (about 2 pounds), or two 16-ounce packages frozen unsweetened sliced rhubarb

1   cup sugar

$^1/_2$ cup white grape juice or apple juice

$^1/_2$ teaspoon finely shredded orange peel

$^1/_4$ teaspoon ground ginger

3   inches stick cinnamon

2   cups fresh strawberries, halved

Vanilla ice cream or frozen yogurt

1 In a 3$^1/_2$- to 4-quart slow cooker place rhubarb. Stir in sugar, grape or apple juice, orange peel, ginger, and stick cinnamon.

2 Cover; cook on low-heat setting for 5$^1/_2$ to 6 hours or on high-heat setting for 2$^1/_2$ to 3 hours.

3 Remove stick cinnamon. If using low-heat setting, turn to high-heat setting. Stir in strawberries. Cover and cook 15 minutes longer. Serve the warm sauce over ice cream or frozen yogurt.*

Nutrition Facts per serving: 236 cal., 8 g total fat (4 g sat. fat), 29 mg chol., 58 mg sodium, 41 g carbo., 2 g fiber, 3 g pro. **Daily Values:** 7% vit. A, 41% vit. C, 15% calcium, 2% iron

PREP:

10 minutes

COOK:

Low 5$^1/_2$ hours, High 2$^1/_2$ hours; plus 15 minutes on High

MAKES:

10 servings

SLOW COOKER:

3$^1/_2$- to 4-quart

*NOTE
Sauce may be transferred to a freezer container and frozen for up to 3 months.

Serve this pretty and colorful fruit dessert warm or chilled over shortcake, pound cake, angel food cake, or vanilla ice cream.

BERRY COMPOTE

PREP:

10 minutes

COOK:

Low 8 hours, High 4 hours

STAND:

10 minutes

MAKES:

10 servings

SLOW COOKER:

3¹/₂- to 4-quart

2¹/₂ cups cranberry-raspberry drink or cranberry juice cocktail

1 7-ounce package mixed dried fruit, cut into 1-inch pieces

²/₃ cup dried cranberries or raisins

¹/₃ cup packed brown sugar

3 inches stick cinnamon

1 12-ounce package loose-pack frozen red raspberries

1 In a 3¹/₂- to 4-quart slow cooker combine the cranberry-raspberry drink, dried fruit, dried cranberries, brown sugar, and stick cinnamon.

2 Cover; cook on low-heat setting for 8 to 10 hours or on high-heat setting for 4 to 5 hours. Stir in frozen raspberries; let stand 10 minutes. Discard cinnamon stick. Spoon compote into bowls.

Nutrition Facts per serving: 149 cal., 0 g total fat (0 g sat. fat), 0 mg chol., 16 mg sodium, 38 g carbo., 3 g fiber, 1 g pro. **Daily Values:** 10% vit. A, 3% vit. C, 2% calcium, 5% iron

Try this yummy, homey dessert over vanilla ice cream for the ideal finale to a relaxed Sunday dinner.

ORANGE-APPLE-RUM COMPOTE

6 cups peeled and cored cooking apples cut into ¹/₂-inch slices (about 2 pounds)

1 7-ounce package mixed dried fruit bits

¹/₄ cup sugar

2 teaspoons finely shredded orange peel

1 tablespoon quick-cooking tapioca

³/₄ cup orange juice or apple juice

3 tablespoons rum (optional)

³/₄ cup whipping cream

³/₄ cup sliced almonds, toasted

PREP:
15 minutes

COOK:
Low 7 hours, High 3¹/₂ hours

MAKES:
12 servings

SLOW COOKER:
3¹/₂- to 4-quart

1 In a 3¹/₂- to 4-quart slow cooker combine the apples, fruit bits, sugar, and orange peel. Sprinkle with tapioca. Add the orange juice and the rum, if desired.

2 Cover; cook on low-heat setting for 7 to 8 hours or on high-heat setting for 3¹/₂ to 4 hours. Spoon compote into bowls. Top each serving with 1 tablespoon cream and sliced almonds.

Nutrition Facts per serving: 210 cal., 10 g total fat (4 g sat. fat), 21 mg chol., 18 mg sodium, 30 g carbo., 2 g fiber, 3 g pro. **Daily Values:** 5% vit. A, 17% vit. C, 4% calcium, 3% iron

You don't need a fondue pot to make this irresistible fondue. Reheat leftovers—if there are any—to serve over ice cream.

CHOCOLATE-ALMOND FONDUE

PREP:

10 minutes

COOK:

Low 2 hours

MAKES:

about 4 cups

SLOW COOKER:

3¹/₂- to 4-quart

2   7-ounce bars milk chocolate, broken into pieces

3   ounces white baking bar, chopped

1   7-ounce jar marshmallow creme

³/₄   cup whipping cream, half-and-half, or light cream

¹/₄   cup finely chopped almonds, toasted

3   tablespoons amaretto (optional)

Pound cake cubes

Assorted fruit such as strawberries, bananas, orange segments, and/or grapes

1 In a 3¹/₂- to 4-quart slow cooker combine milk chocolate, white baking bar, marshmallow creme, cream, and almonds.

2 Cover; cook on low-heat setting for 2 to 2¹/₂ hours or until chocolate melts, stirring once. Stir until smooth. If desired, stir in amaretto.

3 To serve, spear cake cubes or fruit with fondue forks; dip into chocolate mixture.

Nutrition Facts per 1/4-cup serving of fondue: 260 cal., 15 g total fat (9 g sat. fat), 21 mg chol., 38 mg sodium, 28 g carbo., 1 g fiber, 3 g pro. **Daily Values:** 3% vit. A, 6% calcium, 1% iron

Serve warm mincemeat over ice cream or use it to make mincemeat pie and muffins. Excellent apple choices for this recipe include Jonathan, Rome, and golden delicious.

SLOW COOKER MINCEMEAT

¾	pound boneless beef chuck or round rump roast
2	pounds cooking apples, peeled, cored, and chopped (about 6 cups)
1¼	cups dark raisins
1¼	cups golden raisins
1	cup currants
⅓	cup diced candied citron
⅓	cup diced mixed candied fruits and peels
2	tablespoons quick-cooking tapioca
2	tablespoons butter
1	cup sugar
¾	cup apple juice
½	cup dry sherry
¼	cup brandy
¼	cup molasses
2	teaspoons ground cinnamon
1	teaspoon ground nutmeg
1	teaspoon ground mace
⅛	teaspoon pepper

PREP:
30 minutes

COOK:
Low 8 hours, High 4 hours

MAKES:
about 8 cups

SLOW COOKER:
3½- to 5-quart

1 Trim fat from meat; chop meat. In a 3½- to 5-quart slow cooker combine chopped meat, apples, raisins, currants, citron, candied fruits and peels, tapioca, and butter. Add sugar, apple juice, sherry, brandy, molasses, cinnamon, nutmeg, mace, and pepper. Stir well.

2 Cover; cook on low-heat setting for 8 to 10 hours or on high-heat setting for 4 to 5 hours. Skim off fat.

3 Divide mincemeat into 1-, 2-, or 4-cup portions. Use immediately. (Or place in freezer containers, seal, and label. Freeze for up to 3 months. Thaw frozen mincemeat in the refrigerator overnight before using.)

Nutrition Facts per 1/2-cup serving: 298 cal., 3 g total fat (1 g sat. fat), 14 mg chol., 38 mg sodium, 59 g carbo., 3 g fiber, 6 g pro. **Daily Values:** 2% vit. A, 5% vit. C, 4% calcium, 9% iron

This sweet, yet tart, cranberry sauce and ice cream topping is the perfect complement to succulent pears.

POACHED PEARS IN CRAN-AMARETTO SAUCE

PREP:

25 minutes.

COOK:

Low 4 hours, High 2 hours

MAKES:

6 servings

SLOW COOKER:

3¹/₂- to 4-quart

1¹/₂ cups cranberries

²/₃ cup water

¹/₂ cup sugar

¹/₃ cup amaretto or hazelnut liqueur

6 ripe medium pears, peeled, cored, and halved

Vanilla ice cream (optional)

Sliced or slivered almonds, toasted

Fresh mint (optional)

1 In a 3¹/₂- to 4-quart slow cooker, combine cranberries, water, sugar, and amaretto or hazelnut liqueur. Add pears, stirring to coat. Cover and cook on low-heat setting for 4 to 5 hours or on high-heat setting for 2 to 2¹/₂ hours.

2 To serve, divide cranberry sauce among six dessert plates; place two pear halves on each plate. If desired, serve with ice cream and garnish with toasted almonds and mint.

Nutrition Facts per serving: 241 cal., 4 g total fat (0 g sat. fat), 0 mg chol., 1 mg sodium, 490 g carbo., 6 g fiber, 2 g pro. **Daily Values:** 1% vit. A, 14% vit. C, 3% calcium, 4% iron

These nachos have a sugar-and-spice twist. Serve the apple dip with cinnamon-spiced tortilla crisps and top with vanilla yogurt and toasted pecans.

CARAMEL-APPLE DESSERT DIP

⅔	cup packed brown sugar
¼	cup granulated sugar
1	tablespoon quick-cooking tapioca
1	teaspoon ground cinnamon
1½	cups apple juice or apple cider
2	pounds cooking apples, peeled, cored, and cut into ½-inch-thick slices (6 cups)
1	tablespoon butter or margarine, cut up
1	8-ounce carton vanilla yogurt
¼	cup chopped pecans, toasted
1	recipe Cinnamon Tortilla Crisps

PREP:
40 minutes

COOK:
Low 6 hours, High 3 hours

MAKES:
8 servings

SLOW COOKER:
3½- to 4-quart

1 In a 3½- to 4-quart slow cooker stir together brown sugar, granulated sugar, tapioca, and cinnamon. Stir in the apple juice. Add apple slices and butter; stir to mix.

2 Cover; cook on low-heat setting for 6 to 7 hours or on high-heat setting for 3 to 3½ hours. To serve, divide apples and syrup among eight dessert dishes. Top each serving with vanilla yogurt and pecans. Serve with Cinnamon Tortilla Crisps.

CINNAMON TORTILLA CRISPS: In a bowl combine 4 teaspoons granulated sugar and 1 teaspoon ground cinnamon. Cut two 7- to 8-inch flour tortillas into eight wedges each. (Or cut three 6-inch corn tortillas into six wedges each.) Lightly spray wedges with nonstick coating. Place wedges in a single layer on an ungreased baking sheet. Sprinkle with sugar-cinnamon mixture. Bake in a 350° oven about 12 minutes or until crisp. (Or bake corn tortillas about 8 minutes.)

Nutrition Facts per serving: 280 cal., 5 g total fat (1 g sat. fat), 1 mg chol., 85 mg sodium, 60 g carbo., 2 g fiber, 3 g pro. **Daily Values:** 40% vit. C, 7% calcium, 8% iron

This gingerbread is updated with crystallized ginger and dried cherries for a sophisticated flavor. The lemon whipped cream adds tartness.

GINGERBREAD WITH LEMON CREAM

PREP:

20 minutes

COOK:

High 1³/₄ hours

COOL:

30 minutes

MAKES:

6 servings

SLOW COOKER:

3¹/₂- to 4-quart

USE CANNING JARS AS BAKING MOLDS

Create a simple baking or steaming mold with a straight-sided, wide-mouth canning jar. To ensure that the baked cake or bread will slip out easily, grease well the inside of the jar. Lining the bottom of the jar with waxed paper will help, also. Grease a piece of foil on one side. Place the greased side down over the top of the jar and press the foil around the edges to seal tightly.

³/₄ cup all-purpose flour

¹/₄ teaspoon baking powder

¹/₄ teaspoon baking soda

¹/₄ teaspoon ground cinnamon

Dash salt

Dash ground allspice

¹/₄ cup shortening

2 tablespoons brown sugar

1 egg

3 tablespoons molasses

¹/₄ cup boiling water

2 tablespoons snipped dried cherries or mixed dried fruit bits

2 teaspoons finely chopped crystallized ginger

³/₄ cup whipped cream

1 teaspoon finely shredded lemon peel

1 Generously grease the bottom and halfway up the sides of a 1-pint straight-sided, wide-mouth canning jar. Flour the jar; set aside.

2 In a bowl stir together flour, baking powder, baking soda, cinnamon, salt, and allspice. In a mixing bowl beat shortening and brown sugar with an electric mixer on medium speed until combined. Add egg and molasses. Beat 1 minute more. Alternately add flour mixture and boiling water, beating on low speed after each addition. Stir in cherries or fruit bits and ginger. Pour into prepared canning jar. Cover jar tightly with greased foil, greased side down. Place in a 3¹/₂- to 4-quart slow cooker. Pour 1 cup water around jar.

3 Cover; cook on high-heat setting 1³/₄ hours or until a toothpick inserted near the center comes out clean.

4 Remove jar from cooker; cool 10 minutes. Using a small spatula, loosen bread from sides of jar; remove from jar. Cool 20 minutes on a wire rack. Cut bread into 12 slices; place two slices on a dessert plate. Combine the whipped cream and lemon peel; top each serving with whipped cream mixture.

Nutrition Facts per serving: 189 cal., 10 g total fat (2 g sat. fat), 36 mg chol., 104 mg sodium, 24 g carbo., 1 g fiber, 3 g pro. **Daily Values:** 3% calcium, 9% iron

Summertime is berry time, and that means cobbler—warmed jewels of sun-kissed flavor beneath a soft, sweet bread that soaks the juice. Be sure to top it with ice cream.

DOUBLE-BERRY COBBLER

1	cup all-purpose flour
3/4	cup sugar
1	teaspoon baking powder
1/4	teaspoon salt
1/4	teaspoon ground cinnamon
1/4	teaspoon ground nutmeg
2	slightly beaten eggs
3	tablespoons cooking oil
2	tablespoons milk
3	cups fresh or one 16-ounce bag frozen blueberries
3	cups fresh or one 16-ounce bag frozen blackberries
1	cup sugar
1	cup water
3	tablespoons quick-cooking tapioca
	Vanilla ice cream, whipped cream, half-and-half, or light cream (optional)

PREP:
25 minutes
COOK:
High 1³/₄ hours
STAND:
1 hour
MAKES:
6 servings
SLOW COOKER:
3¹/₂- to 4-quart

1 In a medium bowl stir together flour, ³/₄ cup sugar, baking powder, salt, cinnamon, and nutmeg. In a small bowl combine eggs, oil, and milk; add to dry ingredients. Stir just until moistened. Set aside.

2 In a large saucepan combine blueberries, blackberries, 1 cup sugar, water, and tapioca. Bring to boiling. Pour hot fruit mixture into a 3¹/₂- to 4-quart slow cooker. Immediately spoon the batter over the top of the fruit mixture.

3 Cover; cook on high-heat setting for 1³/₄ to 2 hours or until a toothpick inserted into the center of the cake comes out clean. Remove liner from cooker, if possible, and let stand for about 1 hour to cool slightly before serving.

4 To serve, spoon the warm cobbler into bowls. Serve with ice cream, if desired.

Nutrition Facts per serving: 478 cal., 10 g total fat (2 g sat. fat), 71 mg chol., 194 mg sodium, 97 g carbo., 6 g fiber, 6 g pro. **Daily Values:** 41% vit. C, 9% calcium, 11% iron

Slow cookers help eliminate the problem of overcooking custard, producing one with a deliciously creamy texture.

ORANGE-FLAVORED PUMPKIN CUSTARD

PREP:

15 minutes

COOK:

Low 4 hours

STAND:

20 minutes

MAKES:

6 servings

SLOW COOKER:

4- to 6-quart

2	slightly beaten eggs
1	cup canned pumpkin
½	cup sugar
½	teaspoon ground cinnamon
½	teaspoon finely shredded orange peel
¼	teaspoon ground allspice
1	12-ounce can evaporated milk
	Whipped cream (optional)
	Chopped pecans, toasted (optional)

1 In a large mixing bowl combine eggs, pumpkin, sugar, cinnamon, orange peel, and allspice. Stir in evaporated milk. Pour into a 1-quart soufflé dish. Cover the dish tightly with foil.

2 Tear off two 20×6-inch pieces of heavy foil. Fold each piece in thirds lengthwise. Crisscross the strips and place the soufflé dish in the center. Bring up foil strips, lift the ends of the strips, and transfer the dish and foil to a 4- to 6-quart slow cooker. (Leave foil strips under dish.) Pour warm water into the cooker around the dish to a depth of 1½ inches.

3 Cover; cook on low-heat setting about 4 hours or until a knife inserted near the center comes out clean.

4 Using the foil strips, carefully lift the dish out of the cooker. Let stand 20 minutes. Serve warm or chilled. If desired, top each serving with a tablespoon of whipped cream and pecans.

Nutrition Facts per serving: 186 cal., 7 g total fat (3 g sat. fat), 89 mg chol., 90 mg sodium, 26 g carbo., 1 g fiber, 7 g pro. **Daily Values:** 185% vit. A, 5% vit. C, 19% calcium, 6% iron

Caramel, pear, and ginger give an old-fashioned favorite a tantalizing twist. The warm caramel sauce warrants a scoop of ice cream!

PEAR-CARAMEL PUDDING CAKE

1	cup all-purpose flour
1/3	cup granulated sugar
1	teaspoon baking powder
1/4	teaspoon ground cardamom or 1/2 teaspoon ground cinnamon
1/2	cup milk
2	tablespoons cooking oil
1/2	cup chopped pecans, toasted
1/4	cup dried pears or apples
1	cup packed brown sugar
1	cup water
1	cup pear nectar or apple juice
2	tablespoons butter or margarine
1	tablespoon finely chopped crystallized ginger
	Vanilla ice cream or light cream (optional)

PREP:
20 minutes

COOK:
High 2 hours

STAND:
30 minutes

MAKES:
6 to 8 servings

SLOW COOKER:
$3^{1}/2$- to 4-quart

1 In a bowl stir together flour, granulated sugar, baking powder, and cardamom. Add the milk and oil; stir until combined. Stir in the nuts and dried fruit. Spread the batter evenly in the bottom of a $3^{1}/2$- to 4-quart slow cooker.

2 In a small saucepan combine brown sugar, water, nectar, butter, and ginger. Bring to boiling; boil for 2 minutes. Pour mixture evenly over the batter in the cooker.

3 Cover; cook on high-heat setting for 2 to $2^{1}/2$ hours or until a toothpick inserted 1 inch into the center of cake comes out clean. Let stand, uncovered, for 30 to 40 minutes to cool slightly before serving. If desired, serve warm with ice cream or light cream.

Nutrition Facts per serving: 483 cal., 19 g total fat (4 g sat. fat), 16 mg chol., 155 mg sodium, 78 g carbo., 2 g fiber, 5 g pro. **Daily Values:** 3% vit. C, 13% calcium, 15% iron

This pudding cake is a dessert lover's dream. Warm chocolate–peanut butter pudding develops under the cake layer as it bakes. Spooned over ice cream, it's the best!

PEANUTTY CHOCOLATE PUDDING CAKE

PREP:
25 minutes

COOK:
High 2 hours

STAND:
30 minutes

MAKES:
8 servings

SLOW COOKER:
3¹/₂- to 4-quart

1	cup all-purpose flour
¹/₂	cup sugar
2	tablespoons unsweetened cocoa powder
1¹/₂	teaspoons baking powder
¹/₂	cup milk
2	tablespoons cooking oil
1	teaspoon vanilla
³/₄	cup peanut-butter-flavored pieces
³/₄	cup sugar
¹/₄	cup unsweetened cocoa powder
2	cups boiling water
¹/₂	cup chunky peanut butter
2	tablespoons chopped unsalted, dry-roasted peanuts
	Vanilla ice cream (optional)

1 In a bowl stir together flour, the ¹/₂ cup sugar, the 2 tablespoons cocoa powder, and baking powder. Add the milk, oil, and vanilla; stir until batter is smooth. Stir in the peanut butter pieces. Spread batter evenly in the bottom of a greased 3¹/₂- to 4-quart slow cooker.

2 In a bowl combine the ³/₄ cup sugar and the ¹/₄ cup cocoa powder. Stir together boiling water and peanut butter; stir into the cocoa mixture. Pour evenly over the batter in the cooker.

3 Cover; cook on high-heat setting for 2 to 2¹/₂ hours or until a toothpick inserted 1 inch into the center of the cake comes out clean. Let stand, uncovered, for 30 to 40 minutes to cool slightly.

4 To serve, spoon pudding cake into dessert dishes. Sprinkle with peanuts. If desired, serve with ice cream.

Nutrition Facts per serving: 417 cal., 18 g total fat (4 g sat. fat), 1 mg chol., 196 mg sodium, 56 g carbo., 2 g fiber, 10 g pro. **Daily Values:** 1% vit. C, 12% calcium, 12% iron

This homey dessert makes an ideal finale to your next family dinner. Serve it with scoops of vanilla ice cream for the ultimate indulgence.

RAISIN PUDDING CAKE

1	package 2-layer-size spice cake mix
²⁄₃	cup milk
1	cup raisins
½	cup chopped pecans
1½	cups water
½	cup packed brown sugar
½	cup butter or margarine
1	teaspoon vanilla
	Vanilla ice cream (optional)

1 In a large bowl, using a wooden spoon, stir together cake mix and milk until smooth. Stir in raisins and pecans (batter will be thick); set aside.

2 In a small saucepan combine water, brown sugar, and butter; bring to boiling. Remove from heat. Stir in vanilla. Pour into a 3½- to 4-quart slow cooker. Carefully drop large spoonfuls of batter into sugar mixture. Cover and cook on high-heat setting for 2½ hours (center may appear moist but will set upon standing). Remove liner from cooker, if possible, and let stand 45 minutes to cool slightly before serving.

3 If desired, serve warm with ice cream.

Nutrition Facts per serving: 527 cal., 22 g total fat (10 g sat. fat), 34 mg chol., 548 mg sodium, 82 g carbo., 1 g fiber, 4 g pro. **Daily Values:** 10% vit. A, 1% vit. C, 17% calcium, 11% iron

PREP:
15 minutes

COOK:
High 2½ hours

STAND:
45 minutes

MAKES:
8 to 10 servings

SLOW COOKER:
3½- to 4-quart

This decadent dessert is a classic combination—moist, tender cake smothered in rich caramel sauce. Serve in bowls topped with cream.

ORANGE PUDDING CAKE & CARAMEL SAUCE

PREP:

25 minutes

COOK:

High 2½ hours

STAND:

30 minutes

MAKES:

6 servings

SLOW COOKER:

3½- to 4-quart

1	cup all-purpose flour
⅓	cup granulated sugar
1	teaspoon baking powder
½	teaspoon ground cinnamon
¼	teaspoon salt
½	cup milk
2	tablespoons butter, melted
½	cup chopped pecans
¼	cup currants or raisins
⅔	cup packed brown sugar
¾	cup water
½	teaspoon finely shredded orange peel
¾	cup orange juice
1	tablespoon butter
	Half-and-half or light cream

1 In a medium bowl stir together flour, granulated sugar, baking powder, cinnamon, and salt. Add milk and the 2 tablespoons melted butter. Stir until batter is combined. Stir in pecans and currants. Spread batter evenly in the bottom of a 3½- to 4-quart slow cooker.

2 In a medium saucepan combine brown sugar, water, orange peel, orange juice, and the 1 tablespoon butter. Bring to boiling; boil 2 minutes. Pour carefully over batter in cooker.

3 Cover; cook on high-heat setting for 2½ hours (center may appear moist but will set upon standing). Let stand 30 minutes to cool slightly before serving.

4 To serve, spoon the warm cake and sauce into dessert dishes. Serve with half-and-half or light cream.

Nutrition Facts per serving: 390 cal., 15 g total fat (6 g sat. fat), 23 mg chol., 255 mg sodium, 61 g carbo., 2 g fiber, 5 g pro. **Daily Values:** 8% vit. A, 27% vit. C, 12% calcium, 11% iron

Pair this double-chocolate, nut-studded cake and warm mocha sauce with cappuccino or caffe latte for a truly grand finale.

NUTTY MOCHA PUDDING CAKE

1	cup all-purpose flour
½	cup sugar
2	tablespoons unsweetened cocoa powder
1½	teaspoons baking powder
½	cup milk
2	tablespoons butter, melted
1	teaspoon vanilla
½	cup miniature semisweet chocolate pieces
½	cup broken pecans
¾	cup sugar
¼	cup unsweetened cocoa powder
1	tablespoon instant coffee crystals
1½	cups boiling water
¼	cup coffee liqueur (optional)
	Vanilla ice cream

PREP:
25 minutes

COOK:
High 2½ hours

STAND:
30 minutes

MAKES:
8 servings

SLOW COOKER:
3½- to 4-quart

1 In a bowl stir together flour, ½ cup sugar, 2 tablespoons cocoa powder, and baking powder. Add milk, melted butter, and vanilla. Stir until batter is smooth. Stir in chocolate pieces and pecans. Spread batter evenly in the bottom of a 3½- to 4-quart slow cooker.

2 Combine the ¾ cup sugar and ¼ cup cocoa powder. Dissolve coffee crystals in boiling water; stir in coffee liqueur, if desired. Gradually stir coffee mixture into the sugar-cocoa mixture. Pour evenly over batter in slow cooker.

3 Cover; cook on high-heat setting for 2½ hours (center may appear moist but will set upon standing). Let stand 30 minutes to cool slightly before serving.

4 To serve, spoon warm cake into dessert dishes; spoon pudding over cake. Top with a scoop of vanilla ice cream.

Nutrition Facts per serving: 487 cal., 20 g total fat (10 g sat. fat), 38 mg chol., 169 mg sodium, 71 g carbo., 1 g fiber, 7 g pro. **Daily Values:** 8% vit. A, 1% vit. C, 20% calcium, 11% iron

Combine chocolate and cinnamon to make a wonderfully new version of a familiar dessert. Don't be alarmed when the pudding falls as it cools; this is normal.

CHOCOLATE BREAD PUDDING

PREP:

25 minutes

COOK:

Low 4 hours, High 2 hours

STAND:

30 minutes

MAKES:

6 servings

SLOW COOKER:

3¹/₂- to 5-quart

1½   cups half-and-half or light cream

2   ounces unsweetened chocolate, coarsely chopped

    Nonstick cooking spray

2   beaten eggs

½   cup sugar

¾   teaspoon ground cinnamon

3   cups bread cubes (about 4 slices)

1   cup sweetened whipped cream

¼   cup chopped nuts

1 In a small saucepan combine half-and-half and chocolate; heat and stir until chocolate is melted. Cool slightly. Lightly coat a 1-quart soufflé dish and a 12-inch square of heavy foil with nonstick cooking spray.

2 In a medium mixing bowl whisk together eggs, sugar, and cinnamon. Whisk in cream mixture. Gently stir in bread cubes. Pour into prepared dish. Cover the dish tightly with foil, sprayed side down.

3 Tear off two 18×6-inch pieces of heavy foil. Fold each piece in thirds lengthwise. Crisscross the strips and place the soufflé dish in the center. Bring up foil strips, lift the ends of the strips, and transfer the dish and foil to a 3½- to 5-quart slow cooker (leaving foil strips under dish). Pour warm water around the dish in the cooker to a depth of 2 inches.

4 Cover; cook on low-heat setting for about 4 hours or on high-heat setting for about 2 hours or until a knife inserted near the center comes out clean.

5 Using foil strips, carefully lift dish out of cooker. Let stand 30 to 45 minutes (pudding will fall as it cools). Serve bread pudding warm with a tablespoon of whipped cream and sprinkle of nuts.

Nutrition Facts per serving: 365 cal., 25 g total fat (13 g sat. fat), 121 mg chol., 144 mg sodium, 32 g carbo., 2 g fiber, 7 g pro. **Daily Values:** 13% vit. A, 1% vit. C, 12% calcium, 9% iron

Use a slow cooker as your partner to create spectacular desserts. This bread pudding steams unattended. Return home to an out-of-this-world taste treat.

WHITE CHOCOLATE BREAD PUDDING

1½ cups half-and-half or light cream

½ of a 6-ounce package white baking bar or squares, coarsely chopped

⅓ cup snipped dried cranberries or dried cherries

2 beaten eggs

½ cup sugar

½ teaspoon ground ginger

3 cups dry bread cut into ½-inch cubes (about 4½ slices)

¼ cup coarsely chopped pecans or hazelnuts

Whipped cream (optional)

Grated white baking bar (optional)

Ground ginger (optional)

PREP:

25 minutes

COOK:

Low 4 hours, High 2 hours

MAKES:

6 servings

SLOW COOKER:

3½- to 5-quart

1 In a small saucepan heat half-and-half over medium heat until very warm but not boiling. Remove from heat; add chopped white baking bar and cranberries or cherries. Stir until baking bar is melted.

2 In a bowl combine eggs, sugar, and ½ teaspoon ginger. Whisk in the cream mixture. Gently stir in bread cubes and nuts. Pour mixture into a 1-quart soufflé dish (dish will be full). Cover the dish tightly with foil.

3 Pour 1 cup warm water into a 3½ to 5-quart slow cooker. Tear off an 18×12-inch piece of heavy foil. Divide in half lengthwise. Fold each piece into thirds lengthwise. Crisscross the strips and place the soufflé dish in the center of the foil cross. Bringing up foil strips, lift the ends of the strips to transfer the dish and foil to the cooker. (Leave foil strips under dish.)

4 Cover; cook on low-heat setting for 4 hours or on high-heat setting for 2 hours. Using foil strips, carefully lift dish out of cooker. Serve pudding warm or chilled. If desired, serve with whipped cream and sprinkle with grated white baking bar and additional ground ginger.

Nutrition Facts per serving: 360 cal., 17 g total fat (8 g sat. fat), 98 mg chol., 177 mg sodium, 45 g carbo., 1 g fiber, 7 g pro. **Daily Values:** 1% vit. C, 9% calcium, 7% iron

This warm bread pudding is full of dessert favorites—raisins, pecans, coconut, and candied pineapple. Top with caramel ice cream topping for good measure.

BREAD PUDDING WITH FRUIT & NUTS

PREP:

15 minutes

COOK:

Low 4 hours, High 2 hours

MAKES:

6 servings

SLOW COOKER:

3¹/₂- to 5-quart

2   beaten eggs

¹/₂   cup sugar

¹/₂   teaspoon ground cinnamon

¹/₂   teaspoon vanilla

1¹/₂   cups whole milk, half-and-half, or light cream

3   cups dry cinnamon-raisin bread cut into ¹/₂-inch cubes (about 6 slices of bread)*

¹/₃   cup raisins

¹/₃   cup chopped pecans

¹/₃   cup flaked coconut (optional)

¹/₃   cup chopped candied pineapple (optional)

¹/₂   cup caramel ice cream topping (optional)

1 In a bowl combine eggs, sugar, cinnamon, and vanilla. Whisk in milk. Gently stir in bread cubes, raisins, and pecans. If desired, add coconut and candied pineapple. Pour mixture into a 1-quart soufflé dish (dish will be full). Cover the dish tightly with foil.

2 Pour 1 cup warm water into a 3¹/₂- to 5-quart slow cooker. Tear off an 18×12-inch piece of heavy foil. Divide in half lengthwise. Fold each piece into thirds lengthwise. Crisscross the strips and place the soufflé dish in the center of the foil cross. Bringing up foil strips, lift the ends of the strips to transfer the dish and foil to the cooker (leave foil strips under dish).

3 Cover and cook on low-heat setting for 4 hours or on high-heat setting for 2 hours. Using the foil strips, carefully lift dish from cooker. Serve pudding warm or chilled with caramel ice cream topping, if desired.

Nutrition Facts per serving: 395 cal., 9 g total fat (2 g sat. fat), 79 mg chol., 63 mg sodium, 71 g carbo., 6 g fiber, 12 g pro. **Daily Values:** 3% vit. C, 12% calcium, 17% iron

*NOTE
To make dry bread cubes, cut bread into ¹/₂-inch square pieces. Use about 4 cups fresh bread cubes to make 3 cups dry cubes. Spread in a single layer in a 15×10×1-inch baking pan. Bake, uncovered, in a 300° oven for 10 to 15 minutes or until dry, stirring twice; cool.

The only downside to making these fix-'em-and-forget-'em brownies is you probably won't have any leftovers for tomorrow's dessert!

DECADENT RASPBERRY BROWNIES

½ cup margarine or butter

2 ounces unsweetened chocolate

2 eggs

¾ cup sugar

⅓ cup seedless red raspberry jam

1 teaspoon vanilla

¾ cup all-purpose flour

¼ teaspoon baking powder

Vanilla ice cream (optional)

Chocolate ice cream topping (optional)

Fresh raspberries (optional)

1 Generously grease two 1-pint straight-sided, wide-mouth canning jars. Flour the greased jars; set aside.

2 In a saucepan melt margarine or butter and chocolate over low heat. Remove from heat. Stir in eggs, sugar, jam, and vanilla. Using a spoon, beat lightly just until combined. Stir in flour and baking powder. Pour batter into prepared jars. Cover jars tightly with greased foil, greased side down. Place jars in a 3½- to 4-quart slow cooker. Pour 1 cup water around jars.

3 Cover; cook on high-heat setting for 3 to 3½ hours or until a toothpick inserted near the centers of brownie rolls comes out clean. Remove jars from cooker; cool for 10 minutes. Using a metal spatula, loosen brownies from sides of jars. Carefully remove rolls from jars. Place rolls on their sides on a wire rack; cool completely. To serve, cut each roll into 6 slices. If desired, serve with ice cream, chocolate ice cream topping, and fresh raspberries.

Nutrition Facts per serving: 204 cal., 11 g total fat (0 g sat. fat), 36 mg chol., 109 mg sodium, 26 g carbo., 1 g fiber, 2 g pro. **Daily Values:** 1% calcium, 5% iron

PREP:
15 minutes

COOK:
High 3 hours

COOL:
10 minutes

MAKES:
12 brownie slices

SLOW COOKER:
3½- to 4-quart

INDEX

W

Zucchini

METRIC INFORMATION

The charts on this page provide a guide for converting measurements from the U.S. customary system, which is used throughout this book, to the metric system.

Product Differences

Most of the ingredients called for in the recipes in this book are available in most countries. However, some are known by different names. Here are some common American ingredients and their possible counterparts:

- Sugar (white) is granulated, fine granulated, or castor sugar.
- Powdered sugar is icing sugar.
- All-purpose flour is enriched, bleached or unbleached white household flour. When self-rising flour is used in place of all-purpose flour in a recipe that calls for leavening, omit the leavening agent (baking soda or baking powder) and salt.
- Light-colored corn syrup is golden syrup.
- Cornstarch is cornflour.
- Baking soda is bicarbonate of soda.
- Vanilla or vanilla extract is vanilla essence.
- Green, red, or yellow sweet peppers are capsicums or bell peppers.
- Golden raisins are sultanas.

Volume and Weight

The United States traditionally uses cup measures for liquid and solid ingredients. The chart below shows the approximate imperial and metric equivalents. If you are accustomed to weighing solid ingredients, the following approximate equivalents will be helpful.

- 1 cup butter, castor sugar, or rice = 8 ounces = $\frac{1}{2}$ pound = 250 grams
- 1 cup flour = 4 ounces = $\frac{1}{4}$ pound = 125 grams
- 1 cup icing sugar = 5 ounces = 150 grams

Canadian and U.S. volume for a cup measure is 8 fluid ounces (237 ml), but the standard metric equivalent is 250 ml.

1 British imperial cup is 10 fluid ounces.

In Australia, 1 tablespoon equals 20 ml, and there are 4 teaspoons in the Australian tablespoon.

Spoon measures are used for smaller amounts of ingredients. Although the size of the tablespoon varies slightly in different countries, for practical purposes and for recipes in this book, a straight substitution is all that's necessary. Measurements made using cups or spoons always should be level unless stated otherwise.

Common Weight Range Replacements

Imperial / U.S.	Metric
$\frac{1}{2}$ ounce	15 g
1 ounce	25 g or 30 g
4 ounces ($\frac{1}{4}$ pound)	115 g or 125 g
8 ounces ($\frac{1}{2}$ pound)	225 g or 250 g
16 ounces (1 pound)	450 g or 500 g
$1\frac{1}{4}$ pounds	625 g
$1\frac{1}{2}$ pounds	750 g
2 pounds or $2\frac{1}{4}$ pounds	1,000 g or 1 Kg

Oven Temperature Equivalents

Fahrenheit Setting	Celsius Setting*	Gas Setting
300°F	150°C	Gas Mark 2 (very low)
325°F	160°C	Gas Mark 3 (low)
350°F	180°C	Gas Mark 4 (moderate)
375°F	190°C	Gas Mark 5 (moderate)
400°F	200°C	Gas Mark 6 (hot)
425°F	220°C	Gas Mark 7 (hot)
450°F	230°C	Gas Mark 8 (very hot)
475°F	240°C	Gas Mark 9 (very hot)
500°F	260°C	Gas Mark 10 (extremely hot)
Broil	Broil	Grill

*Electric and gas ovens may be calibrated using celsius. However, for an electric oven, increase celsius setting 10 to 20 degrees when cooking above 160°C. For convection or forced air ovens (gas or electric) lower the temperature setting 25°F/10°C when cooking at all heat levels.

Baking Pan Sizes

Imperial / U.S.	Metric
9×1$\frac{1}{2}$-inch round cake pan	22- or 23×4-cm (1.5 L)
9×1$\frac{1}{2}$-inch pie plate	22- or 23×4-cm (1 L)
8×8×2-inch square cake pan	20×5-cm (2 L)
9×9×2-inch square cake pan	22- or 23×4.5-cm (2.5 L)
11×7×1$\frac{1}{2}$-inch baking pan	28×17×4-cm (2 L)
2-quart rectangular baking pan	30×19×4.5-cm (3 L)
13×9×2-inch baking pan	34×22×4.5-cm (3.5 L)
15×10×1-inch jelly roll pan	40×25×2-cm
9×5×3-inch loaf pan	23×13×8-cm (2 L)
2-quart casserole	2 L

U.S. / Standard Metric Equivalents

$\frac{1}{8}$ teaspoon = 0.5 ml	
$\frac{1}{4}$ teaspoon = 1 ml	
$\frac{1}{2}$ teaspoon = 2 ml	
1 teaspoon = 5 ml	
1 tablespoon = 15 ml	
2 tablespoons = 25 ml	
$\frac{1}{4}$ cup = 2 fluid ounces = 50 ml	
$\frac{1}{3}$ cup = 3 fluid ounces = 75 ml	
$\frac{1}{2}$ cup = 4 fluid ounces = 125 ml	
$\frac{2}{3}$ cup = 5 fluid ounces = 150 ml	
$\frac{3}{4}$ cup = 6 fluid ounces = 175 ml	
1 cup = 8 fluid ounces = 250 ml	
2 cups = 1 pint = 500 ml	
1 quart = 1 litre	